SOCIAL INSTITUTIONS
Their Emergence, Maintenance and Effects

SOCIOLOGY AND ECONOMICS
Controversy and Integration

An Aldine de Gruyter Series of Texts and Monographs

Series Editors

Paula S. England, *Department of Sociology, University of Arizona, Tucson*
George Farkas, *School of Social Sciences, University of Texas, Dallas*
Kevin Lang, *Department of Economics, Boston University*

Beyond the Marketplace:
Rethinking Economy and Society
Roger Friedland and A. F. Robertson (eds.)

Social Institutions:
Their Emergence, Maintenance and Effects
Michael Hechter, Karl-Dieter Opp and Reinhard Wippler (eds.)

SOCIAL INSTITUTIONS

Their Emergence, Maintenance and Effects

Edited by

Michael Hechter, Karl-Dieter Opp and Reinhard Wippler

Aldine de Gruyter
New York

About the Editors

Michael Hechter is Professor of Sociology and Director of the Research Group for Institutional Analysis at The University of Arizona.

Karl-Dieter Opp is Professor of Sociology at the University of Hamburg.

Reinhard Wippler is Professor of Theoretical Sociology at the University of Utrecht and the scientific director of the Interuniversity Center for Sociological Theory and Methodology.

Copyright © 1990 Walter de Gruyter, Inc., New York
All rights reserved. No part of this publication may be reproduced or transmitted in any form or by any means, electronic or mechanical, including photocopy, recording, or any information storage and retrieval system, without permission in writing from the publisher.

ALDINE DE GRUYTER
A Division of Walter de Gruyter, Inc.
200 Saw Mill River Road
Hawthorne, New York 10532

Library of Congress Cataloging-in-Publication Data
Social institutions : their emergence, maintenance, and effects /
    edited by Michael Hechter, Karl-Dieter Opp, and Reinhard Wippler.
        p. cm.—(Sociology and economics)
    Based on papers from a meeting held in Bad Homburg, West Germany in Jan. 1988 under the sponsorship of the Werner Reimers Foundation, the American Sociological Association, and the National Science Foundation (U.S.).
    Includes bibliographical references.
    ISBN 0-202-30409-4
    1. Social institutions—Congresses. 2. Social choice—Congresses.
  3. Rational expectations (Economic theory)—Congresses.
  I. Hechter, Michael. II. Opp, Karl-Dieter. III. Wippler, Reinhard.
  IV. Warner-Reimers-Stiftung. V. American Sociological Association.
  VI. National Science Foundation (U.S.) VII. Series.
  HM131.S5847 1990
  306'.01—dc20   89-17836
                                                                  CIP

Manufactured in the United States of America

10 9 8 7 6 5 4 3 2 1

Contents

Acknowledgment   vii

INTRODUCTION
Michael Hechter, Karl-Dieter Opp, and Reinhard Wippler   1

**PART I
ALTERNATIVE EXPLANATIONS OF
NORMS AND INSTITUTIONS**

1. THE EMERGENCE OF COOPERATIVE SOCIAL INSTITUTIONS
   Michael Hechter   13

2. THE EMERGENCE OF NORMS
   James S. Coleman   35

3. THE COSTS OF ORGANIZING SOCIAL COOPERATION
   Hartmut Kliemt   61

4. INDIVIDUAL INTERESTS AND MORAL INSTITUTIONS: AN ENDOGENOUS APPROACH TO THE MODIFICATION OF PREFERENCES
   Werner Raub and Thomas Voss   81

5. THE ATTENUATION OF CUSTOMS
   Karl-Dieter Opp   119

6. THE KULA: SOCIAL ORDER, BARTER AND CEREMONIAL EXCHANGE
   Rolf Ziegler   141

PART II
THE COMPARATIVE ANALYSIS OF INSTITUTIONS

7. A COMPARATIVE INSTITUTIONAL ANALYSIS
   IN THE ARTS: THE THEATER
   Bruno S. Frey and Werner Pommerehne — 171

8. CULTURAL RESOURCES AND PARTICIPATION IN
   HIGH CULTURE
   Reinhard Wippler — 187

9. THE WELFARE STATE AND UNEMPLOYMENT:
   A THEORETICAL ANALYSIS
   Henk de Vos — 205

PART III
THE EFFECTS OF INSTITUTIONS IN A MULTIPLEX SOCIETAL CONTEXT

10. PATRONAGE: AN INSTITUTION IN ITS OWN RIGHT
    H. D. Flap — 225

11. THE POLITICAL GEOGRAPHY OF FASCIST PARTY
    MEMBERSHIP IN GERMANY AND ITALY
    William Brustein — 245

12. INCENTIVES, GOVERNANCE AND DEVELOPMENT
    IN CHINESE COLLECTIVE AGRICULTURE
    Anthony Oberschall — 265

13. TOWARD A THEORY OF UNION EMERGENCE
    AND DEMISE
    Debra Friedman — 291

14. INTRAFAMILIAL MARKETS FOR EDUCATION
    IN JAPAN
    Mary C. Brinton — 307

BIOGRAPHICAL SKETCHES OF THE CONTRIBUTORS — 331

INDEX — 334

Acknowledgment

This volume owes its existence to the support of several institutions and individuals. The Werner Reimers Stiftung and the American Sociological Association (through its "Problems of the Discipline" grant program) funded the Bad Homburg Conference. In addition to the contributors, Hartmut Esser, Carol Heimer, Siegwart Lindenberg and Karol Sołtan were participants. The senior editor is grateful to the Russell Sage Foundation for its support.

Introduction

Michael Hechter
Karl-Dieter Opp
Reinhard Wippler

The analysis of social institutions is a central enterprise in sociology. At least since Durkheim, sociologists have regarded conventions, norms and laws as the crucial sources of social stability:

> Since [social] activity takes place outside each one of us (for a plurality of consciousnesses enters into it), its necessary effect is to fix, to institute outside us, certain ways of acting and certain judgments which do not depend on each particular will taken separately. . . . One can, indeed, without distorting the meaning of this expression, designate as 'institutions' all the beliefs and all the modes of conduct instituted by the collectivity. Sociology can then be defined as the science of institutions, of their genesis and of their functioning (Durkheim [1895] 1938:lvi).

Two sorts of questions lie at the heart of this putative science of institutions.

The first set of questions centers on the emergence of institutions. At the most general level, sociologists can agree that most institutions derive from pre-existing ones. Yet this answer is far from a sufficient explanation: which institutions, out of all possible ones, will arise? And by what means do existing institutions spawn new ones?

There is considerable institutional diversity, both territorial and historical, that calls for explanation. Some of this diversity can be traced to environmental constraints. For example, political institutions such as tribes, clans, and states sometimes arise in territories inhabited by populations of relatively autonomous nuclear families, but at other times they do not (Johnson and Earle, 1987). That states *somehow* evolve from nuclear families is undoubtedly true, but how does this development occur? Further, why is it that states do not always emerge in territories with nuclear family systems?

The second set of questions focus on the ways that institutions produce stable relations and social order. The most familiar sociological approach maintains that the substantive content of institutions—especially those residing in commonly shared norms—is internalized within individuals. When internalized, norms hold a privileged position in the individual's cognitive structure: by being at the very fountainhead of action, they help to socialize behavior. It is not difficult to imagine how normative behavior contributes to cooperative social outcomes. Yet persistent antisocial behavior and instances of social disorganization are also stable outcomes in nearly every society, and their existence makes this normative account seem too optimistic. In any case, skeptics are unlikely to be persuaded by explanations based on internalization, for in their opinion these run the great risk of appearing to be unfalsifiable.

In the wake of these well-appreciated difficulties, some sociologists have found in rational choice theory a more adequate approach to the study of social institutions. This volume presents the first collection of original essays by sociologists that apply rational choice theories to the analysis of norms and other institutions. Since there are many different versions of rational choice in the literature, it will be useful to outline a version of the theory that serves as the common core of the essays in this volume. We regard this version of rational choice the most fruitful one for the analysis of social behavior in general.

Rational Choice Theory

Rational choice comes from one of the oldest theoretical traditions in social science. Its origins can be traced back at least to Nicholas Bernoulli (Stigler, 1950b:373), if not to Thomas Hobbes before him. The period of rapid advance dates from the last quarter of the 18th century. Stigler (1950a, 1950b) begins his review of the development of utility theory—as he calls it—in the year 1776, when Adam Smith's *The Wealth of Nations* was first published. Since that time a voluminous literature has developed. Different versions of the theory have been proposed and applied to a wide range of economic and social phenomena. Whereas economists and psychologists were most involved in the initial development of rational choice, during the last thirty years other social scientists—particularly political scientists, sociologists, and anthropologists—have joined in the enterprise.

Since rational choice is a general theory, a host of different hypotheses can be included under its umbrella (compare, for example, Alchian and Allen, 1974: ch. 3; Becker, 1976: ch. 1; Frey, 1980; Kirchgaessner, 1980; Meckling, 1976). Despite this, there are common elements in all rational choice theories. These include actors, their preferences and opportunity costs, constraints upon their action (for an extended discussion of the underpinnings of rational choice explanations of social outcomes, see Friedman and Hechter, 1988; Opp, 1989: Ch. 2). Most scholars agree that three hypotheses lie at the core of rational choice:

1. *The preference hypothesis:* Individuals act in order to attain preferred ends.
2. *The constraint hypothesis:* Constraints and opportunities also affect actions by influencing the probability that actors' preferred ends can be attained. These constraints derive either from resources under an individual's control (opportunity costs), or from social institutions to which the individuals are subject.
3. *The utility maximization hypothesis:* subject to extant constraints, individuals choose the course of action, among those that are available to them, that realizes to the greatest extent their most preferred ends.

These three hypotheses constitute the basis of all of the models used in the chapters in this volume. This version of rational choice is much less restrictive than the alternatives currently found in the literature: no sweeping assumptions need be made about perfect information, or about frictionless markets, for instance. Several implications follow from these hypotheses, some of which even the proponents of the theory regard as controversial.

First, *all kinds of preferences may serve as explanatory variables.* The preference hypothesis does not limit the kinds of preferences that may serve as the causes of individual action and social outcomes. In rational choice, individuals may have egoistic preferences, but they may also have altruistic ones. Individuals may adhere to norms of legal rules not only because they wish to avoid negative external sanctions, but also because following a norm may be a value of its own. Actions themselves may also acquire an intrinsic reward value.

The openness of the theory to all kinds of preferences is considered problematic by some. These writers fear that this openness permits rational choice explanations to be ad hoc, and as a result, tautological. Indeed, tautology occurs whenever preferences are implicated as causes but are not independently measured. It is fair to say that the proponents of rational choice disagree about the adequacy of explanations of social outcomes based on preferences alone.

Second, *all kinds of constraints and opportunities may be explanatory variables.* Available income and market prices are far from the only relevant constraints that individual actors face. Other relevant constraints include enforceable laws and informal normative expectations. Both the material goods that individuals possess and their intellectual capabilities (those, for instance, that permit them to have control over the behavior of other actors) serve as an important class of constraints or opportunities.

Third, *subjective assessments of constraints are the direct determinants of action.* When individuals expect the probability of receiving punishment for participating in an illegal demonstration to be higher than it actually is, it is the perceived and not the objective probability that affects their participation.

Fourth, *the relative contribution of constraints and preferences to the explanation of individual behavior and social outcomes is principally an empirical, and not a theoretical, issue.* Nevertheless, the difficulties involved in measuring preferences often hinder this empirical determination.

Finally, *individual actors do not calculate their costs and benefits, but act as if they calculated them.* Rational choice does not pretend to describe the actual processes by which individuals make their decisions. The theory assumes that individuals choose the behavioral alternatives that are relatively most advantageous. As long as it satisfies this criterion, habitual or traditional action may be classified as rational action.

The role of norms and institutions is firmly embedded in rational choice models. Norms and institutions affect the behavior of actors by altering benefit/cost calculations. Therefore, norms and institutions are, as traditional sociology asserts, key determinants of behavior. Contrary to traditional sociology, however, rational choice implies that the extent to which these elements influence the behavior of actors depends on the other costs and benefits facing these actors. This implication leads to a variety of hypotheses about the conditions for the variable effectiveness of norms and institutions.

This volume is concerned not only with the effects of social institutions, but also with their origins. While recent research in the rational choice tradition has helped to elucidate the effects of particular institutions on a wide range of issues—including social cooperation, collective decisions, crime, and organizational behavior—it has not provided sufficient understanding of the social dynamics that lead to the rise of these institutions. It is seldom appreciated that institutional constraints represent the results of prior collective action as much as they are producers of subsequent social outcomes. The crucial intellectual failing of both the sociological and rational choice traditions is that they take institutional constraints as given, rather than considering them as outcomes to be

Introduction

explained in their own right. Research focused on developing dynamic theories of institutions is critical to understanding why and how institutions arise in the first place.

What implications, then, does rational choice logic have for the problem of institutional genesis? Basically, it predicts that *institutions will emerge only when it is in the private interests of individuals to establish them*. The chapters in this volume explore how the interaction of rational, self-interested agents spontaneously yields new institutional arrangements and structures, and how institutional innovation and institutional reform come about.

To answer these questions, a group of social scientists from the United States, West Germany and the Netherlands met in Bad Homburg, West Germany in January of 1988 under the sponsorship of the Werner Reimers Foundation (F.R.G.), the American Sociological Association and the National Science Foundation (U.S.). These scholars shared both a substantive interest in institutions, as well as a common commitment to rational choice as a theoretical orientation. The new research in sociological rational choice that this volume represents developed independently in loosely connected European (especially Dutch and West German) and American groups. The first joint meeting of the European and American groups took place at the 1986 International Sociological Association meetings held in New Delhi. The Bad Homburg conference, which is the basis for this volume, was the second occasion for the joint meeting of these two groups.

The chapters that follow attempt to combine social structural elements with individual action and, as such, provide one type of solution to one of the most frequently mentioned problems in sociological discourse—the micro/macro problem. Neither the individual nor the structural level are slighted; rather, the common focus of these chapters lies on linking these two levels of analysis into a coherent whole. The specific linking mechanisms suggested by the various authors, however, do differ notably. Some writers argue for game-theoretic analyses that link individual agents and social outcomes (either institutions or the effects of institutions) via payoff matrices and other rules of the game; others look to collective action to bridge these different levels of analysis; still others concentrate on the relationship between demand and structurally-provided opportunities.

Although the subjects and social settings of these essays diverge widely, all of the chapters exemplify a novel type of institutional analysis, one that is informed both by rational choice and by sociology. Despite the substantive diversity of the collection, the coherence of the book as whole results from the high level of theoretical agreement among the authors.

Alternative Explanations of Norms and Institutions

The first three chapters—by Michael Hechter, James S. Coleman, and Hartmut Kliemt—discuss the emergence of institutions in a state of nature. These chapters share at least two analytical elements in common. In the first place, they explicitly deal with the public goods questions of social institutions. In the second place—and more controversially—they tend to impugn the adequacy of explanations of institutional genesis based on the elegant but simple models of repeated game theory.

Since these chapters consider institutions as bearing some of the aspects of public goods (termed control capacity by Hechter, and heroic and instrumental sanctioning by Coleman), each author must explain how rational individuals would ever provide themselves with such goods in the face of the free-rider problem. Hechter's solution emphasizes the role of the visibility of production and consumption, which provides monitoring economies; Coleman's solution stresses the interdependence of potential sanctioners; and Kliemt advocates an approach based on the technology of commitment.

The next three chapters are written firmly in the game-theoretic tradition. Werner Raub and Thomas Voss seek to understand how self-interested individuals may also behave morally. Their strategy is to construct a game-theoretic model that accounts endogenously for the emergence of morality among such individuals.

Karl-Dieter Opp's paper deals with the conditions leading to decreased compliance to already-extant customs. He regards compliance to customs as the outcome of a coordination game. Thus, for every actor noncompliance to a custom is more advantageous than compliance.

Rolf Ziegler attempts to put some empirical flesh on this range of problems in his game-theoretic analysis of the generalized reciprocal social relations in the South Sea Islands initially described by Malinowski as the Kula Ring. He explores the rational basis of the Kula Ring as well as its peculiar structure. Ziegler claims that the ring-like structure of exchange is one that offers significant monitoring economies, and that the ceremonial exchange of gifts acts as an efficient signalling device to maintain social order among participants.

The Comparative Analysis of Institutions

The next section of the volume features a number of new analyses of a variety of different social institutions. Bruno S. Frey and Werner Pommerehne argue that decisions about the quantity and quality of theater performances, as well as about the types and methods of production, are crucially affected by the institutional constraints faced by the relevant decision-makers. Whether a theater is profit-making, is a cooperative, or is supported by the government thus turns out to have predictable effects on the fare that is likely to be presented.

Reinhard Wippler seeks to understand why schooling is such a good predictor of aesthetic and artistic interest and participation by utilizing a rational choice argument. His analysis flows from two kinds of assumptions. First, the appreciation of culture depends to a large degree on an individual's endowment in cultural resources. Second, people are held to maximize two different kinds of values—pleasure and comfort. People are less inclined to seek physical well-being of the pleasure kind the more they experience physical well-being of the comfort kind. Since comfort is positively associated with wealth and high socioeconomic status, people who are well-off are not highly dependent on artistic enjoyment as a means of realizing physical well-being relative to those who have equivalent cultural capital, but who live in less material comfort.

Henk de Vos uses Gary Becker's theory of social interactions to develop predictions about the consequences of long-term unemployment in two different institutional settings—one during the 1930's, and the other during the 1980's.

The Effects of Institutions in a Multiplex Societal Context

The chapters in this last section of the volume examine the effects of existing institutions on a variety of social outcomes.

H.D. Flap interprets patronage as a network phenomenon in which personal networks are conceived to represent social resources. The emergence and maintenance of patronage are seen to depend, to a large extent, on the value of social capital. The concept of social capital is then related to agency and transactions cost theories, yielding the implication that, under certain conditions, patronage relations constitute efficient solutions to contracting problems in industrial societies.

William Brustein seeks to provide a rational choice explanation for the rise of fascist political movements in twentieth century Germany and Italy—an outcome that many historians consider to be collectively irrational. He claims that regional variation in fascist party membership in these two countries can be attributed to systematic variations in the demand for social policies advocated by these parties in these regions, to differences in the opportunities available for membership, to the party's store of selective incentives, and finally, to the density of local social networks. These factors affected fascist party membership, according to Brustein, because they helped shape individuals' benefit/cost calculations.

Anthony Oberschall traces the effects of a series of major swings of central government policy in the wake of the Chinese revolution on agricultural output and development in one specific Chinese village. The twenty five years of collective agriculture in the Peoples Republic of China represent a vast social experiment in institutional forms varying from the mutual aid teams and cooperatives of the mid-1950's, to the household responsibility system of the late-1970's. Oberschall attempts to explain the different fortunes of each of these institutional forms by utilizing a rational choice model in which incentives for collective output and governance costs help determine agricultural productivity and the village standard of living.

Debra Friedman seeks to account for patterns of the emergence and decline of quite a different kind of institution—American trade unions. In her model, unions are expected to emerge in a given industry to provide workers with insurance against high levels of contextual uncertainty. Once established, however, existing unions are likely to be threatened by the same kinds of contextual uncertainty that helped foster their emergence, for as new institutions arise to help spread the new sources of risk (such as new trade unions or the welfare state), workers' initial motives to participate in the original union are attenuated.

Finally, Mary C. Brinton wants to understand the reasons behind institutionalized differences in the amounts of human capital found in men and women. To this end, she examines the case of Japan, a society in which patterns of gender stratification are particularly marked. Brinton constructs a rational choice model that links the institutional level with individual perceptions, motivations and resources, thereby generating individual decisions that produce stable macro level outcomes.

The promise of sociological rational choice as a research program lies in two quite different directions. As this volume demonstrates, rational choice can help to generate explanations for a wide variety of the substantive concerns of those who are interested in the genesis and demise of institutions. At the same time this volume underscores trends emphasizing the importance of analyzing institutions in real-world settings.

The explanations that are advanced here should be regarded as tentative. Each of the models is bound to be amended to a greater or lesser extent as it is tested against more systematic evidence. But this is a fate common to theoretical work in all successful research programs.

References

Alchian, Armen A., and William R. Allen. (1974). *University Economics: Elements of Inquiry*, London: Prentice Hall.
Becker, Gary S. (1976). *The Economic Approach to Human Behavior*, Chicago and London: Chicago University Press.
Demsetz, Harold [1957] 1974. "Toward a Theory of Property Rights." Pp. 31–42 in E. Furobotn, S. Pejovich eds., *The Economics of Property Rights*, Cambridge, Mass.: Ballinger.
Durkheim, Emile. [1895] (1938). *The Rules of the Sociological Method*. 8th Ed. Edited by George E.G. Catlin. Translated by Sarah A. Solovay and John H. Mueller. Chicago: University of Chicago Press.
Elster, Jon. (1979). *Ulysses and the Sirens*, Cambridge: Cambridge University Press.
Friedman, Debra, and Michael Hechter. (1988). "The Contribution of Rational Choice Theory to Macrosociological Research." *Sociological Theory* 6 2:201–18.
Frey, Bruno S.S. (1980). "Ökonomie als Verhaltenswissenschaft. Ansatz, Kritik und der europäische Beitrag," *Jahrbuch für Sozialwissenschaft* 31:21–25.
Johnson, Allen W., and Timothy Earle. (1987). *The Evolution of Human Societies*. Standford: Standford University Press.
Kahneman, Daniel, Paul Slovic and Amos Tversky, eds. (1982). *Judgment under Uncertainty: Heuristics and Biases*, Cambridge: Cambridge University Press.
Kirchgaessner, Gebhard. (1980). "Können Ökonomie und Soziologie voneinander lernen?" *Kyklos* 33:420–448.
Meckling, W.H. (1976). "Values and the Choice of Model of the Individual in the Social Sciences," *Schweizerische Zeitschrift für Volkswirtschaft und Statistik* 112: 545–559.
Opp, Karl-Dieter, with Peter and Petra Hargmann. (1989). *The Rationality of Political Protest*. Boulder, CO: Westview Press.
Schoemaker, Paul J.H. (1982). "The Expected Utility Model: Its Variants, Purposes, Evidence and Limitations," *Journal of Economic Literature* 20:529–63.
Simon, Herbert A. (1985). "Human Nature in Politics: The Dialogue of Psychology with Political Science," *American Political Science Review* 79:293–304.
Stigler, George J. (1950a). "The Development of Utility Theory. I," *Journal of Political Economy* 58:307–327.
Stigler, George J. (1950b). "The Development of Utility Theory. II," *Journal of Political Economy* 58:373–396.

I
ALTERNATIVE EXPLANATIONS OF
NORMS AND INSTITUTIONS

1

The Emergence of Cooperative Social Institutions

Michael Hechter

The origin of social institutions is a very old concern in social theory. Currently it has re-emerged as one of the most intensely debated issues in social science. Among economists and rational choice theorists, there is growing awareness that most, if not all, of the social outcomes that are of interest to explain are at least partly a function of institutional constraints. Yet the role of institutions is negligible both in general equilibrium theory and in most neoclassical economic models. Among other social scientists, there is a burgeoning substantive interest in institutions ranging from social movements, to formal organizations, to states, and even international regimes.

This chapter discusses the two principal approaches to the problem of institutional genesis—*invisible-hand* and *solidaristic*. It further argues that the second of these is likely to afford us with a better means of attacking the problem than the first. Finally, one particular solidaristic explanation that holds promise for future research on institutional genesis is introduced.

The Concept of Social Institutions

Although the term *institution* is bandied about quite liberally in contemporary social science, no consensual definition of it has as yet emerged. The ambiguity of the term gives authors both the obligation and the license to adopt their favorite definition. At the most general level, I will take the existence of a social institution to be revealed by the appearance of *some regularity in collective behavior*. *Collective behavior* may be said to occur if different individuals behave similarly when placed in the same social situation;[1] *regularity*, for its part, indicates that this collective behavior endures over some long but indefinite period of time.

If institutions are revealed by the appearance of collective behavioral regularities, then one naturally wonders both about their origins and about the mechanisms responsible for their persistence. In institutionally rich environments, new institutions can arise from old ones through modification or diffusion processes (White, 1981; DiMaggio and Powell, 1983). Such solutions to the problem of institutional genesis are limited, however, because they are exogenous and thus beg the question of the prime mover.

What is most challenging to account for theoretically is just how institutions emerge out of anarchy, that is, from a state of nature. How, in other words, do institutions ever arise from a *noninstitutional* environment? Two types of explanations have been advanced to address this hoary old Hobbesian problem.

The *invisible-hand* approach to institutional genesis, advocated to a greater or lesser degree by Menger [1883] (1963), Hayek (1973; 1976), and Nozick (1974), among others, views the emergence of institutions as a spontaneous by-product of the voluntary actions of self-interested individuals who share *no common ends or values* (see Hayek, 1976: 111). In such accounts, existing social institutions are usually conceived as Pareto-efficient equilibria; therefore they are self-sustaining (because no one who is subject to them has an incentive to change them), rather than dependent on some third-party enforcement apparatus (like the state) who existence, in turn, requires additional explanation.

Since invisible-hand arguments can offer an entirely endogenous explanation for the emergence of social institutions, they are to be admired for their parsimony and elegance (Nozick, 1974:18–22; Ullmann-Margalit, 1978). Their principal advantage is that they rely on fewer assumptions than do other kinds of explanations.

The alternative approach to the problem of institutional genesis rests on quite different premises. Rather than emerging spontaneously among self-interested actors each pursuing their own ends, institutions in this view are a product of *solidarity*. Solidarity can only arise among individuals who share some common end (Hechter, 1987). To attain this common end, actors must establish a set of obligations as well as a mechanism that enforces compliance to these obligations (Hobbes, [1651] 1968; Durkheim [1897]; 1951; Blau, 1964:253; Hayek, 1976). From the solidaristic perspective, institutions persist not because they constitute self-enforcing equilibria, but because they are supported by consciously-designed controls.

There are two varieties of solidaristic explanations. On the one hand, institutions can be *imposed* upon a given population by some conqueror or overlord. Since it is easy to explain institutional emergence in the face of significant power differentials among individuals, this solution begs too many questions to be theoretically interesting (as Hobbes well understood). On the other hand, individuals with roughly equal power can create institutions *voluntarily*, in effect binding themselves to a joint project. This contractarian process is theoretically interesting precisely because it is such a problematic outcome.

Which approach is superior, the invisible-hand or solidaristic one? There is a great deal of debate in the literature on this question. Most of the advocates of invisible-hand explanations of institutional genesis rest their arguments on repeated game theory.

Yet, these arguments only suffice for the establishment and maintenance of *conventions* (Lewis, 1969)—such as the rule that we all drive on the right hand side of the road[2]—rather than for the establishment of *n*-person *cooperative institutions*. By cooperative institution, I refer to an institution, principally serving nonclosely related kin,[3] that enables those who are subject to it to reap a surplus by agreeing on a jointly maximizing strategy that is otherwise unavailable due to the absence or inappropriateness of markets.

There is an essential difference between conventions and cooperative institutions. Cooperation is the dominant strategy in conventions because there is no free-rider problem. Compliance with a convention provides its own private reward: for example, drivers who ignore conventional rules of the road take their own lives in hand. Hence, conventions indeed can be conceived of as equilibria. In cooperative institutions (which resemble Prisoner's Dilemmas), however, defection is the dominant strategy. Hence, these institutions can persist only by precluding free riders, or by assuring would-be cooperators that they are not liable to be exploited by defectors.

Contrary to the rhetoric of Taylor (1976), Hardin (1982), and Axelrod (1984), repeated game theory offers no adequate solution to the emergence of cooperation among *n* players of a Prisoner's Dilemma supergame (Hechter, 1990). The inadequacy of repeated game theory in this respect is due to two separate problems. In the first place, there are multiple equilibria in the supergame, some of which are efficient and some inefficient (Aumann, 1985).[4] Yet under most conditions it is difficult to determine which of these multiple equilibria will be realized. In the second place, unique cooperative solutions to the supergame rest on a most unrealistic assumption—that players are endowed with perfect monitoring capacity (Bendor and Mookherjee, 1987). This assumption limits the application of game-theoretic solutions to the evolution of cooperative institutions to the smallest of groups.[5]

In the wake of these current difficulties with the invisible-hand approach, it is best to consider the merits of solidaristic explanations, even though they require much stronger initial conditions. From a solidaristic point of view, the emergence of cooperative institutions requires individual agreement on some common end, acceptance of corporate obligations, and the establishment of formal controls to preclude free riding.

Can these admittedly strong initial conditions be explained on the basis of the typical self-interested behavioral assumptions of rational choice theory?[6] I believe that the answer to this question is a qualified *yes*. Using the relatively weak assumptions that are traditional in rational choice, it is indeed possible to explain the emergence of cooperative institutions on the basis of solidaristic logic. The remainder of this chapter sketches out the basic argument, and then suggests that the argument can be applied to several types of empirical situations.

A Solidaristic Approach to the Emergence of Cooperative Institutions

Briefly, the genesis of cooperative institutions depends on the conjunction of (1) individuals' *demands* to provide themselves with jointly-produced private (that is, excludable) goods, as well as on (2) these individuals' potential *control capacity*—that is, their opportunities either to dissuade each other from free riding, or to assure each other of their intent to cooperate. Both demand and control capacity are necessary for the emergence of cooperative institutions; without either, this kind of institutional genesis is doomed.

The demand for cooperative institutions arises from individuals' desires to consume jointly-produced private goods (hereafter termed *joint goods*) that cannot be obtained by following individual strategies. Cooperative institutions are generally formed to take advantage of positive externalities, such as increasing returns to scale, risk-sharing, and cost-sharing. The demand for joint goods is heightened by contextual events like wars, invasions, epidemics, and natural disasters, as well as by endogenous processes like rapid demographic growth. These events and processes are commonly experienced by a number of people, and on this account stimulate demand for goods that spread risk—such as the protection afforded by walls around a settlement, and the insurance provided the establishment of a mutual benefit society.

But the mere existence of demand for a joint good is insufficient to guarantee its production. One of the firmest conclusions of rational choice is that whereas the production of private goods is hardly problematic, in general public goods will not be produced at optimal levels, if they are produced at all. Whether a joint good is public or private is largely a function of its excludability from potential consumers. With respect to producers, both the protection afforded by town walls and the insurance offered by mutual benefit associations are *collective* goods, but with respect to consumers they are *private* goods in that these consumers (under certain conditions) can be readily excluded from them.

Whether or not a joint good is excludable is, at least in part, due to the control capacity of the potential producers of the good. This control capacity depends upon formal controls that must emerge endogenously. The establishment of these formal controls may be seen as a series of solutions to a three-tier free-rider problem. All three of these free-rider problems must be solved before a cooperative institution can emerge. Since the first two of these problems are already well-appreciated in the literature, this chapter focuses on the third of these.

The First Tier Free-Rider Problem—Design-Making

In the first place, at least one design or plan must be devised that promises to yield the joint good. Each plan must comprise a set of *production rules* that specify what must get done by whom in order to provide an adequate supply of the good.[7] Yet since these designs are themselves a collective good, who will devise them? Although X is eager to consume the joint good, X can spend her time more profitably by attempting to add to her resource endowment than by thinking up designs for newfangled institutions.

The solution to this first-order free-rider problem is the entrepreneurial one; it lies in the individuals' incentive to think up designs that—were their design implemented—would provide them with private benefits greatly exceeding the cost of design-making. For example, ambitious individuals would gamble by formulating plans whose adoption requires either expertise or resources that they alone can claim to have.

The Second Tier Free-Rider Problem: Establishment of an
Initial Constitution

One particular design then must be selected by the relevant population. The desire to consume the joint good motivates individuals to make such a selection, for if they fail to do so, too little of the good will be produced. It is probable that each rational individual will prefer a realistic design that seems to offer the greatest amount of the good at the least (private) cost. These individual preferences must then be aggregated into a collective design. Under the conditions of the state of nature—that is, in the absence of any prior institutional framework, and in the absence of any significant resource imbalance among participants—agreement on a unanimity rule is likeliest among a relatively small group of rational egoists, because this kind of rule is most consistent with each member's private interest (Buchanan and Tullock, 1962).

The Third Tier Free-Rider Problem:
Implementation of the Design

Even though all institution-builders want to consume the joint good, each rational actor will prefer to free ride on the others' contributions. This preference may not, however, characterize those contingent cooperators who would willingly contribute to the establishment of a cooperative institution if they were assured that others would do likewise (this is often known as the *assurance problem*). If there is no means of deterring free riders, then there will be suboptimal production of the joint good—either because everyone prefers to free ride, or because the assurance problem cannot be resolved to the satisfaction of contingent cooperators.[8]

Whatever its specific causes, suboptimal production of the joint good leads the group to unravel. In order to attain optimal production, formal controls that assure high levels of compliance with production (and distribution) rules by monitoring and sanctioning group members must be adopted.

Yet since these controls are themselves a collective good, their establishment has been difficult to explain from choice-theoretic premises. One solution (the solution I have been working on) flows from the *visibility* of the production and distribution of the joint good.

For a joint good to be maximally excludable, both individual production and distribution must be highly visible. In the absence of visibility, neither free riding (a production problem), nor overconsumption (a distribution problem) can be precluded. Production visibility is at a maximum when individual effort can be well-measured by output assessment. Distribution visibility, however, is at a maximum when individuals must draw measurable shares of the joint good publically from some central store or repository.

Most (if not all) of the positive externalities of cooperative institutions rest on the advantages of pooling individual assets so that a common central store, or bank, is thereby established. The individual depositor expects to draw some net private benefit from this central store (either interest, or—most likely in the state of nature—access to a wholly different kind of good than that deposited, such as a share of the meat of a large game animal, or insurance against some loss).

Two examples should suffice to illustrate how control is attained in cooperative institutions. In hunting and gathering societies hunters pool individual inputs of time and labor in drives to kill large game that yield meat. Both the production and distribution of killed meat is highly visible to the other hunters. The effort that each hunter contributes to the drive is difficult to conceal: individual roles in the drive are agreed upon before it takes place, and whether a given person is performing his assigned role is relatively visible (although this is a less accurate way to judge his contribution than output assessment would provide). As for distribution, the meat that is produced by the drive is usually spatially concentrated—and thereby constitutes a central fund—for, given the technology of hunter-gatherers, the most efficient way to kill large animals is to stampede them into shallow arroyos or pits (Wheat, 1967; Lee, 1979).

In rotating credit associations (Hechter, 1987: Chap. 6), individuals pool a given amount of money (which is maximally visible because it is an archetypical output) for the right to draw upon the common store of money to increase their purchasing power. In this way the monetary contributions of individual participants generate what is in effect a credit line, access to which is highly visible to all other participants.

Once individual assets are pooled in a central place, however, another free-rider problem occurs: how is it possible to stop a depositor from taking more than her fair share, or from consuming the entire central fund? This is a question that faces all rational investors—would you be likely to deposit your paycheck in a bank that you believe will soon be robbed? Presumably, only if you had some assurance that your deposit is secure. *Hence it is rational for individuals to establish formal controls in cooperative institutions so as to preserve the integrity of their investment* (which, after all, is a private good). By establishing these controls, individuals inadvertently provide themselves with a collective good—namely, security of the common fund.

But who will monitor the depositors; who will sanction them; and how will the requisite sanctioning resources be produced?

All members will take on the burden of monitoring in the initial cooperative institution. Since anyone who consumes more than their fair share of the common fund appropriates some of my own assets, I am motivated to try to get my own (augmented) investment back. There is no free-rider problem here. Whereas I can assume that other members also have an interest in getting their own investment back, I have no assurance that they won't take my share, split it among themselves, and claim that my share was never found. There is no guarantee that anyone else will look after my interests.

Likewise, *all members* will sanction the noncompliant depositor; no depositor has anything to gain by associating with a rule-breaker whose assets have already been stripped—and presumably much to lose (if it is discovered that the deviant has been helped, the helper herself is then subject to sanctioning).[9] Finally, the ultimate sanctioning resource is easily produced, for it lies entirely within the control of the members themselves—ostracism from the group.[10]

By-Products of Extant Cooperative Institutions:
A Fourth Tier in Institutional Genesis

It is likely that the institutionalized group may come to produce different goods than those providing its initial rationale. This is because the group now has the immense comparative advantage that is is *already organized*[11] and therefore can produce new joint goods much more efficiently than can unorganized individuals.[12]

In certain situations, the group may even come to produce *public* (nonexcludable) goods. This can occur if members gain so much from the production of a public good that they are willing to provide it even to non-contributors.[13] In larger groups, this can also occur due to *agency* considerations. This will happen if the agent is not fully constrained by her principals, and if she can increase her own reputation by transforming some of the assets of the central fund into public goods.[14]

All told, this analysis suggests that cooperative institutions indeed can arise from the interaction of rational egoists in a state of nature. In such an environment, however, cooperative institutions will emerge only in a contractarian fashion. Without prior cooperative institutions, there can be no entrepreneurial route to new ones. This is why the earliest institutions tend to be of the "primitive communist" variety.[15] In institutionally rich environments where, for example, individual private property rights have been established, it is far simpler for these institutions to emerge via an entrepreneurial rather than a contractarian route on account of decision-making costs, and of the costs of specifying fully adequate contracts (Williamson, 1975; North, 1981).

This discussion of the emergence of cooperative institutions has two principal implications. If institutions emerge as a result of the demand for joint private goods, then *shifts in a variety of environmental and demo-*

graphic conditions will heighten demand for certain kinds of joint goods and favor the emergence of institutions supplying these goods.

Thus, the members of foraging societies tend to form local groups in the dry season—when the scarcity of water increases the benefits of cooperation among different nuclear families—but these groups disband when there is sufficient water to meet the subsistence needs of individual families (Johnson and Earle, 1987). Likewise, as markets penetrate into economically isolated territories this leads to the establishment of insurance institutions (Hechter, 1987). Finally, the rise of insecurity (due to the threat of invasion, piracy, and so forth) promotes the establishment of protective associations. Other kinds of shifts will diminish the demand for such institutions. Hence the growth of insurance markets in the late nineteenth century is associated with the decline of fraternal insurance institutions. If some public good-providing organization in a territory did not go through the first stage (that is, if it did not grow from the roots of some private good-producing institution), such evidence would contradict the thrust of this analysis.

Yet demand alone is insufficient to produce cooperative institutions: *both in their roles as producers and consumers, individuals must be highly visible to one another in order to reduce the severity of the free-rider and assurance problems.*

In the state of nature, bulky goods that must be cooperatively acquired are likely to promote both kinds of visibility. This is consistent with the finding that meat (at least some of which is often cooperatively acquired) is more widely shared among hunter-gatherers than other types of food (Kaplan and Hill, 1985). Irrigation systems provide a graphic example of a cooperative institution that develops to provide access to a bulky joint good. Wittfogel (1957:18), for example, notes that water is a distinctive resource in that it has a tendency to gather in bulk.[16] Further research into the visibility of the production of different kinds of joint goods, and of the potential centricity of these goods, doubtless will provide a richer body of empirical implications for the genesis of cooperative institutions.

It should be emphasized that the analysis in this chapter is quite different from Mancur Olson's (1965) well-known explanation of the development of collective goods-seeking organizations like trade unions and farm organizations. Insofar as these groups sought to raise the wages of whole classes of workers, they aimed to produce a collective good. Given this, the optimal strategy for any given worker is to free ride and cash in on the (presumably successful) efforts of union organizers and their credulous followers. How, then, did these groups emerge? Olson's explanation is that the early trade unions (in the days before the passage of closed-shop legislation) could lure members only if they provided them with desirable selective incentives, including insurance. In Olson's account, therefore, insurance is considered to be the by-product of trade unions.

The problem with Olson's explanation is that, like formal controls, selective incentives are themselves a collective good. This means that they, too, have to be produced by rational egoists. How is it that a group aiming to provide a public good can attract any rational members at all, let alone manage to produce selective incentives? As the previous analysis shows, the rise of groups providing immanent joint goods entails no such liability. Since they are formed for the provision of *private* goods, there is no initial free-rider problem. To obtain their goods, members are led to adopt formal controls that make possible production of the goods. Once the goods have been produced, they can be used in a variety of ways. For example, there is no inherent reason why the members of an insurance group cannot convert their common assets into a strike fund and reconstitute themselves as a trade union.

Empirical Applications

While there is little hard evidence about the state of nature, there are at least three kinds of data that we can look to for corroboration of this explanation of cooperative institutional development. These are archeological and ethnographic evidence about the formation of multi-family groups among hunters and gatherers, and historical evidence about the emergence of cooperative institutions in the absence of an extensive institutional infrastructure—as in territories (like early medieval western Europe) where a pre-existing institutional infrastructure has virtually collapsed, where one can study the origin of towns, guilds, and urban leagues, or in frontier regions (such as in 19th century western territories of the United States), where one can study the formation of cattlemen's associations, miners' associations, land clubs, and wagon trains.[17] In the remainder of the chapter, I will briefly apply some of these ideas to the rise of town partnerships and guilds in medieval Europe.

The Rise of Town Trade Partnerships, Guilds, and Merchant Leagues in Medieval Europe

Given opportunities for long-distance trade (for reasons that lie entirely beyond the scope of the present inquiry), individual merchants attempting to attain maximum profits were forced into a variety of joint ventures. Some of these were short-lived joint ventures providing protection against pirates and highwaymen. Others provided credit that was otherwise unavailable, for this was an era in which there were no banks or other financial institutions:[18]

> In a society still as crude as that of the eleventh century, private initiative could succeed only by having recourse to cooperation. Too many perils threatened the wandering existence of the merchant not to impose on him first of all the fundamental necessity of forming in groups for the sake of common defense. Still other motives impelled him to unite with his fellows. At fairs and markets, should a dispute arise, he found in them favorable witnesses, or bondsmen who would be security for him in a court of justice. In common with them he was able to buy at wholesale merchandise which, left to his own resources, he would have been unable to get. His credit was increased by the collective credit of which he supplied a part, and thanks thereto he was able more easily to come out on top in competition with his rivals . . . Trade in the late Middle Ages was known only in that primitive form of which the caravan is the characteristic manifestation. Maritime or land trade was possible only by grace of the mutual assurance an association inspired in its members, of the discipline which it imposed upon them, of the regulations to which it subjected them. And this feature was always in evidence. Boats sailed only when assembled in flotillas, just as merchants travelled the country only in bands. Security existed for them only if guaranteed by force, and force was an attribute of collectivity (Pirenne, 1956:84–85).

The most characteristic twelfth and thirteenth century method of investment was to form partnerships (*soceitas*). By distributing shares, partnerships were able to mobilize considerable capital for specific enterprises. Most of these partnerships were small-scale affairs:

> All partners bore full responsibility. Within the terms of the contract, each was guarantor for the debts of the whole. Such societies lacked perpetuity, also, being created for a specific voyage, for example, or a state length of time. Everything depended upon the personal relationships of the partners (Mundy and Riesenberg, 1958:38).

The capital requirements for overseas trade during this period were formidable. In Venice, for example, a fleet of three or four galleys employed a crew of 600 to 800 men (Lane, 1966:44–45). The voyage to Flanders took at least a year, and often as much as two. The cargo carried by a fleet of the Flemish galleys was worth about 250,000 ducats. The relatively short voyage to Alexandria required only 3–6 months, but the cargoes were often valued at half a million ducats. The cost of these galleys, of their fittings, of food and wages for the crews, and especially of the cargoes exceeded the resources of the richest of families.

Whereas these partnerships were temporary associations that were disbanded after the successful completion of a voyage, the establishment of longer lasting cooperative institutions—the town guilds—can be explained in similar fashion. Max Weber's analysis of the origins of the guilds bears a striking resemblance to the role of demand in the previous discussion:

> [These guilds] had by no means been primarily created for the purpose of influencing political conditions. Originally they were substitutes for something their members frequently very much missed in the early medieval city: the backing of a clan, and its protective guarantees. They provided the services otherwise supplied by the clan: help in the case of personal injury or threats, aid in economic distress, elimination of feuds between members by means of peaceful conciliation, and payment of the wergild liabilities of members (in an English case). The guilds provided for the [member's] social needs by holding periodic feasts—a practice traceable to pagan ritual meals—and for his funeral with the participation of the brethren; they guaranteed salvation of his soul through good deeds and secured for him from the common treasury indulgences and the benevolence of powerful saints. It goes without saying that such protective associations also represented joint interests ... The effect of all these associations [mutual protection guilds, and religious and social fraternities] was essentially indirect. They facilitated the city union by habituating the burghers to the formation of coalitions in the pursuit of common interests, and by providing models for the cumulation of leadership positions in the hands of persons who had gained experience and social influence in the direction of such associations (Weber, [1922] 1968:1257–1258).

Guilds also were fostered by the organization of caravans that were required for overland trade. Note how visibility is maximized by the structure of the caravan:

> Essentially travellers, merchants could not venture abroad alone without running the risk of forthwith falling a prey to some robber. They were therefore compelled to form regular caravans in order to make their long journeys with safety. In each town they assembled before their departure under the command of a chief. At their head marched a standard-bearer, behind whom stretched the train of wagons and beasts of burden. To the packages and bales were bound the tents and tent-poles that were to be set up for the camp at night, as well as the weapons, bows, arrows and swords, to which the comrades would have recourse at the first alarm. Naturally such an organization implied rigorous and practically military discipline. Like the modern caravans in the East, these medieval caravans obeyed regulations, which laid down not only their order of march, but also each man's position and rights at the markets and fairs where they stopped. The dangers they ran together, the obedience rendered to the same chief, the community of interest and sentiment, maintained among their members a powerful corporate spirit. When it returned home the association was not dissolved. It became a gild, a *hansa*, a brotherhood, a *carité*. Now these phenomena were certainly not isolated. Probability compels us to admit that, as like causes produce like effects, all the places devoted to external trade learnt to develop similar institutions (Pirenne, 1963:22).

But if this account explains the motivations for the origins of the guilds, why were these associations not dissolved thereafter? Part of the answer is provided by a study of the parish guilds of London, which offered their members a variety of other kinds of joint private goods—including welfare benefits, health insurance, loans, and the settlement of disputes between members without recourse to the law (Unwin, 1963: 118–22). When these benefit-providing groups were composed of established craftsmen in the same calling they often organized to enforce a monopoly on their goods (Williams, 1963:174). The guilds regulated entry into the trade by setting rules for apprentices and the inheritance of tools, among others. Compliance to these rules was increased by the use of informers (Thrupp, 1963:238–40). The officers of the guild could levy fines for the breaking of certain rules on the basis of one anonymous informer, who sometimes received part of the fine. (The guilds borrowed this practice from the Medieval church.) Finally, solidarity could also be fostered by public ostracism, as in the case of the butchers' guilds. Butchers practiced their craft at their own homes, so they usually lived apart from the rest of the town (Thrupp, 1963:249). In these circumstances visibility was high and the greatest economies of control could be realized.

The merchant guilds came to take responsibility for public goods such as the upkeep of the knights charged with town defenses and the collection of the tolls levied on all merchandise brought by land or water. Their advantage, in this respect, was due not only to their superior wealth, but also to the strength of their organization:

> The prosperity of trade was so intimately bound up with the organization of the towns in which it had located that the members of the gild were almost automatically charged with making provision for the needs that were most pressing. The castellans had no reason to restrain them from meeting, through their own resources, those emergencies that were clearly apparent. They permitted them to "extemporize," as it were, in official communal administration. . . . Thus, without having any legal warrant therefor, the merchant association devoted itself of its own accord to the organization and the management of the nascent city. It made up for the impotence of public power. At St. Omer the gild devoted a part of its revenues to the construction of defense works and to the maintenance of the streets. There is no doubt but that other Flemish towns, its neighbors, did the same. The name of "counts of the hanse" which the treasurers of the city of Lille kept all through the Middle Ages is sufficient proof, in the absence of other records, that there also the chiefs of the voluntary corporation of merchants drew upon the treasury of the gild for the benefit of their fellow citizens. . . . The result of all this, manifestly, was that the gilds were, in the region of Flanders, the initiators of city autonomy. Of their own accord they charged themselves with a task which no one else had been able to carry out. Officially they had no right to act as they did; their intervention is to be explained solely by the cohesion which existed among their members, by the influence their group enjoyed, by the resources they disbursed, and finally by the understanding they had of the collective needs of the middle-class population. It can be stated, without exaggeration, that in the course of the eleventh century the chiefs of the gild performed, *de facto*, the functions of communal magistrates in every town (Pirenne, 1956:133–35).

A town that tried to abolish guilds permanently would have had to expand its permanent administrative staff (Thrupp, 1963:245).

The development of those proto-state institutions known as merchant leagues (such as the League of the Rhine, the Swabian League, and the Hanseatic League) shows that institutional development at a higher level of aggregation can also be explained by this kind of logic. Like the guilds, these merchant leagues also arose to provide joint private goods—especially protection for their members—and to increase the profitability of trade. The perilous conditions of overland trade made merchant leagues desirable, for it was beyond the resources of any single city's merchant association to improve or construct roads, to subsidize maritime navigational aids, to minimize the risks of piracy, to overcome fluctuating currency rates, and to enforce contracts in multiple locales. Evidence that merchant leagues were much more common in Germany, where there was a notable absence of strong central authority, than in France, where there central authority was less problematic in this era (Thompson, 1931:129–130) is consistent with the thesis that the rise of these leagues was due to the demand for protection.

In addition to the existence of a strong demand condition, the Hansa exercised strong control over its members:

> The statutes of the Hansa were strict. Any person who captured a member of the League could trade in none of the cities. The citizens of one town could obtain justice in another. A member of the League could demand help from a city if molested. One who broke his word with one city was boycotted by all. Any one who purchased stolen goods was likewise held guilty. Whoever married a foreigner forfeited his rights in the League. Not only was marriage prohibited with foreigners, but not even a foreign commercial partnership could be formed. In the markets of the League sales could not take place between two merchants not members of the League. In this way the Hansa acted as a middleman. Foreign merchants in vain sought permission to settle in Hansa towns. In Cologne foreign merchants were permitted to reside for only six weeks at a time and that only three times a year, and other cities had similar restrictions. The Hansers were always exceedingly jealous of competition, and employed every means to keep absolute and exclusive commercial control so far as possible (Thompson, 1931:163–64).

This control was made possible by arrangements that heightened the visibility of Hansers trading in foreign cities. A description of London's Steelyard—one of the most famous Hanseatic trading posts—provides a graphic illustration:

> The Steelyard was situated on the banks of the Thames, just above London Bridge, so the merchants had their own docks. The houses of the company were protected by a high wall strongly fortified. . . . Neighboring buildings outside of the Steelyard proper were rented and controlled by the League. The clerks and servants lived here as in a monastery. The working staff of employees was divided into units

designated as "families," each having a head called a "husband" who was responsible for the members thereof. Each "family" had its own table and its own sleeping quarters. Discipline was severe. There were heavy fines for disobedience of rules, for drunkenness, for keeping late hours, for going out of bounds. No woman was allowed within the compound under any circumstances. Married members had to leave their wives at home (Thompson, 1931:166–7).

Once established, the leagues could act for other collective ends—to promote war and to provide trade monopolization (ends that were especially prominent in the case of the Hanseatic League), as well as for wholly *public* ends. Thus the Hanseatic League, the most famous and powerful of these merchant leagues: "built lighthouses, marked channels, fixed buoys off reefs and rocks and established licensed pilots. In the fifteenth century a 'Sea Book' was compiled which described channels, harbors and lighthouses, even the tides, from Reval to Cadiz" (Thompson, 1931:173–74).

Conclusion

The driving force in this explanation of the origin of cooperative institutions is the rational egoist's desire to consume a small number of private goods—like security, insurance, and credit—which can only be produced jointly and therefore induce these individuals to enter into cooperative social relations. No doubt the character of the social context plays an important role in determining the demand for these particular goods. The inhabitants of territories where security is problematic are likely to desire security; those who live through drastic fluctuations in contextual conditions are likely to desire insurance; those who live in capital-poor environments demand credit, and so forth.

In effect, the demand for these joint goods serves as a series of "Schelling points" that enable otherwise unconnected individuals to "coordinate predictions, to read the same message in the common situation, to identify the one course of action that their expectations of each other can converge on" (Schelling, 1960:54). Linked by their common interest in consuming some joint good, these individuals are, however, reluctant to invest their own time and other assets in cooperative efforts in the absence of third-party enforcement, for they want to be assured that their investment will yield a positive return. This assurance can only be provided if it is expected that free riding can be deterred. Hence, in order to consume these joint goods, individuals must create their own controls.

I have argued that an essential determinant of the rise of controls lies in conditions allowing for visibility in both the production and consumption of given joint goods. In the state of nature, this visibility will be at a maximum when joint goods are collected and disbursed from some central place. The collection and disbursement of killed meat among hunter-gatherers, the collection and disbursement of irrigated water among horticulturalists, the formation of partnerships to engage in long-distance trade, and the establishment of caravans on the American frontier all satisfy this key requirement, and therefore provide for high visibility.[19] Visibility, in turn, is a necessary condition for the development of controls. From these controls, cooperative institutions are born.

Acknowledgment

I would like to thank Mary Brinton, Allen Buchanan, and Debra Friedman for their helpful comments.

Notes

1. Consider an elevator having male and female passengers. If male passengers are observed to allow the females to exit first, this is a collective behavioral regularity. Whether this behavioral regularity is due to the presence of a norm or to explicit rules is beside the point.

2. For the purposes of this chapter, language itself may be considered to be a convention.

3. This restriction is due to the fact that the rise of institutions among close relations can be explained easily by evolutionary arguments based on genetic relatedness. Such reasoning is, however, generally insufficient to account for institutions whose scope surpasses the members of a nuclear family.

4. The problem of multiple equilibria is double-barrelled. On the one hand, cooperation may not emerge because some of these equilibria are inefficient. On the other hand, cooperation may not emerge even if the various equilibria are all efficient, since they are unlikely to be equally preferred by all the players or the game. This situation then leads to a noncooperative bargaining problem.

5. In the absence of perfect monitoring capacity, a player can never be certain of the moves that other players have taken in past plays of the game. Thus, she cannot infer that cooperation is ever rational.

6. This question is critical, for if we suspend self-interested behavioral assumptions—and allow individuals to have internalized values or some small but positive amount of altruism—then there is an all too easy way to overcome the assurance problem, and thereby to account for the emergence of cooperative institutions. This strategy is akin to invoking a *deus ex machina*, but there can be no theoretical justification for so doing.

7. I ignore the obvious complication that the initial production functions for the joint good will be estimates, and that disagreements may well result about the accuracy of these estimates.

8. There is a growing experimental literature on the use of provision points and

money-back guarantees as means of resolving the assurance problem. Whereas there is evidence that some of these arrangements do, in fact, result in the production of greater public goods, each of them is imposed *exogenously* in the experiments. Hence these solutions to the free-rider and assurance problems are inconsistent with the premises of this analysis.

9. In more complex situations where there are alternative benefit-providing institutions, deviant actors often gain a negative reputation that makes them unsuitable for admission to any such institution. After other participants get their investment back, what is their incentive to ruin the deviant's reputation? Why should rational egoists be concerned about the fortunes of the participants in *other* institutions? This kind of problem is endemic in academic hiring situations, where the members of sending departments often provide misleading information to receiving departments in hopes of getting rid of a troublesome colleague or a sub-par student. The only force that can counter this free-rider problem is the damage that such deceit might bring to the information provider in further repeat dealings. Hence, the less frequent the contact between the members of two academic departments, the less reliable the information supplied about potential colleagues and students, *ceteris paribus*. The multiplexity of ties between groups increases the probability of this intergroup sanctioning.

10. It should be noted that this solution to the emergence of cooperative institutions is practicable only in relatively small groups. In essence, the creation of a central store of resources commits participants to involvement in a repeated game. As such, many of the mechanisms that produce cooperation in the literature on repeated games (Taylor, 1976; Axelrod, 1984) are employed here to the same effect. The reader may wonder wherein this approach differs from the invisible-hand approach. Whereas repeated game theorists take the existence of the supergame (and sometimes the existence of a specific discount rate) as a given, this analysis explains how it is that rational egoists voluntarily commit themselves to social situations involving repeated exchange.

11. The connection between pre-existing organizations founded to produce joint private goods and public good-providing organizations often has been stressed in the literature on social movements (Oberschall, 1973; McAdam *et al.*, 1988). Thus in her analysis of the emergence of the contemporary women's movement, Evans (1980) locates its roots in informal networks of women who had come to know one another in the context of prior civil rights and New Left political organizations. Black churches (which offered insurance benefits) played an important crystallizing role in the development of the civil rights movement (Oberschall, 1973:126–27; MacAdam, 1982; Morris, 1984). Fraternal-service groups played a similar role in the emergence of local anti-pornography movements (Curtis and Zurcher, 1973:56); and mosques played this kind of role in the early days of the Iranian Revolution (Snow and Marshall, 1984).

12. Naturally, this kind of an argument has its limits, otherwise all production would be concentrated in just one institution. For an interesting discussion of the limits of integration in firms, see Hart (1987).

13. Thus, to satisfy his desire to watch movies in the middle of the night, Howard Hughes bought a local Las Vegas station (Hardin, 1982).

14. For example, the agents of some American ethnically-based fraternal societies had political aspirations in their communities, and by judiciously investing these funds they could further these political aspirations (Stolarik, 1980). Likewise, the managers of large Minneapolis corporations are motivated to provide charitable donations in the community by the access to high prestige social circles that these donations uniquely provide (Galaskiewicz, 1985). The provision of public goods also can be a by-product of relatively homogeneous groups. In such groups, access to the joint good may be limited only to those members who contribute to specific public goods that are unrelated to the group's

initial rationale. Thus some Pittsburgh fraternal associations expelled members who had committed crimes or treason, or who hired out as strikebreakers (Galey, 1977). This then explains how the self-interest of rational egoists can lead them to produce collective (and sometimes even public) goods.

15. In contrast, the Marxian explanation for primitive communism rests on questionable arguments about the absence of a surplus beyond that necessary for subsistence.

16. Clearly, the demand for a predictable water supply is insufficient to account for actual irrigation works, for many peoples who would have gained from it did not adopt such practices. Whether the adopters of irrigation had a visibility advantage over nonadoptors remains to be explored in further research.

17. Discussions of the emergence of land clubs, cattlemen's associations, wagon trains (Anderson and Hill, 1979), as well as of the development of property rights in mining claims on the American frontier are (Umbeck, 1981; Libecap, 1978a, b) consistent with those of the origin of medieval guilds.

18. For other explanations of the origins of the medieval guilds, see Thrupp (1963: 230–236).

19. This provides a simple explanation for one of Karl Polanyi's (1977) key empirical findings, namely that *social systems based on the principles of reciprocity or redistribution historically precede those based on the market*. Whereas both conventions and cooperative institutions can emerge in the state of nature, this is quite impossible for a market system in which production and distribution are decentralized—and therefore have low visibility. The enforcement of contracts in market society requires the establishment of a cooperative institution—the state—which must evolve in a nonmarket setting.

References

Anderson, Terry L. and P. J. Hill (1979). "An American experiment in anarcho-capitalism: The *not* so wild, wild west." *The Journal of Libertarian Studies*, 3(1):9–29.

Aumann, Robert J. (1985). "Repeated Games". Pp. 209–242 in George R. Feiwel, ed., *Issues in Contemporary Microeconomics and Welfare*. Albany, NY: State University of New York Press.

Axelrod, Robert. (1984). *The Evolution of Cooperation*. New York: Basic Books.

Bendor, Jonathan, and Dilip Mookherjee. (1987). "Institutional structure and the logic of ongoing collective action." *American Political Science Review*, 81(1): 129–54.

Blau, Peter M. (1964). *Exchange and Power in Social Life*. New York: John Wiley.

Buchanan, James M. (1975). *The Limits of Liberty*. Chicago: University of Chicago Press.

Buchanan, James M. and Gordon Tullock. (1962). *The Calculus of Consent*. Ann Arbor: University of Michigan Press.

Curtis, Russell L. and Louis A. Zurcher, Jr. (1973). "Stable resources of protest movement: The multi-organizational field." *Social Forces*, 52(1):53–60.

DiMaggio, Paul J. and Walter W. Powell. (1983). "Institutional isomorphism." *American Sociological Review*, 48(2):147–160.

Durkheim, Emile. (1951). *Suicide*. New York: Free Press. [Originally published 1897.]
Evans, Sarah. (1980). *Personal Politics*. New York: Vintage Books.
Galaskiewicz, Joseph. (1985). *Social Organization of an Urban Grants Economy: A Study of Business Philanthropy and Nonprofit Organizations*. Orlando, FL: Academic Press.
Galey, Margaret E. (1977). "Ethnicity, fraternalism, social and mental health." *Ethnicity*, 4(1):19–53.
Hardin, Russell. (1982). *Collective Action*. Baltimore: Johns Hopkins University Press (for Resources for the Future).
Hart, Oliver. (1987). "Incomplete contracts and the theory of the firm". Paper presented at the Conference on Knowledge and Institutional Change, University of Minnesota.
Hayek, Friedrich A. (1973). *Law, Legislation and Liberty*, Vol. I. Chicago: University of Chicago Press.
Hayek, Friedrich A. (1976). *Law, Legislation and Liberty*, Vol. II. Chicago: University of Chicago Press.
Hechter, Michael. (1987). *Principles of Group Solidarity*. Berkeley and London: University of California Press.
Hechter, Michael. (1990). "On the inadequacy of game theory for the resolution of real-world collective action problems." In M. Levi and K.S. Cook, eds., *The Limits of Rationality*. Chicago: University of Chicago Press. In press.
Hobbes, Thomas. (1968). *Leviathan*, edited by C. B. Macpherson. Harmondsworth, England: Penguin. [Originally published 1651.]
Jensen, Michael C. and William H. Meckling. (1976). "Theory of the firm: Managerial behavior, agency costs and ownership structure." *Journal of Financial Economics*, 3(4):305–360.
Johnson, Allen W. and Timothy Earle. (1987). *The Evolution of Human Societies*. Stanford: Stanford University Press.
Kaplan, Hillard and Kim Hill. (1985). "Food sharing among Ache foragers: Tests of explanatory hypotheses." *Current Anthropology*, 26(2):223–239.
Lane, Frederic C. (1966). "Economic consequences of organized violence." Pp. 412–428 in *Venice and History*. Baltimore: Johns Hopkins University Press. [Originally published (1958) in the *Journal of Economic History*, 18:401–17.]
Lee, Richard B. (1979). *The !Kung San*. Cambridge: Cambridge University Press.
Lewis, David. (1969). *Convention: A Philosophical Study*. Cambridge: Harvard University Press.
Libecap, Gary D. (1978a). "Economic variables and the development of the law: The case of western mineral rights." *Journal of Economic History*, 38:338–62.
Libecap, Gary D. (1978b). *The Evolution of Private Mineral Rights*. New York: Arno Press.
McAdam, Doug. (1982). *Political Process and the Development of Black Insurgency, 1930–1970*. Chicago: University of Chicago Press.
McAdam, Doug, John D. McCarthy, and Mayer N. Zald. (1988). "Social movements and collective behavior: Building micro-macro bridges." In Neil J. Smelser, ed., *Handbook of Sociology*. Newbury Park, CA: Sage. pp. 695–738.

Menger, Carl. (1963). *Investigations into the Method of the Social Sciences with Special Reference to Economics*, edited by Louis Schneider. Translated by Francis J. Nock. Campaign-Urbana: University of Illinois Press. [Originally published 1883.]

Morris, Aldon. (1984). *The Origins of the Civil Rights Movement*. New York: Free Press.

Mundy, John H. and Peter Riesenberg. (1958). *The Medieval Town*. Princeton: D. Van Nostrand.

North, Douglass C. (1981). *Structure and Change in Economic History*. New York: Norton.

Nozick, Robert. (1974). *Anarchy, State and Utopia*. New York: Basic Books.

Oberschall, Anthony. (1973). *Social Conflict and Social Movements*. Englewood Cliffs, N.J.: Prentice-Hall.

Olson, Mancur. (1965). *The Logic of Collective Action*. Cambridge: Harvard University Press.

Parsons, Talcott. (1937). *The Structure of Social Action*. New York: McGraw-Hill.

Pirenne, Henri. (1956). *Medieval Cities: Their Origins and the Revival of Trade*. Translated by Frank D. Halsey. New York: Anchor Books. [Originally published 1925.]

Pirenne, Henri. (1963). *Early Democracies in the Low Countries: Urban Society and Political Conflict in the Middle Ages and the Renaissance*. Translated by J. V. Saunders. New York: Harper Torchbooks. [Originally published 1915.]

Polanyi, Karl. (1977). *The Livelihood of Man*, edited by Harry W. Pearson. New York: Academic Press.

Schelling, Thomas C. (1960). *The Strategy of Conflict*. Cambridge: Harvard University Press.

Snow, David A. and Susan Marshall. (1984). "Cultural imperialism, social movements, and the Islamic revival." Pp. 131–152 in Louis Kriesberg, ed., *Social Movements, Conflicts and Change*, Vol. 7. Greenwich CT: JAI Press.

Stolarik, M. Mark. (1980). "Slovak fraternal benefit societies." Pp. 130–145 in Scott Cummings, ed., *Urban Self-Help in America*. Port Washington, NY: Kennikat Press.

Taylor, Michael. (1976). *Anarchy and Cooperation*. London: John Wiley.

Thompson, James Westfall. (1931). *Economic and Social History of Europe in the Later Middle Ages*. New York: The Century Co.

Thrupp, Sylvia L. (1963). "The gilds." Pp. 230–280 in M. M. Postan, E. E. Rich, and Edward Miller, eds., *The Cambridge Economic History of Europe*. Vol. III Cambridge: Cambridge University Press.

Ullman-Margalit, Edna. (1978). "Invisible hand explanations." *Synthese*, 39:263–91.

Umbeck, John R. (1981). *A Theory of Property Rights with Application to the California Gold Rush*. Ames, Iowa: Iowa State University Press.

Unwin, George. (1963). *The Gilds and Companies of London*. London: Frank Cass & Co. [Originally published 1908.]

Weber, Max (1968). *Economy and Society*, edited by Guenther Roth and Claus Wittich. New York: Bedminster Press. [originally published 1922]

Wheat, J. B. (1967). "A Paleo-Indian bison kill". *Scientific American*, January.
White, Harrison C. (1981). "Where do markets come from?" *American Journal of Sociology*, 87(3):517–547.
Williams, Gwyn A. (1963). *Medieval London: From Commune to Capital*. London: The Athlone Press.
Williamson, Oliver. (1975). *Markets and Hierarchies*. New York: Free Press.
Wittfogel, Karl A. (1957). *Oriental Despotism: A Comparative Study of Total Power*. New Haven: Yale University Press.

2

The Emergence of Norms*

James S. Coleman

Much of sociological theory takes social norms as given, and proceeds to examine individual behavior or the behavior of social systems when norms exist. Yet to do this without raising at some point the question of why norms exist at all, and how they came into existence, is to forsake the more important sociological problems in order to address the less important.

Whatever the reason for neglect of this question (and the reason differs for different sets of theorists), I will show in what follows that the emergence of norms can be accounted for by two simple principles. The first of these concerns the conditions in which a demand for effective norms will arise; the second concerns the conditions under which the demand will be satisfied. Both sets of conditions may be described as social structural.

As much as any single concept in the social sciences, a "norm" is a property of a social system, not of an actor within it. In part because it bears a correspondence, at the level of a social system, to "value" at the level of an individual, and because norms may affect individuals' values, this concept has come to play an extensive role in theories developed by

---

*An extension of the work described here can be found in Chapters 10, 11, and 30 of Coleman (1990).

some sociologists. The reasons are even more fundamental. The concept of a norm at a macrosocial level, governing the behavior of individuals at a microsocial level, provides a convenient device for explaining individual behavior, taking the social system as given. It is a device especially useful for those sociologists characterized by Sorokin (1928) as members of the sociologistic school of social theorists. This is a school of which Emile Durkheim was the most prominent member, for he began with social organization and in a part of his work asked the question, "How is an individual's behavior affected by the social system within which he finds himself?"

For another school of social theory, of which Talcott Parsons was the most prominent member, the concept of norm provides a basis for a principle of action that plays a role in the theory comparable to that of maximizing utility for rational choice theory. The principle is approximately, "Persons behave in accordance with social norms," leaving examination of the content of norms as the theoretical task at the macro level.

Quite apart from its role in social theory, the use of the concept of norm in describing how societies function is important. This is especially so for the description of traditional stable societies. A description of the functioning of caste India without the concept of *dharma* (meaning "duty" or "appropriate behavior," or "behavior in accordance with accepted norms"), would hardly be possible.[1] In stable societies, fixed or slowly changing norms constitute an important component of the society's self-governing mechanisms.

Both the evident relevance of norms for the functioning of societies, and the importance of norm as a concept throughout the history of social theory, provide bases for its position in contemporary social theory. It has not one but *two* entries in the *International Encyclopedia of the Social Sciences* (both written by sociologists), one of which begins, "No concept is invoked more often by social scientists in explanations of human behavior than 'norm.'" As an example, Ralf Dahrendorf (by no means one of those sociologists most wedded to the concept) in an essay "On the origin of social inequality," states

> The origin of inequality is thus to be found in the existence in all human societies of norms of behavior to which sanctions are attached . . . (T)he derivation suggested here has the advantage of leading back to presuppositions (the existence of norms and the necessity of sanctions) which at least in the context of social theory may be taken as axiomatic" (1968, p. 104).

Though norms and sanctions may be taken as axiomatic by many sociologists, they constitute an unacceptable *deus ex machina* for other social scientists—a concept brought in to explain social behavior, yet itself left unexplained. Some rational choice theorists, armed with utility maximization as a principle of action, regard the concept as altogether unnecessary. To take this stance, however, is to ignore important processes in the functioning of social systems, and thus to cripple the theory. It is one thing to refuse to take norms as given, as starting points in social theory; it is quite another to ignore their existence altogether. Here I refuse to take norms as given, but I ask how they can emerge and be maintained among a set of rational individuals.

In the present theory, social norms enter in the following way: They specify what actions are regarded by a set of persons as proper or correct, or what actions are improper or incorrect. They are purposively generated, in that those persons who initiate or help maintain a norm see themselves as benefitting from its being observed, or harmed by its being violated. They are ordinarily enforced by sanctions, which are either rewards for carrying out those actions regarded as correct, or punishments for carrying out actions regarded as incorrect. Those holding the norm claim a right to apply sanctions, and recognize the right of others holding the norm to do so as well. Persons whose actions are subject to norms (who themselves may or may not hold the norm) take into account the norms, with their potential rewards or punishments, not as absolute determinants of their actions, but as elements which enter their decision about what actions are in their interest to carry out.

Furthermore, a norm may be embedded in a social system in a more fundamental way that is internal to the individual, with sanctions applied by the individual to his own actions. In such a case, a norm is said to be internalized, and the individual feels internally applied rewards for actions held to be proper by an internalized norm, or internally applied punishments for actions held to be improper by an internalized norm.

Beyond individual norms there is interdependence among norms, such that many are part of a "structure of norms." The most elaborate such structures are those described by *dharma* in India or analogous systems in other societies with long cultural traditions.

Viewed in this way, the tasks for the theorist are substantial. First, one must establish the conditions under which a norm with a particular content will arise. This includes answering the question of why a norm does not always arise when the existence of an effective norm would be in the interests of all or most persons. Related to this are the tasks of specifying who will come to hold the norm, and specifying whose actions will be its target.

Second, is the determination of the strength of sanctions and their prevalence, recognizing that applying a sanction may entail costs for the sanctioner. Related to this is the question of what kinds of sanctions will be applied, since there is a variety (and, empirically, it is evident that various kinds of sanctions are in fact applied, ranging from those that damage or enhance reputations to those that impose physical damage or provide material benefits).

Examples of Norms and Sanctions

To gain some sense of what is meant by norms and sanctions, it is useful to begin with examples.

1. A child aged three, walking with its mother on a sidewalk in Berlin, unwraps a small piece of candy and drops the cellophane on the sidewalk. An older woman, passing, scolds the child for dropping the cellophane and admonishes the mother for not disciplining the child. A child aged three and a half, walking with its mother on a sidewalk in New York City, unwraps a piece of cellophane and drops the paper on the sidewalk. An older woman is passing by, but says nothing, not even noticing the action of the child.

Several questions are raised by this example. Why does the older woman in Berlin assume the right to scold the child and admonish the mother? Why does a woman in a similar circumstance in New York not do the same? Does the woman in New York not feel the right to discipline the child, or does her failure to act arise from other sources?

2. In an organization that provides free coffee and tea to its employees, one employee who drinks tea takes his cup to obtain hot water to get some tea. All tea bags are gone. He expresses no dismay, remarking to another person standing there: "This often happens, but I have taken some tea bags back to my office just for such occasions." The other person responds in a disapproving way, "It's people like you, stashing tea bags away, who create the problem."

This example also raises questions. Again, how did the second person come to acquire a right to express disapproval? And why did the first person leave himself open for such a comment, by his remarks? Further, why did he accept the disapproval of the second person, apparently acknowledging the right of the second person to impose this sanction?

3. A high school girl on a date at a beach house on the lake finds herself in a crowd in which the others, including her date, are smoking marijuana. The others encourage her to do so as well, showing disap-

proval and disdain at her reluctance. The reluctance, in turn, is produced by her knowledge that her parents would disapprove.

This example raises questions about conflict: Can there be two conflicting norms governing the same actions? If so, then what determines which will govern the action, if either does? And if conflicting norms do occur, what is the class of situations in which they arise?

Classes of and Distinctions among Norms

The diversity among the examples above suggests that some definitions and some classifications among norms will be useful at this point.

First, norms are directed at certain actions, which I will call *focal actions*. These are the actions over which persons other than the actor assume rights of partial control. In the first example of the 3-year-old and the cellophane candy wrapper in Berlin, the focal action was dropping the wrapper on the sidewalk, or more generally any action that had the effect of littering the sidewalk.

Some norms such as this one discourage or proscribe the focal action; I will call these *proscriptive* norms. Other norms, such as the norm of smoking marijuana held by the young people at the lake, presented in example 3, encourage or prescribe the focal action (*prescriptive* norms). Norms of the first type provide a negative feedback in the system, damping out the focal action, while norms of the second type provide positive feedback, thus encouraging the focal action. When there are only two possible actions, of course, one is prescribed and the other is proscribed by the same norm. For example, the norm of walking to the right when encountering another pedestrian walking in the opposite direction is simultaneously prescriptive and proscriptive, making this distinction meaningless. The distinction is meaningful only when the number of alternative courses of action is greater than two.

For any norm, there is a certain class of actors whose actions or potential actions are the focal actions for a norm. The statement, "Children are to be seen and not heard," specifies a norm in which children constitute this class. I will call members of this class *targets* of the norm, or target actors. There is also a class of actors who benefit from others' observance of the norm and are potential sanctioners of the target actors. These are actors who assume the right to partially control the focal action, and are seen by others who hold the norm to have this right. In the norm given by this statement, parents or adults more generally are those who benefit. It is possible that children also hold the norm, but its operation and supporting sanctions do not depend on this. I will call those who benefit from the norm (who are also ordinarily the potential sanctioners) *beneficiaries* of the norm. The current beneficiaries of the norm may be those who initiated it, or they may have merely continued the enforcement of a norm initiated by others who preceded them.

For some norms, like the one for children described above, the targets of the norm are not the beneficiaries. The norm is held by one set of actors and directed toward actions of another set. These will be labeled *disjoint* norms, both because the set of holders and the set of targets are disjoint (or largely so), and because their interests are as well: The beneficiaries have an interest in the norm being observed, and the targets have an interest in the focal action being unmodified by the norm.

For many norms, however, including all those in the earlier examples (except for the norm about their daughter smoking marijuana, held by the parents of the girl at the lake), the set of beneficiaries of the norm coincides with the set of targets. Actors hold a norm about their own actions. Here, the interests favoring observance of the norm and those opposing its observance are contained within the same actors. Each is simultaneously beneficiary and target of the norm—*conjoint* norms.

A clarification of what is meant by the term "sanction" is also useful. If holding a norm is assumption of the right to partially control a focal action and recognition of other norm beneficiaries' similar rights, then a sanction is the exercise of that right. A sanction may be negative, directed at inhibiting a focal action which is proscribed by a norm, or positive, directed at inducing a focal action toward which there is a positive norm. The terms "sanction" and "effective sanction" will be used interchangeably, indicating by either an action on the part of a norm beneficiary that has some effect in moving the focal action in the direction intended by the sanctioner.

One final distinction concerns selection of a focal action from among a set of mutually exclusive actions to be discouraged or encouraged by the norm. In some cases, the focal action is largely arbitrary, while in others it is not. The first is exemplified by the convention of driving on the right side of the road (or in England and Australia, on the left). It is arbitrary whether the action to be defined as "correct" is driving on the right or on the left. Once that convention has been established, however, all are better off if each follows the convention. The interests in a particular direction of action depend on whether that is the one being carried out by others. If it is merely a convention which established the direction of the norm, I will call this a *conventional* norm.[2]

For many norms, the focal action is not arbitrary. The target's interests lie in a direction of action opposing observance of the norm, while the holder's interests lie in the direction of action favoring observance of the norm. These interests in a particular direction of action would remain, whether or not the norm were in existence, and independent of others' directions of action. In this case, the direction of the norm depends on more than convention. I will call these *essential* norms. This last distinction can be illustrated, as Ullmann-Margalit (1977) has done (and as I will do shortly), by use of simple payoff matrices from the theory of games.[3]

Externalities and the Genesis of Interests in a Norm

Actions that have externalities generate interests in the action among those actors who experience the externalities. Yet there is no general way in which the consequences of the action for the other affected actors can enter the utility function of the actor taking the action. Actors harmed by the action that benefits the actor in control of the action experience negative externalities, as exemplified by nonsmokers sitting near a smoker. Those benefitted by it experience positive externalities, as exemplified by passers-by who benefit from a householder's cleaning snow from his sidewalk. The social problem in the first case is how to limit the action (and how much to limit it) that is harming others. The problem in the second case is how to encourage and increase the action, and to what level. A special case of the latter is the problem of paying the cost of a public good, when each actor's action has beneficial consequences for others, but the benefits to himself are less than the costs he will incur. Only if enough actors can be induced to carry out the action to bring the benefits above the costs for each will the public good be provided. A parallel problem exists for a public bad, as in overgrazing of a commons, in which each herd-owner's expanded grazing will bring him a his own benefit, but at a cost to others. Only if the herd-owners can all be induced to limit their grazing will the levels be reduced to that which will provide maximum nutrition.

When an action generates externalities for others, they may be able to make their interests felt through wholly individualistic means. One of these actors may engage in an exchange with the actor whose action imposes externalities, offering something to bring about the outcome he desires, or threatening this actor with an outcome on another event that goes against his interest. But this may not be possible, if the externalities are spread among several actors, no one of whom can profitably make such an exchange.

This solution is a special case of that introduced in Coase's 1960 paper, "The Problem of Social Cost." The general solution is to develop a market in rights of control, in which the actors who do not have control of the action may purchase rights of control from those who do, limited only by their interest in the action and their resources. It is easy to see that if there are no transaction costs in such a market, then the outcome will be a social optimum (which is defined only relative to the initial resource endowments of the various parties in the market), at which no further exchanges are mutually beneficial. Those harmed by this level of action would be even more hurt by parting with the resources that the actor controlling it would take to limit it further.

In the case of a public good, each of the actors who is benefitted by the actions of others would exchange rights of partial control of his own action for rights of partial control of the actions of each of the others. For example, they might unanimously vote to adopt a highway speed limit. This in effect would make each actor's action controlled by all the potentially affected parties.

Related markets have been developed in regulation of environmental pollution, not with the amount of total pollution allowed set by market forces, but with marketing of rights to pollute among those who operate pollution-generating plants. And it is likely that the process by which the provision of public goods comes under the control of a collective decision (that is, the shift of activities from individual control to governmental control) can usefully be conceptualized as exchange, among those affected, of rights of partial control over their actions. This results in each having a vote in determining the actions of each.

Yet there are many activities in society in which markets in rights of control cannot easily come into being, for one or another reason, and in which collective decisions are not feasible. In a social situation where one person is smoking and another finds it irritating, the second can hardly come to the first and say, "How much will you take to stop smoking?" Or a high school girl on a date in which all others present would like her to smoke marijuana while her parents would not can hardly ask for bids from the two parties for control of her action. There is a wide range of situations in which an action has extensive external effects, but in which a market in rights of control of the action is either impracticable or illegal.

The first principle referred to at the outset is that interests in a norm arise when an action has similar externalities for a set of others, when markets in rights of control of the action cannot easily be established, and when no single actor can profitably engage in an exchange to gain such rights. Such interests do not themselves constitute a norm, nor ensure that one will come into being. They create a basis, a demand for a norm on the part of those experiencing externalities.

The externalities created by the action may, as indicated earlier, be positive or negative. In high schools, for example, positive externalities are created by athletes who contribute to the success of a team, which in turn contributes to the school's general standing in the community (which, in turn, contributes to the other students' feeling of well-being or pride). Often a norm does arise, one which encourages potentially good athletes to devote their energies to interscholastic sports.

In contrast, scholars who obtain especially high grades create negative externalities for other students, insofar as the teacher grades on the curve. High-performing students increase the effort necessary to produce the same grade for other students, thus making matters more difficult for them. Often a norm also arises in this case, with students imposing norms to restrict the amount of effort put into schoolwork.[4]

How a norm actually comes into being once a demand is created by externalities is altogether another matter, which will be examined later. But the genesis of a norm lies in externalities of actions that cannot be overcome by simple transactions which would put control of the action in the hands of those experiencing the externalities.

Several points follow from the central premise stated above, that interests in a norm arise when actions have external effects. The implication of this premise is that the potential norm will be held by all those who are affected in the same direction by the action. If a norm does arise, it will be those persons who claim a right to have partial control over the action, and it will be they who will exercise the claim by attempting to impose normative sanctions upon the actor to induce the direction of action that benefits them, though often at the actor's expense. A further implication is that a potential conflict of norms arises when an action has positive externalities for one set of persons, and negative ones for another. Such opposing externalities can be seen in the example of the girl whose friends' approval is contingent on her smoking marijuana, and her parents' is contingent on her not doing so (or their ignorance of her doing so). If she does not smoke, she dampens the party, destroys the consensus, and perhaps reminds some of those present of the normative conflicts they are under. If she does smoke (and her parents learn of it), they are made unhappy as their hopes and aspirations for her are undercut.

The structure of interests created by externalities in which norms have their genesis may be seen more systematically by use of simple situations the outcomes of which can be described by payoff matrices as used in theory of games. Here I will use this device in a context that is examined more fully in Coleman (1990).

Suppose two persons are each told, "You make take either of two actions, contribute $9 to a common project, or contribute nothing. For each $3 that is contributed, an additional $1 will be earned by the project (altogether $4 return for each $3 contributed). Then the total will be divided between the two of you, regardless of who made a contribution."

	A_2	
A_1	Contribute	Not contribute
Contribute	3, 3	-3, 6
Not contribute	6, -3	0, 0

Diagram 2.1.

Each can assess the net gains or losses for himself and for the other, for each combination of actions of the two. These are expressed in dollars in Diagram 2.1, with the value of the outcome for A_1 and A_2 listed in that order in each cell.[5]

If neither contributes, there is no gain or loss for either. If A_1 contributes and A_2 does not, A_1's $9 contribution plus the $3 earned will be divided equally, giving $6 to each. For A_2, this will be a net gain, as listed in the upper right-hand cell of the diagram. But for A_1, the size of the original $9 contribution must be subtracted, giving him a net loss of $3. The same outcome in reverse occurs for the case in which A_2 contributes and A_1 does not.

This situation creates a pair of actions each of which has externalities for the other actor. As Diagram 2.1 indicates, A_1's action of contributing or not makes a difference of $6 (between 3 and −3 or between 6 and 0) to A_2, and A_2's action makes a difference of $6 to A_1. Furthermore, in both cases, the externalities move in the direction that opposes the actor's own interests. A_1 is better off if he does not contribute (whichever action A_2 takes), but this makes A_2 worse off. A similar situation exists for the effects of A_2's preferred action on A_1. Finally, the result of this situation is that the external effects of the other's action are greater for each than are the direct effects of his own action. For A_1, his own action only makes a difference of $3 to him, while A_2's action makes a difference of $6. Similarly, the reverse is true for A_2.

The result of this condition is that each will have an incentive not to contribute (since one is $3 worse off by so doing), with the result that each gets $0. Yet if both contributed, each would gain $3. The optimal action for each actor gives a social outcome which is not optimum. Both would be better off if both took actions which were *not* individually optimum, that is, if each contributed to the project.

Much has been written about this structure of outcomes, most of which need not concern us here. (For references to some of this literature, see Axelrod, 1984.) What is of interest is Ullmann-Margalit's discussion of this structure as "calling for" or "generating" one type of norm, which she calls prisoner's-dilemma (or PD) norms. Her argument is that such a structure of outcomes creates an incentive on the part of all parties to have a norm that will constrain the behavior of each toward carrying out the action that is better for the others—in this case to contribute to the joint project. Using the terminology introduced earlier, such a structure of interdependence of actions creates externalities for each and thus an individual interest in the creation of a norm.

However, in situations of this sort, where two persons' actions affect each other in the way shown in Diagram 2.1, a norm is not necessary at all. Either can propose an exchange in which each gives the other rights of control to his action and gets rights of control of the other's action.[6] Each has resources (his own action) that are of more value to the other than the resources held by the other (the other's action). Thus by exchanging rights of control, each gets something that is worth more to him than what he gives up. In exercising that control over the other's action, each does so in the direction which benefits himself, and in so doing brings about a social optimum. A_1 contributes A_2's $9, A_2 contributes A_1's $9, and both gain $3 from the double contribution.

It is always true that with a pair of interdependent actions in which the self-interested action of each imposes negative externalities on the other that are greater than the benefits that the other's own self-interested action brings, a mutually profitable exchange is possible.

Logistics may, of course, preclude exchange. In the game-theoretic analysis of this structure, the possibility of exchange is excluded, because by assumption the players cannot communicate. But no such constraint is necessary here. Because norms can arise only where there is communication, two-person exchange is possible in all those two-actor cases where the possibility for a norm exists. There is an apparent exception in those cases where communication exists before and after the action, but not during the action itself. However, whatever agreements are reached before the action, whatever retributions are taken after the action, need make no reference to a "norm," but can be treated wholly within the framework of bilateral exchange—although possibly of course requiring introduction of notions of trust and mutual trust.

The one true exception, in which the social optimum is neither reached by an individualistic solution nor by a bilateral exchange, is that in which interactions are indeed pairwise, but the two actors are not in contact both before and after the action (or will meet only in the distant future), and thus have no opportunity either to make an agreement or to carry out the terms of a prior agreement.[7] In that case a norm, in which sanctions are imposed by others who are in contact with the actors after the action, can bring about a social optimum while a pairwise exchange cannot.[8]

Before proceeding, it is wise to clarify what "exchange" ordinarily implies in the current context, for the example may otherwise be misleading. The imagery evoked by exchange in the context of this example is one in which one actor approaches another with an offer, "You let me make your decision, and I will let you make mine," or "Let us contribute together," or something similar. This is certainly what happens in some cases. But in an examination of the emergence of norms, it is appropriate to think of a succession of comparable projects, extending over time, with a new decision taken each time. Then the possibilities expand to bring about exchanges, implicit or explicit, that cover two or more projects (for example, "If you fail to contribute this time, I will not contribute next time"). This possibility is especially relevant for those cases in which it is not logistically possible to exchange control or rights to control on a given occasion. It is also relevant for those cases in which there is not a "project" involving simultaneous contribution, but separate actions of each actor which exhibit the same pattern of internal and external effects. That is, actor A_1 must decide whether to take an action (such as watching his neighbor's house while he is gone) that constitute a net cost for him of $3 but benefits his neighbor by $6. His neighbor, in a similar situation, must make the same decision.

There is another implicit exchange beyond this, one which may be more frequent empirically, and that is not precisely equivalent to the others. If the two actors have a social relationship, consisting of a set of obligations and expectations (assumed for the present to be symmetric), various other exchanges are possible. If A_1 is to prevent an action of A_2, which imposes a cost on him of $6, while A_2 benefits only by $3 from the action, A_1 need only introduce into the negotiations some other event that he controls that has a cost for him of less than $6 and a benefit for A_2 of more than $3. A promise or a threat with respect to this event can serve A_1 perhaps as well as, perhaps better than, the action which is analogous to the action of A_2 which he wants to control. To state it differently, he need not use as a sanction for A_2 the same kind of action as the one he is sanctioning. If A_2 shows up late for a meeting, A_1 need not show up late for the next meeting; he can express disapproval, he can threaten to break off the meetings altogether, or he can offer A_2 a special benefit if he arrives on time for the next meeting. A_2 is in a similar position, so long as he has control over events that meet the

The Emergence of Norms

necessary criteria (of less cost to him than $6, and of more benefit to A_1 than $3).

Note how this changes matters. If A_1 has used an extrinsic event as a sanction for A_2, he has made no commitment on his original action. He remains free to contribute or not, or in the case of the meeting, free to show up late at the next meeting himself. But there is a second change as well: The other events may include some which have quite different internal and external effects than those of the original action at issue. In particular, the costs to A_1 of using one of these events as a sanction for A_2 may be very small, yet A_2's interest in the event may be sufficiently great that the sanction is effective.

It is important to recognize these additional sanctioning possibilities that actors may have for one another, because of the importance they lend to the existence of other events linking these actors. Attention to these additional possible sanctions is also important because of the potential sanctioning asymmetries that result from inequalities in their control of events of interest to one another.[9]

Beyond Two Actors

It is when pairwise exchanges (either isolated or in a market context) cannot bring about a social optimum that interests in a norm arise. This may be illustrated by expanding the joint project described earlier to a common project of three actors. Again, each has the alternative of contributing $9 or nothing. For every $3 contributed, the product will be $4, an earning of $1. The social product will be divided equally among the three.

Diagram 2.2 shows the outcomes for each combination of actions. Since the situation is symmetric for the three, the outcomes can be summarized more compactly, as shown in the tabulation given below.

	Gains or losses	
Number of contributions	Contributors	Noncontributors
0	—	0
1	−5	4
2	−1	8
3	3	—

Here, the situation is fundamentally different from before. It is no longer possible for two actors to exchange control over their actions and to gain by so doing. If there are no contributions, with a net gain or loss

		A_3 Contribute		A_3 Not contribute	
		A_2 Contribute	A_2 Not contribute	A_2 Contribute	A_2 Not contribute
A_1	Contribute	3, 3, 3	-1, 8, -1	-1, -1, 8	-5, 4, 4
A_1	Not contribute	8, -1, -1	4, 4, -5	4, -5, 4	0, 0, 0

Diagram 2.2.

to each of $0, and A_1 exchanges control with A_2, each contributing for the other, they end up losing $1, with A_3 gaining $8. If A_3 is already contributing, then A_1 and A_2 each gain $4 before an exchange. If they exchange control, with each contributing for the other, the gain for each is $3, making them $1 worse off than without the exchange.

It is only if *both* A_2 and A_3 can be induced to change their actions from not contributing to contributing, contingent on A_1's contribution, that it becomes profitable for A_1 to join such an arrangement. In such a case, the outcome for each changes from a gain of $0 to a gain of $3. Thus a compact among the three is necessary to bring about a gain to each. One form of compact is a norm, with sanctions attached to enforce it. It is in this way that we can say that each comes to have interests in a norm.

The structure of interdependence in this case is one in which, if a norm arises at all, it will be a conjoint norm, with the same actors as both targets and beneficiaries. It will be an essential norm, not a conventional one, because there is one direction of action that benefits each (contributing), and one which does not. It would be possible to construct a similar artificial example and a similar matrix of outcomes with interdependence that generates interest in a conventional norm that is straightforward and self-evident and will not be presented here. For a disjoint norm, the matter is somewhat different; examination of such norms will be discussed later in the chapter.

Until this point, I have examined the conditions which lead to interest in the creation of a norm and the imposition of sanctions to bring about its observance. I have said nothing about the conditions which allow this interest to be realized by the bringing into being of a norm and sanctions. The question that must be answered is this: What is required to get from interests in a norm to the actual existence of a norm backed by sanctions?

Social Structure and the Realization of Norms

The fundamental problem exhibited by the common project involving three actors in the example of the preceding section is a problem of social organization. In the two-actor project, each has the resources to prevent the other from imposing negative externalities upon him (or equivalently in this case, to induce the other to act in a way that brings positive externalities).[10] This is no longer so in the three-actor project. No single actor can exchange control with a single other to their mutual benefit. The externalities of the action of each for any one other actor are less than the actor's own effect on his gains. If a social optimum is to be achieved, something beyond pairwise exchange is necessary. One solution would be a sequence of pairwise exchanges in which first A_1 and A_2 exchanged rights of control, then A_2, with the right to control A_1's action, exchanged *this* for the right to control A_3's action. The rights of control are then distributed as follows:

A_3 controls a_1
A_2 controls a_3
A_1 controls a_2

If this pair of exchanges took place, then each would exercise the control he possessed in a way that benefitted him (as well as one of the other two): A_3 would commit A_1, A_2 would commit A_3, and A_1 would commit A_2. But the first exchange would take place only if both actors knew that a second exchange was possible—for without it, each gives up something worth more to him for something worth less. Furthermore, after the exchange between A_1 and A_2 has been made, A_3 finds it *not* to his benefit to exchange control with either. Thus the transactions would end after the A_1—A_2 trade, and both would end up losing $1, while A_3 gained $8.

Even if this were not so, the solution depends critically on a condition often not found: the knowledge that further transactions will be available to make an initially unprofitable exchange a profitable one. As is evident from the study of primitive systems of economic exchange, the development of such exchanges (in which objects come to have a "value" in exchange apart from their utility for the actor, leading the actor to acquire them for further exchange) is not a simple one (see Einzig, 1966).

There is one common device that is sometimes used by individuals who anticipate benefits from a common activity to which all contribute, but have difficulty in overcoming the problem that each is better off by not contributing. This is to vest rights of control of their actions in a leader. This requires, of course, a high level of trust in the leader to act in terms of the followers' interests, trust which sometimes occurs when an actor is viewed as having charismatic qualities.

In the absence of such a "collective" solution to the public goods problem, some kind of combined action is necessary if a social optimum is to be obtained. This, in turn, depends on the existence of a relation between at least two of the three. As a first way of looking at this, Figure 2.1 shows two cases: In (a), actor A_1's action has an effect on A_2 and A_3 (as shown by the arrows) who have no social relationship with one another. Their social relations are with other actors A_4 and A_5. In (b), there are the same effects of A_1's actions, but actors A_2 and A_3 have a social relationship (the content of which I will discuss shortly). In figure 2.1(a), any sanction from A_2 or A_3 to direct A_1's action so it is not inimical to their interests must be applied by either independently; and in the three-actor common project the only actions available to A_2 and A_3 are the actions of contributing or not. Can either use that action as a sanction to bring about A_1's contribution? There are two obstacles to doing so.

First, there is a sequencing problem: If each acts independently and simultaneously, then A_2 and A_3 will already have acted when they discover A_1's noncontribution. The sequencing problem is too complex to go into here, except for two comments. First, since a sanction by A_2 and A_3 of not contributing cannot affect A_1's contribution in this project, it is necessary to consider an unlimited sequence of projects, with the sanction for the current project affecting A_1's contribution in the next project. Luce and Raiffa (1957) point this out for the case of a two-person

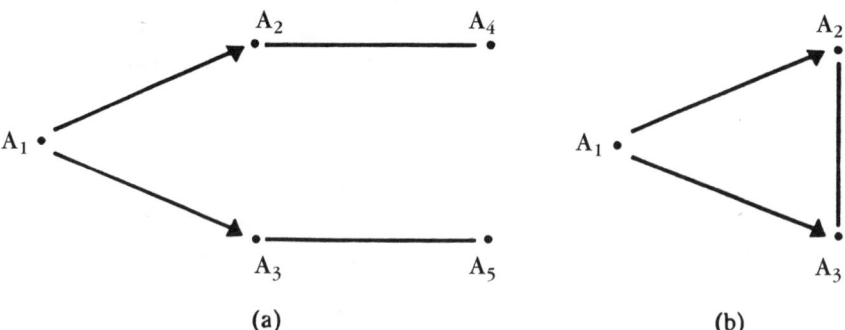

Figure 2.1. Two social structures within which an actor's (A_1's) actions have external effects.

prisoner's dilemma, having the same payoff structure as the common project. (The force of the assumption of an unlimited sequence is softened if the next project only occurs with probability less than 1.) In the subsequent discussion, I will ignore the sequencing problem for purposes of exposition, while recognizing that any effect of a sanction on a project has its effect on the next, and that the credibility of a sanction depends on a future in which there is an indefinite sequence of projects.

The second problem is that A_2's threat not to contribute is not a serious one: A_1 gains $5 by not contributing, and A_2's sanction (not contributing) costs A_1 only $4. Thus A_1 is still better off not to contribute, even if A_2 were to sanction by not contributing.

If, however, there is a social relationship between A_2 and A_3, as indicated in Figure 2.1(b), then, neglecting the problem of sequence, there is the possibility of joint action on the part of A_2 and A_3. A_2 and A_3 may jointly threaten not to contribute if A_1 does not contribute. This sanction would cost A_1 $8, while the benefit of not contributing is only $5. The threat is also a credible one, for A_2 and A_3 would gain $1 by carrying it out. Thus apart from the sequencing problem, the relationship between A_2 and A_3 makes possible a joint sanction that would be effective for A_1. But what is meant by the unanalyzed term "social relationship"?

Unless it is possible to unpack the term "social relationship" and discover within it some interests and control that give one or both actors leverage vis-à-vis the other, the term can have no explanatory value in a theory based on rational choice. Because social relationships consist of obligations and expectations, either asymmetrically or symmetrically held, and because each actor continues to hold control of some events in which the other is interested, there exists inherently in each social relationship leverage to obtain a commitment from the other. If in Figure 2.1, actor A_2 has obligations toward A_3, then A_2 may pay off a portion of those obligations by sanctioning A_1. Or A_3 may initiate such an action by calling A_2's obligations. Or if A_2 has control of some event in which A_3 is interested (which may be nothing more than A_2's approval), A_2 and A_3 can carry out an implicit exchange, with A_3 incurring the cost of sanctioning A_1 in return for control of the event currently controlled by A_2. Note, however, that the discussion of a social relationship goes outside the payoff structure of Diagram 2.2. Introduction of "obligations" of A_2 toward A_3, or "some event" over which A_2 has control and in which A_3 is interested, introduces elements not shown in the payoff matrix.

This answer to the analytical question about how social relationships may be used to aid the employment of sanctions does not indicate how sanctions actually take place. I will state, in general, the problem of applying sanctions when neither can afford to do so separately, but will not discuss the kinds of sanctions that actually are applied to enforce a norm, these are discussed in Coleman (1990, Chapter 11).

The Second-Order Public Goods Problem in the Enforcement of Norms

The sanctioning problem is what has been called the "second-order public goods problem," or the "second-order free-rider problem." To see just what is meant, it is useful to go back to one of Aesop's fables, *The Mice in Council*. The council meeting was called to discuss a problem faced by the mouse society: how to control the cat who was slowly decimating the population. In the terms used in this chapter, the cat's action imposed severe externalities upon the mice, and constituted, in effect, a public bad, creating constant danger for each. This is the first-order public goods (or in this case, public bad) problem.

The *second-order* public goods problem is indicated by the statement of the wise old mouse who finally rose in the council, after a proposed solution (that a bell be put around the cat's neck to warn of its approach) had been roundly applauded. He suggested that the council consider how the bell was to be fastened about the cat's neck, and who would undertake the task. The second-order public goods problem is the fact that, just as the cat's action imposes externalities upon all, an effective sanctioning of the cat's actions also has externalities (positive in this case) for all those experiencing the benefits of the sanction. Yet the benefits to the mouse who would undertake to bell the cat would not be sufficient to overcome the costs. Or in the case of the three-actor project shown in Diagram 2.2 the first-order public goods problem is the fact that each will benefit from the contribution of others; and the second-order public goods problem is the fact that if A_1 does not contribute, then the sanctioning of A_1 is a public good for A_3 and A_2. Neither receives sufficient benefits from his own action to motivate sanctioning A_1. The problem may not appear to be a serious one for the three-person common project. Just as sanctioning may be effected through an implicit or explicit exchange—without any notion of a norm—in a two-person common project like that in Diagram 2.1 the sanctioning public goods problem for one actor's failure to contribute to a three-actor common project is reduced to a two-actor common project. This may be solved whenever there is the possibility of exchange between the two actors who experience externalities from the third. One can compensate the other for the net costs of applying the sanction (that is, the costs, to A_2 say, of sanctioning A_1, less the benefits that A_2 will derive directly from the effects of the sanction). More generally, the second-order public goods problem of sanctioning is always one actor smaller than the original public goods problem.

It is now possible to state the second principle referred to at the beginning of this chapter, which concerns the conditions under which the demand for an effective norm will be satisfied. Stated simply, these are the conditions under which the second-order free-rider problem will be overcome by rational actors.

If there is a social relationship between actors, as between A_2 and A_3 in the example, then this overcomes the second-order free-rider problem for A_1's contribution. If there is a social relationship between A_1 and A_2, and between A_1 and A_3, which may or may not be strong enough to ensure A_1's contribution, but is strong enough to ensure A_1's joint sanctioning with A_2 or A_3, then the contributions of each are assured. The threat of sanctions exists, although they need not be applied.

The existence of a norm facilitates achievement of the social optimum by making use of the social relationships that exist in a social system to overcome the second-order free-rider problem. The existence of a norm implies that each has the right to sanction others for violating the norm, and the right to sanction others for not sanctioning those who violate the norm. It allows the introduction of other resources to be used in sanctioning, so that even when the conditions do not exist for a credible sanctioning threat within the resources of an activity like the common project shown in Diagram 2.2, the social optimum may be achieved through the use of other resources.

Heroic versus Incremental Sanctioning

In the examination of ways in which norms are characteristically enforced, it becomes clear that a common mode of sanctioning is one that can be characterized as incremental. This is exemplified in unions such as the typographical union by putting "in Coventry" scabs and others who seriously violate union norms (Lipset et al., 1956). It is exemplified in communes like Bruderhof by sending a serious offender to an isolated dwelling and cutting off all communication (Zablocki, 1971). It is exemplified by the development of "reputations" followed by avoidance, or more generally what Merry (1984, p. 279) terms the third phase of gossip: some form of sanction such as snubbing, in which each participates as a result of the informal consensus achieved in the second phase of gossip. In incremental sanctioning, the cost incurred by each sanctioner is small, as are the effects, but they are additive, giving a total effect equivalent to that of a single large sanction.

Aesop's fable of the Council of mice, however, is a reminder that it is not always possible to sanction incrementally. To bell the cat was not an activity that could be engaged in by additive increments. It required what I will call a heroic sanction, that is a sanction in which the total effect occurs through a single actor's sanctioning action. And in the examples of norms and sanctions given earlier in the chapter, the sanctions were imposed by single individuals.

In this section, I will use the example of the common project to examine the structure of action when sanctions are incremental, carried out by all the actors in the collectivity other than the one being sanctioned.

If sanctions can be additive in their effects, as the empirical evidence suggests they are in many cases, A_2 can bring about a contribution of half of the $9 from A_1 through a sanction costing A_2 $2 ½, and bringing benefits of $2 each to A_2 and A_3. The net cost to A_2 is only $½. This structure is shown in Diagram 2.3. Here there continues to be a prisoner's dilemma, but one with extensive possibilities for mutually beneficial arrangements, because of the disparity in the sanctioner's net loss (only $½ and the other's gain ($2) from the sanction. This example, however,

		A_3	
		Sanction	Not sanction
A_2	Sanction	.5, .5	-1.5, 1
	Not Sanction	1, -1.5	-1, -1

Diagram 2.3.

does not show the virtues of incremental sanctions as sharply as does a case with a larger number of actors. Consider the same common project, but now with six participants, each contributing 0 or $9, with $1 earned for every $3 contributed, and the total product divided equally among the six. The net gain for each contributor and noncontributor in each configuration of contributions is shown in Diagram 2.4.

Here, the net loss incurred by contributing is no longer $5, but $7. (For

| | Net gain ($) for: | |
Number of contributions	Noncontributors	Contributors
6	—	3
5	10	1
4	8	−1
3	6	−3
2	4	−5
1	2	−7
0	0	—

Diagram 2.4

example, if five actors are contributing, the noncontributor's gain is $10. If he contributes, he ends up with $3, making him $7 worse off.) The net gain experienced by the others from an actor's sanction is no longer $4—it is only $2. (For example, if the sixth actor does contribute, their net gain increases from $1 to $3.) If sanctioning cannot be incremental, the heroic sanctioner must incur a cost of $7 to achieve a gain of only $2. He has a net loss of $5, rather than the $1 for the heroic sanctioner in the three-actor project. Furthermore, this net loss of $5 cannot be made up without loss by another who benefitted because that actor's benefit too from the heroic action is only $2. Not even *two* others could provide sufficient rewards to the heroic sanctioner to make his action anything other than foolhardy. If they rewarded him with all their gains, he would still have a net loss of $1. It would take three others, that is, all but one of the four who gained by his heroic sanction, to make his sanction no longer constitute a net loss.

If the sanctions can be incremental, the degree of exposure of the sanctioner is much less. A sanctioner, say A_2, would incur a cost of $7/5, or $1.4, and would gain from his sanctions alone $0.4 from the incremental contribution made by A_1, the actor that is sanctioned (although he gains $2 altogether from the total set of sanctions if others sanction as well). Thus each experiences a net loss of $1 by sanctioning. As before, it would be possible for this to be made up by a sequence of rewards from others, of $0.4 each, which would again require participation by at least three of the other four. Alternatively, additional incremental sanctions from the others would make up A_2's loss, each incremental sanction reducing A_2's loss by $0.4. If all sanction incrementally, he gains $0.6. Thus for incremental sanctions to pay the sanctioner, some prior collective decision that all (or at least many) will sanction (as in the "consensus" which Merry describes as the second stage of gossip) is required.

For an example, suppose all members of a club are expected to clean up after meetings, but one member consistently fails to help. If one person expresses disapproval, this might induce a small effort on the offender's part, but would also worsen the relation between these two, an effect that could be more important to the potential sanctioner than the benefit from the offender's efforts. But if all concurred in expressing disapproval, inducing the offender to make his full contribution, the benefits to each would outweight the costs of the worsened relation with the offender.[11]

Returning to the example of the common project, suppose there were not a binding collective decision, and all but one sanctioned. Then the sanctions could go one stage deeper. A_1 is the noncontributor, and suppose that A_2 is the nonincremental sanctioner. Each of the others has provided an incremental sanction, and A_1 has made four fifths of his total contribution. A_2, who is $1 better off by not sanctioning, can be induced to sanction again either by a heroic second-stage sanction of $1, which works out to a net cost of $0.6 to the second-stage sanctioner, or by incremental sanctions of $0.25, which work out to a net cost of $0.15 for each of the sanctioners.

The overall difference between the heroic and the incremental sanctions lies in the magnitude of sanction required at every stage. At the first stage, in the six-actor project, the heroic sanctioner must incur a loss five times that of each incremental sanctioner. In this project, A_2, the heroic sanctioner, incurs a cost of $5. At the second stage, for A_3 to reward the heroic sanctioner heroically imposes a net loss of $3 on A_3.

If sanctioning is incremental, the free-rider problem remains, but at a greatly reduced magnitude. The net cost to each sanctioner is $1, rather than $5. If the second-stage sanction (the reward to the incremental sanctioner) is heroic, that means only a net cost of $0.6 to the second-stage heroic sanctioner, rather than $3. If the second-stage sanction is also incremental, the net cost to each of the four sanctioners is only $0.15.

What this means in practice is that in many circumstances in which heroic sanctions are beyond the resources of any sanctioner, they are readily available for incremental sanctioning. These resources may consist of other events which are controlled by each of the potential sanctioners. The values specified above indicate only the maximum costs that the sanction can impose on the sanctioner, and the value it must have to the sanctionee. When the sanctions are of such small cost as they come to be in a large group, a positive sanction may consist of nothing more than a credit slip in the form of gratitude for what the other has done, or a negative sanction may consist of nothing more than a withdrawal of credit in the form of displeasure ("Wait till you ask me to do something for you.")

Other possibilities exist as well with incremental sanctioning. If there is some heterogeneity among the potential sanctioners the free-rider problem may be overcome at some stage, and in any case will constitute a lesser obstacle. The complex possibilities that exist can only be alluded to here.

There is one additional point: the use of the term "heroic" here refers to a single sanction by a single sanctioner of sufficient size to bring about A_1's contribution. If the set of five contributors, or a large enough subset, can act as a single actor, there can be a single sanction from that set sufficient to bring about the contribution and yet bringing a net benefit to each. The frequent institution, in communes, of meetings once a week or at another regular interval, at which the whole membership gathers to hear self-criticism or criticism by others suggests that in such settings this method of sanctioning is easier to organize than either heroic or independent incremental sanctioning.

Conclusion

I have attempted to show that two principles can account for emergence of norms with effective sanctions. One of those is a principle concerning the conditions under which a demand for norms will arise. The conditions involve the existence of similar externalities from a focal action for a set of potential holders of the norm.

The second principle concerns the conditions under which the demand will be satisfied by effective sanctions. These conditions involve the potential for sanctions internal to the set of norm holders, to overcome the "second-order free-rider problem."

Notes

1. See O'Flaherty and Derrett (1978), and Kunst (1978).
2. Ullmann-Margalit (1977:97) calls these coordination norms, and distinguishes between those that arise through convention and those adopted by decree. I will not make use of this distinction.
3. Ullmann-Margalit distinguishes three kinds of norms, which she calls "prisoner's dilemma norms" "coordination norms," and "norms of partiality." These correspond approximately to what I have termed essential norms, conventional norms, and disjoint norms, respectively. However, the correspondence is not complete, because essential norms, to use my terminology, may be disjoint or conjoint, while Ullmann-Margalit's three classes are mutually exclusive.

4. It is, of course, the case that when academic activities are organized interscholastically, they too can generate a prescriptive norm. Striking cases of this may be found in a description of rural schools in Kentucky engaging in statewide competition in academic subjects (Stuart, 1949, p. 90ff).

5. A game with payoffs showing this structure is called a prisoner's dilemma. See Luce and Raiffa (1957) or Rapaport and Chammah (1965) for a discussion of this game.

6. So far as I know, Erling Schild and Gudmund Hernes were the first to (independently, in 1971) point out that the simplest social solution to the prisoner's dilemma is exchange of control between the two players, an action which is rational for each. Peter Bernholz (1987) has shown that the Sen paradox of a paretian liberal, where the payoff structure is that of a prisoner's dilemma, is solved in the same way.

7. This is a fundamental point on which Axelrod (1984:49), who discusses the growth of cooperation in two-person prisoner's dilemmas, exhibits confusion. At some points he can be interpreted as asserting that pairwise interactions in large populations where the same two parties meet only very infrequently, will generate the same cooperation as found in his pairwise "tournaments." In general, however, Axelrod's work in that book demonstrates the point made here: that bilateral exchanges, explicit or implicit, are sufficient, without introduction of a norm, to arrive at a social optimum in pairwise interactions with externalities. See Coleman (1986) for examination of social structural conditions in which the contact does not allow such agreements, implicit or explicit, to be effective.

8. It is worth noting that in Ullmann-Margalit's two-person example (two mortarmen in isolated outposts) in which a norm of "honor" is seen as one solution where a bilateral exchange cannot be, the latter is precluded because no prior agreement can be carried out after the fact since in her example, one mortarman is dead. It is also true that the norm of "honor" arises more broadly in military units, where one soldier may be risking his life save the lives of a number of his fellow soldiers, not merely one.

9. This exposes also another source of asymmetry, hidden by the symmetry of the example. Even for activities in which all actors' similar actions impose externalities on one another, the externalities may be unequal, providing sanctioning opportunities for some actors that do not exist for others. This is related to questions of interpersonal comparison of utilities, and as will be evident later, a correct untangling of that issue will be important for the analysis of norms as for other aspects of the social system.

10. As indicated earlier, when there are only two alternative actions, as in this case, there is no distinction between prescriptive and proscriptive norms.

11. Empirically the costs might also be reduced, for disapproval from all might lead the offender to accept the collective verdict, and not respond unpleasantly to the members expressing disapproval. However, in the example of Diagrams 2.2 and 2.3, the net gain from incremental sanctioning by all does not depend on such reduced costs.

References

Axelrod, Robert. (1984). *The Evolution of Cooperation*. New York: Basic Books.
Bernholz, P. (1987). "A general constitutional possibility theorem." Pp. 383–400 in G. Radnitzky and P. Bernholz, eds., *Economic Imperialism*. New York: Paragon House.
Coase, Ronald H. (1960). "The problem of social cost." *Journal of Law and Economics* V(3):1–44.
Coleman, James S. (1986). "Social structure and the emergence of norms among

rational actors." In *Paradoxical Effects of Social Behavior: Essays in Honor of Anatol Rapoport*. eds. A. Diekmann and P. Mitter. Pp 55–83. Vienna: Physica-Verlag.

Coleman, James S. (1987). "Norms as social capital." Pp. 133–155 in G. Radnitzky and R. Bernholz, eds., *Economic Imperialism*. New York: Paragon House.

Coleman, James S. (1990). *Foundations of Social Theory*. Cambridge, MA: Harvard University Press.

Dahrendorf, Ralf. (1968). *Essays in the Theory of Society*. Stanford: Stanford University Press.

Einzig, Paul. (1966). *Primitive Money*, 2nd ed. London.

Garnsey, Peter. (1973). "Legal privilege in the Roman Empire." Pp. 146–166 in Donald Black and Maureen Mileski, eds., *The Social Organization of Law*. New York: Seminar Press.

Kunst, Arnold. (1978). "Use and misuse of Dharma." Pp. 3–17 in O'Flaherty, W. D., and J. D. M. Derritt, eds., *The Concept of Duty in South Asia*. New Delhi: Vikas.

Lipset, S. M., M. A. Trow, and J. S. Coleman. (1956). *Union Democracy*. New York: Free Press.

Luce, R. D., and Howard Raiffa. (1957). *Games and Decisions*. New York: John Wiley and Sons.

Merry, Sally E. (1984). "Rethinking Gossip and Scandal." Pp. 271–302 in D. Black, ed., *Toward a General Theory of Social Control, Vol 1*. New York; Academic Press.

O'Flaherty, W. D. and J. D. M. Derrett (eds.). (1978). *The Concept of Duty in South Asia*, p. xiv. New Delhi: Vikas.

Rapaport, A., and A. M. Chammah. (1965). *Prisoner's Dilemma*. Ann Arbor: University of Michigan Press.

Sorokin, P. (1928). *Contemporary Sociological Theories*. New York: Harper and Row.

Stuart, J. (1949). *The Thread That Runs So True*. New York: Charles Scribner.

Ullmann-Margalit, Edna. (1977). *The Emergence of Norms*. Oxford: Clarendon Press.

Zablocki, B. (1971). *The Joyful Community*. Baltimore, Maryland: Penguin Books.

3

The Costs of Organizing Social Cooperation

Hartmut Kliemt

In his recent autobiographical essay "Better than plowing" James Buchanan (1986, 373 ff.) remarks

> the ideas that capture my attention are those that, directly or indirectly, explain how freely choosing individuals can secure jointly desired goals. The simple exchange of apples and oranges between two traders—this institutional model is the starting point for all that I have done. Contrast this with the choice between apples and oranges in the utility-maximizing calculus of Robinson Crusoe. The second model is the starting point of what most economists do.

Taking James Buchanan's remark as my starting point, I will subsequently deviate from the world view of most economists. I will also deviate from Buchanan's line of argument and discuss how the institutions that are presupposed in his simple institutional model of exchange conceivably can emerge among rational actors. Contrary to what most economists seem to assume, this is neither an easy nor an unimportant question to answer. In the first step, I will go through a numerical example illustrating comparative advantages and the possible gains from exchange in the conventional manner. This type of analysis tacitly assumes that rules of commitment are exogenously supplied and that the premises of cooperative game theory thus apply. In the second step, I will look at the example from the point of view of noncooperative game theory. These preliminary considerations set the stage for an argument that applies to problems of rule creation in general. It will be argued that the creation of rules poses some difficult problems for any game-theoretically inspired political theory. Some of the problems of classical political theory that modern analyses of iterated games or supergames are designed to solve seem to show up again within the realm of game theory itself. It will be suggested that an effort to solve these problems might be of interest not only for the political theorist, but for the game theorist as well.

Rules and Markets

The Cooperative View of Exchange

Suppose there are two individuals A and B. A can produce up to 5 apples or up to 10 oranges. For A the rate of transformation is 1 apple to 2 oranges. All alternatives are discretely measured. Person B can either produce 10 apples or 5 oranges with a transformation rate of 2 apples to 1 orange. The condition of nonsatiation prevails through the relevant sets of choice for both individuals and both goods.

The technology of A and B, respectively, is shown in the tabulation below:

A's Technology		B's Technology	
Apples	Oranges	Apples	Oranges
0	10	10	0
1	8	8	1
2	6	6	2
3	4	4	3
4	2	2	4
5	0	0	5

Without completely specifying the utility functions of the individual producers let us assume that under conditions of isolated production and consumption the favorite positions on the individual production possibility frontiers according to the preferences of A and B could be:

A: 3 apples; 4 oranges; B: 2 apples; 4 oranges

Assume now that A and B agree that each would specialize in the production of one good (according to the assumptions at least one should specialize completely if Pareto efficiency is to be reached) and, further,

The Costs of Organizing Social Cooperation 63

that they agree to share the fruits of their efforts equally afterward. Then we would have

        A: 0 apples; 10 oranges; B: 10 apples; 0 oranges

which amounts to

        A,B: 10 apples; 10 oranges

with joint or cooperative production of this coalition of producers. After exchange and the apportioning (according to the equality of shares agreement):

        A: 5 apples; 5 oranges; B: 5 apples; 5 oranges

will accrue to the two persons for consumption.

Both individuals are better off. These are the simple Ricardian economics of comparative advantage and exchange in a cooperative setting. If, however, we drop the implicit assumption that the game of life is a cooperative game providing commitment facilities for free, we will have to look differently at the model of exchange. The cooperative exploitation of comparative advantages in production which Ludwig von Mises (1949: 158) called "the Ricardian law of association" will no longer work smoothly in an uncooperative setting.

The Invisible Prisoner's Dilemma in the Invisible Hand

Assume that production is not reversible. Assume, too, that exchange takes place only in the time period after production. Assume further that the two actors cannot simultaneously monitor each other's efforts, but have to produce without knowing what the other actor actually does. Thus they cannot make their own efforts directly contingent on those of the other producer.

Being involved in a noncooperative game the actors cannot commit themselves effectively to one of their production strategies or to certain courses of production. If we model them as rational individuals in the sense of game theory, they will look at the production and the exchange decision as *separate* events. But, then, they will find themselves locked into a prisoner's dilemma. A, for instance, might make the following deliberations:

> If I will not completely specialize but rather go to a position of, say (2 apples; 6 oranges) (*marginal specialization*), then I have to consider—restriction to these two alternatives is made here merely for convenience—two alternative actions of B.
>
> /:(B: 10 apples; 0 oranges) (B sticks to the terms agreed on in advance)

//:(B: 6 apples; 2 oranges) (B does not stick to the terms and also specializes only marginally).

From the point of view of A it is clear that in case / he is in a quite strong bargaining position and can hold up B. He can, so to say "squeeze" lots of apples "out of" B without giving away many oranges. Say, for instance, that this would result in an exchange of 1 orange for 9 apples. The result would be (A: 11; 5), (B: 1; 1), which clearly is better for A than the result from a cooperative full specialization of A.

In case // A would at least be ensured against exploitation. This means that A is again better off than he would be after choosing the agreed on cooperative strategy of full specialization.

The same considerations would apply in the case of B. Thus, both individuals would specialize only marginally, if at all. Should both individuals be willing to incur the risk of marginal specialization (or perhaps react on some sort of anticipation of the other's behavior) then after exchange there may still come about a situation of, (A: 4; 4), (B: 4; 4). There are eight quantities of both goods "in the system" if both specialize "marginally."

This is a Pareto improvement of the original situation of isolated individual choices. Nevertheless, the result of interaction is not Pareto optimal. Both individuals could have (5; 5) of both products if they had specialized fully as agreed on in advance and had shared equally afterward. Further, one cannot trust that a process of marginal specialization is marginally proceeding if the old *status quo* position remains feasible. Because this deviant solution is, so to say, "in the game" all the time, rational actors cannot gradually get away from it. For, in the choice situation itself, all choices remain open. Rational actors of our standard model of noncooperative game theory who are deciding according to the exigencies of the situation will not be in a position to exclude deliberately in advance any alternative from any of their own future choice sets (see also below).

The following table and the graph, which is part of the extensive form of the game, summarizes the discussion.

		A	
		(0, 10)	(2, 6)
B	(10,0)	5,5 5,5	1,1 11,5
	(6,2)	5,11 1,1	4,4 4,4

Diagram 3.1. Illustration of the prisoner's dilemma (PD) character of the specialization game.

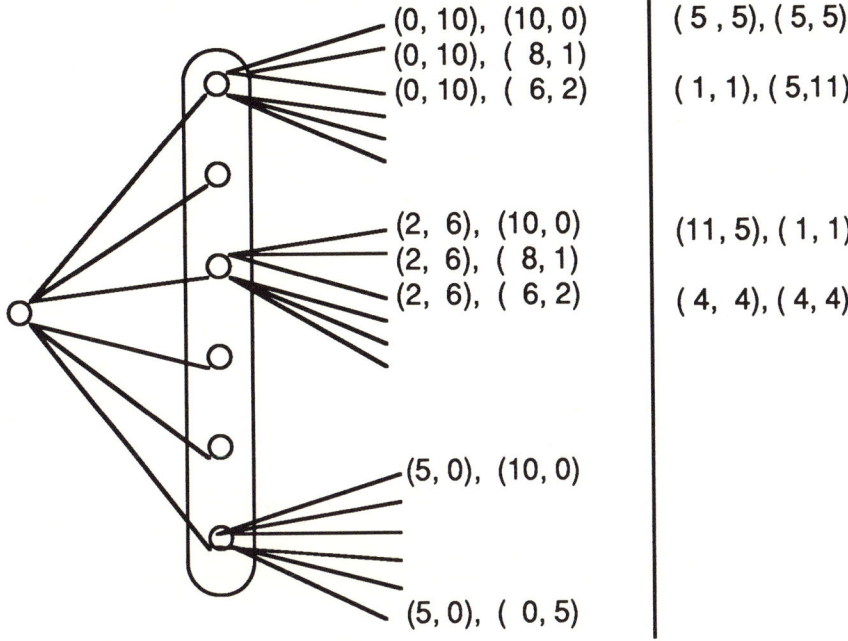

Figure 3.1. The extensive form of the game of exchanging apples and oranges.

The diagram as well as the figure are reduced to only very few strategies. A less simple view could easily be reached. For instance, one could assume that zero production is possible for both players as well as the viability of all convex combinations of the, then, seven pure strategies. This would lead to the following, shown in Figure 3.2.

But these refinements, as well as looking more closely at the bargaining game before and after production, will not add much to the analysis of the commitment problem in the specialization game. Without introducing such refinements, the PD character of an institution-free game of specialization that takes production and exchange as separate decisions, and not implicitly as one decision, should be clear in any case.

Extending the Argument

The Hobbesian Problem of Social Order

The previous statements raise the fundamental Hobbesian problem of social order in a less abstract setting than that in which it is usually

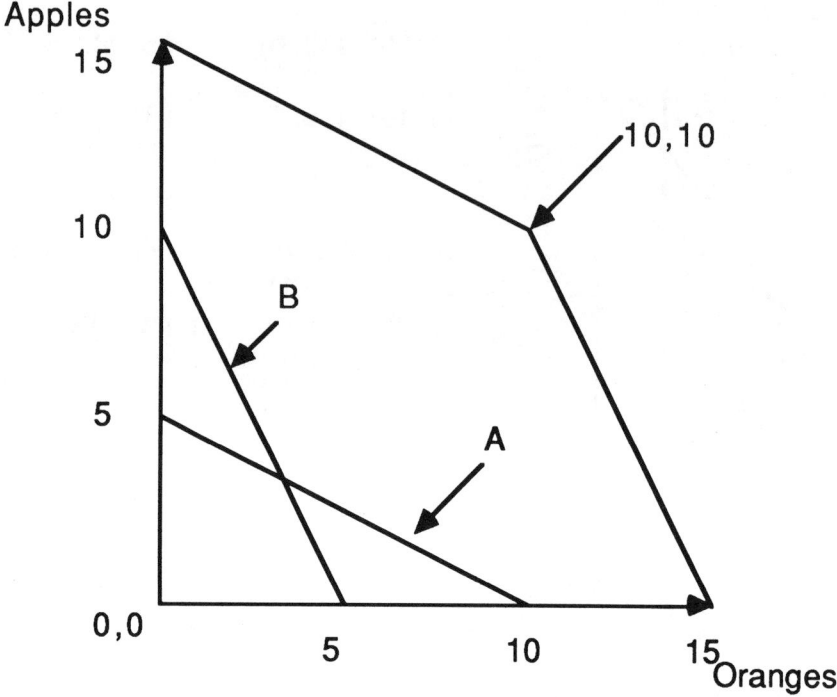

Figure 3.2 Coordinated production possibility space of *A* and *B*.

discussed. We may ask, how did humans manage to exploit comparative advantages regardless of the PD in the division of labor game? Assuming that humans basically are, and have always been, rational actors, there must have been some conditions favorable to overcoming the previously mentioned PD structure.

Conditions favorable for overcoming the prisoner's dilemma in the specialization and division of labor game can come about either naturally or artificially (i.e., institutionally). The first case would be exemplified if behavior of a small group of individuals is scrutinized based on the assumption that the participants of this small numbers' game know that they will interact for some time. The setting in which the game of exchange takes place, then, can provide a functional equivalent to commitment power and the facilities of coalition formation. In discussions of so called "simple cases" that begin by restricting themselves to exchanges between two persons, these functional equivalents (to commitment power or coalition formation) are often introduced into the analysis without notice. If, for instance, Robinson Crusoe and Friday are permanently on the island without an exit option this, of course, is a natural condition favorable to overcoming the PD. The two individuals are committed to an interaction with each other as if they would have agreed on a perfectly binding contract to interact exclusively with each other. In a real market with many participants, such conditions will not typically prevail. In this second case, commitment power must be bestowed on individuals by the rules of the legal order of the market game. Though at its "limits," the market game may contain some of the natural functional equivalents to commitment power mentioned before any modern market, and, in particular, any large market, is basically an artificial arrangement of rules or institutions that is "artificially" organized by a group.

The members of a group that organize a market game must themselves be involved in a different game, and it is within this game that the rules of the market game are produced. It could be hardly assumed that there always exists a market for organizing markets. But, even then, if we want to fully understand what a market is from a game-theoretic point of view we should try to understand both games simultaneously—the rule-creating game, and the game within the rules that are created within a further or more fundamental game (which sometimes might be a market game itself leading to a still higher nonmarket game).

This line of thought can be extended beyond the illustrative example of the market. In almost any other realistic social game there are some rules that are produced or artificial, in the sense previously introduced before. Of course, some rules may be given by nature. They are not the outcome of human choices that could, in principle, be otherwise. These natural rules are beyond the choice of rational actors. But, in addition to this, usually a game as played in social reality is defined by some rules that could be otherwise only if the producers and enforcers of the rules would behave differently. The rules are not necessarily, or even typically the outcome of intentional design or collective action designed to bring about their existence. They can be unintended outcomes or side effects of individual choices that are intentionally directed toward other ends. Still, such rules of a game are different from those that are beyond any kind of human choice; thus they are different from natural rules.

For two reasons, it is convenient to use the classical distinction between the "natural" and the "artificial" that played such a prominent role in the discussion among the British Moralists. On the one hand, it aptly illustrates the continuity between classical individualistic social philosophy based on a rational choice perspective, like the theories of Thomas Hobbes, David Hume, and Adam Smith, and modern game-theoretical analyses. On the other hand, using this distinction we can state the problem of social order in a concise manner: How and under what conditions can artificially organized games arise among rational actors who act according to the precepts of game-theoretic rationality?

The Limits of Rule Creation among Strictly Opportunistic Rational Players

In the example of the interaction between Robinson Crusoe and Friday, we first could imagine that a clever device drops down from heaven one day. This device accomplishes the task of producing some sort of commitment power for the two players. Let us assume that it modifies the payoffs of the two players contingent on any agreement they might reach, such that adhering to the agreed-upon terms becomes the dominant strategy for each of the players. Evidently, it would be advantageous for both players if the rules of the game could be transformed in this way. But, as we all know, our world does not provide clever devices for free; nor does human nature. Thus, commitment power as well as other rules of the game of life have to be artificially or socially provided by regular actions of human beings.

Suppose, therefore, that Robinson Crusoe and Friday are joined by a third individual who, for convenience, might be called Saturday. The three of them play a game in which each has two pure strategies, namely, to cooperate "C" or to defect "D." If Saturday cooperates he is in a position to modify the payoffs of the other individuals such that cooperation or sticking to agreed upon terms becomes a dominant strategy for *them*. However, Saturday can do this only at a cost to *himself*. Therefore, the question arises why he should incur this cost.

More specifically, let us assume that Saturday can choose between two different games that are played afterward by the three players. On the one hand, Saturday can choose to play a game in which he must act in the same ways as do the other players. This interaction will be called the *unmodified game*. It is a three-person PD interaction of Crusoe, Friday, and Saturday. On the other hand, Saturday can choose a game to play in which his cooperative alternative is somewhat stronger than in the original game. This modified game contains the punishment of other individuals' deviant behavior.

After introducing the common single-valued utility representation of preferences for the players, it can be assumed that we have for $N = 3$ and all $j \leq N$, $N \leq -1$:

$$f_j(i) < g_j(i) \text{ and } f_j(N-1) > g_j(0)$$

where f_j is related to the cooperative action C_j, and g_j to the deviant action D_j of the player j, if i other players cooperate. This is a PD structure with dominant strategies leading to a Pareto-dominated result. (With $N = 2$, the usual PD indeed would emerge.) In the present example, it is also assumed that the functions f_j and g_j are strictly monotonically increasing in i on the finite set $i = 0, 1, \ldots, N - 1$ and thus are not only continuous but also, in a plausible sense, well behaved.

The payoffs of the modified game are assumed to be the same as those of the unmodified game as long as player $m = 3$ (who is the "modifier" in this game) chooses to deviate from cooperation or chooses to defect. In that case he does not modify either. If m cooperates, then modified payoffs for himself as well as for the other players will result from his efforts. For illustrative purposes let us assume that this leads to the following payoff functions. If m (the modifier) deviates, then for all $j \le N$

$$f_j^*(i) := f_j(i),$$

for $j \ne m$, and $g_j^*(i) := g_j(i)$; if m cooperates and if $i = N - 1$ (no other deviates), then

$$f_j^*(i) := f_j(i)$$

for all $j \le N$; if m cooperates and if $i \le N - 2$ (at least one other deviates) then with sufficiently small $e, s > 0$, representing the effort of sanctioning and the ("net") sanction respectively,

$$f_m^*(i) := f_m(i) - e$$

and for all $j \le N, j \ne m$

$$g_j^*(i) := f_j(i) - s \text{ and } f_j^*(i) := f_j(i)$$

It is important to note that for $j = m$, we have

$$g_m^*(i) = g_m(i) > f_m(i) > f_m(i) - e = f_m(i)$$

if $i \le N - 2$, and

$$g_j^*(i) = g_m(i) > f_m(i) = f_m^*(i)$$

for $i = N - 1$; therefore, the deviant alternative is dominant for m in the modified as well as in the unmodified game.

For the other players $j \le N, j \ne m$, we get

$$g_j^*(i) = f_j(i) - s < f_j(i)$$

Thus, the dominance of the uncooperative alternative for players other than m vanishes if m cooperates in the second game (i.e., if he cooperates in the strong sense of cooperating himself *and* imposing sanctions on others). But this choice of m is subject to the condition that if any of the other players should deviate, then m's payoff will be less than in the case where he would deviate himself. It is also less than his expectation in the first game.

The effects of these illustrative assumptions are shown in Diagram 3.2 and in the numerical example below—both are for three individuals. By adopting the convention that the payoffs of the players are given in their natural order, the following is noted:

	C_2		D_2	
	C_3	D_3	C_3	D_3
C_1	$f(2), f(2), f(2)$	$f(1), f(1), g(2)$	$f(1), g(2), f(1)$	$f(0), g(1), g(1)$
D_1	$g(2), f(1), f(1)$	$g(1), f(0), g(1)$	$g(1), g(1), f(0)$	$g(0), g(0), g(0)$
C_1	$f(2), f(2), f(2)$	$f(1), f(1), g(2)$	$f(1), g^*(2), f^*(1)$	$f(0), g(1), g(1)$
D_1	$g^*(2), f(1), f^*(1)$	$g(1), f(0), g(1)$	$g^*(1), g^*(1), f^*(0)$	$g(0), g(0), g(0)$

Diagram 3.2. Production possibility space under coordinated action.

In the numerical example, the payoffs of the resulting three-person game for any player $j = 1,2,3$ in terms of other individuals i who are cooperating might be the following:

$$f_j(i) := 3i + 3$$

for $i \leq N - 1 = 2$, and

$$g_j(i) := 3i + 5, \; e := 1, \; s := 1$$

The starred payoff functions of the modified game can be easily calculated after setting $m = 3$, and one obtains the normal form of the game.

	C_2		D_2	
	C_3	D_3	C_3	D_3
without				
C_1	9,9,9	6,6,11	6,11,6	3,8,8
D_1	11,6,6	8,3,8	8,8,3	5,5,5
with				
C_1	9,9,9	6,6,11	6,8,5	3,8,8
D_1	8,6,5	8,3,8	5,5,2	5,5,5

Diagram 3.3. Three-person PD without and with modifier. Player 3 can choose whether he will modify the payoffs of the other players at some cost to him.

If Saturday or player 3 does not choose the modification game, and if taking the upper branch is always the cooperative action whereas taking the lower one is tantamount to defection, then the extensive form of that game is as shown in Figure 3.3.

The Costs of Organizing Social Cooperation 71

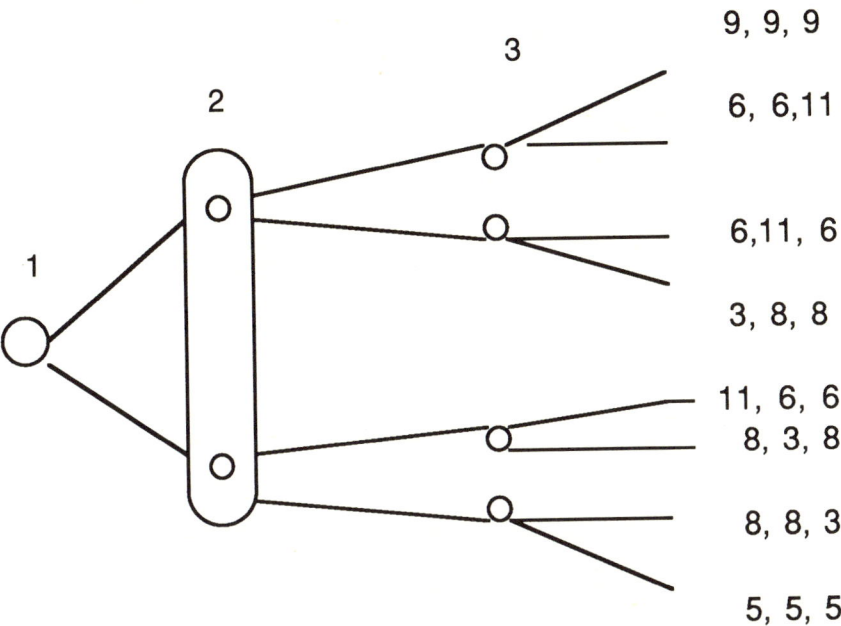

Figure 3.3 Extensive form of game without modification.

If player 3 chooses to play the modification game we get Figure 3.4.

It should be noted here that Saturday has a dominant strategy of deviation in both the modification game and the game without modification. Therefore, introducing a third player who can punish the other players for their defection is not very helpful. Even if the punishing player knows perfectly what the other players have done, the threat of punishment will not be credible. Saturday would not behave in a rational manner at his decision points should he deviate from his dominant strategy.

It would also not be helpful to introduce incomplete information here. Even if the other players do not know whether or not they are in a game with a modifying player, they would still know that defection is a dominant strategy for Saturday. As long as Saturday is opportunistic he will choose his dominant strategy. The interaction between the remaining players will be a conventional prisoner's dilemma with an identical payoff matrix for both the unmodified and the modified game. The matrix of this game is presented in Diagram 3.4.

Even the fact that it was assumed in the model that the modifier is committed to imposing sanctions if he himself cooperates is not sufficient to make playing the modified game attractive. The situation would change only if the enforcing player could commit himself in advance to

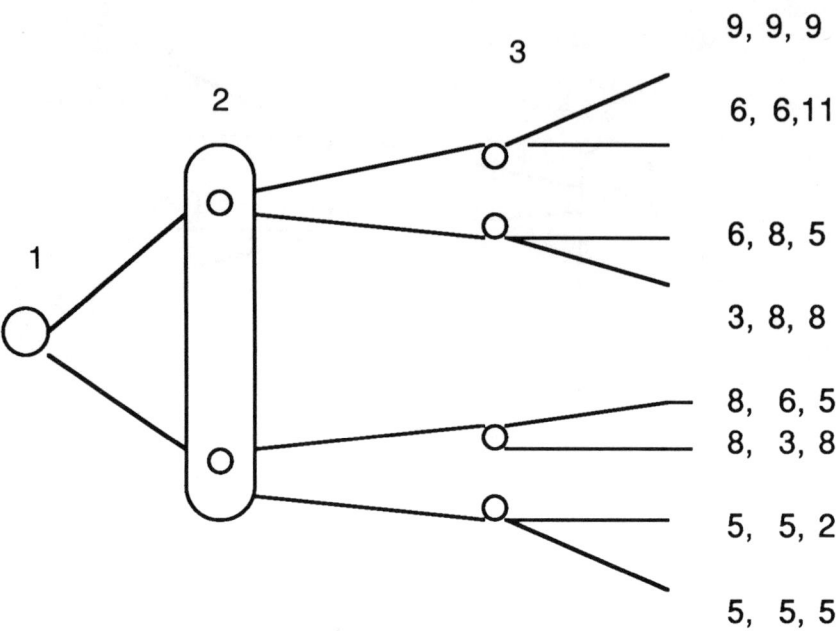

Figure 3.4 Extensive form of modified subgame.

	C_2	D_2
C_1	6,6	3,8
D_1	8,3	5,5

Diagram 3.4. PD among the remaining players.

play his cooperative strategy. In that case the relevant strategic two-person interaction of 1 and 2 would be characterized by the pay off matrix (Diagram 3.5):

	C_2	D_2
C_1	9,9	6,8
D_1	8,6	5,5

Diagram 3.5. Modified game among the remaining players.

Under these circumstances, the predictable result is the completely cooperative one. Cooperation will arise from dominant strategies of both players 1 and 2. But this result comes about only if player 3 can behave in a nonstrategic manner. Saturday must be able to become part of the environment. Then Saturday behaves like the clever device falling from heaven. He no longer acts as a rational individual in the actual play of the game.

However, providing such a choice for the modifier amounts to the assumption that there are additional strategies in the game that as yet have not been explicitly modeled. If one assumes that the modifier, as a matter of fact, has the faculties to commit himself before the game is played, why should not the other players be able to do the same thing? In that case no artificial or social enforcement would be necessary. However, if we want to understand how the division of labor is extended to the enforcement of norms in game-theoretic terms then we should be in a position to explain how players or groups of players can exit the normal strategic interaction.

If the constitutive rules of a game (including preferences) were not beyond the choices of the players of that game, they would not be the rules of the game. Thus, if we want to understand how parts of the rules of a game can be created within a more comprehensive game, then nonstrategic behavior in organizing one partial game must be the outcome of another partial game. As a general principle, it may be noted that those individuals who create a game by their own behavior must not behave strategically in the full sense of that term within the game they are creating. They must be "locked in" in a game that is separated from the created game. But, the foregoing remarks show that this poses a severe difficulty for any theory that sticks to the original game-theoretic model of individually rational behavior. For, then, individuals are modeled as perfectly opportunistic choosers who simply cannot predecide any of their own future choices, or influence any of their own future payoffs except for those cases that provide some form of commitment power as part of the rules of the game already in progress. Noting that the application of rational choice models to social interaction have provided some of the most illuminating insights of recent social theory, at the same time, we have to admit that, these insights are basically confined to within rule choices. To use the same model for the explanation of those choices that create the rules themselves will ultimately present limitations that cannot be overcome within a purely rational choice perspective. If it is not reason, as such, on which social order is founded then adherents of rational choice theory have to amend their theory.

Ways of Amending the Rational Choice Model

It should be fairly obvious that the argument previously introduced is not specific to the example of exchange and specialization nor to the specific choice of values in the subsequent example of an interaction between three individuals. Problems of commitment power will arise almost everywhere if social interaction of rational players is subject to closer scrutiny. According to the game-theoretic model of choice, individually rational behavior is motivated by the expected causal consequences of individual acts. Expediency prevails at any instance of decision. Not only are bygones bygones, but it is also impossible to virtually predecide a future decision at some preceding decision point. It is impossible to commit oneself to some future course of action or to restrict any of one's own future choice sets if the rules of the game do not explicitly allow for this.

Rational individuals do have full control over all choices open to them at any instance. They cannot give up full control over their strategy sets deliberately even if this should be in their own long-term interest. They can and—at least according to our game-theoretical model of rational behavior—they "must" react opportunistically to the exigencies of each choice situation they might enter. It is exactly this fact that is tentatively concealed in the normal form representation of a game and that is deliberately neglected in cooperative modeling. But, in the last resort, the game of life is an uncooperative one and should be understood in terms of uncooperative game theory.

This again raises the question whether there are elements in the game of life that provide some form of commitment power that exists naturally and in a purely *individual* way and thus do not require that it is artificially bestowed on individuals by *social* rules. From everyday experience we are well aware of such rules of prudent self-management, for example, *never drink as long as the sun is shining*. Individuals who have invested in the observation of such rules in the past indeed may be kept from effectively surrendering to the incentives of the moment. They are not motivated by considerations of expediency alone. They partly act as if run by a program. This psychologically appealing line of thought, however, does not really fit into our rational choice perspective of individually rational behavior. Even game theorists seem to fall into a trap here.

Evolutionary Explanations of the Emergence of Institutions

In his entertaining book on *The Evolution of Cooperation*, Robert Axelrod (1984) has tried to apply basically biological ideas to the question of whether stable patterns of cooperation in iterated games of the prisoner's dilemma variety may be expected to arise among rational strategists. Axelrod's idea of inviting people to send in strategies to compete in computer tournaments was doubtless a brilliant one. The aim was to find out which strategy would fare best if consecutively paired with all the other strategies. How the frequency of strategies would change in such an environment, if frequency was made dependent on success in dyadic interactions was scrutinized. Considerations about evolutionary stable strategies also took a prominent place within Axelrod's book.

Apparently this kind of analysis is framed in terms of uncooperative game theory. But, at closer scrutiny, this claim becomes doubtful. First, there are many functional equivalents to commitment power that are assumed to exist without explaining why they should or could be expected to exist. That interaction is always dyadic with no exit option is presumably the strongest of these assumptions. After a pair of strategies has been formed, they interact like Robinson and Friday on their island. What Axelrod has aptly called "the shadow of the future" only emerges because the individuals know that they are going to interact with the same individual for many rounds of the game without knowing when the interaction will end. This is tantamount to assuming that they made a long-term contract to interact with each other exclusively. For Robinson Crusoe and Friday such an assumption is innocuous and certainly sheds some light on the good sense of such institutions as marriage. However, it does not seem to be particularly helpful for understanding how social structure within an N-person interaction of opportunistic players can arise.

Second, modeling strategies as programs, as Axelrod does from the point of view of game theory, is tentatively misleading. For instance, it is quite problematic to assume that players adopt the same strategy across all dyadic interactions they might enter without any in-between choices. Of course, there are interactions in biology that can be modeled very well this way. A program even might be written in such a complex manner that it perfectly matches opportunistic behavior of a rational chooser. (Turing computability allows for a lot of things.) Still, a program can be written as simple as one wants it to be. And, above all, the chooser "run" by the program is stuck with it. All decisions at future points can be made initially. Typically, a rational chooser in the sense of game theory cannot do this. This assumption brings about a very substantial deviation from game-theoretical modeling in the proper sense. (For instance, if rational individuals could preprogram themselves in any way that should seem fit to them, they evidently could make credible any threat and arbitrarily restrict any of their future choice sets in advance.)

Now, one might wonder whether this insistence on the assumption of opportunism in game-theoretic modeling does not distort our view of social reality. It might be true that individual behavior as a matter of fact is closer to programmed behavior than to strategic behavior in the classical sense. This raises some deeper issues about how rational choice models based on strictly opportunistic behavior are related to explanatory models. In an effort to avoid these issues, let me only state that there seem to be quite good reasons for both types of analysis: one based on the strict model of perfect rationality at any instance of choice, and the other one based on psychological assumptions about human nature. At the present moment, I am only concerned with the classical rational choice approach, because I think that from the point of view of a truly general theory of social interaction we should make any effort to rescue it before we are willing to enter the zoo of specific psychological motives.

Within classical models it remains an open question how opportunism, which is presumed to prevail in choices within existing rules, can be overcome in providing the rules themselves. One might be tempted here to take up the notion of a gradual evolution of rules. Looking again at the model of the exchange of apples and oranges, it has to be noted, however, that this notion raises some difficulties of its own. As has been stated before, the chances of gradually getting away from Pareto-inferior situations look dim as long as all strategies of deviation remain in the game. How could completely informed opportunistic players gradually exclude alternatives from their choice sets? How could we model this without giving up the premise of full control?

The assumptions of the classical model also seem to restrict the use of such concepts as "frequency dependency" in solving the problem of how to model a gradual emergence of norms. If, for instance, the frequency of the application of certain strategies within a population of rational players changes, the expected payoffs may also change. We may ask, therefore, whether the process of change in frequencies may be modeled in a fruitful way. To look at this, let us start again with a very pedestrian example.

Assume that the number of players is finite but very large, i.e., $N \gg 0$. The interaction is symmetric in the sense that the payoff functions for all players are identical. The game is a sequence of simple normal or constituent games that are played indefinitely. In each round of play each player can choose between three strategies: Cc, Dc, Dd. The interpretation of the first strategy is: "Cooperate in some material sense and cooperate in sanctioning others for cooperation or noncooperation." The interpretation of Dc is: "Defect and cooperate in sanctioning other individuals." Dd means: "Defect and do not participate in the sanctioning process either." The pay offs for all $i \leq N$ are:

$$f(i) < g(i) < h(i)$$

up to some threshold t_1 with $0 < t_1 < N$.

The Costs of Organizing Social Cooperation

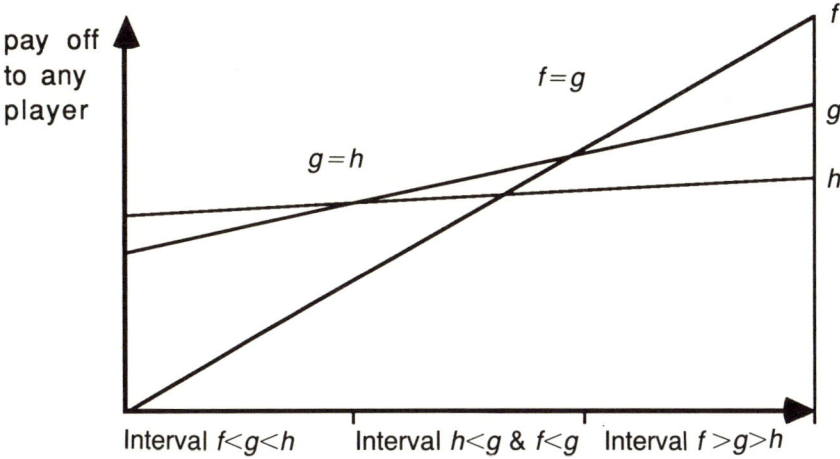

Figure 3.5 Payoff functions of alternative "degrees" of cooperation.

$$g(i) > h(i) \text{ and } g(i) > f(i)$$

up to t_2, $t_1 \leq t_2 < N$.

$$f(i) > g(i) > h(i)$$

for $i \geq t_2$.

If we assume linear functions f, g, h, the payoffs from the point of view of an arbitrary player can be illustrated as shown in Figure 3.5.

The payoffs f, g, h that are shown are related to the strategies Cc, Dc, Dd, respectively. If we illustrate the nine cells with numbers corresponding to the order between the payoffs (from the point of view of the chooser or row player) we get, for instance, something like that shown in Diagram 3.6 (higher numbers indicating preferred results):

	$0 \rightarrow$ Number of other cooperators $\rightarrow N - 1$		
	Almost no other	Approx. half of all	Almost all others
Cc	1	2 or 1	3
Dc	2	3	2
Dd	3	2 or 1	1
	$f(i) < g(i) < h(i)$	$g(i) > h(i)$ $g(i) > f(i)$	$f(i) > g(i) > h(i)$

Diagram 3.6. Order of payoffs functions as number of cooperators increases.

Still, it remains an open question whether and, if so, how we can model that in the course of time the state of interaction is transformed such that from a state corresponding to column 1 we gradually reach column 3. If the change in frequencies of the strategies that are displayed by the players has to be explained endogenously, then it is perplexing why such deviations from former equilibrium points should occur among rational and fully informed players who have full control over their choice sets. Of course, if we assume that strategies are adopted like programs, that there are individuals who experiment, and who innovate in the realm of behavioral programs, then an evolutionary perspective might be helpful. But, this comes about only at the cost of violating or relaxing the fundamental assumption of opportunity-taking behavior.

A Switching Model of Rational Choice

As far as I can see, chances are slight that modern game-theoretical analyses of the emergence and maintenance of social institutions will be able to solve the problem of explaining the emergence of nonstrategic rule-providing behavior without already assuming this kind of behavior on the level of individual choice. There should be at least some choices that are not guided by considerations of expediency, but rather by adopted rules. To avoid going all the way to a model of preprogrammed individual behavior, we should perhaps take a closer look at the behavioral technology of human actors or at human nature. If our rational decision maker is not the observable person anymore but rather a rational chooser "in" a human body then this "person within the person" may be viewed as making use of a behavioral technology that contains some commitment facilities. These, for instance, might be based on retributive emotions. We could model the effects of these emotions explicitly as certain strategic possibilities of the rational actor. The drawback of this, of course, is that the behavior of such an actor is no longer directly observable. The advantage is that to the fictitious person within the person, traditional game-theoretical analysis applies directly. In his ingenious attempt to analyze the "strategic role of the emotions," Robert Frank (1988) has shown that this broadly Humean line of argument may be a very promising one.

In order to avoid the drawback of a fictitious actor running the person as well as the other problems previously discussed, one has to modify the model of traditional behavior. Now, usually one would do this by introducing some kind of limited rationality assumption. Although this is a sound procedure, one should not neglect different ways of introducing the assumption. The most promising way might be to introduce it by stating that human individuals tentatively switch between two different modes of behavior. If the opportunity costs involved in a decision are low, then nonopportunistic behavior should be expected to prevail. If opportunity costs are high, opportunism should prevail. This hypothesis is merely ad hoc in that it is meant to apply to within-rule choices as well as to choices that are involved in rule creation. Undoubtedly, the hypothesis is problematic. However, it would solve many different puzzles that commonly plague a rational choice perspective—like the question why people go to the polls, or why judges prefer one decision to another one, etc. It would accomplish this without throwing "out the baby with the bath." It would not assume that people act in certain ways no matter what.

A sound approach to explaining the emergence and maintenance of social institutions must avoid two extreme assumptions—the assumption of completely opportunistic rational behavior that is motivated exclusively by future expected consequences, as well as the assumption that behavior is completely programmed by past experiences or internalized norms. On the one hand, perfectly rational individuals have little need for social institutions specialized in providing enforcement services. These services could be rendered by rational players themselves using contingent strategies. On the other hand, if complete internalization of norms suppressed any kind of opportunism—or at least led to completely changed utilities—there would be no need to impose sanctions on overt behavior by specialized institutions. At least, those who think that the peaceful anarchic existence of free men is not beyond the scope of viable social arrangements will have to base their claim on some model of the rational individual that is a compromise between the two extreme models of human behavior. Neither perfectly rational, and thus perfectly opportunistic, nor perfectly norm-guided behavior will do as a sole basic model in a unified theory of social cooperation.

Acknowledgments

I am indebted to Werner Raub, Elinor Ostrom, James Buchanan, Viktor Vanberg, and Reinhard Selten for their comments. I am grateful for the hospitality and the financial support of the Center for Study of Public Choice, Fairfax, and the Zentrum für Interdisziplinäre Forschung, Bielefeld.

References

Axelrod, R. (1984). *The Evolution of Cooperation*. New York: Basic Books
Buchanan, J.M. (1986). "Better than plowing." Pp. 359 ff. in *Banca Nazionale del Lavoro Quarterly Review (Roma)* No. 159.
Frank, R. (1988). *Passions Within Reason: The Strategic Role of the Emotions*. New York: W. W. Norton.
Mises, L. v. (1949). *Human Action*. New Haven: Yale University Press.

4

Individual Interests and Moral Institutions: An Endogenous Approach to the Modification of Preferences

Werner Raub
Thomas Voss

The analysis of "problematic social situations" is a topic in the study of social institutions. A social situation is defined as problematic (cf. Raub and Voss, 1986) if there is a conflict between the outcomes resulting from individually rational behavior of strategically interdependent actors and those outcomes which are efficient (Pareto-optimal). The prisoner's dilemma is a paradigmatic—although not the only—situation of this kind.

It is useful to distinguish three kinds of mechanisms which may lead to cooperation (i.e., efficiency) in problematic social situations. The first one focuses on binding agreements enforced by external, third parties. Solutions of this kind are commonly described as *coercive* or *exogenous*. Consider the Hobbesian problem of order as a typical case. According to Hobbes's coercive solution, the state as an enforcing agency emerges in order to police those individuals who deviate from mutually profitable cooperation. Parsons has criticized this approach because no explanation is given of the emergence of the external authority. In particular, the Hobbesian approach fails to demonstrate the existence of individual incentives to contribute to the cost of constructing the Leviathan. More generally, all approaches referring to a cooperative game context and merely suggesting certain binding agreements as a means to improve the outcomes of problematic situations are liable to similar criticism if they do not explain how opportunities for binding agreements are brought about.

A second mechanism is the iteration of a problematic social situation. If appropriate conditions are met, iteration provides actors with incentives to cooperate (cf. *inter alia* Axelrod, 1984). This *endogenous* approach is attractive if one wants to explain a moral praxis which is due to a regularity of behavior in a repeated situation. Nevertheless, there are some limitations. For example, one would hesitate to deny the occurrence of any moral behavior in situations which are not repeated or at least do not fulfill the conditions for cooperation as required by an iterative game approach (cf. e.g., Raub and Voss, 1986, for a description of these conditions).

In this chapter therefore we focus on a *third* kind of mechanism. Cooperation would emerge if actors were endowed with preferences such that a cooperative action becomes individually rational. Suitable preference changes may be due to changes in (physical) outcomes, or to a direct modification of actors' preferences, which may correspond to an adoption of a moral point of view or to a recognition of others' interests (i.e., some kind of altruism). This approach, of course, must provide an endogenous conceptualization of these processes such that preference changes are not assumed but are derived as a consequence of individual adaptation to situational incentives. We suggest a game theoretical model for the analysis of this problem. The model assumes that morality can be a matter of choice motivated entirely by (perhaps even purely selfish) individual interests.

The Problem of Moral Institutions

The sociological tradition of Durkheim and Parsons emphasizes morality as a means to achieve social order. According to Parsons, an essential requirement for a satisfactory solution of the Hobbesian problem is to recognize that obedience to certain moral rules is a necessary condition for the emergence of cooperation. Considering this claim, one will concede that sufficiently goal-directed, and in this sense rational, actors notice the positive effects (in terms of efficiency gains) resulting from the acceptance of moral rules. However, one may object that an incentive remains for a selfish individual to let the others act in consonance with norms. If there exist moral rules prescribing cooperative behavior, it may still pay individually to defect. Thus, a dilemma still remains.

Upon closer inspection, a conception of moral behavior arises within the sociological tradition, which in principle might escape this criticism. Parsons claimed that cooperation stems from an *internalized* commitment to moral norms and values, learned in some process of socialization. Parsons even conjectures that individuals must accept some categorical, unconditional commitment to moral values (cf. Münch, 1982). In a rational action perspective, this would imply that moral rules somehow guide behavior via preferences with a moral component. At this point, then, one might suspect a new difficulty generated by these kinds of normative solutions to the problem of order. The difficulty consists in the proper specification of a mechanism motivating rational individuals to adopt such moral preferences.

The problem of explaining moral institutions (cf. Kliemt, 1985 for a historical discussion of the concept) via preferences with a moral component has not only been posed within the Durkheim–Parsons tradition. Using a rational action framework, a growing body of literature attempts to clarify the interrelations between self-interested behavior and morality. It is often argued that morality can be conceived as an argument of an actor's utility function. Unfortunately, explanations of the emergence of preferences underlying such utility functions are scarce. Simply assuming the existence of moral preferences in order to explain the occurrence of moral actions is liable to result in an ad hoc explanation. In this way, any kind of behavior might be "explained" by an immunizing stratagem. Merely remarking upon efficiency gains brought about by moral preferences provides a quasi-functionalistic argument, at best.

The need for an improvement of rational action models by properly accounting for instrumental as well as moral behavior has recently been stressed (e.g. Wippler, 1985:72). Taking for granted that moral behavior may be mediated by moral preferences, an obvious approach to an endogenous explanation of morality within a rational action paradigm would be to conceive preferences as objects or at least as consequences of choice and to consider the active modification and adaptation of preferences (cf. Frey, 1983).

Some Rational Action Perspectives on Changes in Preferences

There is a somewhat scattered set of contributions relevant to an analysis of morality via preference changes. It may be useful to distinguish between two rather different conceptual frameworks, and to discuss some explanatory sketches using these frameworks by way of specifying mechanisms that can lead to moral preferences. As to *conceptual frameworks*, for the investigation of preference changes, one can either assume that actors are endowed with one set of preferences that change over time, or that they are endowed with two (or more) sets of (possibly conflicting) preferences that are held simultaneously (Elster, 1986).

Various explanatory sketches rest upon the assumption that the actor has but one set of preferences at a time. Contrasting causal with intentional processes of preference change, Elster's (1983:chap. III) "sour grapes" mechanism is an instructive example of a *causal process*. Elster refers to the causal mechanism of adaptive preference formation, or adaptive preference change such that wants or desires (preferences) are shaped by the feasible set. The underlying causal process may be the reduction of cognitive dissonance, as described in Festinger's theory (cf. Elster, 1983:109–110). A mechanism closely related to adaptive preferences and presumably relevant to the discussion of moral behavior is preference change through *learning*. An example of such an approach is Akerlof's (1983) recent discussion of "loyalty filters" (see below).

Assuming an intentional process definitely requires that preferences at least to some extent become, objects of choice. According to endogenous changes in tastes models, the actor experiences a conflict between short- and long-run preferences. He manages to solve this conflict by changing short-run preferences so that they fit into a consistent long-term utility pattern. Therefore, it may pay to sacrifice short-run benefits (e.g., via acting in accordance with a moral rule) in order to collect greater net benefits over a longer period of time.

Other approaches stress that an actor may not change his preferences in time, but may be endowed with two or more conflicting sets of preferences. Adam Smith, in his *Theory of Moral Sentiments*, is one classical author who analyzed the interrelations between morality and self-interest by using such a conception of a "multiple self." According to Smith, the morality of actions is a matter of degree. Virtue, as a high degree of morality, depends on the ability of an actor to achieve a sufficient degree of self-command "over the most ungovernable passions of human nature" (Smith, 1759:25). This self-command seems necessary because of man's weakness of the will. Only if the self is able to "reduce the violence of the passions" (1759:26) to a moderate degree may it partially attain the (moral) perspective of an impartial spectator. This view implies that within the human self two conflicting tendencies may struggle against each other.

More recently, this line of reasoning has been elaborated. According to Frankfurt (1971), the very concept of a person should be defined by reference to the capacity to form preferences of a higher order. In particular, Frankfurt distinguishes between *first-order* desires (preferences), roughly corresponding to Smith's passions, and *second-order* desires. Second-order desires, or desires about desires may be in conflict with the basic preferences. For Frankfurt, the existence of these meta-preferences indicates the human ability of self-evaluation and self-reflection.

An actor experiencing a conflict between two sets of preferences may want to achieve "self-command." An important causal mechanism of "character planning" (Elster, 1983:117) or "egonomics" (Schelling, 1978) is precommitment. For example, consider an actor willing to make a promise to somebody. Recognizing his permanent temptation to break promises, he may want to control his own behavior. This wish may be motivated by purely egoistic preferences, e.g., in order to make the promise convincing to the partner, or not to loose one's good reputation, etc.; or it may be motivated by other, more group-oriented "moral" desires.

As a means to that end, the actor could make a binding commitment. There are different methods of making binding commitments. The most important among them are (1) to restrict the feasible set available at the time of the decision, and (2) to change the incentives (or outcomes) at the time of the decision. The first of these methods may work through physical constraints. Fat people stock their refrigerators with small quantities of food. A change of outcomes may be brought about if a third party is involved who enforces the promise by penalizing acts that run counter to the promise. In this way, an indirect change of preferences may result.

Assuming that there is a technique to achieve the goal of self-control, a crucial question remains. Given two sets of competing preferences, how are they allocated to a determinate decision, even a decision to bind oneself? Schelling (1983:93–94), who is aware of this problem, suggests that there be something like collective choice to resolve this conflict between competing preferences. Margolis (1982) has presented a sophisticated dual self model which involves a kind of social welfare rule for the individual (cf. Lindenberg, 1983, for a related but alternative approach).

Other advocates of dual self models use analogies from larger social systems. Thaler and Shefrin (1981) describe the person as a business firm. In particular, they take the viewpoint of agency theory and distinguish between a *doer*- and a *planner*-self. The doer exists for just one period and is completely selfish and myopic. The planner has a long-run utility function. The planner has the capacity to modify the doer's behavior—at some costs for both selves. Thaler and Shefrin's model comes closest to Elster's concept of "character planning," because it describes the modification of the doer's preferences (and incentives) as basic techniques, the alternative being to change constraints. They consider the internalization of a norm as a way of modifying the doer's interests. Notice that such an adoption of a moral point of view is merely due to the individual's long-run interests (as represented by the planner's utility function).

Sen (1974) suggests that moral behavior may be understood by allowing actors to be able to form meta-preferences. A moral view can then be expressed not as an ordering of outcomes but "through a ranking of the possible *orderings* of outcomes" (Sen, 1974:80). The adoption of a moral point of view may lead to the selection of orderings which are morally more desirable than an ordering dictated by the natural preferences of an actor. With regard to this conception, the question arises again about which set of preferences will determine the action: the set of natural preferences or a set of modified preferences selected by a moral meta-ranking of orderings? In other words, considering different sets of preference orderings as the different "selves" of an actor, how are the selves within each actor related?

Admittedly, Sen is quite vague with regard to this point (cf. e.g., Bolle, 1983; Nida-Rümelin, 1987:chap. 16), but he offers a stimulating sketch of an argument: People may be motivated to act *as if* their actions were guided by a moral point of view, because in this way they can avoid outcomes which are individually as well as socially undesirable. Thus, actors might serve their primary egoistic preferences better if they adhere to the command of their meta-preferences rather than if they act as pure egoists.

Some Shortcomings

Two main problems seem to arise with rational action perspectives on changing preferences as a means of modeling the emergence of morality. One of these involves the neglect of strategic aspects, while the other one is an inadequate treatment of incentives. To justify this impression, we propose to take a closer look at two of the above approaches. As an example of a multiple self model, we use Sen's approach to point out common inadequacies with respect to the explicit consideration of incentive problems. In order to sketch the implications of strategic aspects, we then turn to Akerlof's model of loyalty filters as an example of those approaches, which assume an actor endowed with a single set of preferences that changes over time.

Let us first examine Sen's approach, which is attractive because it is explicitly suited to a game-theoretical context. Thus, Sen aptly models morality as a mechanism inducing cooperation in problematic social situations. He illustrates his argument with a set of preferences ordered so that a classical two-person prisoner's dilemma (PD) situation is generated. Diagram 4.1 gives the normal form representation of the PD.

		Player 2	
		C_2	D_2
Player 1	C_1	R^n, R^n	S^n, T^n
	D_1	T^n, S^n	P^n, P^n

Diagram 4.1. The prisoner's dilemma.

The entries of the matrix in Diagram 4.1 are the players' payoffs. They are indicated by an upper index "n" because they are interpreted as "natural" payoffs. They are those payoffs imposed on the players by their human nature and may, but need not, represent completely egoistic preferences. We assume that the natural payoffs do not reflect moral values, because we want to provide a model in which moral preferences are an endogenous result of individual adaptation. In the PD the natural preference ordering with respect to outcomes implies that

$$T^n > R^n > P^n > S^n \tag{1}$$

Therefore, in terms of natural preferences, the strategy D_i ("defection"; $i = 1,2$) is the best choice for each player no matter what the other player does. If both players defect by choosing their strictly dominant strategy, however, they are worse off than they would have been had they both chosen strategy C_i ("cooperation"). Sen suggests a situation where players are able to change the natural preference ordering (1) or are at least able to behave as if their natural preference ordering has been changed. To represent different kinds of preference orderings of the outcomes associated with the four combinations of (pure) strategies in the PD, we use a second payoff matrix (see Diagram 4.2).

		Player 2	
		C_2	D_2
Player 1	C_1	R^e_1, R^e_2	S^e_1, T^e_2
	D_1	T^e_1, S^e_2	P^e_1, P^e_2

Diagram 4.2. Payoff matrix for an effective game.

The payoffs in this matrix are indicated with an upper index "e" because they represent those preferences that effectively guide the behavior of the players. The effective preferences may reflect a moral point of view. According to Sen, this is the case if they represent orderings that are morally superior to other orderings (cf. Sen, 1974:80) and are in this sense, a result of a moral meta-ranking of effective preference orderings.

As pointed out by Sen, preference orderings reflecting moral considerations can be of various types. First, imagine moral considerations of a Kantian type, for example, the categorical imperative or other kinds of generalization principles. In this case, the moral rule prescribes unconditional cooperation, that is, cooperation irrespective of the other player's behavior. This type of morality can be described by an ordering of effective preferences such that

$$R^e_i \geq S^e_i > T^e_i \geq P^e_i \qquad (2)$$

Rational players acting in accordance with such an effective preference ordering would cooperate, since to do this is their strictly dominant strategy.

A more modest type of moral valuation can be represented by an effective ordering corresponding to Sen's Assurance Game preferences:

$$R^e_i > T^e_i > P^e_i > S^e_i \qquad (3)$$

Cooperation in this case ceases to be a dominant strategy, but to cooperate is a best reply to the cooperation of the other player. This kind of ordering therefore reflects what might be called a morality of conditional cooperation.

The effects of morality now become obvious. Consider two individuals endowed with natural preference ordering (1) but both acting in consonance either with effective ordering (2) or with ordering (3). It would then be possible for them to cooperate mutually since cooperation is based on dominant strategies (both players with effective ordering (2) or at least on an efficient equilibrium point. Notice that not only is $R^e_i > P^e_i$ according to (2) and (3), but also that $R^n > P^n$ according to (1). Morality thus allows individuals to realize outcomes where everybody is better off not only in terms of effective but also in terms of natural interests.

Can we therefore conclude that rational actors who are motivated by even completely selfish interests, but who are equipped with a technique to act in consonance with effective preferences, which may differ from natural preferences, will adopt moral preferences? Such a conclusion of course, is unwarranted. There are serious incentive problems. For example, imagine player 1 having effective preferences such that cooperation is a dominant choice for him. Notice that, under these circumstances, it would be good advice for player 2 *not* to adopt moral preferences like (2) or (3) but just to stick to his natural preferences (1). The simple reason is that, in this case, player 2's only best reply against any strategy of player 1 would be to defect. Due to his effective preferences, player 1's only best strategy against any strategy of player 2 would be to cooperate. Thus, player 2 would be able to realize his most preferred payoff T'' and would thus be able to exploit player 1. Once again it becomes evident that to point out efficiency gains generated by morality does not in itself constitute a solution to the problem of rational actors adopting moral preferences.

It should be noted that Sen's otherwise attractive conceptual framework is far from being the only one to neglect a proper consideration of such incentive problems. Other models are vulnerable to similar types of criticism. As indicated, most authors do not even consider the strategic aspects of problematic social situations and the strategic aspects in the adaptation of preferences.

Akerlof's model of "loyalty filters" provides a suitable illustration of this point. He considers the change of a set of preferences over time. The basic idea is simple and summarized in the following passage:

> When people go through experiences, frequently their loyalties, or their values, change. I call these value-changing experiences "loyalty filters." This paper considers the case where these values are partially, but not totally, changeable. In addition, persons, by having a choice over their experiences, can exercise some choice over their values; or perhaps more typically, persons may choose for their children experiences that will lead them to have desired values. Insofar as this occurs, values are not fixed, as in standard economics, but are a matter of choice (Akerlof, 1983:175).

Though this idea seems to be powerful, Akerlof does not offer an explicit theoretical argument dealing with the conceptualization of the effect of loyalties on behavior. In his analyses, the actors' utility functions only depend on arguments such as economic welfare. In particular, Akerlof seems to argue that *loyalties are chosen (or learned or evolve) because they may have the effect of maximizing utility with respect to nonmoral (including economic) values*. An example refers to an economy with one type of job. Workers have a chance to embezzle (to act noncooperatively) and increase their income with positive probability. Employers' surveillance costs are prohibitive. Alternatively, workers can become honest (assuming some training costs). Employers can measure an employee's character without error. Then a dishonest worker will get a lower wage (reduced by the expected cost of embezzlement) than an honest worker. Furthermore, Akerlof assumes that it is more costly to acquire the ability of *appearing* honest (which may provide the opportunity of embezzling when there is a chance) than it is to *be* honest. Thus mimicry will not pay. Therefore, under quite general conditions, the expected net utility of being honest will be greater than the expected utility of being dishonest, utility depending only on income.

Though this sketch of an analysis does seem to be internally consistent, Akerlof does not touch some crucial aspects of the problem. He tends to trivialize the task by assuming away any kind of strategic interaction. In particular, Akerlof assumes, first, that the employer predicts with certainty each employee's disposition to cooperate or to defect. Second, it is assumed that the employer is himself honest. He does not refuse to perceive any differences between workers in order to pay honest people less than their marginal product. Under conditions like these, it is not surprising that people will have no significant incentives to defect.

In light of this discussion, some requirements for the analysis of moral preferences from a rational action perspective emerge. What we need is an explicit treatment of strategic aspects of problematic social situations. The framework suggested by Sen nicely meets this requirement, in spite of the shortcomings of his analysis. Furthermore, it is necessary to treat incentive problems that arise when we allow individuals to be able to adopt moral preferences. The adaptation of preferences to moral valuations, then, also must be understood as a strategic interaction problem. In view of these requirements, we suggest a model representing the modification of preferences and their adaptation to moral valuations as a move within a larger strategic game.

A Model for the Strategic Modification of Preferences

Following the previous line of reasoning, our model is motivated by five assumptions. First, we assume that a significant part of empirically observable moral rules concerns types of social situations in which outcomes depend on the *interaction* of two or more actors. Therefore, it is straightforward to model the underlying social situations as game situations of strategic interdependence. Second, we suggest that moral rules are important in situations that are *problematic* in that rational actors following their natural preferences realize an outcome, which is suboptimal in the Pareto sense. Third, we consider moral rules as guiding behavior via individual *preferences*. As Sen points out, actors may want to adopt effective preferences which reflect a moral point of view because they generate a socially preferred outcome. Notice that outcomes are counted as efficient with respect to the actors' natural preferences. We assume, furthermore, that effective preferences can be modeled as objects of *choice behavior*. Finally, we suggest that the choice of effective preferences results from the *rational pursuit of basic natural preferences in a strategic setting*.

Next, we introduce a game **M** which models the strategic modification of natural preferences by allowing for the choice of effective preferences which may, but need not, correspond to moral rules.

Intuitive Sketch and Normal Form of Game **M**

Consider players involved in a classical two-person PD as represented by the matrix in Diagram 4.1. The natural payoffs may, but need not, represent completely selfish interests. In game **M**, players 1 and 2 are able to modify these natural payoffs. With respect to different means of bringing about modifications of natural payoffs, our main focus is on modifications due to the direct adoption of moral rules or values. One easily imagines another, and more indirect kind of mechanism which will be discussed below. According to this mechanism, players will not directly modify preferences for a given set of physical outcomes. Instead, they will modify the physical outcomes associated with given strategy combinations in the underlying PD, and induce in this way a change of preferences corresponding to certain strategy combinations.

Without deciding a priori which of these mechanisms is available for the two players, we characterize their strategies O_i ($i = 1,2$) in game **M** as choices of effective preference orderings of the physical outcomes in the PD.[1] Effective preferences are represented by cardinal effective payoff functions. Thus, a strategy O_i *of player i* in **M** is an ordering of the (cardinal) effective payoffs T^e_i, R^e_i, P^e_i, S^e_i in an effective 2 × 2-game represented by the matrix in Diagram 4.2. We assume that players 1 and 2 choose their effective orderings O_1 and O_2 simultaneously. Of course, we want to analyze the choice of such orderings O_i by rational players and we are especially interested in answering the question whether they are willing to choose orderings like the Kantian ordering (2) or the Assurance Game preference ordering (3), which reflect a moral point of view.

How do rational players choose effective preference orderings? Using the assumption that their choices result from the pursuit of natural preferences, we suggest that the choice of effective preferences depends on the implications of the effective preferences for the outcomes of the effective game. These outcomes can be evaluated in terms of the players' natural payoffs. This allows the players, in turn, to evaluate effective preferences in terms of natural preferences.

Let $O = (O_1, O_2)$ denote a vector of strategies chosen in **M**. Then, O_1 and O_2 are the effective preference orderings of player 1 and player 2 for the effective game. A strategy combination $O = (O_1, O_2)$ in **M** thus determines the payoff functions of the players in the effective game and, therefore, determines its normal form. Intuitively, this means that choices of effective preference orderings in **M** determine the incentive structure of the effective game. With regard to the effective game, we use the standard assumption that it is a noncooperative game with complete information.[2] In effect, this implies that each player's effective preference ordering will be revealed to the other player after both players have chosen their effective orderings and before the effective game itself is played. Furthermore, each player will play the effective game as if his effective preferences were his "true" preferences.

A solution theory for noncooperative games specifies the strategy choices of rational players in different types of such games.[3] Applying a solution theory makes it possible to predict the strategy choices of rational players in the effective game, and also generates the probabilities of cooperation of player 1 and player 2, that is, the probabilities q_i and $(1 - q_i)$ of choosing C_i and D_i, respectively, in the effective game, given the effective preference orderings O_i. Given the natural payoffs T^n, R^n, P^n, S^n, we can calculate the (expected) natural payoffs associated with these probabilities, and we interpret these as the payoffs for players 1 and 2 in game **M**. More precisely, consider rational player i to behave as if he anticipated the consequences of effective preference orderings in the described way. The payoff $U^m_i (O_1, O_2)$ for such a player i in **M** is i's natural payoff associated with those strategies of players 1 and 2 which are the elements of the strategy solution of the effective game if the players' effective preference orderings are O_1 and O_2.

The normal form of **M** can now be characterized by defining the players' strategy sets in **M** as sets of preference orderings O_i for the effective game and by payoff functions $U^m_i (O_1, O_2)$. Figure 4.1 summarizes the players' decision situation in game **M**.

We assume that **M** is a noncooperative game. Therefore, binding and enforceable agreements concerning the choice of effective preference orderings are not feasible. The reason for this assumption is similar to the reason for assuming that the PD itself is a noncooperative game and parallels the objection against the coercive solution of the problem of social order. Binding and enforceable agreements on effective preferences may facilitate the choice of moral preferences and may thus ensure efficiency. However, we do not want to trivialize the modification of preferences by assuming opportunities for the enforcement of agreements without being able to give an endogenous explanation for the emergence of these opportunities. Like Sen, we assume that a player is able to behave in the effective game as if he had certain effective preferences, and that these effective preferences are communciated to the

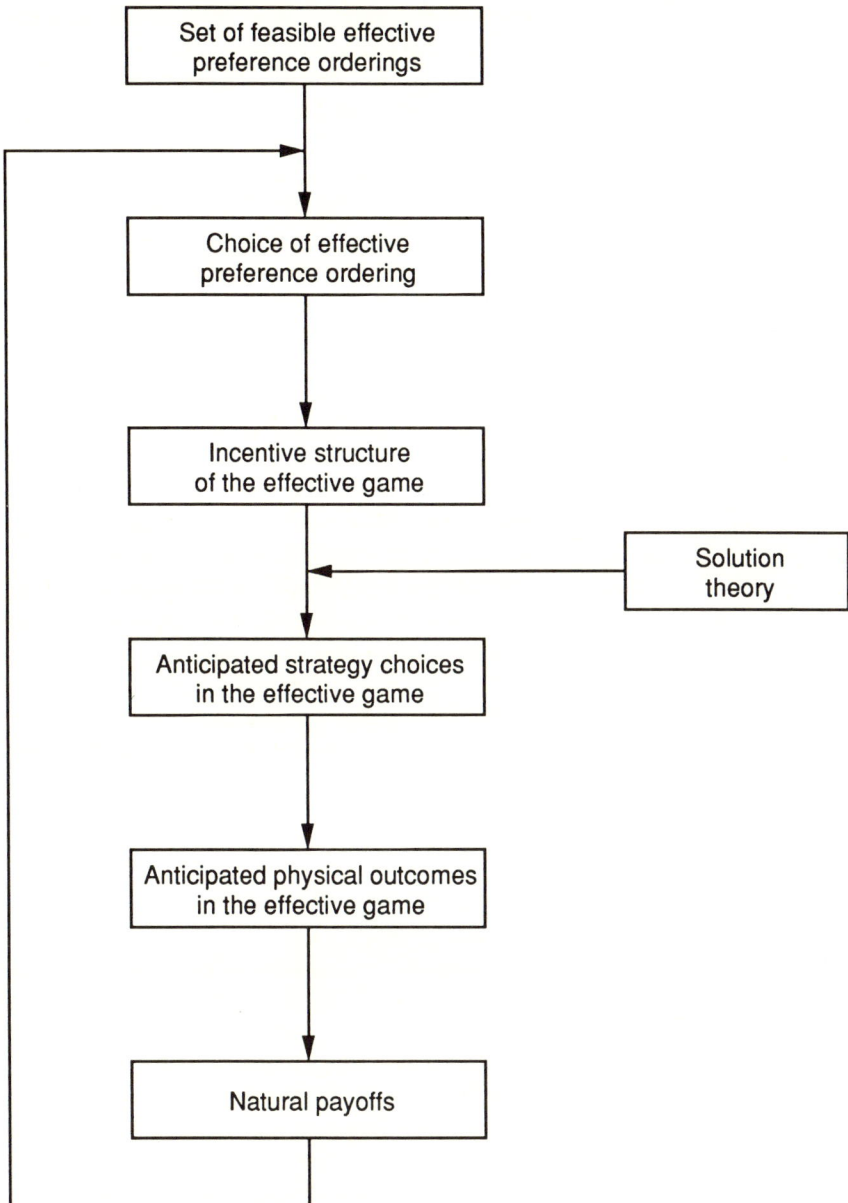

Figure 4.1. The decision situation in game **M**.

other player. We do not assume the opportunity for binding and enforceable agreements of the players on effective preferences. Notice further, that in the framework of the present model, the choice of effective preferences only depends on the players' natural interests.

Analysis of Game **M**: Two Simple Examples and a General Result

We now analyze the players' strategy choices in **M**. Exogenous conditions are, first, appropriately specified strategy sets for the players in **M**, that is, sets of feasible effective preference orderings. A further exogenous condition is the solution theory for the effective game which is used to derive the player's strategy choices in the effective game, given their effective preference orderings.

Considering our characterization of game **M**, two kinds of sensitivity problems relating to the exogenous conditions arise immediately. The first of these concerns the robustness of the results of our analysis with respect to different sets of feasible effective preference orderings in game **M**. We would hesitate to derive general conclusions from the model if outputs, that is, choices of effective preference orderings, were too sensitive to modifications in the opportunity set of feasible strategies.

A second kind of sensitivity problem, to which we will turn first, relates to the solution theory which is used for the effective game. Unfortunately different solution theories for noncooperative games specify rather different solutions for many of these kinds of games.[4] Accordingly, one might suspect that the outcomes of our model will be very sensitive to modifications in the assumptions used for the solution of the effective game. In this case, the outcomes would depend on controversial technical issues in the theory of noncooperative games. This would make the plausibility of the model highly questionable. Therefore, we need to provide for the robustness of our results with respect to assumptions on the solution of noncooperative games.

This suggests an obvious procedure. We do not specify a complete solution theory for all kinds of noncooperative games. Instead, we confine ourselves to simple and compelling assumptions for the solutions of the effective game which are uncontroversial in the sense that they presumably are part of all reasonable solution theories.

Assumptions for the Solution of Noncooperative 2 x 2-Games

[A 1] The strategy solution of a noncooperative 2 x 2-game is an equilibrium point or a maximin point.

[A 2] A strategy combination $\sigma = (\sigma_1, \sigma_2)$ of pure strategies σ_i ($i=1,2$) is the strategy solution of a noncooperative 2 × 2-game if σ is the unique strategy combination which is associated with the highest possible payoff for each player [that is, if $u_i(\sigma) = u_i(\sigma_1, \sigma_2)$ is player i's payoff corresponding to σ, then $u_i(\sigma_1, \sigma_2) > u_i(\sigma'_1, \sigma'_2)$ for all combinations (σ'_1, σ'_2) of—pure or mixed—strategies such that $\sigma'_1 \neq \sigma_1$ and/or $\sigma'_2 \neq \sigma_2$].

From a game-theoretical point of view, [A 1] is uncontroversial. It does not presuppose a definitive answer to the problem of selecting one specific equilibrium point from a set of equilibrium points as the solution of a game. Likewise, it does not presuppose an answer to the question as to whether the solution of a noncooperative game has to be an equilibrium point even if all equilibrium points lack certain stability requirements. Although problems like these might be unresolved in game theory, it is hard to imagine an adequate solution theory for noncooperative games which selects neither equilibrium points nor maximin points.

Consider properties of a strategy combination σ satisfying the condition specified in [A 2]. Such a strategy combination is a strong equilibrium point (in the sense of Harsanyi, 1977:104, that is, both players *only* use their best-reply strategies against the other player's strategy). Furthermore, σ is the unique Pareto-optimal strategy combination and, consequently, also the unique Pareto-optimal equilibrium point. Moreover, σ is a uniformly profitable equilibrium point (it yields a payoff higher than the maximin payoff to both players; cf. Harsanyi, 1977:106). Finally, σ is strictly preferred by both players to *all* other strategy combinations, including all other possible equilibrium points. To summarize, although σ will, in general, neither be a unique equilibrium point nor a maximin point, it fulfills reasonable stability requirements for equilibrium points in noncooperative games (cf. Harsanyi, 1977:124–127 and 273–274 for a discussion of such requirements). In the same way, σ does not give rise to any noncooperative joint-efficiency, bargaining or strategy-coordination problems (cf. Harsanyi, 1977:127–135). Notice one immediate consequence of [A 2] for the problem investigated in this chapter: it implies that mutual cooperation is the strategy solution of Sen's Assurance Game. If both players have Assurance Game preferences [see (3)] then they will choose the cooperative strategy C_i in the effective game.

Our assumptions [A 1] and [A 2] single out a determinate strategy solution only for a few noncooperative games with a rather simple structure. Yet, perhaps somewhat surprisingly, they suffice for the purposes of our analysis. Furthermore, it is an advantage of [A 1] and [A 2] that they are, in fact, rather uncontroversial implications of several solution

Two Simple Examples

We are now prepared to start the analysis of game **M**. First, it is convenient to discuss two simple special cases. In both of these cases we restrict the players' opportunity sets of feasible strategies in **M** to effective preference orderings discussed by Sen. As a first example for the game **M**, consider once again a situation that has been mentioned above in the context of our examination of unresolved incentive problems in Sen's model. Each player i is able to choose one of two effective preference orderings. One of these orderings, which we denote O^c_i, fulfills conditions in (2). According to O^c_i, player i's strictly dominant strategy in the effective game is to cooperate by choosing C_i. Therefore, O^c_i represents a morality of unconditional cooperation. The second feasible effective preference ordering for i, which we denote O^D_i, corresponds to the ordering of the natural payoffs. That is, O^D_i is an effective ordering

$$T^e_i > R^e_i > P^e_i > S^e_i \qquad (4)$$

Thus, the effective preference ordering O^D_i does not change the natural preference ordering. If player i chooses O^D_i, then to defect by choosing D_i is his strictly dominant strategy in the effective game.

What will happen in **M** if both players' sets of feasible strategies just consist of the effective orderings O^c_i and O^D_i? In this case, both players have a strictly dominant strategy in the effective game. The combination of the strictly dominant strategies is the unique equilibrium point and at the same time the unique maximin point of the effective game. Therefore, assumption [A 1] suffices to conclude that the strategy solution of the effective game will be the combination of the strictly dominant strategies. Fig 4.2 can be interpreted as the extensive form of **M** if O^c_i and O^D_i are the feasible effective preference orderings and if [A 1] is used in the solution of the effective game. At his respective first decision node, each player chooses one of two possible effective preference orderings without knowing the other player's decision. The subsequent trivial decision nodes represent players' anticipations of moves in the effective game. A player "chooses" the strategy for the effective game which is dictated by [A 1] and by the effective preference orderings chosen in the first step. For example, if player 1 has chosen O^c_1 and 2 has chosen O^D_2, then the strategy solution for the effective game is the combination (C_1, D_2). That is, in this case player 1 chooses C_1 and 2 chooses D_2 in the effective game

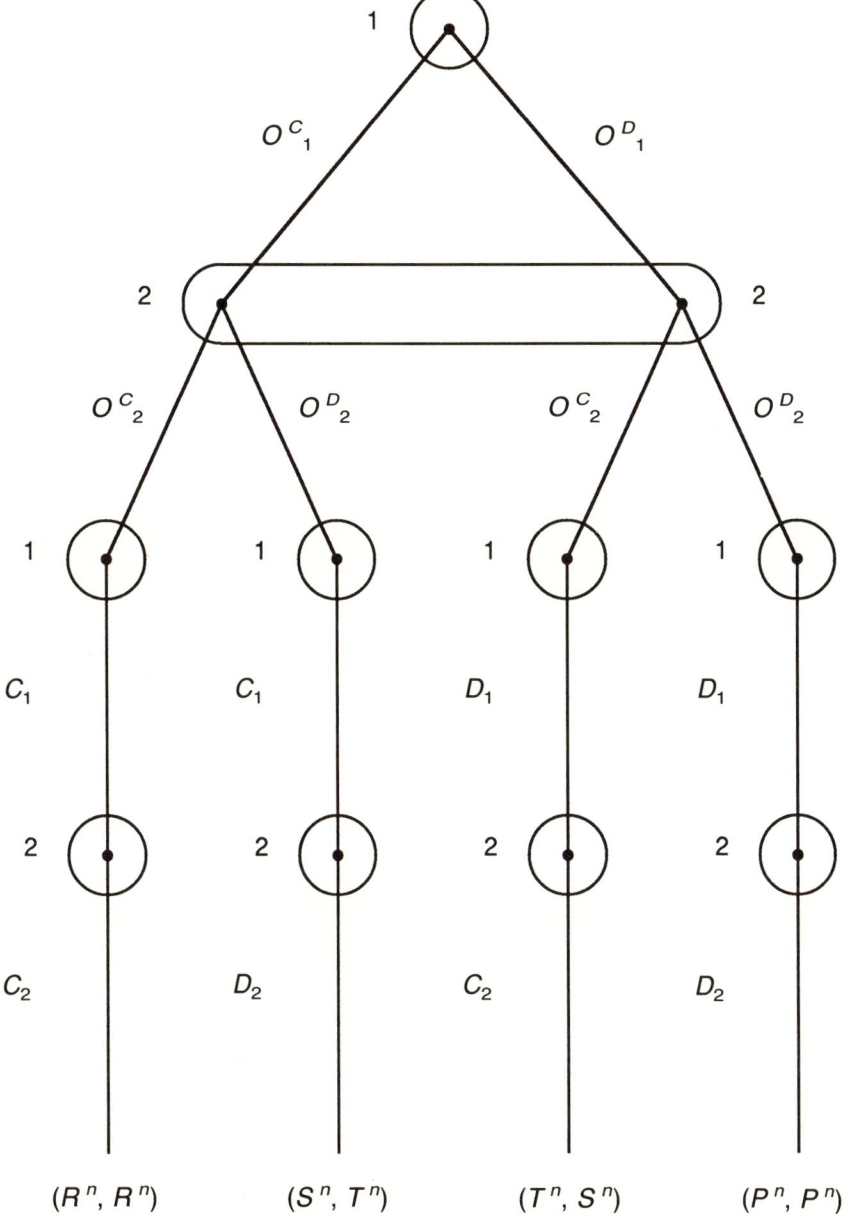

Figure 4.2. Extensive form of **M** if O^c_1 and O^D_1 are the feasible effective preference orderings.

and they mutually expect these moves to take place at their respective second node in Figure 4.2.

The payoffs at the end points of the tree are the natural payoffs corresponding to the solution of the effective game, that is, the natural payoffs corresponding to the physical outcomes of the effective game which result from the players' "choices" at their respective second node. The first payoff at each end point is the natural payoff of player 1, the second one is player 2's natural payoff.

In this example, the normal form of game **M** can be represented by a simple payoff matrix (cf. Diagram 4.3). Rows and columns represent choices of effective preference orderings.

		Player 2	
		O^c_2	O^D_2
Player 1	O^c_1	R^n, R^n	S^n, T^n
	O^D_1	T^n, S^n	P^n, P^n

Diagram 4.3. Payoff matrix for **M** if O^c_i and O^D_i are the feasible effective preference orderings.

Notice that in this example **M** is itself a prisoner's dilemma where O^D_i is the strictly dominant strategy for both players *i*. We therefore conclude that rational players will choose O^D_i in **M** if their feasible preference orderings are restricted to O^c_i and O^D_i. Thus, a rational actor will not endogenously adopt moral preferences if his only feasible moral preference ordering is a morality of unconditional cooperation. In this case, an actor modifying his natural preferences and adopting a moral point of view can and, indeed, will be exploited. In such a situation, a rational actor will not modify his natural preferences and will not be able to achieve efficient outcomes. In spite of its extreme simplicity, our first example for a game **M** seems to exhibit the severe incentive problems facing rational actors that try to adopt moral preferences. We are confronted with a further indication of the general thesis that efficiency gains of moral rules and preferences do not in themselves account for the emergence of such rules and preferences.[7]

In the first example, players are confronted with the alternatives of leaving their natural preferences unchanged, or to adopt a morality of unconditional cooperation. The second example provides an initial glance at the prospects of a modest morality of conditional cooperation. Assume again that each player is able to choose from an opportunity set of two effective preference orderings. Let the effective preference ordering O^D_i corresponding to the ordering of the natural payoffs again be a

Individual Interests and Moral Institutions 99

feasible choice for both players. Contrary to our first example, consider the Assurance Game preference ordering shown in (3) as the second feasible option. Denote such an Assurance Game ordering of effective preferences by O^{AG}_i.

To specify the players' payoff functions U^m_i for this kind of game **M**, use assumptions [A 1] and [A 2] to derive strategy solutions for effective games with the preference orderings (O^D_1, O^D_2), (O^{AG}_1, O^{AG}_2) and (O^D_1, O^{AG}_j). We know that [A 1] implies mutual defection, that is mutual choice of D_i as the strategy solution of the effective game if both players' effective preference ordering is O^D_i. If both players' effective preference orderings are Assurance Game preference orderings O^{AG}_i, we apply [A 2]. In this case, the strategy combination (C_1, C_2) fulfills the condition of [A 2] and is therefore the strategy solution. Thus, if both players have effective Assurance Game preferences, mutual cooperation is the result of the effective game. Finally, consider an effective game such that player i has the effective preference ordering O^D_i and j ($j = 1,2$ and $j \neq i$) has the effective preference ordering O^{AG}_j. Notice that D_i is now a strictly dominant strategy for player i in the effective game. On the other hand, D_j is j's unique best reply against D_i and furthermore, is, j's unique maximin strategy. Thus, the strategy combination (D_i, D_j) is the unique equilibrium point in the effective game and at the same time the unique maximin point. Therefore, [A 1] implies that $D_i, D_j)$, that is mutual defection, is the strategy solution of the effective game.

Using these results, the natural payoffs are easily calculated and an extensive form that parallels Diagram 4.4 could easily be specified. Turning immediately to the normal form representation, consider the matrix in Diagram 4.4.

		Player 2	
		O^{AG}_2	O^D_2
Player 1	O^{AG}_1	R^n, R^n	P^n, P^n
	O^D_1	P^n, P^n	P^n, P^n

Diagram 4.4. Payoff matrix for **M** if O^{AG}_1 and O^D_1 are the feasible effective preference orderings.

Inspection of the matrix reveals significant differences between our two examples and shows that **M** is not a Prisoner's Dilemma in the present case. The strategy combination where both players choose the effective ordering O^D_i is still an equilibrium and a maximin point but it is neither the only equilibrium nor the only maximin point. Notice that (O^{AG}_1, O^{AG}_2), that is, mutual choice of Assurance Game preferences, is an equilibrium point as well. Notice further that the choice of effective Assurance Game preferences is a maximin strategy and even a weakly dominant strategy for both players. In addition, mutual choice of Assurance Game preferences has a number of important properties in contrast to the equilibrium point (O^D_1, O^D_2). Unlike (O^D_1, O^D_2), it is a strong equilibrium point, is uniformly profitable, and is associated with Pareto-optimal payoffs. Thus (O^{AG}_1, O^{AG}_2) even fulfills the condition of assumption [A 2].[8]

Therefore, with respect to our second example, one may reasonably conclude that rational players will modify their natural preferences by choosing an Assurance Game ordering as the effective preference ordering. In this way they do, in fact, adopt a morality of conditional cooperation. The key reason for this result is that a rational player with Assurance Game preferences cooperates in the effective game if the other player likewise has Assurance Game preferences. However, a rational player with Assurance Game preferences cannot be exploited by a player who does not modify his natural preference ordering, because a rational player with Assurance Game preferences defects in the effective game if defection is a strictly dominant strategy for the other player in the effective game. In this way, the incentive problems associated with an endogenous emergence of moral preferences can be overcome.

A General Result

Our first example seems to yield rather convincing evidence for the assumption that rational actors are unable to adopt unconditional moral preferences. However, we should be quite careful in deriving general conclusions concerning the endogenous emergence of a morality of conditional cooperation from our second example. The problem in this context is the following. We have seen that a player adopting effective Assurance Game preferences cannot be exploited by a player who does not modify his preferences at all. Of course, this does not exclude the possibility that there may be other kinds of effective preference orderings that could be effectively used to exploit a player with Assurance Game preferences. Such a consideration leads us back to the first of the two above-mentioned sensitivity problems—the problem of the robustness of the results of our analyses with respect to modifications in the sets of feasible effective preference orderings which the players can choose in game **M**.

In game-theoretical terms, the key question concerns the best-reply properties and the equilibrium properties of choosing Assurance Game preferences as effective preference orderings. In our second example, the choice of Assurance Game preferences is a best reply for player i if the other player j likewise chooses Assurance Game preferences. Therefore, the mutual choice of Assurance Game preferences is an equilibrium point in this example. Allowing for different and, in principle, arbitrary opportunity sets of feasible effective preference orderings, do Assurance Game preferences remain unexploitable in the sense that they are best replies against one another and are thus equilibrium points?

To provide a rather general answer to this question, we begin by adding a third assumption to [A 1] and [A 2]. Our third assumption characterizes the players' opportunity sets in game **M**.

[A 3] All[9] Assurance Game preference orderings are feasible choices for both players in game **M**.

Notice that [A 3] is unrestrictive. According to [A 3], the players' opportunity sets in **M** may contain, in addition to Assurance Game preferences, all logically possible effective preference orderings or any subset of these orderings. Furthermore, we do not require that the players have identical sets of feasible strategies in **M**.

Using only assumptions [A 1] and [A 2] together with [A 3], nothing very general can be said with respect to equilibrium points in game **M** consisting of mutual choices of Assurance Game preference orderings. This is not surprising, since [A 3] requires, in principle, consideration of the strategy solutions of all logically possible 2 x 2-games. As has already been pointed out, our assumptions [A 1] and [A 2] yield determinate solutions only for a small subclass of these games. Therefore, it is not surprising that it would be necessary to substitute a general solution theory for [A 1] and [A 2].[10]

The surprising result is that, even under the weak assumptions [A 1], [A 2], and [A 3], a definitive conclusion can be derived with respect to properties of Assurance Game preferences if we are willing to accept a generalization of the Nash equilibrium concept in noncooperative game theory. The generalization is due to Radner (1980). Using a bounded rationality approach, Radner suggests the concept of an *epsilon-equilibrium*. This generalization of the conventional Nash equilibrium notion implies that players are satisfied with using strategies which, though possibly not strictly best replies against the other players' strategy combination, yield payoffs sufficiently close to the best-reply payoffs. Epsilon-equilibria are combinations of such "sufficiently good" strategies.

To make this idea precise (cf. Radner, 1980:153-154, for a brief discussion), consider an arbitrary noncooperative two-person game (the generalization for the n-person case is straightforward). Strategies of players $i = 1, 2$ and $j = 1, 2$ ($j \neq i$) are again denoted by σ_i and σ_j. Strategy vectors are $\sigma = (\sigma_i, \sigma_j)$. Player i's payoff function is $u_1(\sigma)$. Letting $\epsilon \geq 0$, we then define (cf. Radner, 1980:137,145):

σ_i is an ϵ–best reply against σ_j: $= u_i(\sigma_i, \sigma_j) \geq u_i(\sigma'_i, \sigma_j) - \epsilon$ for all strategies σ'_i of player i.

σ is an ϵ–equilibrium point: $= \sigma_i$ is an ϵ best-reply against σ_j for $i = 1, 2$.

Notice that best-reply strategies are 0-best replies and that Nash equilibrium points are 0–equilibrium points.

We are now in a position to present a general theorem with respect to game **M** (cf. the Appendix in this chapter and Raub, 1987:part IV for proof).

> **Theorem:** Given [A 1], [A 2], and [A 3], there exist feasible Assurance Game preference orderings O^{AG}_1 and O^{AG}_2 for any $\epsilon > 0$ such that (O^{AG}_1, O^{AG}_2) is an ϵ–equilibrium point in game **M**.

The theorem shows that our weak assumptions [A 1] and [A 2] on the solution of the effective game suffice to establish an interesting property of Assurance Game preference orderings which does not depend on the set of other feasible effective preference orderings: If one of the players adopts appropriate Assurance Game preferences, then the other player cannot gain more than ϵ by not adopting Assurance Game preferences himself. It is tempting to consider ϵ as the incentive for the second player not to adopt Assurance Game preferences if the first player does adopt these preferences. The player adopting Assurance Game preferences is able to make this incentive ϵ arbitrarily small.[11]

In this way, an endogenous emergence of moral preferences among rational and possibly completely selfish actors can be based on their mutual adoption of a morality of conditional cooperation. The reason is that mutual adoption of such a morality of conditional cooperation is an ϵ–equilibrium in a strategic setting providing opportunities for the modification of preferences such that these modifications only depend on basic natural interests of the actors. Furthermore, our conclusion is robust in a specific sense. It does not depend on controversial game-theoretical assumptions with respect to the consequences of different kinds of effective preference orderings for effective individual strategy choices. Nor does the conclusion depend on specific assumptions concerning the set of feasible preference orderings.

Consider finally two different, although similar, interpretations of the ϵ–equilibrium property of Assurance Game preference orderings. We have already pointed out that Assurance Game preferences are stable and robust in the sense that the positive incentive ϵ for a deviation from adopting these preferences, when the other player has adopted them, can be made arbitrarily small. Likewise, it can be shown (cf. Raub, 1987: part III) that by choosing appropriate Assurance Game preferences, a player is able to make the loss arbitrarily small which he faces himself if the other player does not likewise adopt Assurance Game preferences.

A related, but apparently not identical interpretation refers to the bounded rationality aspect of the ϵ–equilibrium concept. In the strategic setting considered, players are able to adopt Assurance Game preferences if they are satisfied when getting close enough to, though not necessarily reaching, best-reply payoffs. As Radner (1980:153) states, a reason for such behavior may be

> the various costs of discovering and using alternative strategies, and . . . the possibility that a truly optimal response might be more costly to discover and use than some alternative, "nearly optimal" strategy. In this interpretation the "epsilon" . . . represents a judgement . . . that the additional benefits from improving (the; W.R.,T.V.) strategy would be outweighed by the additional costs.

The possible complexity of game **M** under assumption [A 3] may be a tempting argument for such a line of reasoning: imagine the situation where each player's opportunity set contains *all* logically possible effective preference orderings.

Conditions for the Modification of Preferences

We have conceptualized moral behavior via individual preferences. Moral rules work in a way such that actors attach some moral value to the different outcomes of a social situation. It has been argued that in this context a rational choice approach faces the task of explaining endogenously the emergence of the relevant types of preferences. We have, therefore, assumed individuals' effective preferences to be a matter of choice. Contrary to other approaches, we have considered a strategic interaction situation. A game-theoretical model has been proposed representing the process of selecting effective preferences in a strategic setting. Actors choose among a set of effective preference orderings so that they can be better off in terms of their natural preferences.

Implications of the Game-Theoretical Model: Strategic Requirements and Incentive Problems

The result of the analysis was that even selfish individuals can indeed choose effective preferences with a moral component. In particular, they can adopt Assurance Game preferences as a consequence of rational behavior. Notice the generality of these results. They extend to the two-person PD as well as to n-person games of the PD type. We suspect that the results may also apply to other types of problematic social situations.

Three strategic conditions for the emergence of cooperation via the modification of preferences are implied by the game-theoretical analysis. First, the *set of feasible effective preference orderings* must contain Assurance Game preferences. Considering the nature of morals among rational actors this means that morality guides actors to *conditional* cooperation. Assurance Game preferences induce cooperation with players who have themselves adopted moral preferences. Assurance Game preferences also imply noncooperation with partners who have chosen what might be termed an amorality of unconditional defection. Consequently, there is no incentive for an individual with Assurance Game preferences to exploit other players. In addition, there is no opportunity for a defecting individual to exploit someone who has adopted a morality of conditional cooperation.

Two further strategic conditions refer to informational requirements. Notice that the effective game has been assumed to be a game with *complete information*. This is a conservative assumption characterizing "classical games" in Harsanyi's (1977) sense. Complete information with respect to the effective game means that each actor reflects in game **M** about the effective game under the assumption that it will be impossible to conceal true effective preferences or that "mimicry" with respect to effective preferences is prohibitively costly.

The complete information assumption affects the problem of incentives to delude the other actor as to one's own effective preferences and the problem of incentives to deviate from a given effective preference ordering. If it is possible to conceal one's true effective preferences, one could indeed be better off by cheating. Consider two actors, one of whom has adopted Assurance Game preferences. The other player's true effective preference ordering is of the type O^D_i, which thus corresponds to the ordering of the natural payoffs. If this player is able to cheat his partner into believing that he has also adopted Assurance Game preferences, he would be better off. This is so because he could defect and in this way exploit his cooperating partner. The assumption of complete information rules out opportunities to exhibit this kind of mimicry.

The complete information condition also has consequences for a somewhat similar, but not identical kind of incentive problem. Consider the interaction of a player who has chosen effective preferences of the Assurance Game type with an actor who has also adopted Assurance Game preferences, but who now contemplates a modification of his commitment to those preferences for which defection becomes a dominant choice. The structure of the game along with the condition of complete information implies that it will not be feasible for a deviating player to make the Assurance Game player a "sucker." Under the assumptions specified in defining the game **M**, the Assurance Game player would immediately switch to a defection in the effective game when playing with a defecting partner. In fact, not only are there no incentives to deviate from Assurance Game preferences to effective preferences, which make defection a dominant choice, but moreover there are positive incentives to commit oneself to Assurance Game preferences. It pays to commit oneself to those preferences because one will get a higher payoff in terms of natural preferences. In particular, both players will receive the reward R^n of mutual cooperation instead of the inefficient payoff P^n resulting from mutual defection. In this sense the commitment to Assurance Game preferences is indeed *self-enforcing*.

The two strategic conditions discussed so far (Assurance Game preferences as elements of the set of feasible effective preference orderings, and complete information with respect to the effective game) open up the possibility of cooperation in the effective game via Assurance Game preferences, and guarantee that a player with effective Assurance Game preferences will not be exploited if he cooperates in the effective game while the other player defects. Cooperation in the effective game due to Assurance Game preferences depends, however, on a third strategic condition. This condition can be interpreted as an additional informational requirement which results from the peculiarity of Assurance Game preferences themselves. The peculiarity becomes evident if we contrast players in a conventional PD with players of an Assurance Game. In a PD each player has a strictly dominant strategy. Therefore, it is not necessary to anticipate the other player's strategy. Instead, each player may treat his opponent's behavior as parametric. However, players in an Assurance Game do not have a dominant choice. Consequently, anticipations of the other player's strategy choice are relevant for their own decisions. Therefore, the achievement of a cooperative outcome depends on a sufficient amount of information.

First, the players have to be informed about each other's preferences. Only in this way are they able to recognize that the efficient cooperative outcome is an equilibrium point. Given complete information with respect to the effective game, the players will indeed be able to recognize that the efficient outcome is an equilibrium point. However, an additional problem arises from the fact that this equilibrium point is not unique. In order to choose the cooperative option, rational players thus will need information that their partner's behavior is guided by a sufficient degree of rationality. Mutual information that the players'

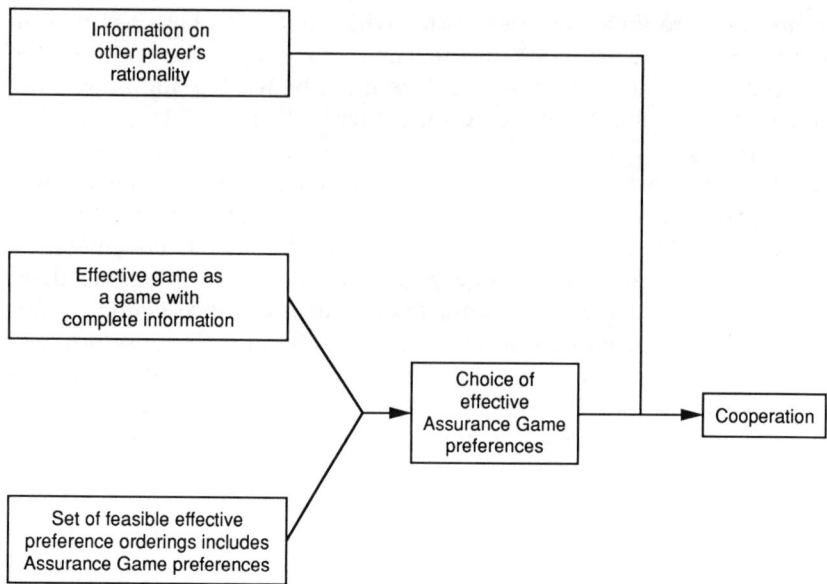

Figure 4.3. Conditions for the modification of preferences in game **M**.

behavior will correspond to conventional rationality postulates for game situations imply the fulfillment of a principle of mutually expected rationality (cf. Harsanyi, 1977). That information produces convergent reciprocal expectations with respect to the choice of the cooperative option. In this way players can be inhibited from choosing their noncooperative maximin strategy.

The strategic requirements that result from our analysis are summarized in Figure 4.3. In a sense, the analysis of game **M** yields a *dilemma*. Cooperation is most easily attained by players whose effective preferences guide them to cooperate due to dominant choices. If cooperation is a (strictly) dominant strategy for both players, mutual cooperation will arise and be stable even if a number of informational requirements are not fulfilled. Yet, such unconditional cooperation requires either a severe and rather implausible restriction of the set of available effective preference orderings (at the least, that this set must not contain preference orderings making defection a dominant choice), or irrational behavior of the players. In a situation without a priori restriction on the set of effective preference orderings, it is impossible for rational actors to achieve unconditional cooperation. Players who are rational and "enlightened" with respect to their strategic situation can only achieve cooperation via "conditional" morality. The dilemma arises from the fact that in this case cooperation becomes more fragile.

This is so because the informational requirements become considerably more severe in cases of conditional cooperation.

Conditions for the Application of the Model

The formal result that rational actors can achieve cooperative behavior in problematic social situations if they are involved in a game situation as described by the game **M** has been established. We would like to point out some conjectures with respect to empirical conditions that presumably affect the strategic requirements for cooperation via Assurance Game preferences.

Considering the set of feasible effective preferences, a general condition for the applicability of the suggested model is that actors are indeed able to perform self-evaluating behavior. They must be endowed with the capacity to perceive a richer set of options than those defined by their natural preferences. It is convenient to conjecture that this capacity can be the product of some suitable training. Notice, however, that the effects of socialization do not at all consist in the direct "internalization" of values. Rather, socialization enables actors to perceive certain situations as suitable to the application of moral rules in order to be better off in terms of their natural preferences. Socialization may, in addition, have the function of accentuating particular moral rules as candidates for the formation of effective preferences. For example, socialization in more advanced societies may lead to the consideration of moral rules of the more sophisticated kind, as expressed in Assurance Game preferences. Thus socialization may primarily be seen as a training which allows an actor "to see the long-term consequences to oneself of particular strategies of action, thus becoming more completely a rational, calculating man" (Coleman, 1964:180).

With regard to the set of feasible effective preferences, a further condition may be of interest. One could argue—analogously to Thaler and Shefrin (1981)—that the adoption of effective preferences may be accompanied by some *cost* due to *effort*. In particular, one might assume that effort increases with the degree of modification of the natural payoffs, which is necessary. This degree may, for example, be measured by a suitable ratio of differences between natural payoffs. Furthermore, if one assumes a reduction of natural payoffs in game **M** as a positive function of modification cost, incentives to cooperate will decrease as modification costs increase.

Consider now mechanisms conducive to satisfying the informational requirements for game **M**. Conditions which contribute to the supply of information about the other player's rationality as well as the other player's effective preferences are direct interactions and a knowledge of the other player's past behavior (reputation). In the present framework these conditions are important not with respect to future opportunities for punishing defection (as in repeated games approaches). They are important because they can serve as a basis for making inferences about a player's rationality and his effective preferences.

A crucial condition for the fulfillment of the complete information condition is that the actors be able to use their effective preferences (which may differ from their natural preferences) when choosing their strategies in the effective game. Consequently, the feasibility of appropriate commitment devices with respect to effective preferences is a condition for the application of our model. As has been pointed out by Schelling (1960:22), the essence of a commitment is that it must entail some "voluntary but irreversible sacrifice of freedom of choice." Furthermore, an effective commitment must also be credibly communicated to the partner.

There are several types of commitment devices which can be considered in our context. The first of them is represented by observable physiological signals emitted by actors' emotional reactions. Certain kinds of personal dispositions (e.g., having a conscience) may generate observable emotional reactions (e.g., expressed by perspiration, pitch and timbre of the voice, movement of the eyes) if an actor breaks a promise or makes a false commitment (cf. Frank, 1987:594–595). Once again, direct interactions may be among those conditions that further the capacity to detect and interpret those signals correctly.

Other kinds of commitment devices, which suggest applications of our model in the field of collective action and of corporate actors, are effective if it is possible to make use of an "agent" (Schelling, 1960:29). The agent can be a third party who gets instructions that are visible to the partner and cannot be changed. Such an agent may have sufficient incentives to carry out orders because he may want to sustain his reputation. A related device would be to use agents who do not get instructions from the actors involved in game **M**, but who have a well-known effective preference structure that can be expected to be stable. These agents then act for the players in the effective game. In this case, game **M** could be regarded as modeling actors who have to choose among agents with certain effective preferences.[12]

The commitment problem has considerable importance with regard to game **M**. However, notice first that according to our theorem a commitment to effective Assurance Game preferences is at least an ϵ-best reply in game **M** against Assurance Game preferences of the other player. Insofar the commitment to effective Assurance Game preferences is self-enforcing up to an arbitrarily small ϵ if one expects the other player to choose appropriate Assurance Game preferences himself.

Furthermore, notice that the commitment problem in game **M** is in a specific sense less severe than those types of commitment problems predominantly discussed by Schelling. Schelling is concerned with bargaining situations where each actor has an incentive to commit himself "first" and "more strongly" than the other player. This results from the fact that Schelling (1960:21) analyzes what he calls the "distributional aspect of bargaining": Players somehow have to agree on one out of several efficient payoff vectors which are not identical so that the players' preferences with respect to these efficient payoff vectors do not coincide (cf. the "payoff-distribution problem" in Harsanyi, 1977:128–132). The player who commits himself "first" or "stronger" can then induce a strategy solution which is associated with an efficient payoff vector favorable to himself (and not to his opponent). In our context, commitment devices do not affect distributional aspects. Rather, they are relevant with respect to the "efficiency aspect of bargaining" (Schelling, 1960:21), i.e., they provide opportunities for the players to achieve a mutually profitable and efficient solution (cf. the "joint-efficiency problem" in Harsanyi, 1977:127–128). Therefore, player i's commitment is beneficial to i and j. Thus, each player has a positive interest in the other player's ability to commit himself.

Given the importance of the informational requirements with respect to the effective game, in general, and especially to the (other player's) effective preferences, our discussion suggests one particular extension of the analysis of game **M**. Such an analysis would have to investigate the consequences of a player's incomplete information with respect to the other player's effective preferences. To illustrate, notice that incomplete information may have the effect of risking exploitation (in terms of natural preferences) in the effective game. Assume that actors form probability estimates of the chances of being misinformed with respect to their partner's effective preferences. Holding these probability estimates constant, one would expect a higher probability for moral behavior if the cost of being exploited is low. This cost again could be measured by means of (ratios of) differences between the natural payoffs.

An Alternative Interpretation of the Model

The most straightforward interpretation of the model is to assume that people have learned to work at their own preferences in order to achieve efficient outcomes. An alternative interpretation is suggested by using the idea of Williamson's (1985: chaps. 7,8) "hostages model" of credible commitments. Instead of interpreting the underlying mechanism as direct preference change, one may take that mechanism to indirectly mediate preference changes by directly changing physical outcomes.

Williamson discusses at length the ways of achieving cooperation among corporate actors (firms) anticipating business transactions. He observes that an important class of business transactions may be exposed to cancellation hazards. These hazards occur if at least one of the parties has irreversibly invested in some special-purpose technology specifically serving the demands of one particular partner. These investments get lost if the business partner cancels his order, because he meets more favorable market conditions from other sellers. Therefore, there is an interest among one or both partners to create safeguards against these hazards. Williamson further observes that there is generally a need for self-enforcing commitments and self-enforcing agreements, because courts and other third parties may not be available as enforcing agents.

In the case of unilateral trade relations, credible commitments can be made by the posting of a hostage to the producer (Williamson, 1985: 171–176). Now consider bilateral transactions, which are a more appropriate example for our discussion. Such reciprocal exchange relations in principle, may, be exposed to similar hazards in case both parties have made specific investments. Williamson (cf. 1985:194–197) stresses the advantages of using "hostages" in the bilateral, as compared to the unilateral, case. Whereas the unilateral transfer of a hostage exposes the transferring party (the buyer) to the risk of being exploited by the seller, in the bilateral case these expropriation hazards do not occur. "Reciprocal trading supported by separate but concurrent investments in specific assets provides a mutual safeguard against this second class of hazards. The hostages thereby created have the interesting property, moreover, that they are never exchanged. Instead, each party retains possession of its dedicated assets should the contract be prematurely terminated" (Williamson, 1985:195).

These observations may serve as an illustration of a mechanism that induces cooperation in problematic situations not by direct modification of preferences, but by the change of physical outcomes. This outcome change, brought about by the parties themselves, results in an indirect change of effective preference orderings. Opportunities to deliver hostages provide a means to include Assurance Game preferences in the set of feasible effective preferences and, at the same time, they provide a specific commitment device with respect to effective preferences. The model **M** may be used to provide a rationale for explaining the application of this mechanism among rational actors. In contrast to Williamson's description and more akin to Schelling's (1960:44, 135–136, 239–240) suggestions, our model emphasizes the strategic problems and incentive problems associated with possible efficiency gains in this context. These problems occur because of each party's incentive to neglect the investment or to invest a smaller amount of resources than necessary for inducing voluntary cooperation.

Conclusion

In this chapter we have provided a game-theoretical model of the endogenous emergence of morality. Figure 4.4 is a summary of our discussion.

We determined that the model's informational assumptions are particularly subject to criticism. However, considering rational choice approaches or, more generally, purposive action approaches to the problem of the explanation of moral preferences, we are not aware of any satisfactory alternative model that is based on weaker assumptions. It is our impression that rejecting the present model without substituting such an alternative would leave two options. One of these would be to abandon a purposive action as well as a more specific rational choice paradigm when accounting for the emergence of moral preferences. Another option would be to restrict the assumption that behavior is guided by moral preferences to situations where convincing arguments (for example, evolutionary one's) suggest that natural preferences themselves sufficiently reflect morality. To assess the prospects of the former option is beyond the scope of this chapter. We are afraid that the prospects of the latter option are dim.

Appendix

For the proof of the theorem, we have to show that for any given $\epsilon > 0$ there is an Assurance Game preference ordering O^{AG}_j for player j such that the choice of an Assurance Game preference ordering O^{AG}_i is an ϵ best-reply for player i in game **M**, that is, $U^m_i (O^{AG}_i, O^{AG}_j) = R^n \geq U^m_i (O_i, O^{AG}_j) - \epsilon$

$$U^m_i (O^{AG}_i, O^{AG}_j) = R^n \geq U^m_i (O_i, O^{AG}_j) - \epsilon$$

for all effective preference orderings O_i of player i $(i,j = 1,2; i \neq j)$. Assume that $U^m_i (O_i, O^{AG}_j) > R^n$. In this case, the application of the solution theory for the effective game, given O_i and O^{AG}_j, must generate a prob-

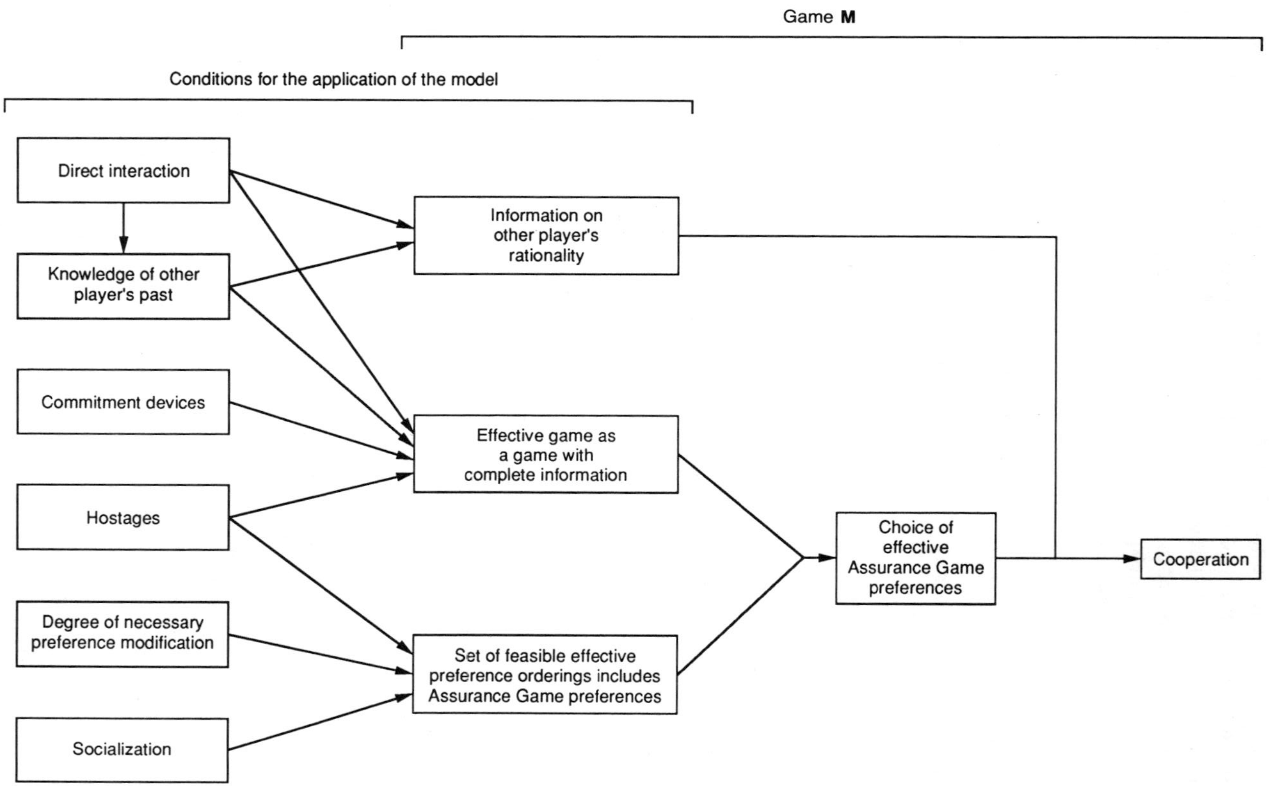

Figure 4.4. Conditions for the modification of preferences.

Individual Interests and Moral Institutions

ability $0 < q_i < 1$ of choosing C_i in the effective game for player i and a probability $0 < q_j \leq 1$ of choosing C_j in the effective game for player j. We must have $0 < q_j$ and $q_i < 1$ because otherwise $U^m_i(O_i, O^{AG}_j) \leq R^n$. The condition $0 < q_i$ follows from [A 1] because, given an effective preference ordering O^{AG}_j, the pure strategy D_j is player j's unique maximin strategy and is furthermore his unique best-reply strategy against the pure strategy C_i of player i in the effective game.

If $0 < q_j$, the strategy solution of the effective game cannot be a maximin point. Thus, [A 1] implies that the strategy solution must be an equilibrium point. Therefore, it must be a best-reply strategy of player j in the effective game to choose C with probability q_j if i chooses C_i with probability q_i. In this case, however, the pure strategy C_j must likewise be a best-reply strategy for j in the effective game. This follows from simple properties of mixed best-reply strategies (cf. Harsanyi, 1977: 102–103, Lemma 2). It is easily seen that this implies, in turn

$$q_i \geq (P^e_j - S^e_j)/(P^e_j - S^e_j + R^e_j - T^e_j) = K_i$$

But then:

$$U^m_i(O_i, O^{AG}_j) = q_i[q_jR^n + (1-q_j)S^n] + [(1-q_i)(q_jT^n + (1-q_j)P^n)]$$
$$\leq q_iR^n + (1-q_i)T^n$$
$$\leq K_iR^n + (1-K_i)T^n$$

Notice that

$$R^n \geq K_iR^n + (1-K_i)T^n - \epsilon \text{ iff } \epsilon \geq (1-K_i)(T^n - R^n)$$

In this case

$$U^m_i(O^{AG}_i, O^{AG}_j) = R^n \geq U^m_i(O_i, O^{AG}_j) - \epsilon$$

and $((O^{AG}_i, O^{AG}_j)$ is an ϵ-equilibrium point in game **M**. If [A 3] holds, player j is able to make the difference $1-K_i$ arbitrarily small. This implies that player j has an Assurance Game preference ordering (O^{AG}_j for any $\epsilon > 0$ such that the choice of an Assurance Game preference ordering (O^{AG}_i is an ϵ best-reply for player i in game **M**.

Acknowledgments

The central idea elaborated in this chapter—the strategic modification of preferences—originated from discussions with Rainer Hegselmann, which are gratefully acknowledged. The idea was first presented in a joint publication (Hegselmann, Raub, and Voss, 1986) that also contained some preliminary analyses similar to the two examples discussed in the section "A Model for Strategic Modification of Preferences." Thomas Voss presented that material in a lecture at the Center for Study of Public Choice, George Mason University, Fairfax (VA) in October 1986. He gratefully acknowledges the Center's financial and intellectual support. Robert Axelrod, Friedel Bolle, Andreas Diekmann, Manfred Holler, Roy Radner, Rudolf Schuessler, and especially Hartmut Kliemt commented on an earlier draft. We also thank the participants of the Bad Homburg conference, particularly Anthony Oberschall, for a vivid discussion and various suggestions. The systematic game-theoretical results partly used and partly just mentioned are due to Raub (1987), which can be obtained from the author.

Notes

1. Hartmut Kliemt (personal communication) has pointed out that the choice of an effective preference ordering in game **M** could be conceived as the choice of an individual constitution.

2. Assuming an effective game with complete information implies, in particular, that each player knows his own and the other player's payoff function for the effective game. This requires, in turn, that players cannot choose proper mixed strategies (probability mixtures of effective preference orderings) in **M**. It may be an interesting extension of the analysis in this chapter to consider an effective game with incomplete information (cf. below).

3. Two examples of general solution theories for noncooperative games have been provided by Harsanyi. According to one of these (Harsanyi, 1977: chaps. 6,7,14), the strategy solution of a noncooperative game is a Nash equilibrium point satisfying special stability requirements or—if such an equilibrium point does not exist—a maximin point. Harsanyi's (1975) tracing procedure, in contrast, always selects an equilibrium point as the strategy solution. A particularly simple solution theory for noncooperative 2 x 2-games, yielding equilibrium points or maximin points as strategy solutions, is the theory of natural outcomes due to Rapoport and Guyer (1966).

4. For example, the theories mentioned in the previous note differ drastically with respect to the solutions they imply for many noncooperative games.

5. Assumptions [A 1] and [A 2] are implied by Rapoport and Guyer's (1966) theory of natural outcomes. Likewise, they are implied by the solution theory set out in Harsanyi (1977). Harsanyi's tracing procedure implies [A 1]. To derive [A 2], it is necessary to add reasonable assumptions on prior probability distributions to the tracing procedure (cf. Harsanyi, 1976).

6. Notice another significant advantage yielded by the simplicity of [A 1] and [A 2]. We analyze choices of rational players behaving as if they use postulates like [A 1] and [A 2] in contemplating the effects of their moves in **M**. Considering obvious qualms about overly strong assumptions on such *as if* capacities of the players, it seems to be good advice to keep them as simple as possible.

7. An intuitive anticipation of incentive problems similar to those arising in our first example may well suggest utterly sceptical conjectures like the following with respect to an endogenous adoption of moral preferences by rational and possibly selfish actors:

"Man darf . . . nicht übersehen, daß die Internalisierung faktischer Moralvorstellungen einer Stützung durch gesellschaftlich durchgesetzte moralische Institutionen bedarf, die grundsätzlich 'indoktrinierenden' Charakter besitzen müssen. Denn es kann gerade nicht interessen-rationale Einsicht sein, die die Individuen dazu führt, ihre Werte individuell und gleichsam 'autosuggestiv' zu verändern" (Kliemt, 1986:181–182). However, in the following analysis we try to show that some caution should be applied to such assessments.

8. It may be useful to note that (O^{AG}_1, O^{AG}_2) is also a (trembling hand) perfect equilibrium point in Selten's sense. This is an immediate consequence of van Damme (1987:48, Theorem 3.2.2). This (Damme's) theorem also implies that (O^D_1, O^D_2) is not a (trembling hand) perfect equilibrium point.

9. Notice that we assume cardinal payoff functions for the effective game.

10. Substituting Rapoport and Guyer's theory of natural outcomes for [A 1] and [A 2], it can be shown (cf. Raub, 1987: part I) that the mutual choice of Assurance Game preferences is an equilibrium point in **M** under assumption [A 3]. The same result holds (cf. Raub, 1987: part II) if the solution theory of Harsanyi (1977) is used and the feasible effective preference orderings are restricted to strict orderings. Using the solution theory of Harsanyi (1977) and allowing for nonstrict effective preferences, mutual choice of Assurance Game preferences is no longer an equilibrium point in **M** (cf. Raub, 1987: part II).

11. In this chapter we analyze the problem of a strategic modification of preferences for the case of the classical two-person PD. It would constitute an important extension to investigate other kinds of dilemma games [cf. Raub (1987: part IV) for the analysis of a general n-person PD.] Even in this general case, a simple generalization of the theorem in the present chapter is available.

12. We are particularly indebted to Hartmut Kliemt for his insistence on the relevance of Schelling's analysis of commitments for the present model. Robert Axelrod suggested to us an application of the "agent"-device to (foreign) policy. The constituency would have the choice among different politicians or political parties (agents) with known preference structures. In democracies these agents would have an incentive to conform to their "effective preferences" (e.g., "moral" conditionally cooperative policies) because they would want to be reelected.

References

Akerlof, George A. (1983). "Loyalty Filters." Reprint. *An Economic Theorist's Book of Tales*, pp. 175–191. Cambridge: University Press, 1984.

Axelrod, Robert. (1984). *The Evolution of Cooperation*. New York: Basic Books.

Bolle, Friedel. (1983). "On Sen's second-order preferences, morals, and decision theory." *Erkenntnis* 20:195–205.

Coleman, James S. (1964). "Collective decisions." *Sociological Inquiry* 34:166–181.

Elster, Jon. (1983). *Sour Grapes. Studies in the Subversion of Rationality*. Cambridge: University Press.

Elster, Jon. (1986). "Introduction." Pp. 1–34 in J. Elster, ed., *The Multiple Self.* Cambridge: University Press.

Frank, Robert H. (1987). "If *Homo Economicus* could choose his own utility function, would he want one with a conscience?" *American Economic Review* 77:593–604.

Frankfurt, Harry G. (1971). "Freedom of the will and the concept of a person." *Journal of Philosophy* 68:5–20.
Frey, Bruno S. (1983). "The Economic Model of Behaviour: Shortcomings and Fruitful Developments." Unpublished.
Harsanyi, John C. (1975). "The tracing procedure." *International Journal of Game Theory* 4:61–94.
Harsanyi, John C. (1976). "A solution concept for n-person noncooperative games." *International Journal of Game Theory* 5:211–225.
Harsanyi, John C. (1977). *Rational Behavior and Bargaining Equilibrium in Games and Social Situations*. Cambridge: University Press.
Hegselmann, Rainer, Werner Raub, and Thomas Voss. (1986). "Zur Entstehung der Moral aus natürlichen Neigungen." *Analyse und Kritik* 8:150–177.
Kliemt, Hartmut. (1985). *Moralische Institutionen*. Freiburg: Alber.
Kliemt, Hartmut. (1986). *Antagonistische Kooperation*. Freiburg: Alber.
Lindenberg, Siegwart. (1983). "Utility and Morality." *Kyklos* 36:450–468.
Margolis, Howard. (1982). *Selfishness, Altruism, and Rationality*. Cambridge: University Press.
Münch, Richard. (1982). *Theorie des Handelns. Zur Rekonstruktion der Beiträge von Talcott Parsons, Emile Durkheim und Max Weber*. Frankfurt a.M.: Suhrkamp.
Nida-Rümelin, Julian. (1987). *Entscheidungstheorie und Ethik*. München: Tuduv.
Radner, Roy. (1980). "Collusive behavior in noncooperative epsilon-equilibria of oligopolies with long but finite lives." *Journal of Economic Theory* 22:136–154.
Rapoport, Anatol and Melvin Guyer. (1966). "A taxonomy of 2x2 games." *General Systems* 11:203–214.
Raub, Werner. (1987). "Spieltheoretische Analysen zur Modifikation von Präferenzen: Spezielle Effekte unterschiedlicher Lösungstheorien und einige allgemeine Resultate." Unpublished.
Raub, Werner and Thomas Voss. (1986). "Conditions for Cooperation in Problematic Social Situations." Pp. 85–104 in A. Diekmann and P. Mitter, eds. *Paradoxical Effects of Social Behavior, Essays in Honor of Anatol Rapoport*. Heidelberg: Physica.
Schelling, Thomas C. (1960). *The Strategy of Conflict*. London: Oxford University Press.
Schelling, Thomas C. (1978). "Egonomics." *American Economic Review (Papers and Proceedings)* 68:290–294.
Schelling, Thomas C. (1984). "Ethics, law, and the exercise of self-command," *Choice and Consequence*, pp. 83–112. Cambridge, Mass.: Harvard University Press.
Sen, Amartya. (1974). "Choice, orderings and morality," reprint. *Choice, Welfare and Measurement*, Oxford: Blackwell, 1982.
Smith, Adam. (1759; 1976). *The Theory of Moral Sentiments*. Glasgow edition, Oxford: Clarendon Press, 1976.
Thaler, Richard H. and H.M. Shefrin. (1981). "An economic theory of self-control." *Journal of Political Economy* 89:392–406.
Van Damme, Eric. (1987). *Stability and Perfection of Nash Equilibria*. Berlin: Springer.

Williamson, Oliver E. (1985). *The Economic Institutions of Capitalism. Firms, Markets, Relational Contracting*. New York: Free Press.

Wippler, Reinhard. (1985). "Explanatory sociology: The development of a theoretically oriented research programme." *Netherlands' Journal of Sociology* 21:63–74.

5

The Attenuation of Customs

Karl-Dieter Opp

This chapter focuses on an issue rarely tackled in the literature: why do norms attenuate, i.e., under what conditions does the extent of compliance to a norm decrease? We proceed from the assumption that norms do exist, i.e., in contrast to the preceding chapters in this volume we are not concerned with the question of why norms emerge. Furthermore, we are not concerned with norms in general, but rather with customs, i.e., with a particular subset of norms as defined by Axelrod (1986:1097).

By definition, a custom exists to the extent that individuals engage in a regular mode of behavior that is (1) neither created by an institution nor by explicit voluntary agreement, (2) mostly enforced by informal sanctions, and (3) normatively expected. Criterion (3) implies that a custom is not only a regular mode of behavior, such as opening an umbrella when it rains, but an internalized norm, i.e., a rule to which adherence is intrinsically rewarding (for it is consciently), whereas deviance is intrinsically costly (for it causes guilt). Examples of customs are table manners, rules referring to the exchange of goods on certain occasions such as at Christmas, rules concerning polite behavior such as greeting or shaking hands, and informal property rights such as the rule "first come first served."

The Custom of Sending Christmas Cards: An Example

In order to examine the conditions for the attenuation of customs consider the sending of Christmas cards is to serve as an example.[1] It is required that cards should be posted to arrive shortly before Christmas or, at the latest, a few days after. Christmas cards have to be sent to a great variety of people, including close friends, business partners etc. People of lower standing (e.g., pupils) send to people of higher standing (e.g., teachers). In general, if personal bonds exist or if someone has sent to you before, sending Christmas cards is considered a necessity.

Sending Christmas cards obviously entails both *costs* and *benefits*. *Costs* include the price of the cards and postage, and the time spent on buying and sending the cards. This time and money could be used for other purposes. *Benefits* of sending include the fun involved in buying and sending cards, the expected approval of the recipient, and the good conscience one has for having done one's duty.

What would happen if an individual decided not to send any Christmas cards? Obviously, he would save the costs of sending them and could use the respective time and money for other purposes. These are benefits forgone if postcards are sent. There are also *costs entailed in not sending:* the disapproval of others who had expected a card and a bad conscience.

The costs and benefits of sending and not sending do not only stem from those to whom cards have to be sent, but also from *third parties* who get to know about the respective compliance or noncompliance. The deviant will experience disapproval, loss of status, and other kinds of informal negative reactions if he does not comply, whereas he will get approval, etc., in case of compliance.

There are many social situations in which the costs and benefits of a type of behavior an individual adopts depend on the *number of people performing this behavior.* Do the costs and benefits of sending cards depend on the number of others who also send them? To answer this question we will describe in a payoff matrix the situation of an actor faced with the alternatives of sending or not sending (see Table 5.1).

Assume that a member of a social group—we will call him Person—is certain that all other members will comply with the custom of sending Christmas cards. Is it more advantageous to Person to send or not to send? On the one hand, sending will yield some approval and other benefits; the costs of sending (price of cards, time spent on buying and sending) are not very high. On the other hand, Person will have to expect strong disapproval for not sending cards: if all group members conform to a custom, deviance will be severely punished. Accordingly, it will be more advantageous for Person to send Christmas cards, if he

Table 5.1. Ranked Payoffs Connected with Sending Christmas cards

Person	All others	
	Send (Compliance)	Do not send (noncompliance)
Sends	3, 3	2, 1
(Compliance)	(a, a)	(b, c)
Does not send	1, 2	5, 5
(Noncompliance)	(c, b)	(d, d)

expects all others to send, too. The respective payoffs in the matrix will arbitrarily be set to 3 and 1 (see the first column). The first payoff in each entry refers, as usual, to the payoff of Person and the second to the payoff of each other member of the group.

Now let us assume that Person is certain that the other members are not likely to send Christmas cards. If Person sends in this situation he will receive little approval and be mainly confronted with negative reactions, because he has, so to speak, made a fool of the others. If Person does not send either, he will get a higher payoff than if he does send being happy that he has saved time and money that can now be used for other purposes. In this case having not sent does not incite disapproval and other negative reactions because the others have not sent either. Moreover, Person will not have a bad conscience because he has apparently not violated a generally accepted custom. He forgoes, to be sure, the approval he would get from the recipients of the Christmas cards. This approval, however, would be so negligible that he is not likely to miss it.

We assigned payoffs 2 and 5 to Person sending and not sending if all others do not send. First, we assume that payoff d is higher than payoff a (see the matrix) indicating that the rewards for complying are relatively low, if all others comply, compared with the costs saved, if the custom were extinct.

We further assume that payoff c is lower than b: if all others comply, noncompliance will result in particularly strong negative sanctions compared with situations where individuals are, in essence, overconforming.

In general, the payoff structure is "d greater than a greater than b greater than c" (see Table 5.1) and thus represents a *coordination game*.[2] This payoff structure exemplifies a *paradoxical social situation*: every member of the group would be better off, if the custom of sending Christmas cards were extinct. If, however, everybody expects the others to send, i.e., if the custom is generally adhered to, it is most advantageous for each member of a social network to send, too.

Customs as Coordination Games

We are not only interested in the custom of sending Christmas cards, but rather in ascertaining the conditions for the attenuation of customs in general. Therefore two questions arise: (1) Are the payoff structures of other customs different? (2) Are the costs and benefits of complying and not complying to other customs different?

In order to answer these questions we argue that the following kinds of customs which regulate most of our everyday life have the above outlined payoff structure: (1) *exchanging gifts* (exemplified in our Christmas card example); (2) *demands of fashion*, such as expectations with regard to the kind of dress one has to wear; (3) *table manners*, ranging from the kind of equipment one should use with certain kinds of food to the kind of conversation permissible at table; (4) *rules of politeness*, such as shaking hands, inquiring about the other's well-being, responding in a certain way to such questions, and offering one's seat to an older person; (5) *informal property rights*, such as the rule "first come first served" or the rule that borrowed things should not be kept too long; (6) *customs related to status changes*, such as the various activities to be performed, if an examination is passed or a child is born, if a person gets married or is promoted or if a member of the family dies.

Is d greater than a? This assumption is plausible for the five customs mentioned above because customs tend to lose their attraction in the course of time, and often turn into a tiresome burden. If such a custom attenuates or becomes extinct, people will regard this situation as more attractive than if the custom is in effect.

Is a greater than b? Let us assume that Person adheres to a custom to which everybody complies and receives payoff a. Assume, furthermore, that after a certain time the respective behavior is no longer performed and Person receives payoff b. There is no question that the net benefit of adhering to a generally accepted custom is higher than conformity to one nobody cares about.

Is b greater than c? This assumption seems plausible because in situations characterized by general compliance defection is usually severely punished. If, however, a custom has already attenuated to a large extent, those exhibiting, so to speak, a "cultural lag" and who still comply will experience relatively little punishment, i.e., receive a relatively high payoff.

However, situations do occur where the above payoff structure does not hold true. Sometimes people are enthusiastically reminiscent about

The Attenuation of Customs 123

the good old days when a certain custom was still in effect (i.e., *a* is regarded as more attractive than *d*). It may also be the case that rewards are attained if attenuated customs are still adhered to (*b* is greater than *a*). Only a few years ago young people were expected to offer their seats in buses, trams, or trains to the elderly, if all other seats were occupied. This custom has virtually disappeared. Nevertheless, offering a seat to an elderly person is still highly rewarded by the respective person as well as by third parties observing this behavior.

Empirical analyses focusing on the payoff structure of compliance to customs are lacking. Although there may be customs that are not coordination games, we assume that by and large the payoff structure of complying and not complying to customs accords with that outlined in Table 5.1. Even if one disagrees, it cannot be denied that there are many customs that display the payoff structure outlined in the above matrix. Our subsequent analysis is based on this structure and thus at least applies to a great number of everyday customs. Further research is needed to ascertain which kinds of customs exactly correspond to coordination games and which do not.

Although the payoff structure of a coordination game is our point of departure, we do not intend to carry out a formal game-theoretical analysis aiming at a solution as Raub and Voss did in their contribution (Chapter 4) to this volume, but rather employ the respective payoff structure to describe the situation of a set of actors. On this basis various assumptions are introduced to develop testable hypotheses not on what would be the best "solution" of the game, but rather on how the actors actually behave.

In discussing the sending of Christmas cards we outlined particular *kinds of costs and benefits* for complying and not complying. Are these kinds of incentives also characteristic of other customs? Our example indicates that there are two types of incentives.

The first type includes *social incentives* that stem from actors. These may arise from those to whom a prescribed action is directed, e.g., the recipient of gifts, of tips in a restaurant or of Christmas cards, and people to whom polite behavior is directed. Social incentives may stem, furthermore, from third parties, who directly observe or are informed about a person engaging in a certain kind of behavior (such as customers who are expected to give tips). These social incentives vary according to the number of persons adhering to the custom.

The second type of incentives are *nonsocial incentives*, i.e., incentives that do not stem from actors. These incentives include internal costs and rewards, such as having a good or bad conscience or having fun in performing an activity, but also material costs such as the time and money that has to be spent. At least in the short run, these incentives

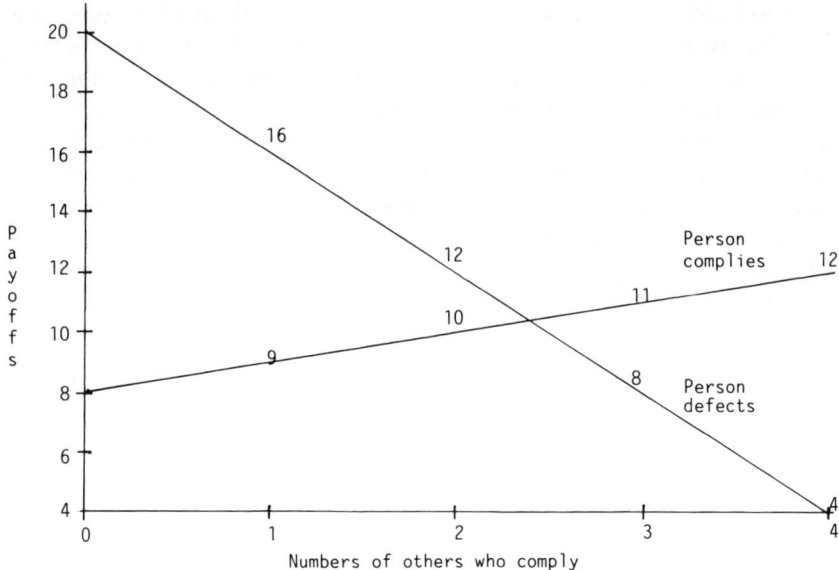

Figure 5.1. Payoffs for a person in a group if more or less others comply.

are not dependent on the number of persons adhering to the respective custom.

The Attenuation of Customs: General Assumptions

In our example we assumed that all others either comply or do not comply to the custom of sending Christmas cards. In order to model the payoffs if the number of others complying varies, we will now change the meaning of the matrix given in Table 5.1: now let us assume that it refers to the payoffs of Person and another member of the group.

If the number of persons complying with the custom varies, we can ascertain the payoffs for each individual member of a group in the following way: if Person interacts with a certain number n of others, we construct n 2 × 2 matrices and add the payoffs Person receives. Let us assume, for example, a group consists of five persons and Person interacts with each of the other four members. If all comply Person receives a payoff of 3 from each other member, i.e., a total payoff of 12. If, however, only two other members comply (and, two others do not comply), Person receives (if he complies) a payoff of 3 from each of the two fellow compliers and a payoff of 2 from each of the two noncompliers for a total payoff of 10. The respective curves for a five-person group are depicted in Figure 5.1.

The Attenuation of Customs

In general, the payoffs for an individual who complies (C) or defects (D) if n others comply can be computed with the following formulas, with the symbols a to d referring to the payoffs in the 2×2 matrix which is the basis of the calculations, and N standing for the size of the group:

$$C(n) = a^*n + b^*(N - n - 1)$$
$$D(n) = c^*n + d^*(N - n - 1)$$

For purposes of illustration let us assume that there is a group of five persons, and Person expects three others to comply. The payoffs are those given in Table 5.1. If Person complies he receives:

$$C(3) = 3^*3 + 2^*(5 - 3 - 1) = 11$$

Accordingly, Person's payoff for noncompliance [$D(3)$] is 8 (see Figure 5.1).

We are now ready to explain the *attenuation* of a custom. By this term we mean the following. Let us assume that a given number of persons comply to a custom. The more general compliance decreases, the greater the attenuation of the respective custom. We will therefore explain the conditions under which the number of those complying to a custom declines.

Our previous argument implies that the attenuation of customs is the result of an individual decision to comply or not to comply. The first step in explaining the attenuation of customs is to examine the alternatives open to an individual in a situation where a given number of others comply.

The first alternative, of course, would be to *comply* as well. If, for example, four other members comply (see Figure 5.1), Person's payoff is 12 for complying and 4 for defecting. Person will thus obtain the highest payoff if he complies.

Person could improve his situation if less than two of the others complied: if the number of compliers decreases, Person's payoff for complying decreases too, whereas the payoff for defecting increases. The two curves in Figure 5.1 intersect between values 2 and 3 on the x axis. If, thus, less than three of the other members comply, the payoff for defecting exceeds that attainable for complying. If only one other group member complies, Person's payoff is 16, if he defects, and 9, if he complies. Person could, therefore, be much better off if the number of compliers decreased to a certain extent.

If Person can improve his situation when the number of compliers decreases, he may attempt to influence others not to comply. He may accomplish this by engaging in some change-oriented action. One possi-

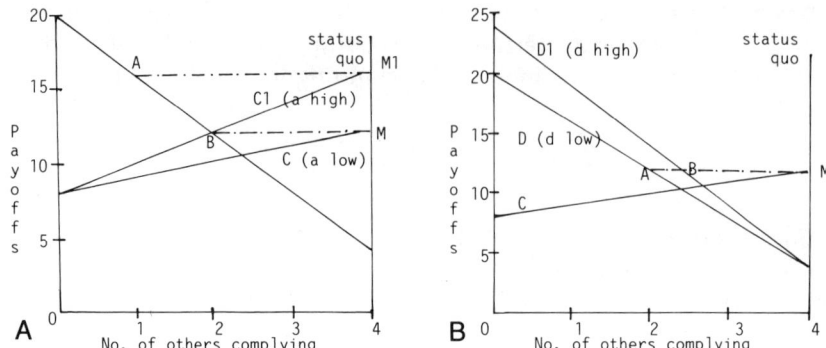

Figure 5.2. Payoffs for complying and not complying for different values of *a* and *d*.

bility is to *defect* and hope that others will imitate his behavior. Although, in the short run, he is bound to lose utility, in the long run he may be better off, if his defection has the expected effect.

A second kind of change-oriented action is to conclude a *contract* with those persons to whom one has certain obligations, i.e., to come to an agreement that a custom will no longer be complied to.

A third kind of change-oriented action could be to attempt to *organize collective action*, such as a social movement for abolishing a custom.

Each of these four alternatives—complying and the three kinds of change-oriented action (defecting, contracting, organizing collective action)—is chosen in everyday life. Apart from simply complying (alternative 1) people sometimes announce that they no longer intend to stick to a custom in the hope that others will follow suit (alternative 2). A further observation is that relatives agree to cease exchanging expensive gifts (alternative 3). Finally, there are examples of collective action: some years ago in Germany there was a certain tendency to stop buying expensive Christmas presents (alternative 4). The womens' movement has also demanded changes in a whole set of customs (and norms).

The payoffs of change-oriented action or compliance depend, as the curves presented in Figure 5.1 indicate, (1) on the *shape of the curves* and (2) on the *number of others who comply*. These relationships are explained in more detail in Figure 5.2.

Let us assume that all members of a group comply to a custom (see the vertical line labeled status quo in Figure 5.2A). If the actors are faced with curves *D* and *C* which are identical to the curves in Figure 5.1, compliance is the best alternative. Everybody receives payoff *M*. If, however, an actor succeeds in moving to position *B*, he gets the same payoffs for defecting. If he moves a little further to the left of B, his payoffs for defecting exceed those attainable for complying. In other words, if Person succeeded in influencing a certain number of others [i.e., more than (M-B) actors] to defect, he could increase his payoffs by switching from compliance to defection.

Assume now, that a increases to a certain amount (say, from 3 to 4), i.e., the payoffs for complying rise if another member also complies. The $C(n)$ equation indicates that for a given n the slope of the curve becomes steeper if a increases. Let the new curve with the higher a be C1 in Figure 5.2A. The payoff for complying is now M1. Curve D remains as before. Person can now increase his payoffs by moving to point A and defecting. The way from M1 to A, however, is longer than in the previous situation where a is smaller. In other words, if a increases and Person wants to attain a higher payoff, a greater number of other members have to be induced to defect. We assume that the costs of change-oriented action increase, if the number of other members who have to be induced to defect increases. *The higher the payoffs for complying if others also comply, the higher the costs of change-oriented action.* As the $C(n)$ equation shows, this proposition also holds true if b increases.

The opposite result can be derived if d increases (say, from 5 to 6), i.e., if the payoff for defecting becomes larger and others defect. Let us proceed from curves D and C in Figure 5.2B. Person has at least to move from M to A in order to raise his payoff. If, however, d becomes larger—see curve D1 in Figure 5.2B—Person has only to move at least to B in order to get a higher payoff if he defects. In other words, *the higher the payoff for defecting if others also defect, the lower the costs for change-oriented action.* The $D(n)$ equation indicates that an increase in c has the same effect.

Let us now assume that the vertical status quo lines in Figures 5.2A and B are moved to the left. The share of other members who have to be brought to defect decreases. That is to say, *if the number of those who comply is relatively small, the costs of change-oriented action are relatively low.*

Proceeding from these general assumptions, more specific propositions referring to endogenous and exogenous changes of customs are developed in the next section.

The Endogenous Attenuation of Customs

What conditions lead to an *endogenous attenuation*, i.e., one which is not caused by any changes in the social or nonsocial incentives mentioned above? Let us initially assume that the status quo is a situation where all group members comply to a custom and where compliance has the highest payoff.

We hypothesize that the range of application of a custom determines the costs of change-oriented action and, thus, the likelihood of endogenous changes of a custom.

Two types of situations are to be distinguished. First, there are customs which apply to anonymous situations: the persons who are expected to perform certain actions and the targets of these actions are permanently changing. Examples include customs regulating behavior in buses, trains, airplanes, restaurants, shops at airports.

In anonymous situations there will not be a big difference between a and c: c will be relatively high (i.e., the costs of nonconformity are low) and a (i.e., the rewards for complying) will be low. But nevertheless noncompliance will be punished and, most importantly, the costs of change-oriented action are prohibitive.

This is even plausible when a custom is already in the process of attenuation (i.e., when the status quo line in the graphs of Figure 5.2 is already far to the left). However, as long as compliance is more beneficial than noncompliance for the majority of group members, there will be too many others who have to be induced to defect for defection to become worthwhile. *The likelihood of change-oriented action in anonymous situations is therefore rather low.*

This is different in the second type of situation where a custom primarily regulates intimate personal relations such as the behavior of married couples, of lovers, relatives, parents, and children. In such recurrent situations where the same actors repeatedly interact, they may agree to abolish certain customs. Couples may agree, for example, no longer to exchange gifts at birthdays, or that the male partner is to do the housework.

Moreover, establishing such agreements is not without costs. Assume a husband suggests to his wife a bilateral defection such as giving up exchanging gifts. This may bring about severe negative sanctions. However, the husband may try to ascertain his wife's opinion by trial and error, for example by asking her what she generally thinks about couples who decide to stop exchanging gifts.

If change-oriented actions are taken in small social networks as opposed to those taken in anonymous situations one type of cost does not occur: negative reactions of third parties can be largely ruled out. The reason is that defection between members of small groups can be kept secret and there are usually no incentives to convey information about defections to third parties. Thus, *the likelihood of change-oriented action occurring with regard to customs applying to intimate personal relationships is rather high.*

If attenuation occurs in intimate relationships the following situation may result: customs that are already extinct may be thought to be still in effect because noncompliance is kept secret. In such cases it will usually take a relatively long time for the expectations with regard to these customs to change. Sociologists sometimes help to accelerate this process by conducting surveys and sending bestsellers such as the Kinsey Report.

The likelihood of defection with regard to customs which apply to intimate personal relationships is particularly high when a custom is already largely attenuated. If it is generally known that many couples no longer exchange gifts, the expected costs of taking the first step of negotiating are low and the expected success of reaching an agreement is high.

The preceding analysis suggests the following conclusions. If no exogenous changes of the costs and benefits of complying or not complying occur, and if a custom is observed by the majority of group members, attenuation is rather unlikely. If it occurs at all, it affects customs regulating intimate personal relationships. Such changes, however, are only likely if a custom is already largely attenuated. Such changes are kept secret and thus remain unperceived. In other words, *endogenous changes of customs are in general unlikely*.

This conclusion is supported by the observation that customs in traditional societies are very stable. Changes only occur if these societies establish contacts with other groups or societies and if, thus, the cost–benefit ratios of various actions change.

The high stability of customs, in view of unaltered exogenous incentives, is due to *the impossibility of secret defection*, i.e., defection where the defectors remain invisible. The costs of metering (Hechter, 1984) are therefore low. If, for example, a person violates other people's ownership rights, he may not be detected and sometimes even the violation itself may not be perceptible. With regard to customs, however, violations as well as violators are visible. There is, therefore, no way of escaping negative reactions on the part of the targets and/or third parties.

The Exogenous Attenuation of Customs

In this section we will explore the effects of two types of exogenous changes that affect the attenuation of customs: changes of social networks, and changes in material incentives.

Changing Networks

What changes of social networks lead to an attenuation of customs? A network changes, by definition, if the composition of a group or the relationship between the members of a group change.

The effects of changing networks on the attenuation of customs can be seen most clearly if we compare two extreme cases. Assume that there is an ethnic group of low social status that migrates into a community, and let this group remain largely isolated from the rest of the community. Assume, furthermore, that their customs differ greatly from those of the other members of the community. Turkish workers in West Germany are an example of such a group of migrants.

The customs of the migrants will only have a negligible effect on the attenuation of the customs prevalent in the community. Although the number of compliers in the community decreases due to the influence of the migrants, noncompliance will remain largely unperceived by the other members of the community. But even if it is known that a segregated group does not comply to certain customs, there will be hardly any changes in the costs and benefits of complying or defecting, because segregated ethnic groups are not regarded as reference groups. We thus predict that there will be no or only a negligible attenuation of customs.

Let us now examine a different case. Assume there is economic growth in a community, and a variety of people of different social status move to that community. These migrants then establish various contacts with the original population. If the migrants share the existing rules of conduct, the customs will be reinforced because the number of compliers increases.

Newcomers do not usually share the whole range of customs they encounter in their new environment because many customs are regionally different. Let us assume that a substantial number of the newcomers hold different customs. What will happen in this situation?

If newcomers enter a community, the first effect on the other members will be an increase in encounters with the newcomers, mainly in anonymous situations. As we have assumed that newcomers will partially defect, the number of defectors rises. The verticle status quo line thus moves to the left (see the "New Status quo" line in Figure 5.3).

In addition, the payoffs for compliance and defection change in the following way: (1) The payoffs for defecting if others comply (c) increase, i.e., reactions to be expected are less negative. The D curve then shifts upward (see the $D1$ curve in Figure 5.3). (2) The benefits of complying, if others comply (a), decrease: the smaller the share of those complying, the lower the rewards for compliance. This means that, the C curve moves downward (see the $C1$ curve in Figure 5.3).

These changes bring about a new status quo in which compliance no longer yields the highest payoff, as Figure 5.3 indicates: the new $D1$ line representing the payoffs for defection is above the new $C1$ line that stands for the payoff for compliance.

The extent to which defecting yields higher payoffs depends on the

The Attenuation of Customs

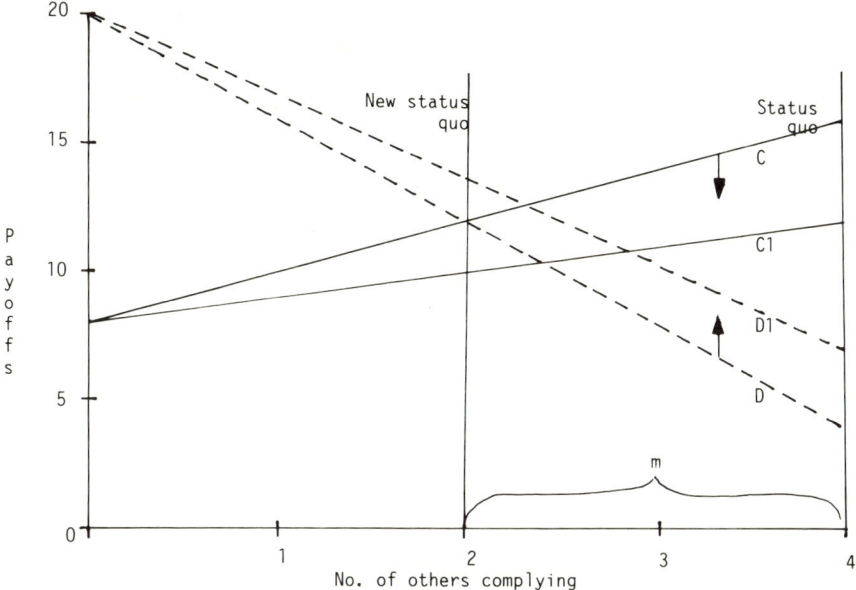

Figure 5.3. Changing payoff curves if the population increases.

extent *m* (see Figure 5.3) to which compliance decreases. If *m* were lower, defecting would be less beneficial.

The degree of attenuation furthermore depends on the extent to which *a* and *c* change, i.e., to which the C and D line shifts. The decline of *a* and the rise of *c* will be quite pronounced if the newcomers have a relatively high status and quickly establish extensive contacts with the other members of the community.

So far we have made a very unrealistic assumption: we presumed identical payoffs for all members of a community. Even if communities are very homogenous, the payoffs for compliance differ among the members.

In order to demonstrate the effects of nonhomogeneous payoffs, two types of actors are distinguished. The first consists of *conservatives* for whom the payoffs of complying (i.e., *a* and *b*) are relatively high and/or the payoffs for defecting (i.e., *c* and *d*) relatively low. For these individuals the C and D curves will intersect if *n* is rather low, as Figure 5.4a indicates: a great many defectors are necessary to induce noncompliance. In other words, their *threshold for noncompliance is high*.

The other extreme consists of individuals we will label *moral entrepreneurs*. For them the payoffs for compliance are generally low, whereas the rewards for defecting are high. These persons will be the first to shift to defection. Their *threshold for noncompliance is low*, as seen in Figure 5.4b.

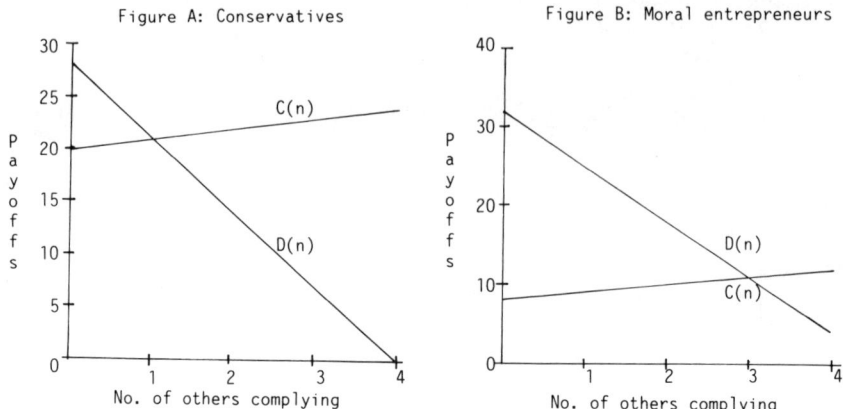

Figure 5.4. Payoff curves for conservatives and moral entrepreneurs.

Let us now assume that a community is highly differentiated, and that there is a clique of stout conservatives and another clique made up of moral entrepreneurs. If culturally homogeneous individuals who partially defect move to this community, the extent of differentiation in the community will increase: A substantial share of moral entrepreneurs will shift to defection, whereas the conservatives will largely remain compliers.

Assume now that the differentiation in a community is far less pronounced: let there be at least one person for every threshold level: At least one person will switch to defection if *one* other person defects; at least one person will switch to defection if *two* other persons defect, etc. When the defection of the migrants is perceived by the other members of the community, the custom will successively attenuate completely: every new defection makes this alternative the most rewarding action for at least one other person.

Based on these considerations a typology of groups may be constructed for which different effects of migration can be expected. In *highly conservative groups* defection of newcomers has only negligible effects on the attenuation of customs, whereas in *highly nonconservative groups* even a small minority of defecting newcomers brings about a high degree of attenuation. In *mixed conservative and nonconservative groups* differentiation increases, because the conservatives will remain compliant whereas the nonconservatives will defect. Where there is *continuous differentiation*, new patterns of behavior (i.e., defection) will slowly lead to large-scale attenuation.

Real groups may certainly include subgroups exemplifying each of these types. There may be a community, for example, that includes a small stoutly conservative, a small highly nonconservative group, as well as a larger subpopulation with continuous differentiation. In this situation the conservatives will largely remain unaffected by the defection of others, whereas the highly nonconservative group will immediately switch to defection. This will instigate a process of complete attenuation for the third group. Some of the stout conservatives with a relatively low threshold will then also defect.

Migration is not the only factor that can lead to exogenous attenuation. Let us assume that a community consists of several largely isolated groups. Let the respective extent of defection be different in these groups and, for some external reason, we will assume that there is *increasing interaction* between some of them. This may be brought about by new public transportation facilities, by new shopping or industrial centers, or by new recreational facilities where the different groups come into contact. Each group is now faced with a higher extent of defection. The processes of attenuation depend on the composition of these groups with regard to the threshold of switching to defection.

A third kind of network shift which may bring about an attenuation of customs is *intergenerational change*. Children are normally not exact copies of their parents. The extent to which they differ from their parents with regard to the acceptance of customs, together with the gradual dying out of the "conservative" parental generation, may bring about an attenuation of customs, depending on the composition of the respective community.

The processes of attenuation outlined above may be exemplified by the development of *norms in the market* since the beginning of industrialization. Expanding markets with high mobility and frequently changing interactions, which affect different sectors of societies in different ways, should have led to a general attenuation of informal norms regulating market relations. However, this attenuation differed in its extent in the various societal sectors. Crafts restricted to local areas can be expected to exhibit stronger adherence to customs than large companies.

The Change of Material Incentives

At first glance, the material costs of complying to customs seem negligible. This assumption, however, is only partly true. If, for example, a large number of people expect to receive a Christmas card, material costs are important. The demands of fashion and customs referring to status changes or to exchanging gifts may impose considerable material costs on the complier. It is, therefore, by no means trivial to explore the effects of changing material costs of compliance on the attenuation of customs.

Material costs include the price of the goods that have to be bought or produced when complying to a custom, as well as the opportunity costs of buying the good. These costs depend on the available income. A given price of a gift is less costly for an individual with a high income than for a person with a low income, because the utility forgone is lower for the person with the high income. In exploring the effects of material costs we therefore also have to consider the income of the targets of a custom, as well as the price of the private goods concerned.

To do so, we proceed from our payoff curves and the pertinent matrices. First, we assume that the magnitude of material costs does not depend on the number of compliers. With regard to this parameter, material costs are therefore fixed. Material costs have only to be borne in case of compliance. In other words, if the material costs increase, the payoffs in the first line of the matrix of Table 5.1 decline. This implies that rising material costs lead to a parallel downward shift of the C curves. Defection will therefore become more attractive.

The extent to which a C curve shifts depends on the cost increase and on the proportion of the material costs in relation to the total costs. If, for example, only negligible material costs are involved, their increase will not lead to a major shift of the C curve.

We furthermore presume that increasing material costs of an "expensive" custom will lead to *differential defection:* actors do not defect equally for all targets of a custom. People generally will not give less expensive gifts or buy less expensive food when guests are invited. Customs are observed in spite of increasing material costs, in particular, for targets for whom the expected benefits of compliance are relatively high and the expected benefits of noncompliance are particularly low. Christmas cards, for example, will no longer be sent to all acquaintances, but only to close friends or to "important" persons. Invitations to dinner will be restricted in a similar way. Increasing material costs of compliance will, therefore, increase social differentiation.

These considerations imply that in times of economic crises "expensive" customs decline. This prediction is supported by newspaper reports stating that the extent of gifts presented by firms to their customers has declined during the last few years, whereas "good" customers still receive expensive gifts.

Problems, Suggestions, and Alternative Explanations

Explaining the Attenuation of Internalization and Sanctions

In this chapter we have focused on the attenuation of customs in the sense of a decreasing number of compliers. If normative phenomena are to be explained, it is not sufficient to only deal with conformity or deviance. Important explanatory issues also include the conditions in which the internalization of customs declines and in which the extent of sanctioning decreases. We suggest that the three variables are positively related: decreasing compliance is coupled with declining internalization and sanctioning (see Opp, 1982). The Ajzen-Fishbein model could be employed to derive hypotheses about these issues (see, e.g., Ajzen and Fishbein, 1980; Opp, 1982, 1983, for an application of this model to explain the emergence of norms).

The Perception of Compliance

Throughout this chapter we have proceeded from the assumption that the actual extent of compliance in a group is correctly perceived by the actors. In many situations this assumption appears questionable. In a recent paper on "Pluralistic ignorance as a factor in racial attitudes," Michael Banton (1986:25) points out: "It is indisputable, firstly, that white people in the United States and Britain significantly overestimate the extent to which other white people wish to maintain social distance in relations with minority members and, secondly, that this miscalculation tends to inhibit them in their own dealings with minority members." With regard to the perception of compliance, similar distortions may be ascertained. If, for example, there is a high extent of compliance in a group, a few instances of defection observed or reported by newspapers may lead to an underestimation of the actual extent of compliance and thus promote attenuation. On the other hand, compliance may be overestimated with regard to customs regulating intimate personal relationships, as was outlined above. One can therefore also ascertain a "pluralistic ignorance" with regard to the compliance to customs.

Compliance to Customs as Prisoner's Dilemma Situations

In the literature, compliance to rules, in general, is often regarded as a prisoner's dilemma situation (see, for example, Axelrod, 1984; Buchanan, 1975; Coleman, 1986 and Chapter 2, this volume; McKenzie and Tullock, 1978; Ullmann-Margalit, 1978). Our analysis suggests that compliance or noncompliance to customs is not a prisoner's dilemma. It is, therefore, not true that it is the best choice of everybody not to send or to comply if everybody else sends Christmas cards (or complies to any other of the customs mentioned above). The main reason for this is that in the case of customs, compliance immediately can be identified, either by one of the targets of a custom or by third parties. However, this does not hold true, for example, for property rights enforced by the state: if all others respect the property rights, stealing can only be the best choice if one can expect to keep the breaking of the law a secret.

Alternative Explanations

The final issue to be raised is whether there are any other plausible explanations for the attenuation of customs. Oberschall's explanation of the emergence of institutional arrangements during the California gold rush (Oberschall, 1986) suggests that transaction cost (e.g., Williamson, 1981) may affect the attenuation of customs. Within the framework of our analysis, transaction costs are relevant for the behavioral alternatives of raising the number of noncompliers by negotiating. However, this alternative is seldom chosen so that transaction costs, therefore, is no major factor in the attenuation of customs.

Rules or the social order, in general, are regarded as public goods in the public choice literature. However, the theory of public goods (see, for example, Olson, 1965; Hardin, 1982) does not seem appropriate to explain the attenuation of customs because some of our assumptions are not compatible with it. In public goods theory, contributing to the provision of a public good is a prisoner's dilemma situation, whereas the compliance to customs is a coordination game. Second, customs are not public goods, but public bads, because all members of a group would be better off if they did not exist. Third, there is no free riding, but only selective incentives: every contribution to the provision of the good, i.e., obeying or breaking a custom, is associated with costs and benefits.

A central variable of the *theory of property rights* is externalities which affect the emergence of property rights (see, e.g., Demsetz, 1974; for summaries see de Alessi, 1980, 1983; see also Coleman, 1986, 1987, and Chapter 2, this volume). If we look at the various types of customs described above, it is difficult to see which externalities might lead to attenuation, unless each cost or benefit imposed on other actors is understood as an externality.

Functional explanations, in which the positive or negative effects of a rule are ascertained are frequently advanced when explaining rules. If it is found that the positive effects outweigh the negative ones, an explanation is regarded as successful (see, for example, Dahlman, 1980; Schotter, 1981; Ullmann-Margalit, 1977). Such types of explanation have been criticized convincingly (see Hardin, 1980; Opp, 1983; Ullmann-Margalit, 1978). A functional account cannot explain how a custom ac tually emerges or becomes attenuated. Our own procedure accords with an evolutionary "invisible hand explanation" (see Ullmann-Margalit, 1978; Vanberg, 1984): It is based on the decisions of individual actors that lead to an overall collective phenomenon, in this case to the attenuation or preservation of a custom.

George Akerlof's (1980:749) theory of social custom is in some respects similar to our own model. He aims at explaining "why social customs that are costly for the individual to follow persist nevertheless" —a situation which is also the starting point of our own model. Furthermore, Akerlof's theory shares some basic assumptions with our own model, for example: "The reputation of an individual depends on his obedience of the code of behavior of the community and also on the portion of the population . . . who believe in that code. The larger the number of believers, the more reputation is lost by disobedience of the code" (p. 754).

However, Akerlof's and our model also differ in many respects, e.g., with regard to the definition of "custom" (see note 1 in Akerlof's article), to assumptions "particularized" to a particular custom in a market (persistence of a fair wage), and with regard to the formal apparatus used. A detailed comparison of the models and their consequences is beyond the scope of this chapter, but would be an interesting task for future research.

Notes

1. The example is taken from Schelling (1978) who, however, fails to provide a thorough analysis. This example is also discussed in Opp (1990). For a detailed description of related customs (giving Christmas gifts) see Caplow, 1982, 1984.

2. See, for example, Lewis, 1969; Ullmann-Margalit, 1977. The situations where customs apply differ in several ways from the usual examples of coordination games. First, the emotional attachment to customs is much greater than that found in normal coordination situations such as driving on the right or left side of the road. Second, the coordination of behavior is much easier to obtain in a normal coordination game than in customs, particularly if the game is repeated. Third, the rewards and costs of coordination in ordinary games differ from those of complying or not complying to customs. Finally, it is doubtful whether customs are self-enforcing.

References

Ajzen, Icek and Martin Fishbein. (1980). *Understanding an Predicting Social Behavior*, Englewood Cliffs, N.J.: Prentice Hall.

Akerlof, George A. (1980). "A theory of social custom, of which unemployment may be one consequence." *Quarterly Journal of Economics* 94:749–775.

Axelrod, Robert. (1984). *The Evolution of Cooperation*. New York: Basic Books.

Axelrod, Robert. (1986). "An evolutionary approach to norms." *Amerian Political Science Review* 80:1095–1111.

Banton, Michael. (1986). "Pluralistic ignorance as a factor in racial attitudes." *New Community* 13(1):18–25.

Buchanan, James M. (1975). *The Limits of Liberty. Between Anarchy and Leviathan.* Chicago and London: University of Chicago Press.

Caplow, Theodore. (1984). "Christmas gifts and kin networks." *American Sociological Review* 47:383–392.

Caplow, Theodore. (1982). "Rule enforcement without visible means: Christmas gift giving in Middletown." *American Journal of Sociology* 89:1306–1323.

Coleman, James S. (1986). "Social structure and the emergence of norms among rational actors." Pp. 55–83 in Andreas Diekmann and Peter Mitter, eds., *Paradoxical Effects of Social Behavior. Essays in Honor of Anatol Rapoport*. Heidelberg and Wien: Physica.

Coleman, James S. (1987). "Norms as social capital." Pp. 133–155 in Gerard Radnitzky and Peter Bernholz, eds., *Economic Imperialism. The Economic Method Applied Outside the Field of Economics*. New York: Paragon House.

Dahlman, Carl J. (1980). *The Open Field System and Beyond. A Property Rights Analysis of an Economic Institution*. Cambridge: Cambridge University Press.

De Alessi, Louis. (1980). "The economics of property rights: A review of the evidence." *Research in Law and Economics* 2:1–47.

De Alessi, Louis. (1983). "Property Rights and transaction costs: A new perspective in economic theory." *The Social Science Journal* 20:59–69.

Demsetz, Harold. (1974). "Toward a theory of property rights." Pp. 31–42 in Eirik G. Furubotn and Svetozar Pejovich eds., *The Economics of Property Rights*. Cambridge, MA: Ballinger.

Hardin, Russell. (1980). "The emergence of norms." *Ethics* 90:575–587.

Hardin, Russell. (1982). *Collective Action*. Baltimore and London: Johns Hopkins University Press.

Hechter, Michael. (1984). "When actors comply: Monitoring costs and the production of social order." *Acta Sociologica* 27:161–183.

Lewis, David K. (1969). *Convention. A Philosophical Study*. Cambridge, MA: Harvard University Press.

McKenzie, Richard B., and Gordon Tullock. (1978). *The New World of Economics. Explorations into the Human Experience*, 2nd Ed., Homewood, IL: Richard D. Irwin.

Oberschall, Anthony. (1986). "The California gold rush: Social structure and transaction costs." Pp. 111–119 in Siegwart Lindenbereg, James S. Coleman, and Stefan Nowak, eds., *Approaches to Social Theory*. New York: Russell Sage Foundation.

Olson, Mancur. (1965). *The Logic of Collective Action*. Cambridge, MA: Harvard University Press.

Opp, Karl-Dieter. (1982). "The evolutionary emergence of norms." *British Journal of Social Psychology* 21:139–149.
Opp, Karl-Dieter. (1983). *Die Entstehung sozialer Normen. Ein Integrationsversuch soziologischer, sozialpsychologischer und ökonomischer Erklärungen.* Tübingen: Mohr Siebeck.
Opp, Karl-Dieter. (1990). "Christmas cards, methodological individualism, rational choice, and social change." *International Review of Sociology,* in press.
Schelling, Thomas C. (1978). *Micromotives and Macrobehavior.* New York & London: W.W. Morton.
Schotter, Andrew. (1981). *The Economic Theory of Institutions.* Cambridge: Cambridge University Press.
Ullmann-Margalit, Edna. (1977). *The Emergence of Norms.* Oxford: Clarendon Press.
Ullmann-Margalit, Edna. (1978). "Invisible-hand explanations." *Synthese* 39: 263–91.
Vanberg, Viktor. (1984). "'Unsichtbare-Hand Erklärung' und soziale Normen." Pp. 115–147 in Horst Todt, ed., *Normengeleitetes Verhalten in den Sozialwissenschaften,* Berlin: Duncker and Humblot.
Williamson, Oliver E. (1981). "The economics of organization: The transaction cost approach." *American Journal of Sociology* 87:548–577.

6

The Kula: Social Order, Barter, and Ceremonial Exchange

Rolf Ziegler

Since its detailed description by Bronislaw Malinowski ([1922] 1953) the Kula Ring has been cited and analyzed over and over again as a classical example of a ceremonial exchange of gifts. In his famous *Essai sur le don*, Marcel Mauss ([1925] 1954) has demonstrated the basic principle of reciprocity: to give, to accept, and to reciprocate. He pointed out its function of establishing and maintaining solidarity and emphasized the noneconomic character of social exchange. Scholars have also been fascinated by the peculiar pattern of the network linking several partners directly and indirectly in a ringlike system of exchanges. This structure has neither been planned by the actors nor deliberately established by a central authority. Rather, it is unintentionally created and maintained by actions and provides favorable conditions for its own maintenance.

Although Malinowski argued decidedly against a simplistic interpretation of the ceremonial exchange of gifts as economic barter by emphasizing its social and psychic functions, he nevertheless stressed the intimate connection between economic and social exchange: "barter of goods and services is carried on mostly within a standing partnership, or is associated with definite social ties or coupled with a mutuality in noneconomic matters. Most if not all economic acts are found to belong to some chain of reciprocal gifts and countergifts, which in the long run balance, benefiting both sides equally" (Malinowski, [1926] 1951:39f.). According to the prevailing view in the anthropological literature, the function of the Kula exchange is the establishment of social order by creating a network of stable relationships among stateless tribal societies, thereby facilitating commercial trade.

We will try to elaborate this functionalist interpretation though this cannot be more than an explanation sketch. We pretend neither to explain all important details of the phenomenon nor to systematically test our hypotheses, especially based on an invisible-hand explanation (Ullmann-Margalit, 1978), which would require historical data about the origin of the Kula.

First, we will briefly describe the basic features of the Kula system which are essential for our explanation sketch. We will then outline the basic problem of social order and the prerequisites for the development of stable bilateral constitutional contracts. We will describe an "organic" process that leads to the observed ring structure of exchanges, given the geographical and economic boundary conditions. Finally, we will analyze the stabilizing function of the ceremonial exchange of gifts and will elaborate the self-enforcing incentive mechanisms inherent in this structure of exchange.

The Social System of the Kula Exchange

The Kula Ring is a system of exchange of gifts among several tribal societies living on different island groups southeast of Papua New Guinea. They are culturally, and especially linguistically heterogenous, characterized predominantly by a matrilineal kinship system, and organized in clans and local communities. As the positions of chiefs, elders, and big-men are not integrated into a unified centralized leadership structure, one speaks of stateless societies.

Malinowski describes the Kula system as follows: "The Kula trade consists of a series of . . . periodic overseas expeditions, which link together the various island groups, and annually bring over big quantities of *vaygu'a* and of subsidiary trade from one district to another. The trade is used and used up, but the *vaygu'a*—the armshells and the necklets—go round and round the ring" ([1922] 1953:103). Quite remarkably, the two ceremonial gifts circulate always in opposite direction: the necklaces (*soulava*) clockwise and the armshells (*mwali*) counterclockwise. Two Kula rings may be distinguished, an outer one of eleven groups of islands and an inner one (on which we concentrate) which consists of the following five groups of islands: Trobriand islands (Vakuta, Sinaketa, Kiriwina, Kitava), Marshall-Bennett islands (among others, Iwa,

Gawa), Woodlark islands (Kaurai), Tubetube, and the Dobu islands (Southeast Dobu, Dobu, Northeast Dobu).

The exchange of gifts is regulated strictly ceremonially. The dates of the expeditions, which take place about twice a year under the leadership of the big-men, are fixed in advance. The visitors do not bring *vaygu'a* with them, but upon their arrival begin the exchange with a small opening gift which the hosts reciprocate by the Kula gift, e.g., necklaces. It is only at the later countervisit that the first, now acting as hosts, return their *vaygu'a*, i.e., armshells, having been offered an opening gift by their guests. By this pattern of *delayed reciprocity* one partner is indebted alternately to the other. When the host does not have *vaygu'a*, he may return an intermediary gift (*basi*) which has to be accepted and also reciprocated. One should not keep a *vaygu'a* too long because one may run the risk of losing his reputation and his partners. "A man who is in the Kula never keeps any article for longer than, say, a year or two. Even this exposes him to the reproach of being niggardly and certain districts have the bad reputation of being 'slow' and 'hard' in the Kula" (Malinowski, [1922] 1953:94). The exchange of gifts is accompanied by public ceremonies and magic rites aimed at influencing the Kula partner to donate generously.

The Kula exchange does not take place in an anonymous market but within stable, usually lifelong, partnerships being transferred to the heirs by mortuary rites symbolizing the stability of the relationship (Uberoi, 1971:107). The number of Kula partners and the distance covered by the exchange vary with social rank. But even the most influential chief only trades within a limited geographical area. The chief as well as the commoners know the names of their partner's partners (Malinowski, 1953:278) and may have an idea of being part of a closed system.

It is possible to establish new exchange relationships with a limited fund of *vaygu'a* by the principle of delayed reciprocity and the strategic use of intermediary gifts:

> I have become a great man by enlarging my exchanges at the expense of blocking theirs for a year. I cannot afford to block their exchange for too long, or my exchanges will never be trusted by anyone again. I am honest in the final issue. (*Fortune*, 1932, p. 217).

Protected by these social relationships, which are stabilized by the ceremonial exchange of gifts, there also is heavy trade of commodities (*gimwali*) among members of different tribes by way of middlemen. However, there is no bartering and haggling among Kula partners themselves but always only within their villages. "The trade takes place between the visitors and local natives, who are not their partners, but who must belong to the community with whom the Kula is made" (Malinowski, [1922] 1953:362). The Kula partner is involved in a threefold relationship. "First, there is his partner, with whom he exchanges general gifts. . . . Then there is the local resident, not his personal Kula partner, with whom he carries *gimwali*. Finally there is the stranger with whom an indirect exchange is carried on through the intermediation of the local men" (Malinowski, [1922] 1953:363). Of course, this short description of the social institution of the Kula, does not give an accurate picture of all the details of this much more complex and differentiated structure, but concentrates only on the essential elements.

A Non-Leviathan Solution to the Problem of Social Order

It is hypothesized that the basic structure of the Kula system can be traced back to the advantages of peaceful commercial trade. By this we do not claim to be able to explain all the details; nor do we assume that this institution has no functions other than economic ones. When Malinowski characterized ordinary trade as a secondary or subsidiary activity, he, too, made it clear that this was a matter of ethnographic description but not of sociological analysis.

> Indeed, it is clear that if we look at the acts from the outside, as comparative sociologists, and gauge their real utility, trade and canoe-building will appear to us the really important achievements, whereas we shall regard the Kula only as an indirect stimulus, impelling the natives to sail and to trade (Malinowski, [1922] 1953:p. 100).

Before peaceful trading can take place, the more fundamental Hobbesian problem of social order has to be solved.

> In order to trade, man must first lay down his spear. When that is done he can succeed in exchanging goods and persons not only between clan and clan but between tribe and tribe and nation and nation, and above all, between individuals. It is only then that people can create, can satisfy their interest mutually and define them without recourse to arms (Mauss, [1922] 1954:80).

As James Buchanan (1975) has stressed, this is the problem of securing an initial agreement on positive claims to goods, to resource endowments, and to specific spheres of activities, i.e., establishing a constitutional contract on property rights in a very general and fundamental sense. "In this initial inclusive contract, all parties gain from the poten-

The Kula

		Actor B	
		Respects rights	Respects no rights
Actor A	Respects rights	R , R	S , T
	Respects no rights	T , S	P , P

Diagram 6.1. The constitutional contract as a prisoner's dilemma game. (The order of preferences is $T > R > P > S$.)

tial elimination of socially wasteful outlays on defense and predation" (Buchanan, 1975:64).

However, this constitutional contract contains a prisoner's dilemma which can be put into the well-known form of a matrix game (see Diagram 6.1). Both actors have two options: a cooperative one, C, respecting rights, and a defecting one, D, abiding by no agreement and using force. Both would prefer peace[1] (R,R) to the "natural anarchistic equilibrium" (P,P) where both have to expend some share of their efforts in defending and predating. But each would be better off taking stocks of a peaceful neighbor by (threat of) force. On the other hand, the worst outcome would be to remain defenseless against an aggressor and unable to attack. Therefore, both actors rank the outcomes[2] $T > R > P > S$. For both of them the defecting alternative is dominant, resulting in the Pareto-inferior outcome (P,P). Rational actors prima facie seem not able to establish a social order. Since there is no way to enforce commitments, both have an incentive to defect.

The Hobbesian solution to this problem—the emergence of Leviathan as the enforcing agency, i.e., the surrender of private coercion in favor of public monopoly of power—has not developed among the stateless tribal societies where wars, raids, and cannibalism are reported to have been widespread before the Kula (e.g., Landa, 1983:146). It is, instead, the social institution of giving which brings peace and makes commercial trade possible at all. As Marshall Sahlins points out in his discussion of Mauss' essay: "The gift is the primitive way of achieving the peace that in civil society is secured by the State" (1972:169). However, how this institution could, *in principle*, have emerged in such a problematic situation is not explained. Drawing on some ideas from evolutionary game theory, we want to outline an explanation sketch.

As shown in detail in the game-theoretic literature,[3] an endogenous solution without assuming an external enforcing mechanism is only possible if the transactions are repeated *indefinitely*. If the number of iterations is fixed and known in advance there always remains an incentive to defect, while there may be an incentive to cooperate if the

		Actor B	
		TIT FOR TAT	ALL D
Actor A	TIT FOR TAT	$R/(1-w), R/(1-w)$ (a_w, a_w)	$S + wP/(1-w), T + wP/(1-w)$ (d_w, b_w)
	ALL D	$T + wP/(1-w), S + wP/(1-w)$ (b_w, d_w)	$P/(1-w), P/(1-w)$ (c_w, c_w)

Diagram 6.2. Cooperative (TFT) and defective (ALL D) strategies and payoffs in a prisoner's dilemma supergame with discount parameter w.

future becomes important enough, e.g., when the probability of the present transaction being the last one is sufficiently low. How the actors judge the stability of their relationship turns out to be the decisive factor. These repeated transactions are modeled by iterated games (so-called supergames).[4]

A strategy (or decision rule) specifies what to do in any situation that might arise. In a supergame there are many strategies available to the actors. By the use of computer tournaments, Robert Axelrod (1984) tried to find out whether in an indefinitely repeated prisoner's dilemma there exist best strategies yielding the highest possible score. A very simple strategy turned out to be extremely successful: it was the rule of the Old Testament's "An eye for an eye, a tooth for a tooth." The TIT-FOR-TAT (TFT) rule combines those elements Axelrod detected in other successful strategies: niceness ("Be not the first to defect"), provocability ("React immediately to the very first defection of the other player"), forgiveness ("Be nice again after retaliating to a single defection"), and clarity ("Be comprehensible to the other player"). As the reaction of an actor only depends upon the previous move, TFT reduces the costs of information storage and processing both for him and his counterpart, who is trying to anticipate that reaction.

The prototype of an extremely uncooperative strategy is ALL D where one always defects. The relationship between cooperative and defecting strategies will now be discussed using these ideal types (TFT and ALL D). The matrix of Diagram 6.2 shows the added payoffs in a prisoner's dilemma supergame. If both actors cooperate by using TFT, in every round each gets R, i.e., a total value of

$$R + wR + w^2R + \ldots = R/(1-w)$$

The discount parameter w shows the weight of the next move relative to the current one; $(1 - w)$ may be interpreted as the probability of the current move being the last one. The total value $R/(1 - w)$ is, therefore, increasing if the importance of the future w or the durability of the relationship rises, i.e., $(1 - w)$ gets lower. $w = 0$ results in the extreme case of a single encounter (the future is totally irrelevant) and reduces the payoff matrix of the supergame to that of the simple prisoner's dilemma. If actor A uses ALL D against B who plays TFT, on the first move A gets the highest payoff, T, but thereafter, P, because B is now reacting uncooperatively to A's defecting behavior. The total value for A is

$$T + wP + w^2P + \ldots = T + wP / (1 - w)$$

while B gets

$$S + wP + w^2P + \ldots = S + wP / (1 - w).$$

Which strategy is the best? The answer to this question depends upon the durability of the relation. If it is low, i.e., if w is small, there remains an incentive to defect. However, if the relation is thought by both actors to be sufficiently stable, more precisely, if $w > [(T-R)/(T-P)]$, TFT is the more advantageous strategy, while the defective strategy ALL D leads to a Pareto-inferior equilibrium. For cooperative behavior to take place, the relationship has to be the more durable the larger the costs of cooperation $(T-R)$ and/or the lower the disadvantages of defecting behavior $(R-P)$ are.

So far the analysis has been restricted to the dyad. Axelrod broadens the scope of analysis to a system of n actors interacting bilaterally between each other. He studies two questions especially relevant to our problem. First, when do cooperative actors succeed in invading a population of notoriously uncooperative individuals? Second, is a population of cooperative players able to prevent a defective strategy from invading and spreading?

Two assumptions are made with regard to this evolutionary process. It is assumed that an actor will stick to his strategy if it turns out to be superior on the average in comparison with the strategies of his partners. It is further assumed that a strategy will be replaced by a more successful one.[5]

Axelrod shows that uncooperative actors cannot invade a population of cooperative individuals.[6] On the contrary, the latter do have a chance to spread in an uncooperative environment if certain precisely stated conditions hold. Essentially the proportion of transactions of cooperative actors among themselves must be sufficiently large to outweigh the disadvantages from transactions with defecting members. This happens either when the proportion of randomly interacting cooperative actors is sufficiently large from the very beginning, or if cooperative actors are clustering, i.e., more frequently interacting among themselves than with defecting players.

At this point, we will briefly summarize the argument put forward so far. The establishment of peaceful social order contains a prisoner's dilemma that can only be solved cooperatively under the conditions of a durable relationship. In an uncooperative environment, there is a chance for the evolution of cooperation if those few cooperative actors present at the beginning form densely interacting clusters. Having succeeded they can resist invasion by defecting strategies. It should again be stressed that neither an external sanctioning mechanism nor the internalization of moral norms is assumed, but only behavior guided by self-interest.

A first prerequisite for applying this explanatory approach is the presence of an incentive for the tribal societies to coexist peacefully, i.e., their situations must be characterized by a prisoner's dilemma. It has already been noted that the relations among the tribes had been hostile rather than peaceful before the emergence of the Kula. Therefore, it seems implausible to assume that they had met with cooperative strategies from the very beginning.

We will now show that the conditions for the evolution of cooperation as elaborated by Axelrod are much more easily fulfilled *if* trading among n actors occurs in a *ringlike pattern*. It is assumed here, for the sake of simplicity, that all neighbors are engaged in (at most) one supergame, and that every actor pursues the same strategy vis-à-vis his neighbors. Then, two conditions are sufficient.

First, all neighbors have to judge their relationship as sufficiently durable, i.e., for both of them it must be $w > [(T-R)/(T-P)]$ and $w > [(T-R)/(R-S)]$. However, this is already a much weaker assumption than is random interaction where these conditions apply to any two actors. For neighbors that are spatially close to each other, these conditions seem to be more easily met.

Second, there must exist two cooperative neighbors, since a single cooperative actor could never "convince" his defecting neighbors of the superiority of his cooperative strategy, but would give it up in favor of the defecting one. This is so because playing TFT against two defecting neighbors always leaves him worse off:[7]

$$V(\text{TFT}|\text{ALL } D) + V(\text{TFT}|\text{ALL } D) < V(\text{ALL } D|\text{TFT}) + V(\text{ALL } D|\text{ALL } D) \quad (1)$$

However, the situation may be different with two cooperative neighbors C_1 and C_2 in a chain $C_2 - C_1 - D_1 - D_2$. C_1 will be able to demonstrate the superiority of his strategy if the sum of payoffs with his cooperative (C_2) and uncooperative (D_1) neighbor is larger than the total value which D_1 is getting out of the transactions with him (C_1) and with his defecting neighbor (D_2). The following inequality must be satisfied:

$$V(TFT|TFT) + V(TFT|ALL\ D) > V(ALL\ D|TFT) + V(ALL\ D|ALL\ D) \quad (2)$$

This happens to be true if and *only* if:

$$w > [(T - R) + (P - S)]/(T - S) = 1 - [(R - P)/(T - S)] \quad (3)$$

The durability w must be the larger the smaller the difference between the two equilibria (R-P) is, and/or the larger the difference gets between exploiting and being exploited (T-S), (3) is a somewhat stronger condition than Axelrod stated for the solution of the iterated prisoner's dilemma because it implies $w > [(T - R) / (T - P)]$.

It may not be obvious that inequality in (3) presupposes the observability of the strategies of one's partners' partners. It is not sufficient to know that one's partner uses the same strategy against his neighbor. In addition, D_1, must know that C_2 plays TFT against C_1. Otherwise, he may judge his defecting strategy to be superior to that of the single cooperative actor as was shown in (1). C_1 must also know that D_1 is playing against a defecting neighbor. If he were to assume D_2 to be cooperative, then he would perceive his cooperative strategy to be superior if and *only* if:

$$V(TFT|TFT) + V(TFT|ALL\ D) > V(ALL\ D|TFT) + V(ALL\ D|TFT) \quad (4)$$

i.e., if

$$w > [(T - R) + (T - S)]/[(T - P) + (T - S)]$$

Yet (4) is even stronger than (3) which it implies. This leaves us with a somewhat surprisingly asymmetric result. The defecting player D_1 has to have information about the strategy of his cooperative neighbor's neighbor (C_2), while the cooperative player C_1 can compensate his lack of information about D_2's strategy by having a sufficiently durable interest in the relationship with his defecting neighbor D_1. However, as far as the need for information is concerned, a ring structure has the additional advantage that this "indirect" information is only necessary about two persons, i.e., the (two) neighbors of one's two neighbors. This is another cost-reducing aspect of that structure.

The two conditions, (3) and $w > [(T - R)/(R - S)]$, are sufficient for the spread of cooperation in a ring structure. Both are independent of the number n of actors. *Two neighboring actors* who cooperate may start a process which gradually "infects" the total population. Whether there are two cooperating neighbors, of course, need not be the case but this seems to be a rather weak assumption.

The Evolution of a Circular System of Bilateral Exchanges

Showing that a ring structure in a sense poses minimal requirements for the evolution of cooperation guided solely by self-interest does not, of course, explain how that ring structure develops. It is here that we have to bring in the advantages of commercial trade. Once social order and property rights have been established, peaceful exchange can develop. Because of the initially uneven endownment of resources and manufactured goods, incentives for mutually advantageous exchange may be assumed.[8] As trading among the islands is a spot transaction (Malinowski, [1922] 1953:362), no additional problems of specifying and enforcing agreements in barter exchange arise.[9] In effect, the prospects of peaceful trading raise the value of R, thereby lowering the threshold of w, and hence reducing the required durability of the relationship.[10]

The internal dynamics of commercial trade under the specific geographical constraints are able to account for the development of a ring structure. Janet Landa (1983) has developed such an explanation. First, she points out some additional efficiencies of a ring structure—given the geographical, economic, and social constraints. She then outlines a mechanism giving rise to the observed ring structure by an evolutionary process.

Besides giving away one's own resources, every trade incurs three kinds of costs: (a) transportation costs; (b) transaction costs of searching, bargaining, and enforcing contracts; (c) set-up costs of establishing and maintaining a basic, reciprocal relationship of cooperation, which is problem-laden (as shown above).

Geographically, the island groups are arranged in a somewhat irregulary shaped "circle" with varying distances (see Figure 6.1). To make matters simple, we assume for the moment that due to the uneven resource endowment, each of n actors is a potential exchange partner for everybody else.[11] Then three ideal-typical institutional arrangements are conceivable (Landa, 1983:148ff).

With n isolated markets, each actor trades directly with all others. Everybody would incur high transportation costs and (n-1) times the transaction and set-up costs. A central marketplace could reduce the costs for everybody. However, a big-man entrepreneur would have to emerge offering a centrally located market, making profits large enough to cover the costs of carrying inventories of all traded goods, and establishing and enforcing law and order in the central marketplace. No big-man was forthcoming to make such a solution unlikely, and, indeed, no central marketplace has emerged in the region.

A third institutional arrangement is a ring of n spatially separated markets where "each big-man in a market performs the role of middle-

The Kula

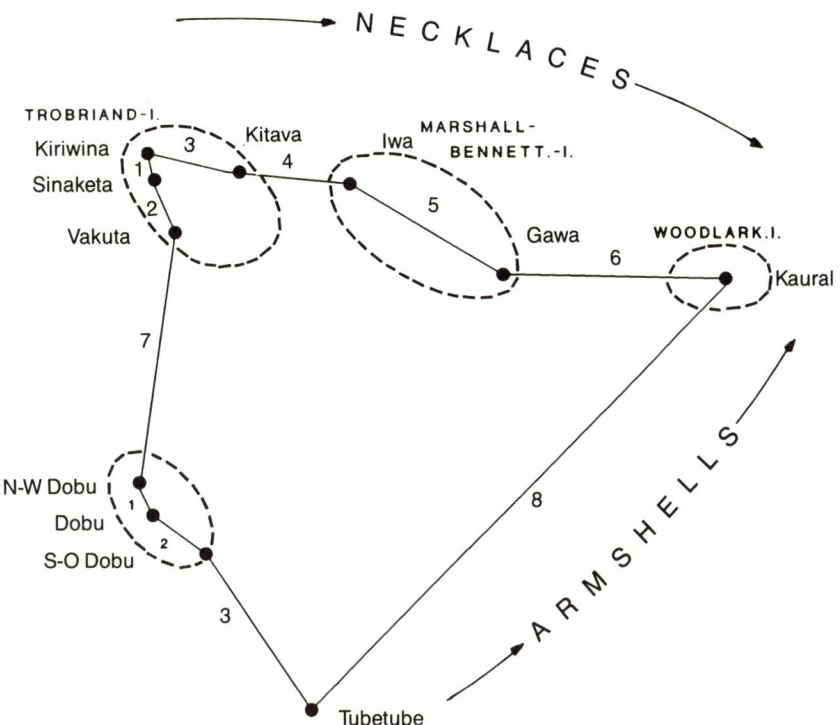

Figure 6.1. Schematic Representation of the inner Kula Ring (with approximate distances; numbers indicate the phases of the hypothetical formation process).

man for its two adjacent markets" (Landa, 1983:150). Everybody reduces not only his transportation costs but also the other two kinds of costs since he has only to trade with two partners instead of up to (n-1) ones. "The institution of *middlemen* eliminates the need for trust between members of different tribes who do not trust each other but trust the local natives who act as the middlemen." (Landa, 1983:151).

Economizing on these costs creates an incentive to act as middleman making profits by arbitrage.[12] In the basic prisoner's dilemma the value R is enhanced still further, thereby raising the chance of establishing and maintaining a cooperative relationship. (In all inequalities, raising R lowers the critical value of w, beyond which the cooperative strategies lead to a Pareto-optimal equilibrium.)

In a second article, Bernard Grofman and Janet Landa (1983:360ff.) specify a mechanism that reproduces the *exact* structure of the Inner Kula ring, taking into account the geographical distances among the islands. This iterative process proceeds in three steps: (a) If A is the nearest island to B and B closest to A they will trade and form a "subsystem." (b) The distance between two subsystems equals the distance between their two nearest islands. (c) Two subsystems unite and form a larger subsystem if they are closest to each other. In eight steps this iterative process[13] leads to a ring structure among the eleven islands (see Figure 6.1). The last step closing the ring requires a distance of 165 miles to be covered between Tubetube and Kaurai. Indeed, the inhabitants of the tiny volcanic island Tubetube are excellent sailors who also hold a strategic location between the inner Kula Ring and the outer Kula Ring southeast of the region. They command the necessary capabilities (or have acquired them) and have an additional incentive from functioning as long-distance middlemen in the outer Kula Ring.

In an earlier article, Grofman (1982) has developed this model for describing an iterative process of coalition formation among parties. However, it is not necessary to introduce the assumptions (a–c) in an ad hoc fashion. They can be derived from the general assumptions of rational action by taking into account transaction costs. Landa (1983:150) succinctly states the essential point:

> This invisible-hand process is, in effect, an entrepreneurial process in which each Big-man entrepreneur . . . perceives opportunities for making a profit by engaging in arbitrage between adjacent markets and seizes the opportunities by linking up a set of all submarkets.

We will briefly outline how to derive the three assumptions. (a) and (c) follow from the *mutual* interest in the reduction of transportation costs provided there exists an incentive for two neighbors to trade at all. Such an incentive arises from the initial distribution of resources or as a result of trading by middlemen, a process implied in assumption (b). The emergence of trading by middlemen is quite likely and is implied by rather weak assumptions about the distribution of demand among individual actors, the supply (either from domestic production or from previous trade) and the information of the actors about supply and demand of their neighbors' neighbors. Let us look at a chain of exchanges A–B–C–D. In order for an indirect exchange between A and D to take place, either C (who is trading with D) must have aquired A's products from B (who is trading them with A) because he needs them himself or he must know about the demand of D for these products and for that reason gets them from B. Actors do not have to have complete information about the distribution of supply and demand in the whole system. Trading by middlemen will gradually spread in "subsystems" making all goods produced or exchanged within each subsystem available at the island closest to another subsystem—as implicitly assumed by (b). Let us now conclude our outline of the explanation of the emergence of a ring structure of exchanges[14] and turn to the problem of explaining the function of the ceremonial exchange of gifts from a structural–individualistic perspective.

The Kula Exchange as an Efficient, Self-Enforcing Signaling System to Maintain Social Order

While the transfer of control over the means of physical coercion to the state changes the structure of the game, the endogenous development of social order by the process described leaves the basic dilemma unchanged.

> The gift, however, would not organize society in a corporate sense, only in a segmentary sense. Reciprocity is a "between" relation. It does not dissolve the separate parties within a higher unity, but on the contrary, in correlating their opposition perpetuates it. Neither does the gift specify a third party standing over and above the separate interests of those who contract. Most important, it does not withdraw their force, for the gift affects only will and not right. (Sahlins, 1972:170)

Therefore, it becomes crucial to correctly estimate the stability of the relationship between the two.

The choice of a strategy in the basic prisoner's dilemma supergame depends on the size of w, i.e., the importance of future transactions as judged by the actors. There are four possible combinations (four different prisoner's dilemma supergames) depending on whether both consider the relationship to be sufficiently durable, i.e., $w > [(T - R)/(R - S)]$, whether only one does or whether both have no lasting interest in the relationship, i.e., $[(T - R)/(R - S)] > \overline{w}$. Diagram 6.3 shows these four supergames.

The payoffs may be calculated from the matrix of Diagram 6.2 and form a partial order: $a_w > b_w > c_w > d_w$, $b_{\overline{w}} > a_{\overline{w}} > c_{\overline{w}} > d_{\overline{w}}$, $a_w > a_{\overline{w}}$, $b_w > b_{\overline{w}}$, $c_w > c_{\overline{w}}$ and $d_w > d_{\overline{w}}$. The analysis of these four supergames shows that only when both actors have a lasting interest in the relationship is it possible to obtain the Pareto-optimal result (a_w, a_w) by solving a (trivial) cooperation game, i.e., avoiding the Pareto-inferior equilibrium (c_w, c_w). In all other cases there exists only one Pareto-inferior equilibrium which leaves both actors worse off than with the cooperative but unstable outcome.

Now let us first assume that both actors have complete information about which supergame they are actually playing. Then two conclusions may be drawn from Diagram 6.3. (1) Every actor recognizes that a durable relationship is preferable to a transient one[15] *independently* of how

		B_w		$B_{\bar{w}}$	
		TFT	ALL D	TFT	ALL D
A_w	TFT	(a_w, a_w)	d_w, b_w	$a_w, a_{\bar{w}}$	$d_w, b_{\bar{w}}$
	ALL D	b_w, d_w	(c_w, c_w)	$b_w, d_{\bar{w}}$	($c_w, c_{\bar{w}}$)
$A_{\bar{w}}$	TFT	$a_{\bar{w}}, a_w$	$d_{\bar{w}}, b_w$	$a_{\bar{w}}, a_{\bar{w}}$	$d_{\bar{w}}, b_{\bar{w}}$
	ALL D	$b_{\bar{w}}, d_w$	($c_{\bar{w}}, c_w$)	$b_{\bar{w}}, d_{\bar{w}}$	($c_{\bar{w}}, c_{\bar{w}}$)

Diagram 6.3. Strategies and payoffs in a prisoner's dilemma supergame with different durations of the relationship (w = high; $\bar{w}$ = low). The meaning of the symbols is as in Diagram 6.2. Pareto-inferior equilibria are shown in dashed, Pareto-optimal ones in solid circles.

the other evaluates its stability, because the equilibria are ordered $a_w \gg c_w > c_{\bar{w}}$. (2) If an actor considers a relationship to be sufficiently durable he would prefer the other to have a lasting interest too ($a_w \gg c_w$), otherwise he is indifferent to the other's estimation of the durability.

We will now drop the assumption of complete information and look at the need for receiving and providing information. Two further hypotheses may then be stated. (3) Every actor wants to obtain reliable information about the other's estimation of durability when he himself has a lasting interest, because without that information he may cooperate erroneously. That information is irrelevant if he regards the relationship to be transient, because then his defecting strategy is dominant. (4) Finally, an actor is interested in reliably informing the other *if* both judge their relationship to be sufficiently durable.

The main result of this analysis is that *if* stable relations have been established, both actors are interested in reducing the uncertainty about what supergame they are in by communicating reliable messages. *The ceremonial exchange of gifts provides such an efficient signaling of the kind required to maintain social order* (Posner, 1981:170; Landa, 1983:152).

This interpretation accounts for many peculiarities that may not be understood when the exchange of gifts is thought of as a form of commercial trade. Goods and services exchanged do not have to have use or exchange value (if traded by middlemen), but have to convey clear and unmistakable meanings. Ritualism in exchanging gifts ensures the unambiguousness of signals. Nor does it help to be niggardly. On the contrary, each has to give generously because a signal not being sent does not convey a message.

Even the pattern of delayed reciprocity now makes sense. Unilateral disarmament may induce the other to take advantage and defect. However, the ceremonial exchange of gifts is not aimed at solving a prisoner's dilemma, but at stabilizing the mutual expectations about what supergame one is engaged in. To be the first to signal one's lasting interest is by no means disadvantageous, but rather raises one's credibility. Accepting a gift demonstrates the same attitude on the receiver's side. A signal becomes more credible if the countergift is of equal value and is bestowed somewhat later, when the uncertainty about the continuing interest in the relationship has again increased. Signals staggered in time and alternately sent by both actors foster the shared trust in the durability of the relationship. Moreover, as Landa (1983:152) points out, the use of two kinds of gifts that always have to be exchanged in one direction prevents the misinterpretation of the signals. With only one kind of gift available in both directions the danger would arise—especially if gift and countergift were to be hastily exchanged—of interpreting the countergift as a rejection of one's own present, thereby fatally misinterpreting the signal. Even the function of the opening gift becomes understandable. By sailing from abroad, the visitors have already demonstrated their interest in the relationship, underlining their friendly intentions by a small opening gift. Their higher uncertainty about the continuing interest of their hosts is best reduced by bestowing generously *vaygu'a*.

Its signaling function also explains why there is no haggling, although the gifts are expected to be of equal value even when "the equivalent rests with the giver, and cannot be enforced" (Malinowski, 1953:98). Haggling presupposes social order and the acknowledgment of property rights, while the gift signals the basic choice between peace and war. "Although the prestations and counter-prestations take place under a voluntary guise they are in essence strictly obligatory, and their sanction is private or open warfare" (Mauss, 1954:3).

So far we have avoided the problem of cheating and mistrust. Therefore our argument has been weak and somewhat contradictory, because if there is perfect information, there is no signaling problem, but if the information is incomplete, cheating and/or mistrust should not be neglected. The situation now becomes much more complex. The two actors not only evaluate the durability of the relationship as either lasting (w) or transient ($\overline{w}$) but also have to decide whether to be honest and whether to trust. While the durability belongs to the restrictions—unknown to Other but known by Ego, though not to be chosen by him—to cheat and/or to trust are matters of choice. The possible combinations are shown in Diagrams 6.4a-d.

Bestowing a gift is assumed to signal the *shared* meaning of having a lasting interest. All actors have a common interest in the unambiguousness of this semantic code, especially, of course, those who want to cheat. What one *should* mean if one presents a gift is shared by all.

The Matrixes in Diagram 6.4a-d are Explained as Follows
[the Example Refers to Diagram 6.4a Cell (2,1)]:

The *first line* shows the situation as perceived by both actors who have no information about honesty and trust of the other:

$w\overline{w}, ww$: EGO perceives (incorrectly) the situation to be $w\overline{w}$
OTHER perceives (correctly) the situation to be ww

The *second line* shows the strategies chosen and expected by the actors depending upon the (Pareto-optimal) equilibria in their perceived situation:

Dd, cC: EGO defects (D) and also expects OTHER to defect (d)
OTHER cooperates (C) and also expects EGO to cooperate (c)

The *third line* shows the payoffs anticipated by the actors depending upon the perceived situation and the choice of strategies:

c_w, a_w: EGO anticipates c_w; OTHER anticipates a_w

The *fourth line* shows the actual payoffs to the actors (in brackets) depending upon the actual situation and their choice of strategies (if different from the anticipated payoffs):

(b_w, d_w): EGO gets b_w; OTHER gets d_w

The Kula

			Other w (durable)			
			Gift (honest)		No gift (dishonest)	
			Trust	Mistrust	Trust	Mistrust
Ego w (durable)	Gift (honest)	Trust	ww,ww Cc,cC a_w,a_w	$ww,\overline{w}w$ Cc,dD a_w,c_w (d_w,b_w)	$w\overline{w},ww$ Dd,cC c_w,a_w (b_w,d_w)	$w\overline{w},\overline{w}w$ Dd,dD c_w,c_w
		Mistrust	$w\overline{w},ww$ Dd,cC c_w,a_w (b_w,d_w)	$w\overline{w},\overline{w}w$ Dd,dD c_w,c_w	ww,ww Cc,cC a_w,a_w	$ww,\overline{w}w$ Cc,dD a_w,c_w (d_w,b_w)
	No gift (dishonest)	Trust	$ww,\overline{w}w$ Cc,dD a_w,c_w (d_w,b_w)	ww,ww Cc,cC a_w,a_w	$w\overline{w},\overline{w}w$ Dd,dD c_w,c_w	$w\overline{w},ww$ Dd,cC c_w,a_w (b_w,d_w)
		Mistrust	$w\overline{w},\overline{w}w$ Dd,dD c_w,c_w	$w\overline{w},ww$ Dd,cC c_w,a_w (b_w,d_w)	$ww,\overline{w}w$ Cc,dD a_w,c_w (d_w,b_w)	ww,ww Cc,cC a_w,a_w

Diagram 6.4a (ww). Perceived situations, choice of strategies, anticipated payoffs, actual payoffs (in brackets if different from anticipated) when both EGO and OTHER estimate the relationship as durable.

158   Rolf Ziegler

			Other $\bar{w}$ (transient)			
			Gift (dishonest)		No gift (honest)	
			Trust	Mistrust	Trust	Mistrust
Ego w (durable)	Gift (honest)	Trust	$ww, w\bar{w}$ Cc, dD $a_w, c_{\bar{w}}$ $(d_w, b_{\bar{w}})$	$ww, \bar{w}\bar{w}$ Cc, dD $a_w, c_{\bar{w}}$ $(d_w, b_{\bar{w}})$	$w\bar{w}, w\bar{w}$ Dd, dD $c_w, c_{\bar{w}}$	$w\bar{w}, \bar{w}\bar{w}$ Dd, dD $c_w, c_{\bar{w}}$
		Mistrust	$w\bar{w}, w\bar{w}$ Dd, dD $c_w, c_{\bar{w}}$	$w\bar{w}, \bar{w}\bar{w}$ Dd, dD $c_w, c_{\bar{w}}$	$ww, w\bar{w}$ Cc, dD $a_w, c_{\bar{w}}$ $(d_w, b_{\bar{w}})$	$ww, \bar{w}\bar{w}$ Cc, dD $a_w, c_{\bar{w}}$ $(d_w, b_{\bar{w}})$
	No gift (dishonest)	Trust	$ww, \bar{w}\bar{w}$ Cc, dD $a_w, c_{\bar{w}}$ $(d_w, b_{\bar{w}})$	$ww, w\bar{w}$ Cc, dD $a_w, c_{\bar{w}}$ $(d_w, b_{\bar{w}})$	$w\bar{w}, \bar{w}\bar{w}$ Dd, dD $c_w, c_{\bar{w}}$	$w\bar{w}, w\bar{w}$ Dd, dD $c_w, c_{\bar{w}}$
		Mistrust	$w\bar{w}, \bar{w}\bar{w}$ Dd, dD $c_w, c_{\bar{w}}$	$w\bar{w}, w\bar{w}$ Dd, dD $c_w, c_{\bar{w}}$	$ww, \bar{w}\bar{w}$ Cc, dD $a_w, c_{\bar{w}}$ $(d_w, b_{\bar{w}})$	$ww, w\bar{w}$ Cc, dD $a_w, c_{\bar{w}}$ $(d_w, b_{\bar{w}})$

Diagram 6.4b ($w\bar{w}$). Perceived situations, choice of strategies, anticipated payoffs, actual payoffs (in brackets if different from anticipated) when EGO estimates the relationship as durable, but OTHER as transient.

The Kula

			Other w (durable)			
			Gift (honest)		No gift (dishonest)	
			Trust	Mistrust	Trust	Mistrust
Ego $\bar{w}$ (transient)	Gift (dishonest)	Trust	$\bar{w}w,ww$ Dd,cC $c_{\bar{w}},a_w$ $(b_{\bar{w}},d_w)$	$\bar{w}w,\bar{w}w$ Dd,dD $c_{\bar{w}},c_w$	$\bar{w}\bar{w},ww$ Dd,cC $c_{\bar{w}},a_w$ $(b_{\bar{w}},d_w)$	$\bar{w}\bar{w},\bar{w}w$ Dd,dD $c_{\bar{w}},c_w$
		Mistrust	$\bar{w}\bar{w},ww$ Dd,cC $c_{\bar{w}},a_w$ $(b_{\bar{w}},d_w)$	$\bar{w}\bar{w},\bar{w}w$ Dd,dD $c_{\bar{w}},c_w$	$\bar{w}w,ww$ Dd,cC $c_{\bar{w}},a_w$ $(b_{\bar{w}},d_w)$	$\bar{w}w,\bar{w}w$ Dd,dD $c_{\bar{w}},c_w$
	No gift (honest)	Trust	$\bar{w}w,\bar{w}w$ Dd,dD $c_{\bar{w}},c_w$	$\bar{w}w,ww$ Dd,cC $c_{\bar{w}},a_w$ $(b_{\bar{w}},d_w)$	$\bar{w}\bar{w},\bar{w}w$ Dd,dD $c_{\bar{w}},c_w$	$\bar{w}\bar{w},ww$ Dd,cC $c_{\bar{w}},a_w$ $(b_{\bar{w}},d_w)$
		Mistrust	$\bar{w}\bar{w},\bar{w}w$ Dd,dD $c_{\bar{w}},c_w$	$\bar{w}\bar{w},ww$ Dd,cC $c_{\bar{w}},a_w$ $(b_{\bar{w}},d_w)$	$\bar{w}w,\bar{w}w$ Dd,dD $c_{\bar{w}},c_w$	$\bar{w}w,ww$ Dd,cC $c_{\bar{w}},a_w$ $(b_{\bar{w}},d_w)$

Diagram 6.4c ($\bar{w}w$). Perceived situations, choice of strategies, anticipated payoffs, actual payoffs (in brackets if different from anticipated) when EGO estimates the relationship as transient but OTHER as durable.

		Other $\bar{w}$ (transient)			
		Gift (dishonest)		No gift (honest)	
		Trust	Mistrust	Trust	Mistrust
Gift (dishonest)	Trust	$\bar{w}w, w\bar{w}$ Dd, dD $c_{\bar{w}}, c_{\bar{w}}$	$\bar{w}w, \bar{w}w$ Dd, dD $c_{\bar{w}}c_{\bar{w}}$	$w\bar{w}, w\bar{w}$ Dd, dD $c_{\bar{w}}, c_{\bar{w}}$	$\bar{w}w, \bar{w}w$ Dd, dD $c_{\bar{w}}, c_{\bar{w}}$
	Mistrust	$\bar{w}\bar{w}, w\bar{w}$ Dd, dD $c_{\bar{w}}, c_{\bar{w}}$	$\bar{w}\bar{w}, \bar{w}\bar{w}$ Dd, dD $c_{\bar{w}}, c_{\bar{w}}$	$\bar{w}w, w\bar{w}$ Dd, dD $c_{\bar{w}}, c_{\bar{w}}$	$\bar{w}w, \bar{w}w$ Dd, dD $c_{\bar{w}}, c_{\bar{w}}$
No gift (honest)	Trust	$\bar{w}w, \bar{w}\bar{w}$ Dd, dD $c_{\bar{w}}, c_{\bar{w}}$	$\bar{w}w, w\bar{w}$ Dd, dD $c_{\bar{w}}, c_{\bar{w}}$	$w\bar{w}, \bar{w}\bar{w}$ Dd, dD $c_{\bar{w}}, c_{\bar{w}}$	$\bar{w}\bar{w}, w\bar{w}$ Dd, dD $c_{\bar{w}}, c_{\bar{w}}$
	Mistrust	$\bar{w}\bar{w}, \bar{w}\bar{w}$ Dd, dD $c_{\bar{w}}, c_{\bar{w}}$	$\bar{w}\bar{w}, w\bar{w}$ Dd, dD $c_{\bar{w}}, c_{\bar{w}}$	$\bar{w}w, \bar{w}\bar{w}$ Dd, dD $c_{\bar{w}}, c_{\bar{w}}$	$\bar{w}w, w\bar{w}$ Dd, dD $c_{\bar{w}}, c_{\bar{w}}$

(Row labels: Ego $\bar{w}$ (transient))

Diagram 6.4d ($\bar{w}\bar{w}$). Perceived situations, choice of strategies, anticipated payoffs, actual payoffs (in brackets if different from anticipated) when both EGO and OTHER estimate the relationship as transient.

The Kula 161

However, without complete information an actor does not know whether his partner is honest and trusting. He only knows whether the other presents a gift or not. Depending on his own evaluation of the durability, on the fact whether a gift was presented or not, and on his choice of being honest and trusting, he "defines the situation," i.e., determines the supergame he thinks they are playing. These estimations are shown in the first line of each cell; the letters before the comma refer to Ego's estimation, those after the comma to Other's definition of the situation. Based on the perceived situation, each actor chooses his equilibrium strategy and expects the other to do the same. This choice is shown in the second line; capital letters indicate the strategy *chosen*, while lower case letters the strategy *expected*. The third line shows the anticipated payoff based on the perceived supergame. If the actual payoff (determined by the chosen strategies and the actual supergame the actors are engaged in) differs from the anticipated one, this is shown in brackets in the fourth line. An example is given in the legend.

Looking at the four actual supergames (presented in the Diagrams 6.4 a-d) the following general conclusions may be stated:

If both actors consider the relationship to be transient (Diagram 6.4d; $\overline{w}\overline{w}$), it is irrelevant whether to cheat and whether to trust or not. Although leading to different "definitions of the situation", both actors always decide to defect, anticipate, and actually get the payoff $c_{\overline{w}}$.

If Ego has no lasting interest, but Other has (Diagram 6.4c; $\overline{w}w$), Ego realizes that there are situations he can take advantage of, i.e., receiving $b_{\overline{w}}$ instead of $c_{\overline{w}}$, at the expense of Other.

If, on the other hand, Ego has a lasting interest but Other does not (Diagram 6.4b; $w\overline{w}$), Ego recognizes the imminent danger that due to incomplete information he might misperceive the situation and actually get the lowest (d_w) instead of the anticipated highest (a_w) payoff. He also realizes that Other has an incentive to bring about those situations that would benefit him (Other gets $b_{\overline{w}}$ instead of $c_{\overline{w}}$).

Finally, if both judge the relationship to be durable (Diagram 6.4a; ww), there exist several (unstable) possibilities of exploiting and being exploited and *four* Pareto-optimal equilibria with both actors receiving the highest payoff a_w. Obviously there exists a coordination problem with many pitfalls.

How should Ego decide? A close analysis of Diagram 6.4 (one must simultaneously look at 6.4a and b, or at c and d, respectively) suggests the following conclusions:

- If Ego has no lasting interest ($\overline{w}$), he should follow the rule: "Be honest *if* Other is *mis*trusting you!" (or equivalently: "Cheat him *if* he trusts you!"). However, there is no need for Ego to decide whether to trust Other or not. His own trust is irrelevant for himself.

- If Ego has a lasting interest (w), he has to obey the following two rules at the same time: "Be honest *if* Other is trusting you!" and "Trust Other *if* he is honest!"

It is now easy to tell what kind of information Ego really needs. If his interest is transient ($\bar{w}$), he only wants to know whether Other is trusting or not. Whether Other is cheating him is irrelevant (because his use of the defecting strategy protects him of being exploited). He wants to cheat but can't be cheated!

If, however, Ego has a lasting interest (w), he needs information both about the honesty and the trust of Other—at least if Other also has a lasting interest. If Other's interest is transient, Ego needs only to know whether Other is honest or not.

If all actors would agree on the following *convention:* "Don't forget to donate if you have a lasting interest!" the situation could be simplified. It would give a clear meaning to nonparticipation in gift exchanges. "To refuse to give, or to fail to invite, is—like refusing to accept—the equivalent of a declaration of war; it is a refusal of friendship and intercourse" (Mauss, 1954:11). This convention would be equivalent to the rule that people with a lasting interest do not cheat. It would in effect mean that the feasible set of "definitions of the situation" would be restricted to the doubly framed parts in Diagram 6.4a-d. A closer look shows that there is a definite *common* interest in such a convention among all actors who estimate the relationship to be durable. It drastically simplifies the coordination problem with other actors who have lasting interests (see Diagram 6.4a) and does not make Ego *more* vulnerable to being cheated by Others with no lasting interest (see Diagram 6.4b). On the other hand, actors with no lasting interest cannot obstruct the convention and do not even have an incentive to do so because the convention does not prevent them from cheating (see Diagram 6.4c).

This convention may, therefore, be considered as the solution of a coordination game of a higher order. If it is established, it will reduce the need for information. For actors with a lasting interest, it now suffices to know whether their partner is honest or not.[16] If Other lies, Ego knows that Other has no lasting interest and he should mistrust him. If Other is honest and donates, Ego knows that Other has a lasting interest and he should trust him.[17] If Other is honest and does not present a gift, Ego knows that Other has no lasting interest but he should nevertheless trust him.

The Kula

For those actors having a lasting interest it is therefore sufficient to know either whether their partner is honest, or (equivalently) how he evaluates the durability of their relationship. But what prevents someone without a lasting interest to donate a Trojan horse, pretending to be interested, and then to exploit the trusting partner? It is the loss of reputation that leads third parties—who are ready to cooperate (i.e., use TFT)—to meet a defecting individual (using ALL D) uncooperatively from the very beginning, since they know that he has no lasting interest, i.e., they know that they are playing the supergame $(A_w B_{\overline{w}})$, or $(A_{\overline{w}} B_{\overline{w}})$, respectively. Even if the defector should change his partners continually like a marriage impostor in order to exploit their initial cooperation, this would not help him very much. Because his bad reputation would precede him, all others would behave as one and the total value received by him would be $T + wP + w^2P + \ldots = T + wP/(1 - w)$.[18] At first, this outcome does not seem to differ from that in Diagram 6.2. However, there is a decisive distinction. There the outcome refers to the transaction between an actor A and a specific partner B and w measures the durability of that particular dyadic relationship. Now, the partners are changing continually, and w refers to the enduring interest of A in remaining in the whole social system. But this will certainly be larger than the stability of a specific dyadic relationship. If the information system is functioning well, the incentive to cooperate will therefore, be sufficiently large even if each pair relation is rather unstable.

But who is ready to bear the costs of an information system? If the information is available to everyone, it is a public good, the provision of which causes problems. The public character of the ceremonial exchange of gifts does reduce costs of information, but only locally. Much more efficient is the ring structure of two distinct gifts, armshells and necklaces, circulating always in opposite directions. This creates a self-enforcing mechanism ensuring the quick and accurate detection of black sheep, and the loss of their reputation. Because of the periodicity of the Kula expeditions and the circulation of gifts, a violation of the principle of reciprocity is quickly detected as it blocks the supply of *vaygu'a*. However, everybody is interested in not being falsely suspected merely because he lacks the "right" kind of gifts. He will inquire and—because of the fixed direction the gifts are circulating—does know where to look.

> The Kula Ring, with its double circuit of two different objects turns out to be a club-like arrangement in which everyone is watching everyone else, gossiping about each other, and monitoring each other's behavior. And because Kula partnerships are passed on from generation to generation, hence excluding outsiders, an "unbroken chain" of Kula partners exists. (Landa, 1983:153)

The endurance of a Kula relationship beyond death, which is symbolized by mortuary rites, enhances the chances of cooperation by raising the value of w, i.e., enlarging the shadow of the future.[19]

Finally, we have to explain that the visiting Kula partners of a local big-man do trade and haggle within his village, but not with him personally. "The overseas partner is . . . a host, patron and ally in a land of danger and insecurity." (Malinowski, [1922] 1953:92) Of course, he also conducts *gimwali*, yet not with his personal partners but with other natives. There seem to be two reasons: first, one avoids using signals strategically in commercial trade, pretending a lasting interest that does not exist; second, the choice of a concrete partner for bartering is left open without endangering the estimation of the durability of the relationship. Flexibility of economic exchange and stability of social relationships are thereby combined.[20]

Let us summarize the argument. If there is imperfect information about what supergame the actors are playing, there exists a need for an efficient and reliable signaling system. The ceremonial exchange of Kula gifts acts as an efficient and self-enforcing information system of the sort required. However, honesty—donating if, and only if one has a lasting interest—and trust, i.e., believing the (shared) meaning of the signal emitted, become problematic and a matter of choice. The rather complex situation becomes simplified by the establishment of the following convention for which a common interest exists: if one has a lasting interest one should present a gift. Then two kinds of information are sufficient: (1) everybody knows whether his partner is honest, and (2) everybody assumes that his partner knows whether he is honest or not. The first kind of information helps those with a lasting interest to solve their decision-problem about whether to trust. The second assumption prevents those with a transient interest from cheating. Both kinds of information are provided for by a well-functioning system of reputation. The peculiar structure of the Kula Ring creates a self-enforcing mechanism for transmitting reliable information. As dishonest members are threatened with ostracism by loss of reputation, this mechanism also raises the effective level of w, which now refers to the interest in remaining in the whole system and not to the durability of any specific dyadic relationship.

There is still another possibility for solving the problem of deciding whether to trust and to be honest. In addition to the second assumption stated above, the following has to be fulfilled: (3) all assume that everybody thinks that his partner knows whether he is honest, i.e., there is a shared belief that everybody else assumes that his cheating is visible. Then everybody has a rational basis for believing that everybody else is induced to be honest. Assumptions (2) and (3) do not require a system of transmitting information about *specific* people as assumption (1) does, but a functioning system of reputation will quite likely give rise to and maintain these shared beliefs.

Conclusions

The phenomenon of the Kula Ring raises two general problems of sociological interest. First, how may we explain the emergence and maintenance of a complex structure from the interdependent behavior of individuals or groups of actors without hypostatizing "the society" as a self-regulating or autopoetic system? From the point of view of an observer, societies may behave "as if" they would have these attributes. But the problem remains and has been succinctly stated by Malinowski ([1922] 1953:83):

> What appears to us an extensive, complicated, and yet well ordered institution is the outcome of ever so many doings and pursuits, carried on by savages, who have no laws or aims or charters definitely laid down. They have no knowledge of the *total outline* of any of their social structure. They know their own motives, know the purpose of individual actions and the rules which apply to them, but how, out of these, the whole collective institution shapes, this is beyond their mental range.

The problem is how to precisely specify and explain the mechanisms and dynamics that give rise to and maintain such complex structures.[21] We have tried to outline such an explanation from a structural-individualistic perspective, using the Kula Ring as an example.

The second problem concerns the relationship between commercial trade and social order. By analyzing the signaling function of the ceremonial exchange of gifts, some of the pecularities of this institution could be accounted for. However, we do not pretend to be able to explain all aspects of the Kula, nor to grasp all distinctions made in the literature between economic and social exchange.[22] The hypothesis put forward ought also to be elaborated and to be tested by ethnographic data. Nevertheless, it has predictive value. Should the interest in trading among the island societies decline because of shifting demand and supply, then the incentive for an efficient signaling system would disappear, and one would expect the Kula Ring to break.

Acknowledgments

I would like to thank Michael Hechter, Manfred Holler, Siegwart Lindenberg, Ulrich Mueller, and Werner Raub for their helpful critique and detailed comments. I hope to have been able to improve the argument. I must also thank Eckehart Köhler for linguistic corrections of the text.

Notes

1. By the constitutional contract, the natives acknowledge "the rights of persons to retain those stocks of goods that they can wrest from the natural environment by their own labor" (Buchanan, 1975:63). As positive property rights to goods directly produced will not necessarily emerge from conceptual contractual agreement, a more detailed analysis would have to show that the direct-production position is Pareto-superior to the natural anarchistic equilibrium.

2. We have taken the notation from Axelrod (1984:8). T stands for temptation, R for reward, P for punishment and S for sucker. These labels are slightly misleading, as "punishment" and "reward" suggests an intermediate "zero-point" where satisfaction turns into dissatisfaction. But only rankings are implied where P stands for the second to worst or third best outcome. Using the same symbols for both actors, of course, does not mean that their utilities are "equal". The use of the same symbols helps only to simplify the notation.

3. For example, Michael Taylor (1976), Edna Ullman-Margalit (1977), Andrew Schotter (1981), Robert Axelrod (1984), and Thomas Voss (1985).

4. See Voss (1985, Chapter 4) and the references therein.

5. Nothing is said (and has to be said!) about the specific mechanisms of selection, e.g., differential fitness of survival, passing on successful patterns of behavior by socialization, operant conditioning or vicarious learning.

6. Besides the requirement already mentioned, $w > [(T - R)/(T - P)]$, the further condition that $w > [(T - R)/(R - S)]$ must be fulfilled (see Axelrod, 1984:207ff.).

7. $V(\text{TFT}|\text{ALL } D)$ designates the total value a cooperative actor receives when playing against a defecting opponent who uses ALL D. It amounts to $S + wP/(1-w)$. The other expressions may be interpreted analogously. Their values may be taken from the matrix of Diagram 6.2.

8. Landa (1983:144f.) presents a short list of goods traded among the islands. Food like yams, taro, sweet potatoes, bananas, coconuts, and sago is traded over shorter distances, while durable goods for consumption and investment (like pots, wooden bowls, baskets or canoes) circulate over a larger portion of the Kula Ring.

9. In an earlier version of this chapter, I argued that the prisoner's dilemma inherent in bilateral *trading* leads to the development of the Kula. However, as barter seems to be a spot transaction, no such problems have to be solved. But the more fundamental problem of social order remains, of course. I thank Siegwart Lindenberg and especially Michael Hechter, whose critique at the Bad Homburg conference helped me to rethink the argument and put it on a much sounder basis.

10. Buchanan (1975:30) argues that there seems little reason to predict a precise correspondence between originally agreed endowments (in the constitutional contract) and optimally preferred bundles (achieved by postconstitutional trading). R could, therefore, be improved while P, T, and S do not change.

11. Here the explanation sketch has to be supplemented by an important boundary condition. Though in its present form the condition is unnecessarily strict—everyone has to be a potential trading partner for everybody else—whether the resources are actually distributed among the islands in such a way that *in all necessary cases* there exists an

The Kula

incentive to act as middleman remains to be determined. A preliminary analysis of the empirical data seems to indicate that this boundary condition is fulfilled.

12. Malinowski ([1922] 1953:363ff.) gives an example of the profits made by intermediary trade between the northern Trobriand islands and Dobu, which passes through Sinaketa.

13. Unintentionally (!), this process, based on dyadic transactions only, leads to a shortest possible path among n actors (see Grofman and Landa, 1983:361).

14. Implicitly we have made a rather strong assumption: the establishment of social order is only problematic among neighbors while there exist *no direct* relationships at all, neither peaceful nor hostile, between more distant actors. If one drops this assumption, one has to elaborate the argument in two directions. First, an actor may have more than two relationships to consider. Two more parameters would therefore have to be included in inequality (2):

$$p_i V(\text{TFT}|\text{TFT}) + (1 - p_i) V(\text{TFT}|\text{ALL } D) > p_j V(\text{ALL } D|\text{TFT}) + (1 - p_j) V(\text{ALL } D|\text{ALL } D)$$

p_i denotes the proportion of relationships of actor i with cooperative partners, $(1-p_i)$ his proportion of contacts with defecting ones. The critical value of w is now also dependent on p_i and p_j. Furthermore, if in a chain A-B-C, where A and B form a peaceful subsystem, the neighbors B and C establish social order among themselves, step (c) in the Grofman/Landa iterative process (i.e., all three form a larger subsystem) requires peaceful relationships to develop between A and C, too. This may happen for two reasons: the proportion of peaceful partners of C has increased or the payoff structure in the basic PD game between A and C may have changed because stock now becomes available by peaceful intermediary trade via B.

However, for reasons of simplicity we keep the strong assumption of a perfect ring structure, which is equivalent to each actor's having exactly two neighbors.

15. The (subjectively evaluated) durability of a relationship is not a matter of choice, but is due to its constraints. A somewhat speculative question may nevertheless be raised. Might an actor try to change that constraint, i.e., his w or that of his partner, if he becomes aware of a situation like that in Diagram 6.3?

16. An equivalent condition would be that Ego has to know how Other evaluates the durability of the relationship, because durability and donating define honesty, while honesty and donating allow for the evaluation of durability.

17. This is the best strategy for Ego to solve the coordination problem left in the situation where he knows that both of them have a lasting interest (see the doubly framed part of Diagram 6.4a). Of course, he does not know whether Other perceives the situation correctly. So, he may still be in doubt whether Other inadvertently does not trust him (because, for example, Other assumes Ego to be dishonest).

18. If he could remain anonymous in a very large population without additional costs, he would receive the maximum total value obtainable in a prisoner's dilemma supergame $T + wT + w^2T + \ldots = T/(1-w)$.

19. Landa cites two other clublike elements of the Kula. Barriers to entry are very high, because one has first to master the rites of the club and the initiation is controlled by the club members. Somebody is only accepted into the Kula if he has received *vaygu'a* from a club member who has tested his reliability.

20. A more extended analysis would have to deal systematically with the internal functions of the Kula within the local communities, clans, and tribes. On the one hand, big-men enforce the constitutional contract with the stranger; among the commoners, on the other hand, the Kula exchange preserves and enhances their internal status.

21. These will, of course, not always be "invisible-hand explanations." However, ex-

plaining the emergence and maintenance of a structure by a visible hand is by no means unproblematic.

22. See Ekeh (1974) and Heath (1976) who compare the work of Blau and Homans with that of Lévi-Strauss and Mauss.

References

Axelrod, Robert. (1984). *The Evolution of Cooperation*. New York: Basic Books.
Buchanan, James M. (1975). *The Limits of Liberty. Between Anarchy and Leviathan*. Chicago and London: The University of Chicago Press.
Ekeh, Peter. (1974). *Social Exchange Theory. The Two Traditions*. London: Heinemann.
Fortune, R.F. (1932). *Sorcerers of Dobu*. London: Routledge & Kegan Paul.
Grofman, Bernard. (1982). "A dynamic model of protocoalition formation in ideological N-space." *Behavioral Science* 27:77–90.
Grofman, Bernard and Janet T. Landa. (1983). "The development of trading networks among spatially separated traders as a process of proto-coalition formation: The Kula trade." *Social Networks* 5:347–365.
Heath, Anthony. (1976). *Rational Choice and Social Exchange. A Critique of Exchange Theory*. Cambridge: Cambridge University Press.
Landa, Janet T. (1983). "The enigma of the Kula ring: Gift-exchanges and primitive law and order." *International Review of Law and Economics* 3:137–160.
Lévi-Strauss, Claude. (1969). *The Elementary Structures of Kinship*. London: Beacon Press (first published 1949).
Malinowski, Bronislow. (1951). *Crime and Custom in Savage Society*. London: Routledge & Kegan Paul (first published 1926).
Malinowski, Bronislow. (1953). *Argonauts of the Western Pacific*. London: Routledge & Kegan Paul (first published 1922).
Mauss, Marcel. (1954). *The Gift. Forms and Functions of Exchange in Archaic Societies*. London: Cohen & West Ltd. (first published 1925).
Posner, Richard A. (1981). *The Economics of Justice*. Cambridge: Harvard University Press.
Sahlins, Marshall. (1972). *Stone Age Economics*. Chicago: Aldine.
Schotter, Andrew. (1981). *The Economic Theory of Social Institutions*. Cambridge: Cambridge University Press.
Taylor, Michael. (1976). *Anarchy and Cooperation*. London: Wiley.
Uberoi, J.P. Singh. (1971). *Politics of the Kula Ring*. Manchester: Manchester University Press.
Ullmann-Margalit, Edna. (1978). "Invisible-hand explanations." *Synthese* 39: 263–291.
Ullmann-Margalit, Edna. (1977). *The Emergence of Norms*. Oxford: Oxford University Press.
Voss, Thomas. (1985). *Rationale Akteure und soziale Institutionen. Beitrag zu einer endogenen Theorie des sozialen Tauschs*, München: Oldenbourg.

II
THE COMPARATIVE ANALYSIS OF INSTITUTIONS

7

A Comparative Institutional Analysis in the Arts: The Theater

Bruno S. Frey

Werner W. Pommerehne

Institutions From The Economic Point of View

Art, and theater in particular, is not solely the result of the creativity of specially gifted individuals. Rather, what is produced and becomes art is strongly determined by the *institutional setting* in which individuals act. This chapter is devoted to showing that the choice of institutions has a predictable impact on the quantity and quality of theatrical performances, as well as on the type and method of their production. The emphasis lies on the supply of art. Compared to the demand for art, which has been the subject of many inquiries within sociology, the supply side has been neglected.

Cultural institutions are analyzed using the economic approach which has two distinctive characteristics: First, individuals are the actors. They pursue their own goals and their behavior is confined by various constraints. The most important constraints are due to income and prices for goods and services, but besides these physical, psychic, and material factors can restrict the possibility set. The wishes (preferences) of the actors are strictly separated from the constraints and are independent from these (except in particular cases like self-imposed restrictions). Changes in behavior are attributed to changes in the constraints, as these are easier to operationalize. Explanations based on changes in preferences are countenanced only when those based on changes in constraints are empirically unsatisfactory or appear to be false. Explaining changes in behavior by means of constraints has a further important advantage. The empirically well-founded rule of relative price effects can be used: a good which becomes comparatively more expensive to buy or an activity which becomes more costly to undertake will be demanded less.

This model of human behavior is not only used by economists (see, in particular, Becker, 1976; Stigler and Becker, 1977), but also increasingly by political scientists (e.g., Riker and Ordeshook, 1973; Hibbs, 1987) and sociologists (e.g., Coleman, 1964; Opp, 1972, 1979; Lindenberg, 1983, 1984). By no means does it conflict with the psychological model of human behavior (see Stroebe and Frey, 1980; Frey and Foppa, 1986).

The second fundamental point of the economic analysis of cultural institutions consists of the comparative view. Institutions are not analyzed or evaluated individually, but are always contrasted with existing alternatives. There is no point in comparing real-world institutions, with all their shortcomings, to utopian fantasies that have never seen the light of day (see Alchian and Demsetz, 1972).

The goal of this chapter is to explain the origin and the behavior, and therewith the effects, of different institutions in the arts. In order to set forth as clearly as possible the characteristics, as well as the advantages and disadvantages of this approach in connection with a concrete problem, the analysis is confined to the area of the stage and music theater.[1]

The economics of the arts[2] has developed greatly in the past few years and has led to an understanding of this field which differs markedly from the traditional view of art historians and sociologists. In the sociology of the arts (e.g., Weber, 1958; Silbermann, 1963, 1973; Wick and Wick-Knoch, 1979) the major emphasis lies on an analysis of, and the motives for, participation in a cultural activity on the basis of the sociological model of human behavior. In contrast, the economics of the arts stresses that the behavior of those attending a cultural activity is not only determined by preferences (particularly class-specified art access), but also that income, prices, and, above all, the amount of time available are also of great importance. Further, the economics of the arts analyzes the behavior of suppliers with the help of the theory of the firm. Finally, demand and supply are explicitly related to each other by investigating the role of the market.

Theater can take the form of a cooperative organization. The next section sets forth the conditions for the existence of this institutional form. It discusses why the cooperative theater, when successful, must nearly always be abandoned and replaced either by a profit-oriented or a government-supported institution. The following two sections are concerned with the characteristics and effects of these two forms, which at present dominate theater institutions.

Cooperative Theater

In the theater labor often hires capital, instead of capital hiring labor, as is the rule in most other areas of society. The typical instance is a small "cooperative" group of persons (say four to five actors) with equal voting rights who look for capital in order to realize a particular commonly-held idea. Often such groups are highly informal and management tasks are shared.

In such performing arts groups, joint production by a team is efficient. The monitoring problem relating effort and remuneration (Alchian and Demsetz, 1972) is solved by mutual control. This set-up is efficient because much or all information is "impacted" within the team (Williamson, 1975, 1980): the input of effort is supervised in a decentralized and informal way, and any unevenness is dealt with amicably. A centralized monitoring arrangement would be more costly: information would have to be gathered and this would have negative effects on productivity and output, since formal monitoring would be resented by the members of the group. A calculative environment is not conducive to high artistic achievement. Accordingly, the profit, if any, is distributed among the group members without problem.

Such an "idyllic" institutional form of theater may exist for a long time. As a rule, however, the purely cooperative form is usually taken over by a more hierarchical set-up in which one member takes a leading (managerial and artistic) role. The main reason for this institutional change is that the monitoring problem becomes more serious when the cooperative performing arts group gets larger. Remuneration is no longer automatically fixed because the input becomes more differentiated (the artistic, technical, and administrative tasks become separated). Group members are no longer able to easily evaluate what effort is put in by each, and a split emerges between those who directly reap the artistic success of the production and those who do the less rewarding auxiliary back-stage technical and administrative work. For both reasons, it is no longer easy to organize the theater in a way that is satisfactory to all group members. Accordingly, with increasing size, tensions increase due to different preferences and work inputs. The result is that cooperation weakens, efficiency drops, and financial losses accumulate. The problems connected with increasing size may be overcome in three different ways:

1. The cooperative group dissolves, and the more enterprising members possibly form new small (cooperative) theater groups.
2. The actors hire a manager whose task is to monitor the effort of individual members (see Putterman, 1984). If each group member retains his voting rights, there is an insufficient incentive to monitor the manager because of the public good problem. This allows the manager to pursue his own goals (one of which is to earn a higher income) which are not necessarily identical, and are possibly in conflict, with the actors' goals. A more definite solution to the monitoring problem is the establishment of a classical capitalist firm in which the group members are the share owners and distribute the residual among themselves. In that case, the manager's behavior (and perhaps discretionary leeway) is also monitored by the (financial) market (Jensen and Meckling, 1979; Grossman and Hart, 1980).
3. A third solution for the survival of a cooperative theater is to gain government funds. This may take many different forms, with specific effects on the behavior of the performing arts institutions it supports.

Which of the three institutional forms will be adopted depends on the politicoeconomic and legal conditions. The first type of institution, theater as a cooperative team, will not be treated further, as it is limited to small organizations. The members of an expanding theater must decide whether they wish to expose themselves mainly to the market or to political and administrative influences. As will be shown in the two following sections, both of these institutional forms have advantages and disadvantages. When an expanding cooperative team wishes to receive public support, early efforts must be made to procure this from the administrative and political decision-makers. This rent-seeking (see Buchanan, Tollison, and Tullock, 1980; Tollison, 1982) is inevitably combined with the rise of a hierarchy, since the public administration, in accordance with the general governmental rules and regulation, is neither prepared nor able to heap subsidies on an ill-defined team as a whole. A responsible discussion partner and a juristically clearly defined corporate body is demanded. A decision in favor of striving for government subsidies always means that an artistic body working on a voluntary basis fundamentally changes its character after restructure—which many subsidized, one-time cooperative theaters only discover later.

When a basic decision to engage in market-oriented theater has been made, adjustments to the legal conditions (e.g., share rights) become necessary. This goes hand-in-hand with the emergence of a hierarchy, for then someone must be designated to assume responsibility for the theater management.

It will be clear from these observations that a transition from a cooperative to a profit-oriented or a subsidized theater always means that the team character will be destroyed, and that a hierarchy will take its place. The following section deals with the behavior of the capitalist, profit-oriented theater institutions.

Profit-Oriented Theater

Conditions for Survival

Profitable production is possible for theaters, although this is not always recognized (see, e.g., DiMaggio, 1986). Indeed, in various areas of theatrical production the following conditions obtain:

1. *Fixed costs are small.* Traveling stage companies have relatively low fixed costs because they eschew the (high) fixed cost of keeping up a house and its technical outfit. Moreover, they often can use the technical and administrative staff of the hosting theater. A higher use of capacity makes it possible to benefit from decreasing average cost.
2. *Audiences are large.* Many spectators can be attracted by performing the same play *en suite* rather than having a broad repertoire. Obviously, large audiences can be reached in large cities. A large audience can also be gained by visiting the potential spectators; that is the solution taken by the touring companies.
3. *Prices are discriminated.* A downward sloping demand curve is a reasonable assumption, for the performing arts presumably have an element of monopoly. Since secondary markets are of minor importance, audiences with a high willingness to pay can be charged a high price. In this way, consumer surplus may be transformed into revenue to a degree sufficient for recovering the total cost.
4. *Other income is gained.* The artistic production may be used as a means to earn income in addition to the box office receipts. An important and promising possibility is the selling of performances to the media, such as to radio, television, video, or to the film. Modern media can reach a huge audience by historical standards. The showing of *Hamlet* on American television (even if viewed by only a small share of all television owners) assembles

an audience that is larger than that which has seen the play since 1601. The main difficulty is that television and film may produce their own versions of the plays and operas[3] so that the theaters have a limited possibility of generating much revenue in this manner.

The four conditions of profitability in the performing arts were and are satisfied in many countries and periods in the past. In England, private theaters have always been of great importance. This applies not only to popular theaters, but also to those producing the (undisputed) highest quality of "serious" plays such as those by Shakespeare. During the reign of Elizabeth I (1558–1603) the first regular playhouses were built in London, including the Globe, Swan, and Red Bull. Operating licences were normally granted to an entrepreneur whose management aimed at making a profit. At present, private theaters still exist in England. One of the reasons are the long runs of successful plays such as Agatha Christie's *Mousetrap*, which has been continually on stage since 1952.

In the United States, private performing arts institutions have been the rule until World War II. Today, Broadway theaters may still be profitable without receiving public support, but profitability varies a great deal. Similarly, most Off-Broadway productions, summer, dinner, and road theaters are commercially viable (Netzer, 1978:188).

On the European Continent, "Boulevard" and "Tournée" theaters are still able to attract sufficiently large audiences to be profitable. They play *en suite* and choose popular plays, mostly comedies. In large cities such as Berlin, the profitable theaters perform in their own houses, but more often stage companies tour the country and attract the audiences by some star known from television or the films.

Behavior

Profit-maximizing theaters choose the quantity, quality, and technology of production so as to meet the marginal conditions; they consider the effects of incremental changes in these variables on revenue and cost. The necessary and sufficient conditions are easy to state formally and are, of course, the same as in any other profit-maximizing firm. What is of interest here are the special and possibly unique features of quantity, quality, and technology in the performing arts.

Quantity

The number of spectators and/or of performances offered to the public within a year constitutes the major quantitative aspect of the theater.

The same attendance can be achieved by various combinations of the number of repeated performances of a particular play, the number of different plays per season, and the repertoire consisting of the plays that may be activated for performance.

The choice among these aspects depends on the particular cost and demand characteristics. As already noted, profit-oriented theaters only have a restricted repertoire and often perform merely one play per season, keeping a particular play on stage as long as there is sufficient demand for it. Historically, this happened when city populations grew large enough for stock companies to keep one play running for a very long time. The number of plays that receive very many performances has strongly increased in recent times. In the season 1927–1928 only 3 out of 156 plays on Broadway attained more than 400 performances. More recently, producers have adjusted to the changed cost situation by either closing a production after a very short period (sometimes after one or two evenings), or letting them run for a very long time. In the 1957–1958 season, for example, 14 out of the 116 Broadway plays had over 400 performances. These figures also document that over this period the producers chose to perform a smaller number of plays (Moore, 1968:10-11). Even more demand can be activated by having the same theater company performing in two locations (mostly towns that share the cost). Equally, guest performances can be given in towns having no theater. American producers used to launch shows on Broadway, where they hoped to cover their production cost; the profits they expected would come from the road company (Moore, 1968:xiv).

Quality

In the theater, the qualitative aspect is of overriding importance. Even a "difficult" play or opera considered to be of high quality by (part of) the potential audience (and therefore willing to pay high entrance prices) may be financially successful.

But what is the "quality" of the performing arts output? While it is difficult to evaluate, quality is determined by rather diffuse processes in the "art world" composed of insiders, namely directors, performing artists, other artistic personnel, and, of course, the professional art critics of local and national newspapers. This assessment of "quality" is the one accepted and produced by an enlightened elite. Economists, however, use another yardstick: the willingness to pay. This individualistic evaluation, while probably not independent of the enlightened elite's one, is certainly not identical with it. The economic approach does not attempt to determine the *content* of "art" or its "quality."

Technology of Production

The production function relating inputs to the quality of performance is insufficiently known and contains strong random elements. The difficulty that spectators, and even members of the "art world," have in evaluating quality may even lead them to measure it by the subjectively perceived quality of the inputs – in particular, the fame of the actors and of the stage director. Consequently, "technology" in the performing arts is not restricted to technical aspects (such as in traditional production functions), but contains aspects of subjective evaluations of demanders.[4]

More is known about the production function relating factor inputs to the quantity of output. A production function for 33 symphony orchestras and 27 theaters in Canada 1971–1972 has revealed strongly increasing economies of scale (Globerman and Book, 1974). For 42 theaters in the United Kingdom (1968-1969) and for 34 theaters in Australia (1971-1974), the estimates of long-run cost functions show decreasing average cost up to a level of output around 150,000 attendances per year in the United Kingdom and 100,000 in Australia. Thereafter, unit costs are found to increase sharply. For opera, ballet, and music companies, at least in Australia, scale economies are even more pronounced over a wide range of company sizes; the minimum of long-run average cost is attained at an attendance of 260,000 per year (Throsby and Withers, 1979:93 *et seq.*).

It is often thought that the performing arts production is characterized by fixed coefficients, and, therefore, that changes in relative factor costs have no effect on input mix. There are obvious limits to substitution for a *given* play. Most performances require an exactly determined number and type of actors, singers, musicians, and time. But there are exceptions even here: In the royal dramas by Shakespeare, which sometimes require large crowds, one actor has been used who holds up a table indicating that the spectator should imagine a crowd of people. Moreover, one actor may perform various roles in the same play.

Additional substitution possibilities arise as soon as the choice between plays is considered. One effect of the relative rise of the cost of labor (actors) relative to capital may be that an increasing number of plays having few actors are chosen. The Experimental Traverse Theatre in Edinburgh cut the average size of its cast from 8.1 (1975–1976) to 4.3 (1980–1981) (Peacock, 1984:206). Recently, in the United States, there seems to be a tendency to substitute less expensive chamber music for more costly symphonies (see Reineccius, 1984). Relative price effects may also have had an effect on playwrights who see a better chance of having their work staged if the cast is small. Other substitution possibilities exist in the preparation of a production, in particular with rehearsals and the use of the stage.

Profit-maximizing performing arts institutions have an incentive to seek revenue from lines of activity that are only indirectly related to art production. While attracting commercial sponsors, selling attractive programs, and running profitable bars and restaurants is an obvious possibility, selling performances to the media may create a problem, because the (future) demand for the particular productions may be reduced. This would have little effect on the decision of an individual company provided its share of the market is small, because then the fall in demand is a public bad. In the performing arts, a supplier may thereby effectively spoil the market. On the other hand, showing a performance in the media (especially on television) increases exposure to the public, thus increasing demand for the live performance. An "addiction" to the arts might be created among the television viewers and radio listeners (see Stigler and Becker, 1977). Again, there is a public good element, because the rise in future demand not only benefits the theater concerned, but all performing arts institutions. The main effect, however, should still fall on the theater presenting the particular performance.

In addition to these possibilities for raising revenue from other sources, profit-oriented theaters have also made a determined effort at facilitating the acquisition of tickets: reservations may be made by telephone and immediately paid by credit card. A centralized ticket office has been instituted for all commercial Broadway theaters. Price discrimination has been introduced by offering unsold tickets on the day of the performance at half the regular price. This experiment resulting in a considerable increase of attendance, turned out to be a financial success. (Baumol, 1979; Cheskin, 1984:79 *et seq.*).

Government-Supported Theaters

The development of a profit-oriented institutional arrangement for theaters is only one—and historically a less important—mode of organization. The dominating institutional form of performing arts has been the establishment in a hierarchical setting by the Church, later by princes and kings, partly emerging from cooperative companies. In Germany, after World War I, these theaters were taken over by governments in the form of the Regietheater. They became part of public administration; their budget is accordingly part of the public household of the Länder, or the municipalities (Herterich, 1937; Jonas, 1972:7 *et seq.*; Wahl-Zieger, 1978). In other European countries, especially in Italy,

France, and Austria with their old and prestigious performing arts traditions, the important institutions have also been public.

In public theaters in Germany, the income from ticket sales dramatically dropped from 63% before World War I to 11% in 1984–1985. Private support has always been low, and is now practically zero. In contrast, government subsidies by the Länder and municipalities increased their share from 27% in 1911 to 84% in 1984–1985. This illustrates the dominant importance of direct monetary government support for German nonprofit public theaters; quite a similar situation exists in most other countries of Continental Western Europe.

Influence of the Type of Government Support on Behavior

Public support has important incentive effects, changing behavior in the performing arts considerably. It brings about a different type of theater with a different content. Public support has an effect on the quantity and quality of the works performed, the prices of admission charged, the technology of production used, the nonticket receipts, and on the internal organization of the theater, including factor payments.

The differences in behavioral modification depend on the particular form of public support that is provided. Three types will be discussed here: lump sum subsidy, ticket subsidies, and deficit coverage. (For a formal analysis of some aspects see Hansmann, 1981 and Le Pen, 1982.)

Lump Sum Government Subsidy

A subsidy is given to a performing arts institution on the sole basis of its *existence* but unrelated to its output, input, or prices. The amount granted cannot be influenced by the receiving organization through its output decision. Such a lump sum subsidy may (at least in the short run) facilitate the survival of a performing arts institution which otherwise would have to close down for commercial reasons. Normally, the subsidy is withheld (or has to be refunded) if there are positive profits. This fact has strong incentive effects on the subsidy recipient. Profits generate a cost to the theater managers in the form of a loss of the subsidy, and, therefore, the incentives to earn profits are strongly diminished. In consequence, a theater policy is chosen in which no financial profits (or at least no visible ones) appear. This is often accomplished by improving quality above the level desired by the audience, distributing rents to employees, concentrating on the "artistic" side and disregarding other possible sources of revenue.

Subsidies and Taxes on Tickets

The public support of the performing arts may take the form of giving a fixed subsidy per admission (independent of the price charged) or, giving a variable subsidy matching total ticket receipts, using a fixed factor.[5] This type of subsidy is uncommon. But its negative counterpart is widespread, namely, a sales tax imposed on box office receipts. Often this negative subsidy not only applies to commercial but also to public performing arts institutions. The change in relative prices induced works against enlarging the size of the audience and in favor of other goals such as raising artistic quality.

Deficit Coverage

Many Continental European theaters are subject to public administration. These theaters have to observe cameralistic budget principles. One principle is that of "specificity" with respect to content and time: the various items of the budget may neither be substituted nor transferred over time. Even more important is the principle of *nonaffectation*, which states that a surplus due to higher receipts and/or lower costs may not be used by the institution for its own purposes. These funds have to flow back to the general public treasury.

The subsidy is granted on the basis of a projected deficit. The likely deficit is not "given" but is the result of a process of bargaining between the particular performing arts institution and the responsible ministry of culture (and the ministry of finance in the case of a substantial deficit). The bargaining process takes place in the context of an information asymmetry in favor of the subsidy-seeking institution (see Dupuis, 1983). On the one hand, cost increases are easy to document because they are in good measure due to the fact that the institution is part of the public administration. Most important, the technical and administrative staff are either public employees or personnel whose wages increase in line with those of public employees. On the other hand, the ministry finds it difficult to demonstrate convincingly that reductions in the projected deficit are feasible. Corresponding suggestions are easily shown to affect the "artistic quality" by the theater managers, and therefore they pertain to an area for which the directorate of the performing arts institution claims exclusive authority. Public officials in the ministries concerned accept this claim because of their lack of competence, but even more because they have little incentive to interfere. They gain more by having an amicable relationship with the theater people, who, in turn, acknowledge this by accepting them in the "art world" (e.g., by providing them with tickets for opening nights, and inviting them to social events).

Given asymmetric information (and incentives), bargaining rules have been established to facilitate the process. Past deficits and subsidies are taken as the cornerstone for projecting the new deficit. Foreseeable cost changes are added. The general financial situation of the public purse represents a countervailing force which also affects the theater. If, for instance, public expenditures have to be reduced across the board, theater subsidies are not exempt.

A direct consequence of linking current subsidies to past deficits is that reducing its deficit has a double cost to the management of the performing arts institution. Achieving a surplus or decreasing a deficit does not benefit the theater; the implicit tax rate applied is 100%. Moreover, future subsidies are reduced.

Therefore, the directors of a public theater have a strong incentive *not* to reduce the deficit, but rather to increase it above the projected level. The sanctions against doing so are low. Sometimes, the unbudgeted deficit is simply covered at the end of the year, and there is a good chance of getting a higher deficit budgeted in the future. Only under unfortunate circumstances is the unbudgeted current deficit (partly) subtracted from the future subsidy. Such a reaction, however, is not in line with the standard budget practices of a public administration. Only if the director of a public theater consistently overruns the budgeted deficit by sizable amounts does he run a risk of being reprimanded and possibly not being reappointed when his contract runs out. Nevertheless, such behavior would endanger the friendly relationship with the money-giving public administrators and may not pay in the longer run.

Subsidies covering deficits have marked effects on the behavior of managers of performing arts institutions. Managers have a low regard for "market efficiency" and can indulge in the pursuit of other goals in their utility function, such as attaining prestige in the "art world," performance excellence, monetary income (mainly indirectly through the use of additional income sources such as directing plays in other theaters, and participating in festivals), and a good atmosphere in the theater (beyond the efficient amount) consisting in satisfied co-workers and employees. For managers, a restricted workload and the possibility of earning outside income are particularly important goals.

An illustrative example of deficit coverage strongly shaping behavior is provided by the *Salzburger Festspiele*. This festival is organized by the "Salzburger Festspielfonds," consisting of four directors and a president (for institutional details see Kaut, 1982 and Wimberger, 1983). According to a law passed in 1950, the federal government, the state, and the city of Salzburg are *required* to cover any deficit of the Festspiele. The budget constraint the organizers must observe is extremely weak, since all the expenditures have to be covered by law irrespective of costs. An effective constraint on the size of the deficit exists only in so far as the organizers must not demand subsidies so high that the financial capacities of the institutions covering the deficit are overtaxed, and consequently the law is changed.

The institutional conditions under which the directorate acts lead the Salzburger Festspiele to enact a redistributive policy. (For a more elaborate analysis with detailed empirical evidence see Frey, 1986.) The Austrian taxpayers are burdened by the subsidies while the gains are shared by the directorate, the staff, and a portion of the spectators. This redistribution is not purposeful from the taxpayers' point of view, but rather is the unintended consequence of institutionalized behavior. The observed behavior is not the result of the directors' personal preferences; indeed, they would act quite differently if the form of subsidy were different.

Concluding Remarks

The central idea of this chapter is that institutional differences affect the behavior of the management of performing arts institutions significantly and systematically. The theoretical analysis of the effect of institutional arrangments on the incentive structure of individuals allows us to derive testable hypotheses about the differences between profit-oriented and publicly run performing arts institutions. Theaters behave differently with respect to output, inputs, and the production process depending on whether they are cooperative, profit-oriented and private, or nonprofit-oriented and public. The type of government subsidy theaters receive also affects their behavior.

Acknowledgments

We acknowledge financial support from the Fritz Thyssen Stiftung. For helpful comments we are grateful to Beat Heggli.

Notes

1. For the area of the museum, see especially Pommerehne and Frey (1980), or Frey and Pommerehne (1980).
2. Baumol and Bowen, 1966; Blaug, 1976; Peacock, 1984; Throsby and Withers, 1979; for recent surveys see Throsby, 1982; Pommerehne and Frey, 1985.

3. Recent examples are *Amadeus* by Shaffer, or *Carmen* which has been produced by Saura, or the *Zauberflöte* by Bergman.
4. In this context, see the discussion of the phenomenon of "superstars" by Rosen (1981) and Adler (1985).
5. It may be shown that in the case of a quality maximizing performing arts supplier subject to a budgetary constraint a ticket subsidy leads to a smaller increase in audience size than would an equivalent lump sum subsidy. In the case of an audience maximizing supplier it may be shown that a ticket subsidy leads to a larger increase in quality than will an equivalent lump sum subsidy (Hansmann, 1981:359).

References

Adler, Moshe. (1985). "Stardom and talent." *American Economic Review*, 75:208-212.
Alchian, Armen A. and Demsetz, Harold. (1972). "Production, information costs, and economic organization." *American Economic Review*, 62:777-795.
Baumol, William J. (1979). "On two experiments in the pricing of theatre tickets." Pp. 41-58 in Michael J. Boskin, ed. *Economics of Human Welfare*. New York: Academic Press.
Baumol, William J. and W.G. Bowen. (1966). *Performing Arts: The Economic Dilemma*. Cambridge, Mass.: Twentieth Century Fund.
Becker, Gary S. (1976). *The Economic Approach to Human Behaviour*. Chicago: University of Chicago Press.
Blaug, Mark (Ed.) (1976). *The Economics of the Arts*. Boulder and London: Westview Press and Martin Robertson.
Buchanan, James M., Robert D. Tollison, and Gordon Tullock (Eds.) (1980). *Toward a Theory of the Rent-Seeking Society*. College Station: Texas A & M University Press.
Cheskin, Irving W. (1984). "The 'Taxpaying' Theater: How Has it Fared during Inflation?" Pp. 71-85 in Hilda Baumol and William J. Baumol, eds. *Inflation and the Performing Arts*. New York and London: New York University Press.
Coleman, James S. (1964). *Introduction to Mathematical Sociology*. New York.
DiMaggio, Paul J. (1986). *Nonprofit Enterprise in the Arts*. Oxford/New York: Oxford University Press.
Dupuis, Xavier. (1983). "La surqualité: le spectacle subventionné malade de la bureaucratie?" *Revue Economique*, 34:1089-1115.
Frey, Bruno S. (1986). "The Salzburg Festival—from the economic point of view." *Journal of Cultural Economics*, 10:27-44.
Frey, Bruno S. and Klaus Foppa. (1986). "Human behavior: Possibilities explain action." *Journal of Economic Psychology*, 7:137-160.
Frey, Bruno S. and Werner W. Pommerehne. (1980). "An economic analysis of the museum." Pp. 248-259 in W.S. Hendon, J.L. Shanahan, and A. MacDonald, eds., *Economic Policy for the Arts*. Cambridge, Mass.: Abt.
Globerman, Steven and Sam Book. (1974). "Statistical cost functions for performing arts organizations." *Southern Economic Journal*, 40:668-671.

Grossman, Sanford J. and Oliver D. Hart. (1980). "Takeover bids, the free-rider problem, and the theory of corporation." *Rand Journal of Economics* 11:42-64.
Hansmann, Henry. (1981). "Nonprofit enterprise in the performing arts." *Bell Journal of Economics*, 12:341-361.
Herterich, Fritz. (1937). *Theater und Volkswirtschaft*. Munich and Leipzig: Duncker and Humblot.
Hibbs, Douglas A. (1987). *The Political Economy of Industrial Democracies*. Cambridge, Mass. and London: Harvard University Press.
Jensen, Michael C. and William H. Meckling. (1979). Rights and production functions: An application to labor-managed firms and codetermination. *Journal of Business*, 52:469-506.
Jonas, Lutz. (1972). *Die Finanzierung der öffentlichen Theater in der Bundesrepublik Deutschland*. Dissertation, University of Mainz.
Kaut, Josef. (1982). *Die Salzburger Festspiele 1920-1981*. Salzburg and Vienna: Residenz Verlag.
Le Pen, Claude. (1982). "L'analyse microéconomique de la production dramatique et l'effet des subventions publiques." *Revue Economique*, 33:639-674.
Lindenberg, Siegwart. (1983). "Utility and morality." *Kyklos*, 36(3):450-468.
Lindenberg, Siegwart. (1984). "Preference versus constraints." *Journal of Institutional and Theoretical Economics*, 140:96-103.
Moore, Thomas G. (1968). *The Economics of American Theatre*. Durham: Duke University Press.
Netzer, Dick. (1978). *The Subsidized Muse: Public Support for the Arts in the United States*. Cambridge, London and Melbourne: Cambridge University Press.
Opp, Karl-Dieter. (1972). *Verhaltenstheoretische Soziologie*. Reinbeck bei Hamburg: Rowohlt.
Opp, Karl-Dieter. (1979). "Das 'ökonomische Programm' in der Soziologie." Pp. 313-350 in H. Albert, and K.H. Stapf, eds. *Theorie und Erfahrung*. Stuttgart: Klett-Cotta.
Peacock, Alan T. (1984). "Economics, inflation, and the performing arts." Pp. 71-85 in Hilda Baumol and William J. Baumol, eds. *Inflation and the Performing Arts*. New York and London: New York University Press.
Pommerehne, Werner W. and Bruno S. Frey. (1980). "The museum from an economist's perspective." *International Social Science Journal*, 32:323-339.
Pommerehne, Werner W. and Bruno S. Frey. (1985). "Kunst: Was sagt der Ökonom dazu?" *Schweizerische Zeitschrift für Volkswirtschaft und Statistik* 121:139-167.
Putterman, Louis. (1984) "On some recent explanations of why capital hires labor." *Economics Inquiry*, 22:171-187.
Reineccius, Richard. (1984). "Inflation, public support, and the far-off broadway theater." Pp. 71-85 in Hilda Baumol and William J. Baumol, eds., *Inflation and the Performing Arts*. New York and London: New York University Press.
Riker, William H. and Peter C. Ordeshook. (1973). *An Introduction to Positive Political Theory*. Prentice Hall: Englewood Cliffs, New Jersey.
Rosen, Sherwin. (1981). "The economics of superstars." *American Economic Review*, 71:845-858.

Silbermann, Alphons. (1963). *The Sociology of Music*. London: Routledge.
Silbermann, Alphons. (1973). *Empirische Kunstsoziologie. Eine Einführung mit kommentierter Bibliographie*. Stuttgart.
Stigler, George J. and Gary S. Becker. (1977). "De gustibus non est disputandum." *American Economic Review*, 67:76-90.
Stroebe, Wolfgang and Bruno S. Frey. (1980). "In defense of economic man: Towards an integration of economics and psychology." *Schweizerische Zeitschrift für Volkswirtschaft und Statistik*, 116:119-148.
Throsby, C. David. (1982). "Economics and the arts: A review of seven years." *Economic Record*, 58:242-252.
Throsby, C. David and Glenn A. Withers. (1979). *The Economics of the Performing Arts*. London and Melbourne: Arnold.
Tollison, Robert D. (1982). "Rent seeking: A survey." *Kyklos*, 35:575-602.
Wahl-Zieger, Erika. (1978). *Theater und Orchester zwischen Marktkräften und Marktkorrektur*. Göttingen: Vandenhoeck and Ruprecht.
Weber, Max. (1958). *The Rational and Social Foundations of Music*. Carbondale: Southern Illinois University Press.
Wick, Rainer and Astrid Wick-Knoch. (eds.) (1979). *Kunstsoziologie. Bildende Kunst und Gesellschaft*. Köln: Du Mont Buchverlag.
Williamson, Oliver E. (1975). *Markets and Hierarchies: Analysis and Anti-Trust Implications*. New York: Free Press.
Williamson, Oliver E. (1980). "The organization of work: A comparative institutional assessment." *Journal of Economic Behavior and Organization*, 1:5-38.
Wimberger, Gerhard. (1983). "Salzburger Festspiele—heute und morgen." Pp. 111-119 in *Salzburger Festspiele 1983*. Salzburg: Landespressebüro.

8

Cultural Resources and Participation in High Culture

Reinhard Wippler

It has repeatedly been observed and empirically established that formal educational attainment is the best predictor we have of a person's participation in the arts and cultural activities: the higher the educational level, the more participation in cultural activities. Although this relationship holds for countries whose educational systems and art institutions are not alike, countries differ considerably with regard to aggregate art involvement (Scitovsky, 1976a:65)—in any case, much more than with regard to educational attainment. Apparently education, though being the best predictor on an aggregate level, does not tell us what motivates people to go to theaters, concert halls, or museums.

This point has recently been made by DiMaggio and Useem. After concluding that with regard to cultural participation "education makes a difference," they agree that we do not yet know "*why* schooling is such a good predictor of aesthetic and artistic interest and participation" (DiMaggio and Useem, 1980:64,68). Expressed in more technical language: strong evidence from empirical research suggests that education affects the degree of art involvement regardless of differences in educational systems and art-related institutions. However, this effect is merely described as an empirical generalization, but not explained.

Seeking an explanation of this effect of formal educational attainment introduces an interesting theoretical problem, for any explanation requires reference to a mechanism. Since, to my knowledge, social scientists have not been able to specify strictly structural or institutional mechanisms (i.e., those that do not refer to acting individuals), the dynamic element in social science explanations has to be sought at the individual level. Since most of the principles governing human behavior are known to social scientists and, at least outside mainstream sociology, have been successfully applied for explanatory purposes, it also seems reasonable to use these principles in sociological explanations.

Rational choice theory represents the most widely used system of behavioral principles in social science explanations. This chapter elaborates rational choice theory in a way that elucidates the mechanisms by which social conditions (such as formal educational attainment) affect the degree of a person's participation in the arts and cultural activities. In the first section, some general aspects of rational choice theory will be discussed, i.e., without reference to cultural participation. The next section deals with the application of that theory to this specific problem area. It is followed by a summary of the results of the theoretical analysis with regard to educational attainment as a predictor for cultural activities. In the final section, some conclusions are drawn with respect to the central question, namely, why and to what extent education has the predictive power shown in empirical research.

Rational Choice Behavior

The most general assumptions of rational choice theory are that individuals have goals which they try to realize by their actions, thereby using resources and acting under social and natural (situational) constraints. Maximizing utility under constraints is assumed to be the general principle governing behavior.

Choices take place within constraints that jointly determine the feasibility set confronting the actor. Usually constraints are regarded as given, but individuals may try to pull down existing constraints or sometimes even voluntarily build up constraints in order to overcome "weakness of will" (Elster, 1979).

In rational choice theory it is not assumed that people consciously calculate the expected costs and benefits of the behavioral alternatives feasible in a particular situation. There are no claims that cognitive processes are being realistically described. It is simply assumed that people display certain consistent and predictable patterns of response to positive and negative incentives, or stated more generally, to changes in their environment, i.e., that people act "as if" they weigh costs and benefits. Rational choice theory is, therefore, by no means restricted to behavior characterized by Max Weber as *zweckrational*. *Rationality* refers only to the assumption of ordered preferences.

In order to apply rational choice theory to particular actors and their specific social circumstances, one has to know something about the goals of these actors, the kinds of resources relevant to these goals, and about the social conditions under which different kinds of resources can be used to realize these goals. Rational choice theory itself does not tell us which goals people have, which resources are relevant, and which social conditions allow the use of resources for goal attainment. Additional assumptions have to be made, and the next sections will be devoted to the introduction of these assumptions.

Assumptions about Goals

The specification of goals is, as Jon Elster (1985:8) rightly states, the crucial step in intentional explanations. There seem to be two main directions in which this step may be taken. On the one hand, one can try to *establish empirically* the various goals people pursue. My objections to this strategy are twofold. First, the advantages of theoretical knowledge, i.e., the possibility of deriving behavioral predictions when situational parameters are known, are lost if each application of rational choice theory has to be preceded by time-consuming and costly empirical research. Second, it is hardly possible to empirically isolate preferences from the circumstances to which they refer, because reported preferences often are already shaped by the opportunities and constraints of the situation.

On the other hand, one may establish theoretically the goals people pursue. This is the strategy Adam Smith employed (cf. the reconstruction of his behavioral assumptions in Lindenberg, 1980). It can be assumed that most people would like to attain given goals and that they differ only with regard to the resources they dispose of and the situational opportunities and constraints that they confront. Recently, this strategy for handling the problem of goal specification has been advocated by Stigler and Becker (1977). I shall follow their lead.

Assuming that there are at least two goals all human beings strive for: *physical well-being* and *social approval*. Regarding these goals, two assumptions about costs can be formulated: (1) strainful exertion reduces physical well-being and will, therefore, be avoided, and (2) socially harmful behavior leads to the loss of social approval and will, therefore, be confined to special occasions.

There are different kinds of physical well-being and social approval, each kind requiring other social conditions for their realization. Since in this context no detailed description is intended, rough distinctions will be sufficient.

Physical well-being can appear in two forms: comfort and pleasure (cf. Scitovsky, 1976b). *Comfort* may be described as a state in which basic needs are satisfied, while *pleasure* refers to a state which is the result of combined external and internal stimulation. In the psychological literature on motivation (an overview is given in Heckhausen, 1980) it is suggested that comfort and pleasure are related to different neurophysiological principles. The degree of physical well-being of the comfort kind increases with need satisfaction up to the point of satiation; this corresponds with the classical idea of drive reduction.

The degree of physical well-being of the pleasure kind, however, is in a complicated way dependent on the stimulation or "arousal potential" to which the individual is exposed. The "arousal potential" (Berlyne and Madsen, 1973) is a hypothetical construct summarizing all peculiarities of a momentary information inflow; it determines the "level of activation," likewise a hypothetical construct referring to a state of the organism. The level of activation, in turn, determines the degree of agreeable sensation, or pleasure, in such a way that changes in the level of activation are experienced as pleasing. These changes may come about either through an increase of a low arousal potential (meaning less monotonous stimulation and boredom) or through a lowering of a high arousal potential toward a middle level (meaning a reduction of an excessive and chaotic stimulation). Or, as Gombrich has aptly stated, "delight lies somewhere between boredom and confusion" (Gombrich, 1979:9). The principles underlying the two kinds of physical well-being are illustrated in Figures 8.1 and 8.2.

According to Lindenberg (1984, 1986) three kinds of social approval can be distinguished: status, behavioral confirmation, and positive affect. *Status* is social approval in the form of ranking. Social approval of this kind is given on the basis of the command of scarce goods such as privilege, power, extraordinary talent, or specialized knowledge. *Behavioral confirmation* is the feeling of having done "the right thing" in the eyes of relevant others. When the reaction of relevant others can easily and accurately be predicted, the actor can feel behavioral confirmation even in the absence of these relevant others. *Positive affect* is what an actor gets if another person cares about him. This kind of social approval implies that indicators of an actor's utility have become goods that

Cultural Resources and Participation in High Culture

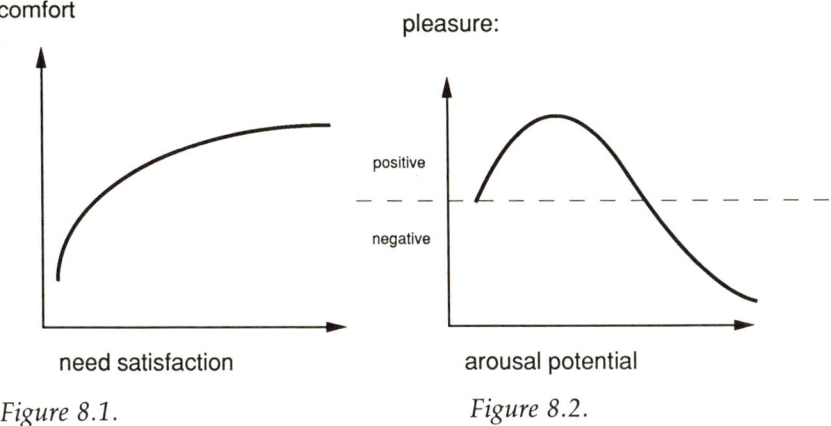

Figure 8.1.   Figure 8.2.

produce a certain amount of physical well-being in that other person (Lindenberg, 1986:300–303).

Assumptions about Resources

Usually three kinds of resources are distinguished (e.g., Bourdieu, 1983): economic, social, and cultural resources.

Economic resources are market goods as well as the financial means needed to acquire those goods. Since financial means may be used for saving time (e.g., hiring people for routine work) and time may be used to compensate scarce financial means (e.g., doing one's own repair work, time can be considered as an equivalent of financial means.

Social resources consist of having direct or indirect access to influential groups or persons (Lin, 1982), and being a part of certain social networks. Actors can mobilize these social networks in order to gain advantages for the realization of their goals (e.g., on the labor market or in the political arena).

As plausible as the idea of *cultural resources* seems to be, it is difficult to define these kinds of resources unambiguously. Under the heading of "cultural resources" or "cultural capital" (Dimaggio, 1982), quite different references can be found in the literature. They range from interest in art events, engaging in cultural activities, having a certain self-image (Dimaggio and Mohr, 1985), objects like paintings, musical instruments and books, to certain competences and dispositions.

From a theoretical point of view, Bourdieu has attempted to bring order to this heterogeneous collection of items. He distinguishes three states in which cultural resources may appear: incorporated, institutionalized, and as objects (Bourdieu, 1983). In the *incorporated* state, cultural resources are lasting dispositions of the organism; they are permanently part of an individual's personality and become perceptible as a person's "habitude." In the *institutionalized* state, cultural resources are academic titles and other certificates of educational accomplishments; they refer to socially recognized and guaranteed competences of their owners. In the state of *objects*, cultural resources are all those material goods that are owned or used by cultivated people in the context of their cultural activities; here Bourdieu mainly refers to books, paintings, monuments, and instruments (1983:185-190).

In the context of rational choice theory, it seems to me that the relevance of cultural resources, both in an institutionalized state and as objects, depends on their relation to cultural resources in an incorporated state. Titles and certificates without corresponding competences may exist, but they are probably exceptions in modern societies. Similarly, ownership of paintings, instruments, and books without any competence for their use as art objects is possible, but then they are stripped of their cultural function and reduced to investment goods.

Given these considerations, I shall concentrate in the following analyses on cultural resources in the form of competences and dispositions. Without a certain cultural competence, objects of art remain inaccessible; titles and certificates cannot, or at least not permanently, compensate for lack of this competence. Cultural resources are therefore treated as a special kind of human capital (Stigler and Becker, 1977).

What does this cultural competence refer to more precisely? For reasons that will become clear later on, cultural competence is conceived of as the *ability to command* aesthetic, cognitive linguistic, and social *codes*. Codes are the keys for symbolically mediated information, and symbols are instruments for ordering and memorizing impressions from the environment, one that often confronts actors with aesthetic, cognitive, and social information too complex to be handled adequately (Gombrich, 1982:16).

The command of *social* codes (i.e., of rules of context-specific social conduct and of proprieties) gives actors access to interaction opportunities and smoothes the course an interaction may take. The command of *cognitive linguistic* codes (i.e., of linguistic expressions allowing consideration of certain details as well as abstraction from irrelevant particularities of a given problem situation; cf. Basil Bernstein's "elaborated code") gives actors access to insight in the structure of problem situations and thereby facilitates effective problem solving. Finally, the command of *aesthetic* codes gives actors access to arts objects and events, enabling them to enjoy aesthetic experiences. Certain characteristics of aesthetic codes will be treated in detail below.

Assumptions about Social Conditions

In the framework sketched above, rational choice refers to the processes wherein resourceful actors attempt to "produce" positively valued states (goals) under constraints particular to their social circumstances (cf. also the new theory of consumer behavior, Becker, 1976). Within this framework, opportunities, constraints, and resources (instead of a variety of individual goals) become central in the explanation of behavior. Which social conditions are then required for the production of comfort, pleasure, status, behavioral confirmation, and positive affect?

There may be many ways to produce a state of *comfort*. However, two conditions have to be met in any case. First, people must have at their disposal a means of guaranteeing their subsistence at a level at least comparable with that of their relevant others. Second, there have to be institutions furnishing a certain degree of protection against health hazards, criminal attack, and exploitation.

Because, a state of *pleasure* according to theories of motivation mentioned above, is the consequence of certain changes in stimulation (i.e., arousal increment and decrement), a varied and changing environment is a precondition for physical well-being of the pleasure kind. Varying tasks in the work situation, diversified living accommodations, and varied informal social relations are means for the production of pleasing experiences. Culturally or intellectually active groups provide a rich, stimulating social setting.

However, the realization of a state of pleasure does not solely require varied and changing influences from the environment, but is also dependent on a person's capacity to actively regulate a momentary information inflow (i.e., to bring about arousal increments and decrements). Since the command of codes is a means of ordering impressions from the environment, the disposal of cultural resources can be considered to be instrumental for the production of physical well-being of the pleasure kind. Pleasure is then brought about in two ways: First, by the reduction of an excessive information inflow (i.e., by making sense of formerly meaningless impressions with the help of the ordering capacity of codes), and second, by providing access to symbolically mediated impressions (i.e., by the application of several codes to the same information inflow, thereby opening up new "levels" of information hitherto inaccessible).

The social conditions conducive to the production of comfort differ from those favoring the production of pleasure. Scitovsky (1976b) has argued that modern Western societies are characterized by comfort without pleasure because of the discrepancy between their enormous wealth and their scarce opportunities for enjoyment. Conversely, one may remember historical constellations of social conditions in which a high level of cultural activities coexisted with extreme deprivation of means of subsistence and a nearly complete lack of institutional protection—the eastern part of Germany in the period immediately following World War II is a case in point. Apparently, comfort and pleasure vary independently.

The conditions that enable a person to produce *status* are largely a function of the historical and geographical context of the particular society under study. In general, not much can be said except that the command of scarce goods forms the basis for the production of status. Societies differ widely with regard to the valuation of scarce goods. The shell armlets and necklaces highly valued by the Trobriand islanders are certainly not status-enhancing in modern societies and, with speed limits introduced in almost every European country, fast cars may soon be obsolete as status-producing goods. In modern meritocratic societies, one may expect that the production of status increasingly depends on acquired scarce goods (conspicuous consumption goods, but also academic titles and certificates) and less on inherited goods.

Small-scale social settings (i.e., face to face relations) play an important role in the production of *behavioral confirmation*, because they provide a person with opportunities for feedback without time delay. Since behavioral choices are restricted by social norms and roles, they will over time bring about conformity of behavior, which, in turn, will create behavioral confirmation as a by-product (Lindenberg, 1986:302). Consequently, two types of social conditions can be specified that favor the production of social approval in the form of behavioral confirmation. First, in traditional, normatively integrated societies, behavioral confirmation is more easily obtained than in less integrated modern societies or under conditions of anomy. Second, in functional systems (Boudon, 1981:39–57), i.e., systems in which interactions are structured by mutual role expectations, behavioral confirmation is produced to a larger extent than in interdependent systems (Boudon, 1981:58–85), where the mutual dependence of actors is brought about by the consequences of individual choices.

The social conditions favorable to the production of *positive affect* are mainly confined to small-scale social settings in which relatively stable primary relations prevail. Informal interactions on a continuous basis, the frequent occurrence of mutually profitable exchange, and a high level of coorientation are conditions under which mutual caring is likely to develop.

Of the three components of social approval, only status is a positional good in that it cannot be acquired by everybody at the same time. However, behavioral confirmation and positive affect could, in principle, be evenly distributed throughout society. Therefore, behavioral confirmation and positive affect are particularly important sources of social approval for people of low status (Lindenberg, 1986:303).

Social Conditions Pertinent to Art Involvement

The considerations of the preceding sections have been of a general kind, and in this form they are applicable to a wide range of explanatory problems. In this chapter, however, they will be applied specifically to the problem of participation in high culture or, more precisely, to art involvement. I will follow the line of argument from the preceding sections and discuss goals, resources, and social conditions conducive to the realization of goal states related to cultural participation as well as social conditions leading to the use and acquisition of a certain kind of resources.

It has been assumed that everybody likes physical well-being and social approval, and that people differ only with regard to the resources they dispose of and the opportunities and constraints with which they are confronted. Certainly art involvement may increase physical well-being and bring social approval, but not to the same degree if the components distinguished earlier are considered separately. Art involvement and aesthetic experiences provide pleasure and enjoyment, but will not significantly enhance comfort. Similarly, participation in high culture confers status to a person and also may procure some behavioral confirmation, but will hardly increase the amount of positive affect received from relevant others.

It is likely that all kinds of resources are used in relation with cultural participation, although the specific combination of these resources will vary with cultural activities. For instance, the frequency of theater attendance depends not only on economic resources, but also on the relative scarcity of time as related to income, as Linder has pointed out in his analysis of the "harried leisure class" (1970). Other authors also have emphasized the role of income and time as cost factors. An analysis of Swiss data shows a 2.7% increase in theater attendance as a consequence of a 1% rise of income and a decrease in attendance as a higher consequence of higher ticket prices and greater scarcity of time (Pommerehne and Frey, 1985:146–147). Social resources (i.e., membership in social networks that can be mobilized) in big cities may play a role in finding the little-known places where the "best" theater group performs or unknown artists exhibit their paintings.

No doubt, cultural resources—especially the command of aesthetic codes—are most pertinent to the enjoyment of cultural activities. Therefore, the handling of these codes, their relation to artistic enjoyment, and the conditions of their acquisition will be discussed in greater detail.

Aesthetic Codes and Artistic Enjoyment

Pleasure, in general, and artistic enjoyment, in particular, are brought about by changes in arousal level, as Berlyne (1974); Berlyne and Madsen (1973) have found in their studies in "New Experimental Aesthetics." These changes come about in two ways. (1) Excessive stimulation is reduced to a middle level by means of some kind of ordering of complexity. (2) A low level of stimulation is increased by the introduction of new ordering schemes adding complexity to former impressions.

Because symbols are ordering instruments for impressions from the environment, and codes serve as keys for symbolically mediated information (Gombrich, 1982), the command of codes becomes important for an *active regulation of pleasure* derived from symbolically transformed objects and events. That is, objects of art are sources of pleasure to the extent that their arousal potential is matched by the corresponding command of codes. If environmental richness is not matched with decoding capacities, then either boredom will result (if the viewer of an art exhibition or the listener at a concert has more cultural resources at his disposal than the paintings or pieces of music require) or irritation (if the unprepared viewer or listener is confronted with art objects of high complexity).

The access to art requires the command of several codes, and from the same object of art one may obtain information at quite different levels depending on the particular code applied to it (Bourdieu, 1970:165). Furthermore, the pleasing experience derived from the confrontation with objects of art seems to be related to an alternation of the codes applied. In the field of comparative literature, the aesthetic experience is described in semiotic terms as "the psychological condition of satisfaction coinciding with the switching of codes or with the successful application of a familiar code to a text yielding substantial information" (Fokkema, 1982:65).

In this same field, it is suggested that there are at least five codes operative in virtually all literary texts:

> (1) the linguistic code, which directs the reader to read the text as, e.g., an English text; (2) the literary code, which predisposes the reader to discover a particular coherence in the text . . . increasing the acceptability of uncommon metaphors and other deviations from standard linguistic usage; (3) the generic code, such as the code of narrative or of poetry, which instructs the reader to activate certain expectations . . . ; (4) the period code or sociocode, which directs the reader to activate his knowledge of the conventions of a period or particular semiotic community; and (5) the idiolect of the author, which insofar as it is distinguishable on the basis of recurrent features also has a code character (Fokkema, 1985:646–647).

The description of a hierarchy of codes underlying literary texts, and the related hypothesis that the greater the knowledge a person has of the codes that have determined the text, the more information he will be able to elicit from that text, are both borrowed from comparative literature (Fokkema, 1984:9). I would, however, suggest that these ideas can be generalized to other art forms, for they make comprehensible how the command of codes is an instrument for arousal increment as well as for arousal decrement. By the alternate application of a series of codes to the same art object, each new code enhances the complexity of the information inflow and thereby increases the enjoyment of the aesthetic experience; since this regulation of stimulation is brought about by the viewer/listener himself, the increase of stimulation will end when the limit of his information-processing capacity is reached. On the other hand, the command of codes enables the viewer/listener to reduce the complexity of information contained in an art object by conferring meaning to hitherto unintelligible impressions. In both cases, however, art involvement requires an active use of cultural resources.

Given the importance of cultural resources for participation in high culture, which social conditions are favorable for the acquisition of cultural competence? There are at least three settings that merit attention: (1) primary social relations, especially the family as an agent of early socialization, (2) institutions with an, at least, partially educational function, like schools and certain mass media, and (3) participation in high culture itself, providing opportunities for acquiring command of aesthetic codes.

A culturally rich environment at home is probably the main source for the acquisition of cultural resources. In most cases, the transmission of the knowledge of codes from parents to their children comes about in a diffuse way and remains unacknowledged by the receiver (Bourdieu, 1983:198). Whether the subsequent transmission of this kind of knowledge, is effective in the context of schools and other educational institutions depends on the degree to which the command of codes has been learned previously in the context of primary relations. A student who, is completely unfamiliar with the enjoyment derived from art objects due to his background does not understand what lessons in the history of art and literature are all about. His family background works as a threshold for his participation in high culture that is not easily demolished.

However, once an initial stock of cultural resources is acquired, using one's command of codes in cultural activities may result in a continuous accumulation of cultural resources at one's disposal. Stigler and Becker demonstrate that in the same way as consumers in general accumulate "consumption capital," consumers of classical music accumulate "music human capital" through learning by doing. According to their new theory of consumer choice, music appreciation depends on the time allocated to music and the music human capital a person has at his disposal, such that an increase in music capital increases the productivity of time spent listening to music (Stigler and Becker, 1977:78).

If attending arts events not only requires the command of aesthetic codes in order to derive pleasure from these events, but at the same time produces a greater understanding and a better knowledge of the codes relevant for aesthetic experiences, then it is an important source for cultural resources. This source is open to everybody once an initial threshold has been passed. How this initial threshold can be overcome, other than by being reared by parents in a culturally rich environment, will be discussed later.

Which social conditions are favorable for experiencing pleasure through art involvement? Following the reasoning presented earlier about the two goals all human beings are striving for, it seems plausible to assume that people are less inclined to seek physical well-being of the pleasure kind the more they experience physical well-being of the comfort kind. Since comfort is strongly related to wealth and to upper class positions, people living in material comfort and occupying high social positions are hardly dependent on artistic enjoyment as a means of realizing physical well-being. Naturally this does not mean that upper class people do not participate in cultural activities—empirical data clearly show that they do. It means only that people living in comfort display a lower level of cultural participation than less privileged people, under the condition that the amount of cultural resources at their disposal is the same for both groups.

For those less privileged with regard to comfort who seek physical well-being through pleasing experiences, it is plausible to expect that the more pleasure they experience from stimulations provided by their work, their living accommodations, or their social relations, the less they are dependent on cultural participation as a means of realizing physical well-being through pleasure. This expectation also applies only when people of the same level of cultural competence are compared.

Social Aspects of Cultural Participation

Cultural activities also serve goals other than enjoyment of aesthetic experience: they confer status and may procure behavioral confirmation. Cultural activities differ with regard to the extent in which they are status enhancing; the specific activities that confer status to the greatest extent vary with time and place. In the Netherlands, empirical data suggest that one actually gains greater status by going to concerts where classical music is played or by attending traditional theater productions; popular reading confers the least status (Ganzeboom, 1986). Conversely, all kinds of cultural participation can, in principle, procure behavioral confirmation to the same degree. Whether this will occur, in fact (i.e., whether a person has the idea of engaging in the "right" kind of activities) depends solely on the behavior of the other group members and on the social norms operative in the group.

What can be said about social conditions conducive to gaining status and/or receiving behavioral confirmation through participation in high culture? In view of the argument previously presented, some hypotheses can be formulated.

For people belonging to low-status groups, status is the least available means (compared with behavioral confirmation and positive affect) to obtain social approval. On the other hand, those belonging to high-status groups can easily attain social approval; if they want more, they have to turn to behavioral confirmation or positive affect. However, the situation differs for those of the middle class. For this group, it is reasonable to expect gains in social approval by engaging in status-enhancing activities. Furthermore, the uneasiness created by a middle-class position (being subordinate and superordinate at the same time) strengthens tendencies of upward mobility. Under these circumstances, behavioral confirmation will not be sought so much by social relations with persons of the same middle-class positions but more by reference to the behavior of high-status people. Thus for members of the middle class, the importance of engaging in status-procuring cultural activities as means of acquiring social approval will be enhanced.

Another condition favorable for status attainment through cultural participation is social isolation. Without a certain amount of informal interaction, neither behavioral confirmation nor positive affect can be used as sources of social approval. The only source of social approval remaining is status. However, social isolation will have this effect on participation in arts events only, if other conditions favoring art involvement—especially the degree of cultural competence—are the same.

With regard to the social conditions relevant for the realization of behavioral confirmation, two have been specified earlier: membership in normatively integrated groups and, producing an effect in the opposite direction, being part of functional systems (i.e., interaction systems structured by mutual role expectations). Membership in culturally active groups provides a highly stimulating environment. However, a member of such a group not only gets the enjoyment derived from the cultural activities themselves, but, in addition, will gain social approval in the form of behavioral confirmation; the higher the normative integration of the group, the greater the degree of behavioral confirmation. Exclusive art circles illustrate this twofold gratification through pleasure and behavioral confirmation. However, this effect of normative integration on cultural participation will be less for those people located in functional systems such as bureaucratic or business organizations (managers, public service clerks).

Educational Attainment and Participation in High Culture

In empirical research educational attainment has been proven to be a good predictor of participation in high culture, even where the theoretical interpretation of this empirical relationship is not given. In light of the argument expressed in the preceding sections, what can be said about the validity of educational attainment as a rough indicator for a variety of social conditions conducive to art involvement?

Before this question can be answered, the hypothesized effects of social conditions on art involvement have to be summarized and related to each other. What overall picture arises from the preceding sections?

When one looks for the constellation of social conditions favorable to the attainment of pleasure, status, or behavioral confirmation through participation in cultural activities, it appears that people belonging to the upper middle and lower upper class are structurally in the most advantageous position for participation; the attainment of pleasure, status or behavioral confirmation is greater if people are integrated in culturally active informal groups and the more they belong to the professional classes instead of being managers or bureaucrats.

This advantage, however, is not a sufficient condition for participation in high culture. The structurally induced inclination to the realization of physical well-being and social approval through art involvement must be matched by cultural competence (especially the command of aesthetic codes) in order to gain access to art objects and events. Thus, people who grow up in a culturally rich environment have a clear lead over those who did not obtain a cultural education from their parents. However, those who have—for idiosyncratic reasons—developed a habit of art involvement will in time have accumulated a certain amount of cultural resources, because participation not only uses but, at the same time, also produces "human capital" (Stigler and Becker, 1977).

There is still another aspect of cultural participation: *costs*. In general, cultural activities are not only rather time consuming, but most of them are also bound to those hours of the day in which many alternative uses of time are available. This means that engaging in cultural activities makes great demands on one's time. Since there is an inverse relationship between discretionary time and income (Linder, 1970), people with the highest incomes are under the greatest time pressure and are, therefore (as members of the harried leisure class), not in a position to participate to a great extent in high culture.

There is, however, a factor working in the opposite direction, namely that a high income is associated with high cultural competence. Thus, people who have cultural competence gain more aesthetic enjoyment from arts events than those with little competence can gain from these same events. This means that the *time costs* incurred by a person with a high income through cultural activities are *compensated* with high benefits from the same activities if that person is also culturally competent.

I now return to my earlier stated question: how valid is educational attainment as an indicator for the social conditions favoring participation in high culture?

To begin with, the conclusion from empirical research that formal educational attainment is the best predictor we have of a person's participation in the arts and cultural activities (Dimaggio and Useem, 1980: 68), has not been undermined by our theoretical analysis. Education is a rough indicator for class position, which, in turn—so the argument states—structurally induces the inclination to realize physical well-being and social approval by means of cultural participation. Nevertheless, schools are not the only, or even the most important, places where cultural competences are acquired, the claims of naive educators notwithstanding.

However, knowledge of a person's educational attainment does not provide cues about other social conditions that also affect art involvement. Knowing the educational level of a person still leaves many issues unanswered: whether this person belongs to the professional classes or to the group of managers and bureaucrats, whether one has been reared in a culturally rich milieu, whether one is integrated into culturally active informal groups, and whether one has, for reasons other than family background or training in school (e.g., loyalty toward friends or identification with an otherwise significant other), frequently attended arts events and thereby built up a stock of cultural capital.

But it is exactly those conditions for which formal educational attainment cannot serve as an indicator that allow a differentiation within the upper middle and upper class between the culturally active part of these classes and the remainder. In light of the theoretical analyses of the preceding sections, it seems doubtful whether this differentiation within the higher social strata has led in our society to the emergence of a identifiable new "cultural" elite alongside of the established politico-economic elite, as was contended by Bourdieu (Bourdieu, 1984). Apparently, Bourdieu did generalize some particularities of intellectual circles in France. The theoretical argument points only to the existence of highly integrated informal groups of culturally competent people. If members of these groups consider themselves to be a "new elite," their claim would have to be recognized by outsiders before the conclusion could be drawn that, in fact, a new elite has emerged. As long as this is not the case, this new elite will not play the role in society it apparently would like to play.

Conclusion

In this chapter, I have set out to elucidate the mechanisms that lie behind the empirical generalization regarding the effect of formal educational attainment on participation in high culture. This has been done with the help of the behavioral principles of rational choice theory, supplemented by assumptions about goals, resources, and social conditions. The theoretical discussions led to a specification of a constellation of social conditions conducive to cultural participation and art involvement.

A comparison of this theoretically derived constellation of circumstances with conditions characterizing people with high educational attainment shows a certain overlap of these two sets of conditions, notably with respect to class position. As far as this overlap is concerned, the theoretical analysis can claim to have given an answer to the question stated in the first section, "why schooling is such a good predictor of aesthetic and artistic interest and participation" (Dimaggio and Useem, 1980).

This rational choice explanation is only outlined and requires further elaboration. The theoretical analysis, however, has yielded more. On the one hand, it points to conditions under which formal educational attainment will have a much weaker effect on cultural participation than would have been generally thought. The effect of education will be less pronounced for those who have high-level positions in industry and public service, whose parents did not care about cultural participation, who had no other opportunities to acquire cultural competency, and who have no connection with culturally active circles.

On the other hand, the theoretical analysis also points to conditions under which the effect of education will be stronger than average. The effect of educational attainment on participation in high culture will be most pronounced for people belonging to the professional classes, who come from cultivated homes and are involved in artistic groups, and who are privileged because of the high returns they get out of their investments in cultural activities.

References

Becker, G.S. (1976). *The Economic Approach to Human Behavior*. Chicago: University of Chicago Press.
Berlyne, D.E. (ed.) (1974). *Studies in the New Experimental Aesthetics*, New York: Wiley.
Berlyne, D.E. and K.B. Madsen. (1973). *Pleasure, Reward, Preference*. New York: Academic Press.
Boudon, R. (1981). *The Logic of Social Action*, London: Routledge & Kegan Paul.
Bourdieu, P. (1970). "Elemente zu einer soziologischen Theorie der Kunstwahrnehmung," Pp. 159–201 in P. Bourdieu, ed., *Zur Soziologie der symbolischen Formen*. Frankfurt a.M.: Suhrkamp.
Bourdieu, P. (1983). "ökonomischen Kapital, kulturelles Kapital, soziales Kapital," Pp. 183–198 in R. Kreckel, Eds., *Soziale Ungleichheiten*. Göttingen: Schwartz.
Bourdieu, P. (1984). *Distinction: A Social Critique of the Judgment of Taste*. Cambridge, MA: Harvard University Press.
DiMaggio, P. (1982). "Cultural capital and school success." *American Sociological Review* 47:189–201.
DiMaggio P. and J. Mohr. (1985). "Cultural capital, educational attainment, and marital selection, *American Journal of Sociology* 90:1231–1261.
DiMaggio P. and M. Useem. (1980). "The arts in education and cultural participation: The social role of aesthetic education and the arts. *Journal of Aesthetic Education* 14:55–72.
Elster, J. (1979). *Ulysses and the Sirens*. Cambridge: Cambridge University Press.
Elster, J. (1985). *Making Sense of Marx*. Cambridge: Cambridge University Press.
Fokkema, D.W. (1982). "A semiotic definition of aesthetic experience and the period code of modernism. *Poetics Today* 3:61–79.
Fokkema, D.W. (1984). *Literary History, Modernism, and Postmodernism*. Philadelphia: Benjamin.

Fokkema, D.W. (1985). "The concept of code in the study of literature." *Poetics Today* 6:643–656.
Ganzeboom, H.B.G. (1986). "Een individueel keuzemodel voor cultuur-deelname." Unpublished manuscript.
Gombrich, E.H. (1979). *The Sense of Order*. Oxford: Phaidon Press.
Gombrich, E.H. (1982). *The Image and the Eye*. Ithaca: Cornell University Press.
Heckhausen, H. (1980). *Motivation und Handeln*. Berlin: Springer Verlag.
Lin, N. (1982). "Social resources and instrumental action." Pp. 131–145 in P.V. Marsden and N. Lin, eds., *Social Structure and Network Analysis*. Beverly Hills: Sage Publications.
Lindenberg, S. (1980). "Instigation of and participation in revolts and revolutions: An analysis of Marx's possible contribution to this problem and analysis of an alternative. Unpublished manuscript.
Lindenberg, S. (1984). "Normen und die Allokation sozialer Wertschätzung." Pp. 169–191 in H. Todt Ed., *Normengeleitetes Verhalten in den Sozialwissenschaften*. Berlin: Duncker & Humblot.
Lindenberg, S. (1986). "The paradox of privatization in consumption. Pp. 297–310 in A. Diekmann and P. Mitter, eds., *Paradoxical Effects of Social Behavior*. Heidelberg: Physica-Verlag.
Linder, S.B. (1970). *The Harried Leisure Class*. New York: Columbia University Press.
Pommerehne W.P. and B.S. Frey (1985). "Kunst: Was sagt der Ökonom dazu? *Schweizerische Zeitschrift für Volkswirtschaft und Statistik*, pp. 139–167.
Scitovsky, T. (1976a). "What's wrong with the arts is what's wrong with society." Pp. 58–69 in M. Blaug, ed., *The Economics of the Arts*, London: Martin Robertson.
Scitovsky, T. (1976b). *The Joyless Economy*. Oxford: Oxford University Press.
Stigler G.J. and G.S. Becker. (1977). "De Gustibus Non Est Disputandum," *The American Economic Review* 67:76–90.

9

The Welfare State and Unemployment: A Theoretical Analysis

Henk de Vos

Introduction: Unemployment in the 1930's and the 1980's

In the 1970's and in the early 1980's in most Western countries unemployment figures rose to levels unheard of in the postwar period. In response to this unexpected development social scientists returned to almost forgotten subjects of interest: The study of how people experience and respond to job-loss and long-term unemployment. A research tradition that started in the economic depression of the 1930's (Bakke, 1940a, 1940b; Jahoda, Lazarsfeld and Zeisel, 1960 [first edition 1933]; Komarovsky, 1940) was abandoned in the postwar decennia of economic growth. Much of the research focused on the problem of identifying individual effects of unemployment, on mental health, life satisfaction, social participation, leisure behavior, social networks, marriage-partner relationship, school performances of children, political attitudes, self-esteem, etc., (see O'Brien, 1988; Furnham and Lewis, 1986, Chapter 7).

A recurrent theme in the recent literature is whether the institutional and social changes occurring between the 1930's and the 1980's had any effects on the impact of job loss and unemployment, and on the behavior of the unemployed. One answer to this question focuses on the institutional developments since the 1930's, particularly the rise of the welfare state. Proponents of this view claim that the social security systems of the welfare states, which were almost completely absent in the 1930's, have fostered voluntary nonemployment. For example, Mead (1986) argues that the high replacement rates in welfare states (the ratios of the size of unemployment benefits and welfare payments to net-earnings from available jobs), especially regarding unskilled, low-income jobs, result in people leaving menial jobs and therefore staying unemployed for longer periods. Because the replacement rates were much lower in the 1930's, it is supposed that there was much less voluntary unemployment. This implies that job loss and unemployment is a lesser hardship nowadays than it was in the 1930's. This view has one shortcoming: it suggests that only monetary aspects are important or that other aspects, such as, the social consequences of job loss and unemployment, have not changed.

Jahoda (1982), one of the authors of the famous study of the Marienthal community in the 1930's, calls attention to the different monetary and nonmonetary consequences of unemployment. According to her, the unemployed not only are deprived of the "manifest" aspects of work, such as earning a living, but also of various "latent" aspects, such as: (1) the provision of a time structure for the waking day, (2) social contact with people other than family members and immediate neighbors, (3) a sense of "collective" purpose, (4) social status and personal identity, and (5) an opportunity for engaging in regular activity (Jahoda, 1982:83). One would expect that her discussion about the different consequences of unemployment is based on an analysis of this inventory of job aspects, and on hypotheses about changes in these job aspects from the 1930's to the 1980's. This, however, is not the case. Jahoda conjectures that, in contrast to the 1930's, the unemployed in the 1980's (1) suffer less absolute deprivation (due to more generous public assistance): (2) have higher job aspirations and blame themselves less (due to increased education and decreased social distance to middle-class and rich people [Jahoda, 1982:33–38]) and therefore, (3) have less resignation and apathy (Jahoda, 1982:98). These conclusions are based on hypotheses about the effects of increased education, rather than on an analysis of changes of the latent, non-monetary aspects of work. Although Jahoda stresses the importance of the non-monetary aspects of work, no implications about the different consequences of unemployment are derived from this source.

The debate over the welfare state could be advanced by explicitly considering implications of the non-monetary aspects of work. The comparison between the 1930's and the 1980's cannot be limited to institutional characteristics such as earnings-replacement ratios, but has to be extended to other characteristics relevant to the non-monetary aspects of work. We have to deal with social changes since the 1930's that could have influenced the degree to which work is a source of positively valued social contacts.

By applying a behavioral model in which money, income, and social amenities are all included, it is possible to take the social as well as monetary value of jobs into account. Becker's theory of social interactions is just such a model (Becker, 1976). It is used here to derive predictions about various responses to job loss under two different sets of institutional and social conditions: first, in which the monetary value of a job is high and the social value low, a situation characterizing the 1930's, and second in which the monetary value is low and the social value high, a situation characterizing the 1980's.

Becker's Theory of Social Interactions

Utility in Becker's theory is equivalent to the degree to which people dispose of basic commodities. Basic commodities are the primary objects of choice from which utility is directly obtained. They are produced with market goods and services, on the one hand, and characteristics of a person's social environment, on the other hand. Characteristics of a social environment are the amount of esteem or blame given by other persons, the opportunities for social contact, social support, and so forth. I consider one commodity, social well-being, that is produced with a single market good and a single characteristic of others: the degree to which others provide opportunities for social contact, called the (positively valued) social environment. Then,

$$U_i = Z(x, R), \qquad (1)$$

is the utility function of person i, Z stands for the commodity well-being, x for market good and R for the positively valued social environment. R consists of two additive components: an endowment part, D_i, and a part h which is dependent on i's efforts:

$$R = D_i + h. \qquad (2)$$

D_i is i's social endowment. The budget constraint for money income is

$$p_x x + p_R h = I_i, \qquad (3)$$

where I_i is i's money income, $p_x X$ is the amount he spends on x given the price p_x and $p_R h$ the amount he spends on R given the price p_R. Since $R - D_i = h$, (3) can be rewritten as

$$p_x x + p_R R = I_i + p_R D_i = S_i. \qquad (4)$$

The right-hand side represents i's social income (S_i), consisting of his

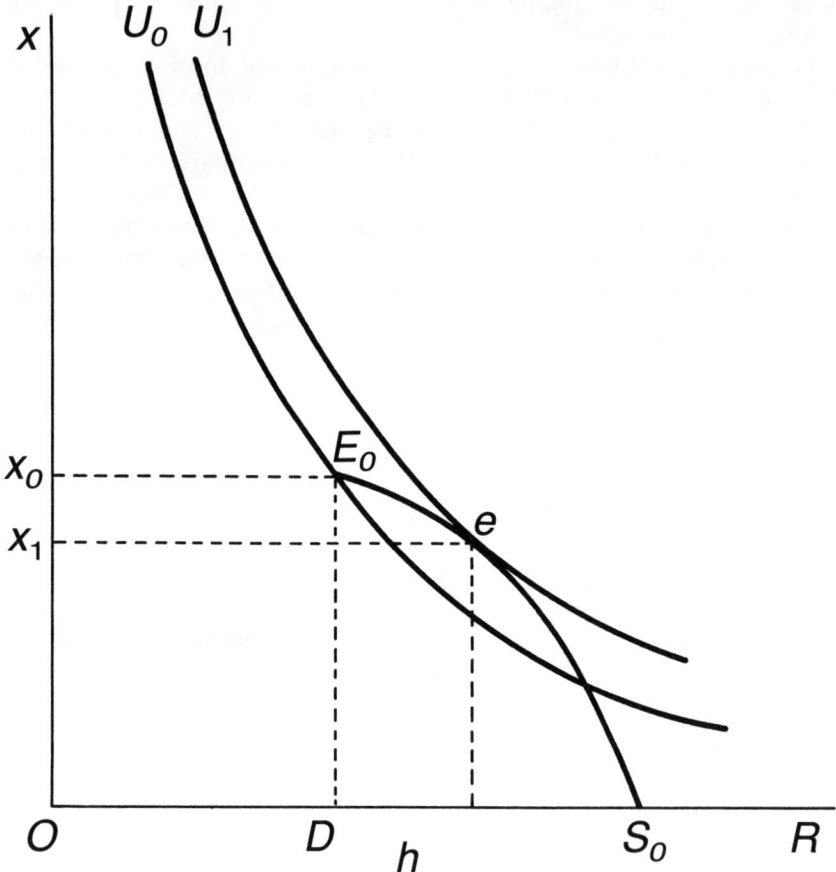

Figure 9.1. Equilibrium position according to social interaction theory. x = market good; R = positive characteristics of others; E_0 = endowed point; e = equilibrium (adapted from: Becker, 1976:258)

money income and the value to him of his social environment. The left-hand side represents his spendings, partly on good x and partly on his social environment.

Figure 9.1 shows i's equilibrium position. If OD is i's social endowment and x_0 his income (in terms of x) then E_0 is the endowed point. It represents i's utility when he spends nothing of his income on his social environment. If we represent i's opportunities for purchasing additional R with the budget line E_0S_0 (assuming a decreasing marginal productivity of spendings on R), then i maximizes his utility by moving to point e_0, where the slope of the budget curve is equal to the slope of the indifference curve U_i. h_0 is the amount of R he purchases and his spendings on x decrease from O_{x_0} to O_{x_1}.

To be able to apply the theory to the problem of the responses to job loss, the monetary and non-monetary aspects of work must be related to the theory. Of course this is, easy for the monetary aspect: having a job provides an income that is spent on x and R. The following section deals with the non-monetary aspects of work.

The Social Value of Work

Jahoda's list of latent functions of work is one of several approaches to the problem of the relation between job or work attributes and job satisfaction, psychological well-being or mental health. These approaches are brought together by Warr (1987a) in nine principal job features, including "availability of money," which have been shown to influence affective well-being of workers. The other eight features are opportunity for control and skill use, provision of goals and task demands, provision of variety and environmental clarity, provision of physical security, opportunity for interpersonal contact and provision of a valued social position. The value of work in general, and of each type of job in particular, can be characterized by a combination of values of each of these characteristics. Job loss and unemployment can be characterized in the same way: as a loss of these valued goods to the degree that the same goods are not provided by nonemployment (Warr, 1987b).

The social value of work is represented by two features, interpersonal contact and valued social position. The latter, however, is strongly conditioned by the monetary aspect. It is not work *per se* that provides a valued social position, but work that is scarce enough to yield monetary rewards. Therefore, I ignore this characteristic and consider opportunities for social contact as constituting the social value of work.

The workplace can be considered as one of the foci around which joint activities are organized. Other foci are voluntary organizations, hangouts, families, and so forth (Feld, 1981). Individuals whose activities are organized around the same focus have frequent social contact and tend to become interpersonally tied. Although there are exceptions (such as bridge-tenders), a significant part of the total number of social contacts an employed adult has consists of contacts with co-workers during working hours. Co-workers can also become a part of a person's social network. Jackson et al. (1977:51) found that 26% of the friendships of working adult males living in primary families in the urbanized sections of the Detroit metropolitan area had the workplace as their source (7% kinship, 20% childhood, 23% neighborhood and 7% voluntary associations). Fischer (1982), whose working adult respondents were scattered among a wide variety of largely urban industries and occupations, also found a considerable degree of co-worker involvement. The average number of co-workers in the respondent's personal social network was 1.8 (the same average number for close kin, 4.3; for other kin, 3.4; for neighbors, 1.9; for voluntary organization members, 1.1; for "just friends," 4.9; and for "other," 1.1) (Fischer, 1982:41).

Although co-workers can become friends, in general, relations with co-workers are not very strong or intimate. Bell and Boat (1956) compared the kind of contacts employed adult men had with their neighbors, co-workers, relative and friends (who were neither neighbors, co-workers or relatives). The frequency of informal contact with co-workers (outside of work) was similar to contacts with neighbors and much less than contacts with relatives and friends. There were fewer informal gatherings at home with co-workers than with members of the three other categories. Also, co-workers (and neighbors) were less called on for care in case of sickness than relatives and friends. A similar pattern is reported in Jackson et al. (1977). Relationships based on work had less frequency of contact (outside the work setting) and were perceived as less intimate than those based on kin and childhood. Although those personal networks based on work ties had a higher degree of density, intimacy and density were not associated for friends from the workplace (Jackson et al., 1977:51–54).

These data indicate that co-worker relationships are a special kind of *weak ties* (Granovetter, 1973). Weak ties are characterized by a low degree of intimacy, dominance of balanced (instead of general) reciprocity, a low density of the parts of the network containing weak ties and restricted ranges of physical and temporal contexts (Adelman, Parks and Albrecht, 1987; Sahlins, 1972). Co-worker relationships have all these characteristics except low density. Therefore, it can be stated that the social value of work is equal to the value of the weak ties that are indissolubly connected with work.

Adelman, Parks,and Albrecht (1987) identify four support functions associated with weak ties: extending access to information, goods and services; promoting social comparison with dissimilar others; facilitating low-risk discussion of high-risk topics, and fostering a sense of community. It seems likely that ties between co-workers indeed have these functions. Although they are generally dense, co-worker ties are not strong and therefore can function as bridges to other networks, providing several kinds of useful information, for example, about sales or new products. Because co-workers are generally dissimilar in several respects (such as in family and cultural background), they provide social comparisons which facilitate self-evaluation. Because co-worker ties are generally not connected with one's strong ties, they provide opportunities to discuss topics that one would rather not, or could not discuss with strong ties (e.g., because of the need for other opinions). Last, because co-worker ties bring a person into contact with a larger social world, they foster identification with a larger community, which enhances feelings of safety and togetherness. Apart from these support functions, co-workers are people with whom one can gossip and exchange information.

It seems safe to conclude that ties with co-workers, a special kind of weak ties, can be a significant part of people's social environment. Among its other effects unemployment causes a loss of these ties and therefore produces, ceteris paribus, a decline of social well-being.

Social Environment and Work in *Bethnal Green* and *Woodford*

Depending on the kinds of social conditions a person lives within, the relative contribution of work to his social well-being (the social value of his job) varies. This becomes clear if we have a closer look at the endowed part of a person's social environment. The major part of a social endowment consists in strong ties, especially ties to close kin. Because these ties are characterized by general reciprocity, a person maintains them without much effort. In this respect co-worker ties of employed people are similar: having a job usually means that you have colleagues in your social environment. Therefore, for an employed person co-worker ties—although typically they are weak—are a part of the person's social endowment. Let us assume that social endowments consist of a part due to strong ties (family members and close kin) and a part due to weak ties (for employed people this can be co-worker ties). Then, if $D_{i(w)}$ is the weak ties-part and $D_{i(s)}$ is the strong ties-part of D_i,

$$D_i = D_{i(w)} + D_{i(s)} \tag{5}$$

I will introduce a distinction between two sets of social conditions, which are labeled *Bethnal Green*, representing the 1930's, and *Woodford*, representing the 1980's. Bethnal Green is a set of conditions that has the social characteristics of the London borough of this name at the time it was studied (between 1953 and 1955) by Young and Willmott (1977). I understand that their description of this working-class borough is a reasonable approximation of districts during the 1930's in which unemployed people lived. Woodford stands for the social characteristics of the London suburb of this name as described by Willmott and Young (1967). Woodford was also studied in the 1950's and was selected in order to determine whether it would have a different, more "modern," kind of family and community life than Bethnal Green. I assume that the description of this suburb is a reasonable approximation of districts in the 1980's in which unemployed people lived.

Bethnal Green is characterized by a low degree of mobility; therefore long-standing residence is typical. People live in localized extended families. Often, married couples not only have their parents living in the same district, but also siblings and other relatives. Although there is a high frequency of contact between members of the same extended family (with the mother in a central position), kinship ties do not exclude ties to outsiders, but are important means of promoting them. For each person, members of his extended family are links to their acquaintances and neighbors and to other families. There is a network of local attachments based on the combination of long-standing residence and localized kinship. People's endowment of strong ties does not isolate them from the outside world, but is on the contrary an important source of weak ties. There is a high probability of belonging to a series of small and overlapping groups, and active social life can be attained without much effort. Bethnal Greeners do not "have to make friends," their friends "are ready made" (Young and Willmott, 1977, Chapters 5 and 7; Willmott and Young, 1967, Chapters 9 and 11).

In social conditions like those of Bethnal Green, co-worker ties are an addition to an endowed large and rich network of strong *and* weak ties based on kinship and vicinity. People have a large social endowment of which co-worker ties are but a small part. $D_{i(s)}$ is a large proportion of D_i and $D_{i(w)}$ consists mainly of weak ties in the neighborhood. In other words, the social value of work is small and a neglegible part of i's social endowment.

Woodford is characterized by more short-standing residence and a much larger geographic distance between members of the wider family. Kinship plays a lesser role than it does in Bethnal Green. For married couples there is certainly no day-to-day interaction with parents, siblings or relatives. Meetings with relatives are specially arranged and are less frequent. Sociability in Woodford is institutionalized and based on membership in clubs, churches and other voluntary organizations. People in Woodford have to work harder to keep their friends. You have to show that you are worthy of being a friend, you have to be "the right sort of person, have a decently furnished home . . . speak with the right accent, be neatly dressed . . . have a readiness to engage in conversation . . ." (Willmott and Young, 1967:112). If you do not meet the standards, you have fewer friends. In Woodford it is easier to be an isolate and class-based social divisions are more likely to exist. Where lower-class people are in a minority, as in Woodford, they have less of a social life outside the family than middle-class residents (Willmott and Young, 1967; Chapters 9 and 10).

The Welfare State and Unemployment

In social conditions like those in Woodford, people have a small kinship-based network of strong ties. So $D_{i(s)}$ is smaller than in Bethnal Green. Further, the strong kinship ties, do not function as intermediates to new friends or acquaintances (weak ties) because of larger distances and infrequent contacts. Therefore, if there is a vicinity-based network of weak ties, it does not have the character of an endowment at all. Friends have to be made and sustained by club membership contributions, expenses to keep up social status, and other costs of conformity. For employed people, however, work-based ties contribute to the social endowment. So the vicinity-based weak ties disappear from i's social endowment, which consists only of few kinshp ties and of work-based weak ties. Not only is D_i smaller, but the social value of work is a larger proportion of D_i than in Bethnal Green.

With constant monetary income, the effects of the different characteristics of Bethnal Green and Woodford on i's equilibrium are represented in Fig. 9.2. As a consequence of the smaller social endowment in Woodford (OD^W) than in Bethnal Green (OD^B), when living in Woodford, i finds himself at a lower indifference curve (U_w) than in Bethnal Green (U^B).

Becoming Unemployed

Disregarding for the moment the direct monetary consequences of becoming unemployed, the social consequences when i lives in Woodford are shown in Fig. 9.3. Job loss in Bethnal Green has little neglegible effect on i's social environment. Therefore, i's position is the same as in Fig. 9.2 (e^B).

In Woodford a much larger part of i's social endowment consists of his work-related social contacts. Therefore, unemployment results in a position at a given point far to the left, where a very large proportion of i's social contacts have to be purchased (e^w). All things being equal, unemployment in Woodford produces a larger decrease of social income than unemployment in Bethnal Green.

Effects of Institutional Contexts

I will now introduce different institutional contexts for the two social conditions: a pre-welfare state context for Bethnal Green and a welfare state context for Woodford.

A pre-welfare state institutional context is characterized by:

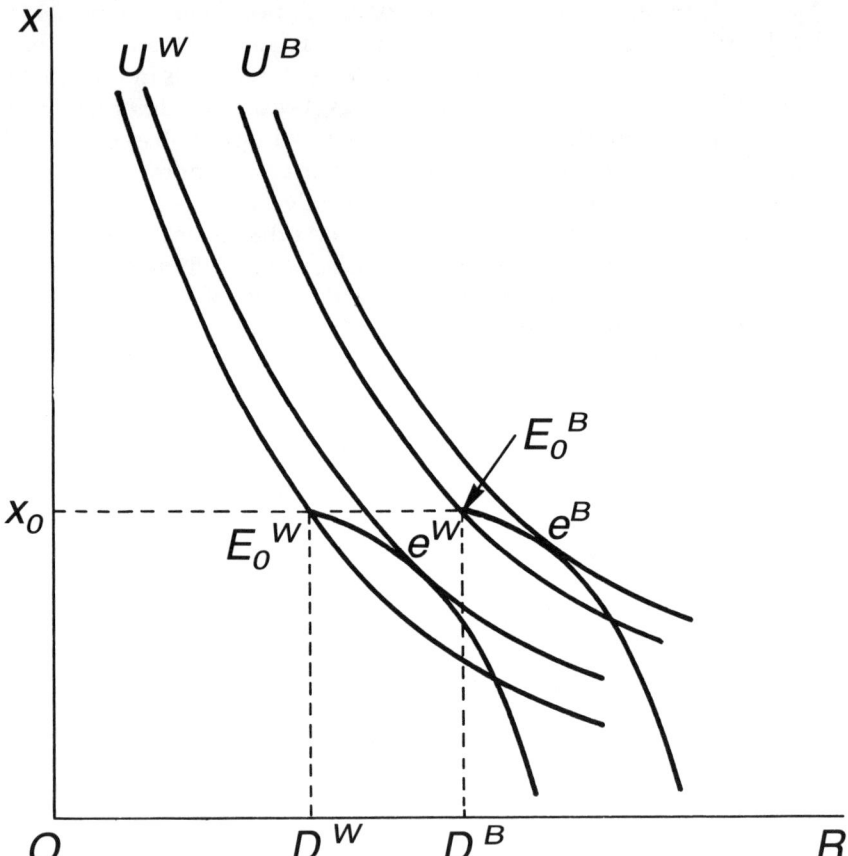

Figure 9.2. Equilibrium of a person with income x_0 living in Woodford (e^W) and living in Bethnal Green (e^B) OD^W = social endowment in Woodford; OD^B = social endowment in Bethnal Green

1. no unemployment benefits or a small maximum duration of benefits with a small earnings-replacement ratio [according to data reported in Egginton (1987), in England these ratios, although rising substantially during the interwar period, were (in the 1930's) well below the standard of the 1970's and 1980's];
2. a means-tested assistance-program (such as the one described by Bakke [1940]):

- with standard budgets that do not provide for spendings on items such as recreation, education and benevolence;

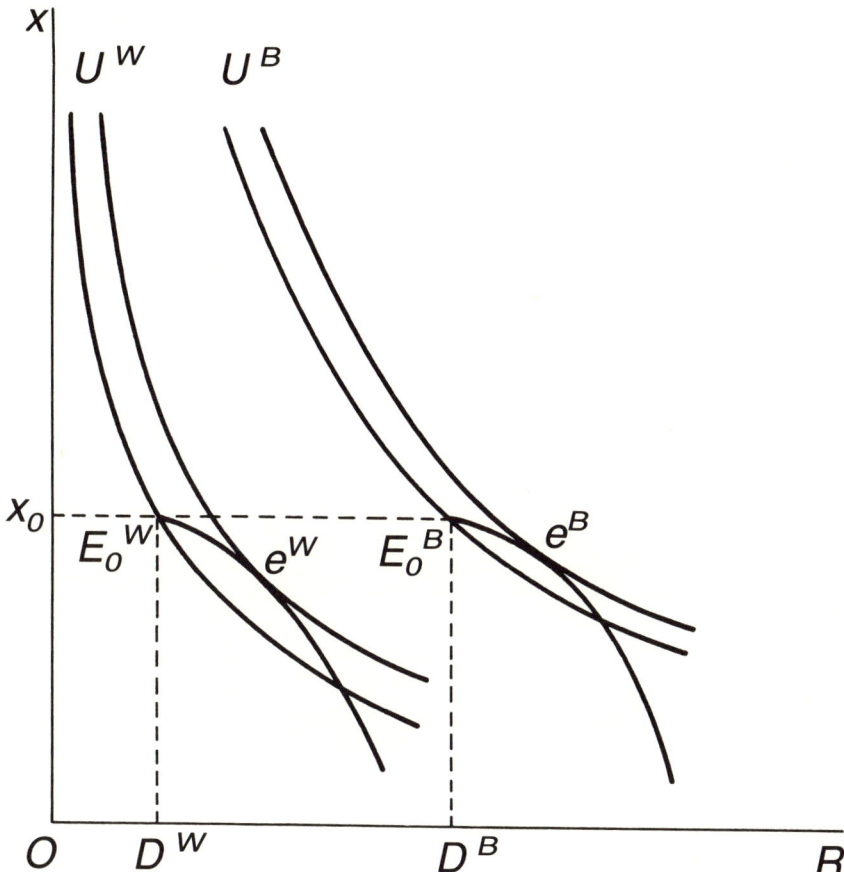

Figure 9.3. Equilibrium of an unemployed person living in Woodford (e^W) and living in Bethnal Green (e^B)

- with partial allowances given in cash, clothing only given as needed and items such as transportation and household expenses not automatically granted;

- with free medical service only in emergencies and bills to be paid by the family or relatives;

- without rent subsidies, implying the necessity of moving if rent can no longer be paid.

This institutional context may be interpreted as having a virtual *absence of a monetary endowment;* therefore work has a high monetary value.

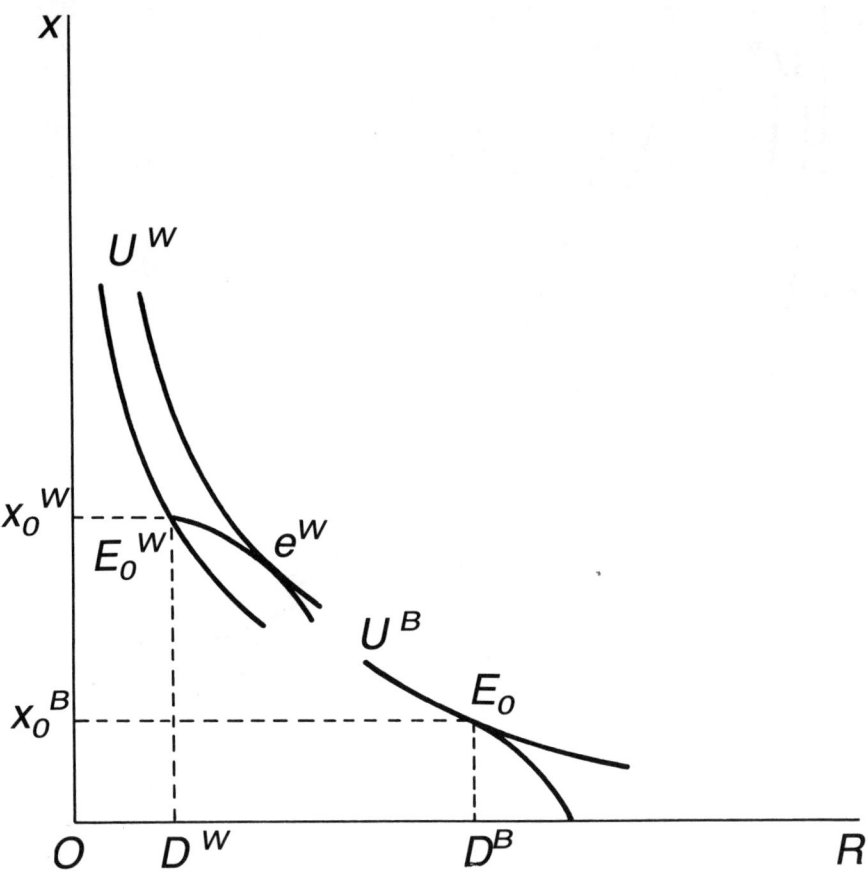

Figure 9.4. Equilibrium of an unemployed person living in welfare state Woodford (e^W) and living in pre-welfare state Bethnal Green (E_0)

If i lives in Bethnal Green and becomes unemployed, his monetary income falls to a very low level, for example x_0^B in Fig. 9.4, a level at which only the barest material necessities are affordable. This extremely low monetary income level, together with a large social endowment, produces an endowed point E_0 in the south-eastern region of the Figure. Here i's indifference curve has a smaller slope than his budget curve: i stays in his endowed position, and no amount of social contacts is purchased. Hence he completely depends on his family and relatives and perhaps on some family-related weak ties. This is the social circle in which i has already spent most of his life. If his unemployment is not of a long duration, i's main problems are to subsist financially and, if most of his relatives and friends are employed, to fight boredom during working-hours. If i becomes a victim of long-term unemployment, things may change. Relatives are willing to help, in cash or in kind, or by letting i's family move in ("doubling up"), or by taking in their young children (e.g., Keyssar, 1986:164). However, the relatives' jobs may be terminated and in the long run, the relatives will expect something in return for their kindness, at least gratitude and humility. These expectations produce informal pressure to search for and accept jobs, even menial or distant ones.

The welfare state institutional context of Woodford is characterized by:

1. a much longer maximum duration of unemployment benefits and a higher earnings-replacement ratio;
2. more lenient means-tested assistance programs with unlimited duration, and a higher earnings-replacement ratio;
3. several other benefits, such as, children's allowances, scholarship programs, income-dependent rent-subsidies, national health insurance acts and/or national health services.

In its entirety this can be interpreted as the *provision of a monetary endowment*. This endowment is taken into account in Fig. 9.4: i's monetary income if he lives in Woodford and is unemployed, x_0^w, has decreased slightly compared to the reduction he would have experienced in Bethnal Green. In consequence, i finds himself at the north-western region of the Figure and will move to a higher indifference curve by purchasing a certain amount of social contact. This movement can be interpreted as expenditure on reputation and respectability (socially induced expenses on such items as clothing, house decoration, gardening and furniture), on participation in voluntary organizations, clubs, and so forth, as well as helping, inviting and entertaining friends. If, for some reason, i's budget curve were steeper, he would be in danger of becoming socially isolated. Factors that affect the slope of the budget curve are discussed in the following section.

In summary, the theory allows us to derive the implications of living in different institutional contexts. The nonwelfare state institutions of Bethnal Green produce a large monetary and a small social loss for the unemployed, together with strong monetary and social incentives to search for and accept jobs. The welfare state context of Woodford produces a small monetary loss and a large social loss for the unemployed.

Opportunities to Purchase Social Contacts

The unemployed person living in Woodford is expected to spend a part of his monetary income on social contacts, because it was assumed that the slope of his budget curve is less steep than the slope of his indifference curve. Whether this is actually so depends on several factors (for example, the relative price level of goods which serve to maintain respectability) as they are defined by current social norms. If fashionable clothes are relatively inexpensive and rents are low or subsidized to such a degree that enforced moving to lower cost housing can be avoided, it is cheaper to maintain respectability as a means to maintain social contacts. Social attributions regarding the causes of unemployment are important, as well. In periods of massive lay-offs, unemployed people are blamed less for their joblessness and are respected more than in times when unemployment is very rare. This was demonstrated in the Netherlands by Maassen and De Goede (1988:161-3) from 1980 to 1984, a period of dramatically increasing unemployment levels. In general, the budget curve will be less steep when status goods are cheaper and the unemployment level is higher.

Another interesting factor to consider is the sheer availability of people for social contact during normal working hours. The unemployed used to spend this time socializing with their weak ties at the workplace. The greater the number of non-working adults, the less costly it is to compensate for this social loss (hence the budget curve will not be as steep). It follows that, given a high unemployment level, unemployed people will have more unemployed or non-working people in their social network than employed people. A study comparing the unemployed and employed in the Netherlands during a period of high unemployment provides some evidence: more than 60% of the unemployed respondents had unemployed people among their family members or friends vs. somewhat less than 40% of the employed (Becker and Vink, 1984:50). In another Dutch study, data were gathered about changes in the social networks of long-term unemployed people. In the first year after job loss there was a net decline of contacts with non-working people, but in the following six years these contacts strongly increased and contacts with working people decreased (Sprengers and Tazelaar, 1988:24-5).

Voluntary Unemployment

The introduction of the social value of work has a straightforward but interesting implication for the conventional budget line analysis of work incentives. In the standard economic analysis of the effects of social security systems and wage rates on decisions to participate in the labor market, it is assumed that individuals optimize "hours worked" and "disposable income," given individual preferences and a budget con-

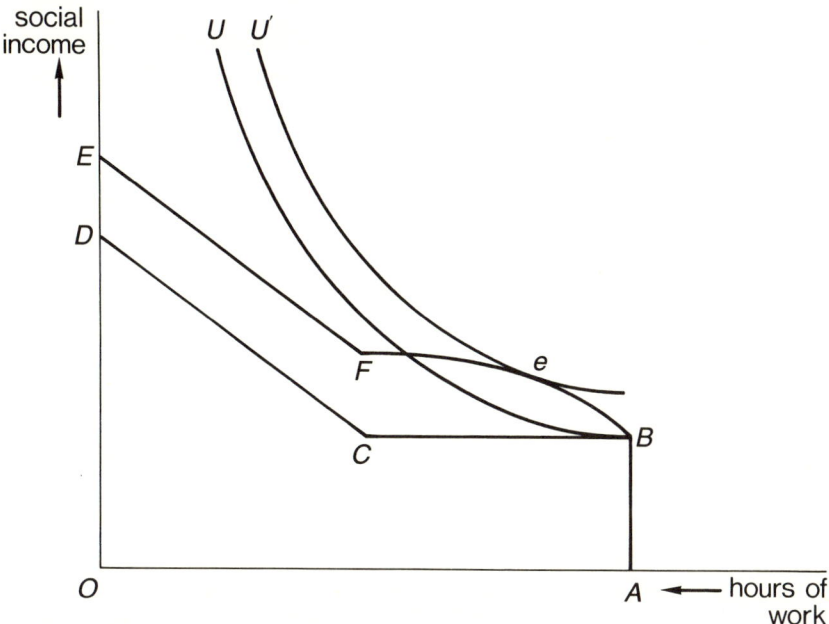

Figure 9.5. Optimization of "social income" and "hours of work" with a stylized welfare state budget line

straint with typical welfare state characteristics (e.g., Ehrenberg and Smith, 1987; Beenstock and Associates, 1987). A stylized budget constraint for a person living in Woodford is shown as the line $ABCD$ in Fig. 9.5, with hours of work from right to left on the horizontal axis and monetary income on the vertical axis. The plateau BC is a consequence of an unemployment benefit system where payments are reduced by $1 for every $1 dollar earned. Because of the plateau there is no incentive to work for a number of hours up to point C. A person with preferences like those of indifference curve U maximizes his utility in B with no hours of work. In a stylized version of the budget line under conditions like those of Bethnal Green, the plateau would be absent or much less conspicuous, and the monetary endowment AB would be very small. Budget line analysis shows that the replacement ratio with full-time work (AB/OD if point O represents full-time) is but one of several factors which determine the degree of voluntary unemployment (others being the length of the plateau, the wage rate, taxation, and, of course, preferences).

The social value of work is taken into account by simply adding it to the monetary income on the vertical axis, assuming that it has a monetary equivalent. This is the same as putting the sum of I and $p_R D$, which is the right-hand side of (4), on the vertical axis, thereby *introducing the time dimension* on the horizontal axis.

The social value of work will increase with the number of hours worked over a significant range of hours (e.g., from zero to four hours a day) thereafter remaining constant (*BFE* in Fig. 9.5). As a consequence, the optimimum of a person with preferences indicated by indifference curve U moves from B to e on the higher indifference curve U', as shown in Fig. 9.5. The negative effect of the "social security-plateau" on work incentives is thereby mitigated. The conclusion is that although the institutional characteristics of the Woodford conditions promote voluntary unemployment, the social characteristics have a positive effect on incentives to work. Which of the two effects dominates, is of course difficult to decide. However, the analysis implies that Woodford conditions produce a demand for part-time jobs, not on the basis of monetary incentives, as is the case under Bethnal Green conditions, but on the basis of social incentives.

Summary and Discussion

On the one hand, the debate over the welfare state is predominantly a debate about the effects of institutions. A well-known argument is that the social security systems of welfare states produce negative incentives to work and therefore maintain a significant degree of voluntary unemployment. On the other hand, it is argued that people in welfare states respond differently to unemployment than in the 1930's, because of increased education and decreased social distance between the unemployed and the employed. The first argument emphasizes the monetary aspect of work and job loss. The second argument rightly stresses that nonmonetary aspects also matter, but it is not based on a systematic analysis of the ways in which the nonmonetary aspects of work have changed since the 1930's. In this chapter I argue that the social value of work has increased. In order to study the effects of the introduction of welfare state institutions with due regard to the increased social value of work, a behavioral model should be used in which money income and social amenities are included. Becker's theory of social interactions is such a model.

Becker's theory was used to derive optima for unemployed people in two different sets of institutional and social conditions. The description of the social conditions was borrowed from Willmott and Young's well-known studies of two London boroughs: a traditional working-class district (Bethnal Green) and a modern suburb (Woodford). The different institutional conditions were introduced by placing Bethnal Green in a pre-welfare state context and Woodford in a welfare state context. From the theory, together with these different conditions, implications were derived about the unemployed's spendings on social contacts and on work incentives. The theory also predicts that several factors influencing the opportunities for social contacts affect responses to job loss, especially for the long-term unemployed. Finally, the time dimension, which was neglected by Becker, was introduced in the analysis. The Woodford conditions were shown to produce a demand for part-time jobs based on social incentives.

Are Bethnal Green and Woodford close enough approximations of the social environments of unemployed people in the 1930's and the 1980's? Of course this is not easy to decide. However, the average unemployed man in the 1930's probably had a larger social endowment of strong and weak ties based on kinship and vicinity than the average unemployed man in the 1980's. In addition, the well-known demographic trend of decreasing family size supports the assumption that people's social endowment of strong ties was larger in the 1930's than it is today.

REFERENCES

Adelman, Mara B., Malcolm R. Parks, and Terrance L. Albrecht. (1987). "Beyond close relationships: support in weak ties." Pp. 126–147 in Terrence L. Albrecht, and Mara B. Adelman, eds., *Communicating Social Support*. Newbury Park, NY: Sage Publications.

Bakke, E.W. (1940a). *The Unemployed Worker: A Study of the Task of Making a Living Without a Job*. New Haven: Yale University Press.

Bakke, E.W. (1940b). *Citizens Without Work: A Study of the Effects of Unemployment upon the Workers' Social Relations and Practices*. New Haven: Yale University Press.

Becker, J.W. and R. Vink. (1984). *Werklozen, Arbeidsongeschikten en Werkenden Vergeleken*. Rijswijk: Sociaal-cultureel Planbureau.

Becker, Gary S. (1976). *The Economic Approach to Human Behavior*. Chicago and London: University of Chicago Press.

Beenstock, Michael and Assoc. (1987). *Work, Welfare and Taxation: A Study of Labour Supply Incentives in the UK*. London: Allen & Unwin.

Bell, Wendell, and Marion D. Boat. (1956). "Urban neighborhoods and informal social relations." *American Journal of Sociology* 62:391–398.

Egginton, Don M. (1987). "A historical analysis of labour supply incentives." Pp. 76–123 in Michael Beenstock and Associates, eds., *Work, Welfare and Taxation: A Study of Labour Supply Incentives in the UK*. London: Allen and Unwin.

Ehrenberg, Ronald G. and Robert S. Smith. (1987). *Modern Labor Economics*, Glenview, Ill.: Scott, Foresman.

Feld, Scott L. (1981). "The focused organization of social ties." *American Journal of Sociology* 86:1015-1035.
Fischer, Claude S. (1982). *To Dwell among Friends: Personal Networks in Town and City*, Chicago and London: University of Chicago Press.
Furnham, A. and A. Lewis. (1986). *The Economic Mind*. New York: St. Martins Press.
Granovetter, Mark S. (1973). "The strength of weak ties." *American Journal of Sociology*, 78:1360-1380.
Jackson, Robert Max, Claude S. Fischer, and Lynne McCallister Jones. (1977). "The dimensions of social networks." Pp. 39-58 in Claude S. Fischer et al., eds., *Networks and Places: Social Relations in the Urban Setting*. New York and London: Free Press.
Jahoda, Marie, Paul F. Lazarsfeld, and Hans Zeisel. 1960 (1933). *Die Arbeitslosen von Marienthal*. Allensbach and Bonn: Verlag für Demoskopie.
Jahoda, Marie. (1982). *Employment and Unemployment: a Social-psychological Analysis*. Cambridge: Cambridge University Press.
Keyssar, Alexander. (1986). *Out of Work: The First Century of Unemployment in Massachusetts*. Cambridge: Cambridge University Press.
Komarovsky, Mirra. (1940). *The Unemployed Man and His Family: The Effect of Unemployment upon the Status of the Man in Fifty-nine Families*. New York: Dryden Press.
Maassen, Gerard H. and M.P.M. de Goede. (1988). *Publieke Opinie over Werklozen en Arbeidsongeschikten: Een Trendstudie*. Utrecht: University of Utrecht, Dissertation.
Mead, Lawrence M. (1986). *Beyond Entitlement: The Social Obligations of Citizenship*. New York and London: Free Press.
O'Brien, Gordon E. (1988). *Psychology of Work and Unemployment*. Chichester: Wiley.
Sahlins, Marshall. (1972). *Stone Age Economics*. Chicago: Aldine.
Sprengers, Maarten and Frits Tazelaar. (1988). *Social Networks and Unemployment*. Paper presented at the MASO conference, June 8–11, Zeist, Netherlands.
Warr, Peter. (1987a). "Job characteristics and mental health." Pp. 247–269 in Peter Warr, ed., *Psychology at Work*. Harmondsworth: Penguin.
Warr, Peter. (1987b). "Workers without a job." Pp. 335–356 in Peter Warr, ed., *Psychology at Work*. Harmondsworth: Penguin.
Willmott, Peter and Michael Young. (1967). *Family and Class in a London Suburb*. London: New English Library. (first printing 1960)
Young, Michael and Peter Willmott. (1977). *Family and Kinship in East London*. Harmondsworth: Penguin. (first printing 1957)

III
THE EFFECTS OF INSTITUTIONS IN A MULTIPLEX SOCIETAL CONTEXT

10

Patronage: An Institution in Its Own Right

H.D. Flap

The question of why patronage allegedly declined in the western world has intrigued me for years. Classic sociologists like John Millar, Vilfredo Pareto, and Max Weber wrote about patronage during their lifetime.[1] However, the subject of patronage or clientelism is virtually neglected in present-day sociology, as evidenced by current relevant literature. Many sociologists obviously believe that these kinds of relations disappear when a nation modernizes and industrializes, considering clientelism more pertinent in preindustrial, mainly peasant societies. Indeed, anthropological and historical studies of preindustrial societies confirm this notion (Schmidt *et al.*, 1977). It is commonly thought that the bonds of patronage can be found elsewhere and in the past, but not in present-day western society.

This chapter presents arguments why this view is mistaken, and unfortunate as well, especially in light of the growing awareness that sociology is the science of how people act under the constraints of different institutional arrangements, and how these institutions are created.

What is patronage? Lemarchand and Legg (1972:151–152) define it as "a more or less personalized relationship between actors or sets of actors, commanding unequal wealth, status or influence, based on conditional loyalties, involving mutually beneficial transactions." There can be differences in ties of patronage in at least three respects: in the degree of intimacy, the extent of inequality in access to resources, and the degree of reciprocity in the transactions. One other aspect should be added, namely, the extent of its diffuseness: "patron-client partners have a relationship that may be invoked for almost any purpose" (Scott, 1972b:95).

What is so intriguing about patronage? In present-day western industrial societies it is considered unusual, i.e., different from the way things are done here, or at least different from the way we think that things are done here. Patronage offends our principles of universalism. For instance, rather than selecting persons deemed most competent for the job in question, a friend is chosen instead. Another example is found in voting. People do not vote because they think a particular candidate or party will realize their ideas, but cast their vote for opportunistic reasons to the candidate that offers most in the way of immediate and concrete material rewards.

Furthermore, it is amazing that patronage constitutes a freely engendered, enduring relation of exchange between socially unequal individuals in which both parties are better off. This deviates from the deeply ingrained idea, especially among sociologists, that social differences lead to strife, whereas likeness produces friendship and consensus. Anthropologist Pitt-Rivers (1954:140) coined the well-chosen term "lopsided friendship" to designate ties of patronage. In contrast to sociologists, economists are inclined to think that social differences are conducive to mutual beneficial exchanges, while similarities lead to competition. Probably, this idea on the part of sociologists is another reason for their relative lack of interest in patronage.

Surprisingly, recent research in anthropology and history reveals that clientelism is not merely an addendum to existing institutions, but a dominant form of social organization in many preindustrial, especially peasant societies.

Much of the literature deals with consequences of patronage, not with its emergence or maintenance. Patronage relations are used to explain why something that should have happened according to one's own favorite theory did not happen. For example, Marxists use patronage to explain why greater social inequality does not produce class solidarity, let alone a revolution. Functionalists use it to explain why democratization and all types of developmental aid do not result in economic development, implying that patronage acts as a brake.

The literature on patronage in preindustrial, peasant societies is abundant and produced mainly by anthropologists (cf. Schmidt *et al.*, 1977). Therefore, it is interesting to cite some examples from Dutch history, for in former days the Low Countries was not a purely agrarian society, but a maritime society with a strongly commercialized agrarian sector.

Koenigsberger (1971:166) begins his analysis of the political situation in the Low Countries during the years before the revolution against the Hapsburg regime of Philip II with the following remark: "patronage was the fuel which kept the wheels of sixteenth century political society turning." According to Koenigsberger, part of the explanation for the uprising in the Low Countries lies in the cessation of patronage relations by the Spanish king to the higher nobility of the Low Countries. The rewards granted by the king also took the form of benefits to third parties, at the request of their patrons. Thus, it now became difficult for the higher nobles to bind the lower nobility through dispensing patronage. Although in those days every king had to rely on cooperation with regional elites, the catholic king did not want to offer patronage to nobles that he did not trust and whom he suspected of heretical ideas.

In a biography on Johan de Witt, grand pensionary of Holland in the 17th century, Rowen (1978:154-169) includes a separate chapter on De Witt as "the master of patronage." According to Rowen, De Witt, successfully dominated the political scene of the Dutch Republic of Seven United Provinces (until he was murdered in 1672) because of his understanding of the art of patronage as a means of power.[2] "Although his instructions specifically forbade him to concern himself with office seekers or elections, De Witt unhesitatingly employed patronage as the grease which enabled the Dutch political system to work." "The giving and withholding of patronage were the carrot and the stick of political life" (p. 163) . . . "a powerful tool, commanding the obedience even of men who do not share the patron's political principles" (p. 157). Patronage also created conflicts, if only because it led to frustration on the part of the persons who did not receive these privileges. In addition, there were other would-be patrons who thought they should be the ones to dispense patronage (in the Republic this was especially true for the Prince of Orange, the *stadholder*).

These examples serve to modify the idea that patronage is restricted to peasant societies with a command economy. More recently, studies indicate that patronage is a prominent feature of all communist societies, not only of the agrarian type like China (Oi, 1984; Walder, 1986), but also of present-day industrial societies (Ionescu, 1977; Willerton, 1979; Baker, 1982). These studies give the impression that patronage is actually rising. (In this respect it is telling that more recent political leaders of some communist societies began public campaigns to reduce the extent of clientelism.)

Patronage is not often explicitly thought of as an institution. Yet, it seems to be an "alternative means for integration where coercive power is not sufficiently coercive to command widespread compliance and where conceptions of legitimacy are as yet too weak or circumscribed to produce consensus" (Lemarchand, 1972:69). People manage to achieve their goals practically without or despite malfunctioning formal institutions. Baumann (1979:186) concisely summarizes the point: "patronage may well be seen as a systemic regulating feature of Communist society: a functional equivalent of law and/or the impersonal marketplace." Because it fulfills many of the same functions as does a market, or a bureaucracy (diffusion of information, allocation of scarce resources, providing some social integration), patronage, although not codified in laws, can be seen as an informal institution or mechanism of integration and distribution that can be placed in between "hierarchy" and "market." It can be added to the well-known typology of Dahl and Lindblom (1953), which is comprised of four institutional decision-making mechanisms: hierarchy or organization, market or price-system, democracy, and bargaining.

In fact, clientelism often takes forms that are illegal, being used in exchange for some service. Wherever a state with laws exists, the possibility arises that political leaders will flaunt the rules, or bypass, bend, or forget the laws selectively, in exchange for future services and deference. In addition, the service delivered by the client might also be illegal (e.g., a political murder). The existence of general laws makes these operations illegal, transforming them to what they are often called, political corruption. They account for some of the moral indignation aroused by patronage, and for its defination of something abnormal that should disappear. Ethical and political judgments about "honesty" are immediately involved. Rather than considering the different forms of clientelism, I will instead concentrate on the elementary forms of patronage.

In order to provide an answer to the question "Why patronage?," the following is necessary. One must acknowledge that patronage implies a specific structure of the social network that people form with each other. This will be shown in the next section. Social networks are then seen from the perspective of a rational choice theory, which brings me to the notion of personal networks as social resources. This idea and some of its implications are then used to specify the conditions under which patronage will emerge and persist. The chapter concludes with a discussion of parallel theoretical developments in economics, and some conclusions about a future research agenda.

Patronage as a Specific Social Network Structure

Many social scientists have noted that patronage relationships are particular forms of social networks. To most of them, this was just a remark without any further consequences for their argument. Scott

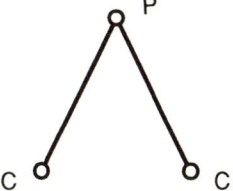 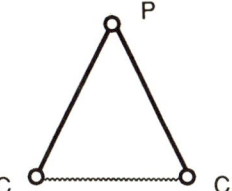

Figure 10.1. The elementary forms of patronage. (a, left) open triangle, (b, right) closed triangle.

(1972a,b) and Singelmann (1975) were among the first sociologists to attempt to specify the kind of network structure that is basic to patronage. Singelmann discerns between a model of the open and the closed triangle, representing situations in which a patron has at least two clients (cf. Figure 10.1). In the situation of an open triangle (that is most often found in reality), the clients do not have contact; in the situation of the closed triangle, clients maintain contact with each other. The question posed by Singelmann (1975) is under what conditions will clients show some solidarity with each other, i.e., when will there be a "closing of the open triangle."

Scott also begins with the situation that a patron usually has more than one client. Thus, he speaks of a patron–client cluster (see Figure 10.2a). When higher placed persons do not control resources of their own, but are themselves clients of other, still higher placed persons. In this situation they function as an intermediary between this higher placed persons and their own clients. These go-betweens that operate with the resources of other persons, are designated as "brokers." Clients, brokers, and patron constitute a patronage-pyramid (see Figure 10.2b) (Scott, 1972a).

In reality, these relationships form complex and extended networks, encompassing whole societies. They create a total social network in the shape of a pyramid with a very broad base. These wider ramifications of patronage networks will not be discussed here.

What is to be gained by a network representation of patronage relations? Generally the structure of social networks acts as a constraint on the behavioral alternatives available to actors. Peter Burke (1974:37–38) best elucidates this in his study on seventeenth century Venice and Amsterdam. To explain the small influence of the lower nobility on the administration of Venice, he refers to the following: "One possible explanation is the strength of cross-cutting social ties. The 'horizontal solidarity' of poor nobles and rich nobles was balanced by the 'vertical solidarity' of patrons and clients." Burke continues by explaining that

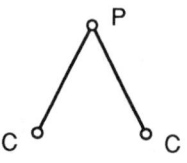 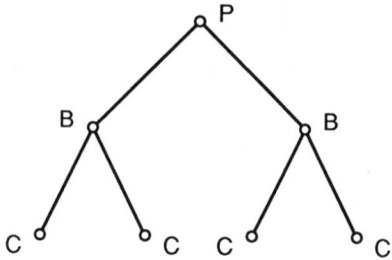

P, Patron;
C, client;
B, broker.

Figure 10.2. Patron-client clusters and patron-client pyramids. (a, left) Patron-client cluster; (b, right) patron-client pyramid.

patronage not only stifles collective action of clients against their patrons but that patronage also drives a wedge between patrons:

> A lesser noble would be torn between allegiance to his social group and allegiance to his patron. As modern social anthropologists like to point out, conflicting allegiances are often a force making for social cohesion, because a man caught in such a conflict has a strong interest in seeing that any given dispute is settled by a compromise. Cross-linking of this kind may well be the fundamental reason for the relative absence of political conflict in Venice. It is also a reminder not to exaggerate the cohesiveness of the elite (Burke, 1974:37–38).

Although the context of patronage relationships may be quite diverse, the basic structure of patronage networks is similar in every context, and imposes similar restrictions on the alternatives of the actors that form these social networks with each other. Since similar clientelistic network structures impose largely similar restrictions on the behavioral alternatives of the actors, the outcomes will be more or less similar across a diversity of social contexts. This helps explain why clientelistic networks can lead to political integration and foreclose violent conflict in diverse institutional contexts. A patronage network as the one that is depicted in Figure 10.3 forms an instance of a network with cross-cutting social cleavages. A more developed explanatory model of the conditions under which such a criss-cross network structure dampens conflicts, is given in Flap (1988).

To consider clientelism as a particular social network structure means that the original explanatory question has to be rephrased: why do persons create these clientelistic social networks? In order to answer this

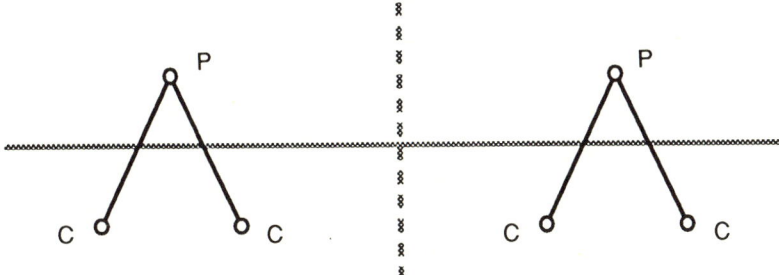

Figure 10.3. The criss-cross network structure of clientelism. Dashed vertical line, cleavage according to social class; solid horizontal line, cleavage according to faction (patron-client clusters).

question—or more generally, to explain the emergence of social networks—rational choice theory.

A Theory of Social Capital

"To have friends is to have power: for they are strengths united." These are words of Thomas Hobbes ([1651] 1961:150) in Chapter 10 *Leviathan*. The assumption has great heuristic value. It serves as a guide of where to look for explanations of social network phenomena. It presents in a "nutshell" a research program in which personal social networks are treated as a specific social resource. Hobbes, of course, emphasized the importance for the problem of order, for the defense of one's life in the struggle for survival. But social resources are important not only for physical safety, but also for most other things that people desire in life: companionship, social esteem, and good health. The idea of social capital is relevant to the explanation of other social phenomena as well, e.g., social inequality. Many violent acts stem from the fact that goods are scarce and not all people can own or consume the goods they want. The idea that someone can produce better life chances if that person has more social resources, relates nicely with the neo-Weberian explanation of social inequality. Weber distinguishes three kinds of resources: economic, symbolic, and political. Personal social networks form a fourth kind of resources that individuals can mobilize in order to achieve their goals and to better their conditions of life (cf. Flap, 1987, 1988; De Graaf and Flap, 1988).

Social capital consists of the expected value of future support. It is the combination of at least the following three factors: (1) the number of persons willing to grant assistance, (2) the resources provided in this indirect manner, and (3) the degree to which the other persons are prepared to help the individual.[3] The second factor has to be stressed, because it is usually neglected in social network research. The question as to which resources personal contacts give access to, is particularly critical to goal achievement. Thus, in a sense, social capital consists of the resources of one's contact persons, which may be called second-order resources. The graphical representations of social networks presented earlier map the distribution of social resources.

The idea of social capital implies that people spend their resources on others, not only for the efficacy of the moment, but also with an eye to the future. Social capital is an entity, consisting of all expected future benefits derived not from one's own labor, but from connections with other persons. It is sensible to view all actions in this light. That is, every human action is equally an investment decision in which actors, whoever they may be, look into the future to justify their current actions. It should be noted that people not only invest in social capital, but also in economic, symbolic, and political capital. They try to combine their investments in a package they hope will maximize their conditions of life. In their investment decisions people will always discount what anticipated future benefits will be, and consider the value these have for them now. People will invest and disinvest in social capital according to the expected value of future support. The greater the value of social capital discounted, the smaller the expected value of support. Taylor (1976:9) calls this the "discount rate." Axelrod (1984:12) nicely captures the meaning of this idea in the image of "the shadow of the future."[4] The value of social capital increases by enlarging the shadow of the future. Several conditions affect the expected value of future social support, for example, the absence of a state, where there is no state. In that situation an extra premium is placed upon the formation and maintenance of social capital, e.g., to ensure physical safety.

How do people acquire social capital? This question and the largely equivalent question of how and why social networks emerge or change, has attracted remarkably little attention in the tradition of social network research. People are likely to invest in each other when the expected value of future support is high, and when they do not anticipate that other resources will greatly improve their future conditions of life. As early as 1923, Marcel Mauss, in his famous *Essai sur le don, forme archaïque de l'échange,* argued that people acquire social capital, namely, by giving, and thereby indebting others to them. Incidentally, Mauss thought that the presence and importance of social capital was restricted to nonwestern, or as he called them, primitive and archaic societies. According to him, social life in these societies consisted of an unremitting give-and-take: *On thesaurise, mais pour dépenser, pour obliger, pour avoir hommes lignes.*

There is another way to gain social capital without having to mobilize one's own resources, that is, through endowment, or more generally, through ascription of rights supported by certain people. An important part of a person's social capital—all the indirect ties that colleagues, acquaintances, friends and kin create by forming relationships with each other and with other persons—develops without their own intervention and conscious knowledge. Even direct ties are not always the product of intentional action. One's weak ties, often grow "at random," as a by-product of actions directed toward other goals.

An Explanation Sketch

The idea of social capital, i.e., of investing and disinvesting in social networks, plays an important part in the explanation of the emergence and maintenance of patronage relations as offered here. The key idea of social capital is that people invest into, and disinvest from, networks if such behavior is expected to improve their ability to attain their goals. These investments are mainly of a local nature. Global patterns that emerge spontaneously from such actions vary widely with social conditions. How can such unintended global aspects, e.g., patronage networks, be explained in terms of individual action?

Before explaining the emergence and maintenance of these patronage networks, I want to discuss my decision to work with a rational choice theory, rather than with some other general behavioral theory, as, for example, a balance theory. Clientelistic network structures aptly illustrate that balance of theory does not offer an adequate explanation of what happens in real-life network structures. As Anderson (1979:469) points out, "a political entrepreneur or broker will make it a point to create imbalanced triads. He will deliberately cultivate persons who are not on speaking terms, because he stands to gain from mediating." Granovetter (1979:510) states the same with regard to clientelistic networks: "the political context is such that it is for instrumental reasons important to maintain unbalanced triads."

I assume that the original situation is one in which there is considerable difference in access to resources so that one can speak of two categories of actors: persons with access to many resources, and those with practically no access to resources. Buchanan (1975) showed that in a world without institutions, exchanges or contracts can be made between two parties that are more rewarding than robbery and theft. It is conceivable that in a world with some institutions both kinds of actors can benefit from engaging in a relation of patronage, say, the exchange of a vote from the client for future services by the patron, or a loan from a bureaucrat in exchange for some favor. This benefit will be greater the higher the value of these goods is for the beneficiary and the less this value is for the benefactor.

But to say that both can benefit from transacting is not sufficient. We have to know what alternatives are open to both potential parties in a contract. In his classic paper on manifest and latent functions, Merton (1949) wrote that the explanation of the maintenance of patronage in industrial America must be due to the fact that the political machine provides its clients with greater services than the official welfare agencies. The client receives immediate help, and does not have to lose his self-respect. In commenting on Merton's paper, Heath (1976:103) remarks that an adequate explanation for the persistence of the political machine requires more than claims about the demand for the machine's services.

Gouldner (1960) emphasized that there are two parties to a transaction, and that the transaction must contain a reward for both. But his account of the persistence of political machines also must be criticized, since "it is not enough to know that the machine gets votes and illegal favors in return for welfare benefits. We also need to show that this bargain is a better one, taking into account the costs of providing the benefits, than could be obtained by, say, legitimate politics" (Heath, 1976:104). The alternatives available set limits to the exchange.

Thus, what are the feasible alternatives to both categories of actors? What is the incentive structure to potential clients and to potential patrons? To determine the feasible alternatives to the potential clients, one can begin with Blau's classic discussion (1964:21–22) of the situation in which someone wants something that another person controls, as was done by Scott in 1972. In such a situation there are four possible alternatives to becoming the other person's client, that is, to being deferential and promising future services in return. The first option could be immediate reciprocation with a service that the potential patron badly needs, thereby restoring the balance of exchange. The potential client may try to secure the needed service elsewhere. Of course, he could possibly coerce the other into providing the service. Finally, he can try to do without the needed service.

The first alternative is practically out of the question since, the original situation is one of an unequal access to diverse resources. For the same reason, coercion is no real alternative, apart from a collective resistance by a whole group of potential clients against potential patrons. Doing without the service is not a prospect that will be freely chosen; it will be the outcome only if the other alternatives prove to be a failure. Seeking the service elsewhere, implies seeking out another patron. Thus, apart from collective action, clientage is the only option. The search for another patron and collective resistance imply that there are other potential patrons and clients present in the situations.

Given unequal access to resources, either in a market or from a bureaucracy, the situation will frequently be one of a society of clients-in-search-for-a-patron, in which clients have no real alternative. Solidarity with other clients would imply a collective solution to individual problems, and hence the closing of the triangle (Figure 10.1). The incentive structure of patronage is such that, from the perspective of a "rational" individual, a political machine is, in fact, the only kind of party to which it makes sense to adhere, because it is striving mainly for benefits that accrue to particular individuals rather than for the common interest of a large group (Graziano, 1976:165; Chubb, 1982:212). This explanation is implicit in the rather famous quotation of a citizen in need of assistance, and duly disappointed with the official institutions: "Help, you understand; none of your law and justice but help" (Merton, 1949:74).

If the number of competing clients is rather large in comparison to the number of potential patrons, there is always another potential client willing to take the place of an unwilling one. Clients and would-be-clients compete for special treatment: lest the patron would decide otherwise, the system can reproduce itself and persist through time. Growing demands on the part of a client can be easily blocked by the patron by excluding these persons from privileged treatment (cf. Figure 10.1).

How many goods and services (e.g., how many jobs per year and how many clients) must be available to keep the clientelistic network intact? A conventional idea is that, if the competition among would-be clients is keener, and/or the supply of material rewards with which to dispense patronage declines, then patronage would wither away, and some kind of collective action on the part of the former potential clients would ensue. Chubb (1982) tries to show that in a situation of scarcity, collective solutions are even less attractive in comparison to private ones, especially because the success of collective solutions become even more uncertain. Clientage gives hope for individual salvation. In her comparative study of the cities Naples and Palermo during the 1970s, Chubb suggests that the Communists could only attain power in Naples under catastrophic circumstances (a malaria epidemic) in which only the Communists proved to have organizations that could act efficiently. Further, they could only remain in power by dispensing some 6000 jobs to the people who voted for them. In Palermo, the reigning Christian Democrats gained an electoral victory even though they provided inefficient public services (without a basic infrastructure like water and electricity) social services (such as schools, clinics, and pharmacies) and deteriorating economic conditions. In addition, there is always nonmonetary patronage (e.g., issuing licenses, and providing police assistance) that can be used as long as the patron controls access to these resources.

If there is more than one potential patron, the possibility arises that one can align with another patron, leading to a factional structure (cf. Figure 10.3). But this will only improve the client's freedom of choice if the number of clients does not increase too.

But what about the potential patron? What alternatives does he have and how will he decide? The existing literature is even more limited than in the analysis of the situation of the client. Boudon (1979) offers an analysis of a tenancy relationship, paraphrasing an economic model presented by Bhaduri: For the potential patron the market is not always a more attractive solution, because producing for the market can mean that his actual or potential clients obtain a better income and become more self-reliant. Thus the patron loses the clients' services, their votes, and the status he may derive. By making his clients more self-reliant, he would be deprived of future services (cf. Popkin, 1979:77). Not only do we have to know which goals the patron has, but there is no special reason to think that he would strive for different goals than do most people. Compared to the situation of the would-be clients, it is more difficult to imagine how the goals of the patron are best served in his particular situation. Yet, if he competes with other potential patrons he needs the support of clients. For they can afford him status, an income, and, at times, physical protection.[5]

Patronage can only thrive under circumstances in which social capital is a means to one's ends (the more so if other resources are not a means to these ends). Thus, all the circumstances that are usually given in the anthropological literature, like "precarious personal security; formalistic or weakly developed institutional and impersonal standards of procedure and behavior; political competition largely confined to a narrow elite group; and weakly developed horizontal class or occupational interests" (Scott, 1972b:42), are indeed conducive to the formation of clientelistic relationships. Another essential condition, for the development of patronage is the existense of unequal access to resources.

To some degree, social capital will always be a means to a higher individual status and more welfare. This, in conjunction with the acknowledgment that unequal access to resources cannot be eradicated in more technologically advanced societies, leads to the conclusion that patronage will probably be more or less omnipresent. Particularism is not on the wane in all industrial societies. Eric Wolf (1966:19) is probably correct in writing, ". . . complex societies in the modern world differ less in the formal organization of their economic and legal and political system than in the character of their supplementary interpersonal sets."

Discussion and Conclusions

The preceding section did not offer a detailed explanatory model of the emergence and maintenance of clientelism. It can only be considered an attempt to indicate the circumstances under which patronage networks emerge and persist.

Recently, a branch of economic literature has developed that presents arguments that describe the conditions under which personal relations are valuable in economic and organizational life, or more generally, that specify the circumstances under which investment logic places a premium on investments in others. This literature is variably described as transaction cost theory, agency theory, and "organizational economics" (Barney and Ouchi, 1986). It can be particularly useful if one wishes to specify the conditions under which potential patrons have an interest in engaging in clientelistic relationships with would-be clients.

Clientelism, or more generally, social capital, is important because social life departs from the assumptions made in economic theory about markets with perfect competition: There may be a small number of buyers and/or sellers, the product or service being exchanged can be heterogeneous, and there are costs to the activity of engaging in an exchange (Barney and Ouchi, 1986:7). This results in asymmetric information and creates possibilities for opportunistic behavior. Resource dependency and other forms of asset specificity also create possibilities for opportunistic behavior. Apart from vertical integration—that is, creating an organization—there are other solutions to the problems of exploitation, e.g., a kind of implicit contracts. One may look at clientelism as just such a contract. In a patronage relationship all investments of both parties in each other are transaction-specific investments, i.e., the value of any good or item invested in a particular transaction is higher than its value in any alternative transaction. Although the patron is in general less dependent than the client but he is also dependent, since he makes transaction-specific investments. The fact that past investments are bygone if one does not keep to the contract, acts as a deterrent to either a breach of the contract or a search for another patron or client. Still another condition under which networks of personal relations will emerge is, when tasks are cooperative undertakings in which not all terms of the contract can be enumerated beforehand, and in which team production is the rule.

That some aspects of life are more patronage-prone than others may depend on the factors discussed earlier, e.g., in the political sphere there are products that do not have exact calculable prices, great uncertainties, etc. But, contrary to what is stated in several texts on patronage (for example, by Gellner, 1977:6), the economic realm is not free from personal relations either, even when it is not politicized. To take an example from a recent publication, Formichella and Thomas (1987:271–274) show in an analysis of economic behavior of shrimp fishermen on the coasts of Alabama. In the absence of market information, these fishermen select buyers not for the economic payoff, but for personal relationships that provide long-term economic security at the expense of short-term economic gain. Whenever the quality of merchandise is highly variable and difficult to access, and when there are high costs connected to further search for a higher bid, lack of information can be compensated for by trust.

Patronage can be seen as an agency relationship between persons of unequal social standing, "a contract under which one or more persons [the principal(s)] engage another person (the agent) to perform some service on their behalf which involves delegating some decision-making authority to the agent" (Jensen and Meckling, 1976:308). It is "a neat kind of social plumbing" (White, 1985), intermediate between formal organization or hierarchy, on the one hand, and market, on the other. White called patronage "a social invention of some note" (1985).

The argument presented can show how the so-called "theory gap" in social network analysis could be closed. Because as Mark Granovetter (1979:501) noted:

> In the rapidly expanding literature on "social networks," one nagging question keeps intruding: where is the theoretical underpinning for all these models and analyses? . . . most network models are constructed in a theoretical vacuum, each on its own terms, and without reference to a broader or common framework. Despite continuing progress, therefore, the point of diminishing returns is approaching, and will rapidly overtake us, unless we pay more attention to what I call the "theory gap" in network studies.

The theory of social capital not only in principle has something to say about the effects of social networks on the behavior of individual actors, but it also can explain the emergence and changes in social networks.

The study of clientelism suffers from lack of empirical documentation, let alone comparative studies. Studies abound with illustrations, taken from field material; at best they present an extended case. This state of affairs makes it difficult to ascertain whether patronage does exist or even constitutes the dominant form of social organization in particular societies. Empirical research into patronage and the like is more or less taboo in societies and organizations with formal charter rules and with an ideology of universalism. Patronage practices in societies without a constitutional state and without universalistic laws were often meticulously recorded since they were not illegal. Comparative research, but especially historical research, can be of help in tests of hypotheses on rise and decline of clientelism (cf. Shefter, 1977). Shefter argues that the precise order in which institutions developed greatly influences the rise and decline of political patronage. Whenever the emergence of a state bureaucracy precedes the development of an electoral democracy, political parties will have to adopt an ideological stance because otherwise they can not gain access to the "spoils of office." If, however, an electoral democracy precedes bureaucratization, parties can use government jobs as patronage (cf. Sombart, 1906). This order is also to be expected on the following grounds: "where a stable network of relations mediates complex transactions and generates standards of behavior between firms, such pressures toward vertical integration in a market should be absent, [and] . . . if something is done well within personal relations no market, no bureaucracy will emerge to deal with these business" (Granovetter, 1985:503). These arguments will also be valid for other realms of social life in addition to the economic one.

In summary, patronage is not something deviant, abnormal, or inherently pathological, nor is it necessarily inefficient in the economic sense. Neither are there grounds to expect that it will disappear. It is not something that only exists in traditional peasant societies, nor is it restricted to the political sphere. For example, results of our network research in the Netherlands show that patronage still enables people to find jobs with higher prestige (Flap and De Graaf, 1986). Patronage is recreated in present times, not despite the existing institutional arrangements but because of them. Apart from the theoretical work (e.g., developing the idea of social capital into a more rigorous theory, and systematically comparing the literature on patronage, and organizational economics), the agenda for future research should include the study of patronage in areas other than the political arena, i.e., in and between economic organizations. Furthermore, state-socialist societies, in particular, offer the possibility to study patronage within the context of a comparative institutional analysis. In these communist societies, several institutional experiments are occurring that all seem to generate patronage, although in different degrees. This is more the case in China than in the USSR, probably because the Chinese are dependent on their jobs for a wider range of their needs than their Russian counterpart while at the same time their superiors seem to have greater discretionary power, unrestricted by legal rules or job-performance qualifications (Walder, 1986).[7] It appears as if Namier's words that "no one bribes, where he can bully" have their counterpart in a situation where outright violence is difficult to practice. Whenever a one-party state becomes less repressive, patronage will be on the rise.

Notes

1. These classic sociologists were more skeptical about the disappearance of patronage. They also were much less inclined to see patronage as a stumbling block along the way to some virtuous goal.
2. Rowen (1978:168) speaks about "patronage as a gift to individuals at the cost of the public." This remark hints at another possible line of explaining variations in clientelism: patronage could be seen as a form of "rent-seeking."
3. There are several aspects to social capital, not all equally important for the achievement of different kinds of goals. For example, the number of weak ties one can dispose of increases the amount of one's information to a considerable extent. On the other hand, if one needs actual support, one fares better with strong ties.
4. Axelrod (1984:12) states that "the future is less important than the present for two reasons. The first is that players tend to value payoffs less as the time of their obtainment recedes in the future. The second is that there is always some chance that the players will not meet again. An ongoing relationship may end when one or the other players moves away, changes jobs, dies, or goes bankrupt. For these reasons, the payoff of the next move always counts less than the payoff of the current move. A natural way to take this into account is to cumulate payoffs over time in such a way that the next move is worth some fraction of the current move. The weight (or importance) of the next move relative to the current move will be called w. It represents the degree to which the payoff of each move is discounted relative to the previous move, and is therefore a discount parameter."
5. Clientelistic systems often meet with great difficulties when incumbents of high office have to be succeeded, since generally there are no formal rules how and who is going to succeed whom at which moment (Goody, 1966). Dutch history illustrates some of the ways in which patrons dealt with these difficulties. During the Republic certain families of regents managed to stay in power for decades by carefully managing their social capital. They succeeded in this by creating affinal relationships with other powerful families and by so-called contracts of correspondence, i.e., official agreements between contending political factions to share power by way of rotation. These agreements were meticulously recorded. In this manner they were able to circumvent laws and moral indictments against family-government, while at the same time keeping conflicts and deceit to a minimum (e.g, van Dijk and Roorda, 1980).
6. There is yet another way in which personal relations attenuate opportunism: they can spread a reputation for being an unreliable partner, thereby making it difficult to obtain new trading partners in the future.
7. Because communist societies represent an integration of patrimonial rule with modern bureaucratic form, Walder calls these forms of clientelism "neo-traditional" (Walder, 1986:251).

References

Anderson, Bo. (1979). "Cognitive balance theory and social network analysis. Remarks on some fundamental theoretical matters." Pp. 453–469 in P.W.

Holland and S. Leinhardt, eds., *Perspectives on Social Network Research*. New York: Academic Press.

Axelrod, R.D. (1984). *The Evolution of Cooperation*. New York: Basic Books.

Baker, R.H. (1982). "Clientelism in the post-revolutionary state: The Soviet Union." Pp. 36–52 in C. Clapham, ed., *Private Patronage and Public Power. Political Clientelism and the State*. London: Francis Pinter.

Barney, Jay B. and William G. Ouchi (eds.). (1986). *Organizational Economics*. London: Jossey-Bass.

Baumann, Z. (1979). "Comment on Eastern Europe." *Studies in Comparative Communism* 12:184–189.

Blau, Peter M. (1964). *Exchange and Power in Social Life*. New York: Wiley.

Boudon, Raymond. (1979). *Le Logique du Social*. Paris: Hachette.

Buchanan, James M. (1975). *The Limits of Liberty: Between Anarchy and Liberty*. Chicago: University of Chicago Press.

Burke, Peter. (1974). *Venice and Amsterdam. A Study of Seventeenth-Century Elites*. London: Temple-Smith.

Chubb, Judith. (1982). *Patronage, Power and Poverty in Southern Italy: A Tale of Two Cities*. Cambridge: Cambridge University Press.

Dahl, Robert, and Charles E. Lindblom. (1953). *Politics, Economics and Welfare*. New York: Harper and Row.

De Graaf, Nan Dirk, and Henrik Derk Flap. (1988). "With a little help from my friends." *Social Forces*, 67:452–472.

Dijk, H. van, and D.J. Roorda. (1980). *Het Patriciaat van Zierikzee Gedurende de Republiek*. Middelburg: Zeeuws Genootschap der Wetenschappen.

Flap, Hendrik Derk. (1987). "De theorie van het sociale kaptiaal." *Antropologische Verkenningen* 6:14–27.

Flap, Henrik Derk. (1988). *Conflict, Loyalty and Violence. Social Networks in Stateless Societies*. Bern: Peter Lang.

Flap, Hendrik Derk, and Nan Dirk De Graaf. (1986). "Social capital and attained occupational status." *Netherlands Journal of Sociology* 22:145–161.

Formichella, Cecilia, and J. Stephen Thomas. (1987). "Personal ties between shrimpers and buyers in a Gulf Coast fishing community." *Sociology and Social Research* 71:271–274.

Gellner, Ernest. (1977). "Patrons and Clients." Pp. 1–6 in E. Gellner and J. Waterbury, eds., *Patrons and Clients*. London: Duckworth.

Goody, Jack (ed). (1966). *Succession to High Office*. Cambridge: Cambridge University Press.

Gouldner, Alvin. (1960). "The norm of reciprocity." *American Sociological Review* 25:161–178.

Granovetter, Mark S. (1979). "The theory gap in social network analysis." Pp. 501–518 in P.W. Holland and S.W. Leinbardt, eds., *Perspectives in Social Network Research*. New York: Academic Press.

Granovetter, Mark S. (1985). "Economic action and social structure: The problem of embeddedness." *American Journal of Sociology* 31:481–510.

Graziano, L. (1976). "A conceptual framework for the study of clientelistic behavior." *European Journal of Political Research* 4:149–165.

Heath, Anthony. (1976). *Rational Choice and Social Exchange: A Critique of Exchange Theory*. Cambridge: Cambridge University Press.

Hobbes, Thomas. (1968). *Leviathan*. Edited with an introduction by C.B. MacPherson. Harmondsworth: Penquin. [Originally published 1651.]

Ionescu, Ghita. (1977). "Patronage under Communism." Pp. 97–102 in E. Gellner and J. Waterbury, eds., *Patrons and Clients*. London: Duckworth.

Jensen, Michael C., and William H. Meckling. (1976). "Theory of the Firm: Managerial behavior, agency costs and ownership structure." *Journal of Financial Economics* 3:305–360.

Koenigsberger, H.G. (1971). "Patronage and bribery during the reign of Charles V." Pp. 166–175 in H.G. Koenigsberger, ed., *Estates and Revolutions*. Cornell University Press: Ithaca and London.

Lemarchand, René. (1972). "Political clientelism and ethnicity in tropical Africa: Competing solidarities in nation-building." *American Political Science Quarterly* 66:68–90.

Lemarchand, René, and Keith Legg. (1972). "Political clientelism and development. A preliminary analysis." *Comparative Politics* 4:149–178.

Merton, Robert K. (1949). *Social Theory and Social Structure*. Glencoe, Ill.: Free Press.

Oi, Jean C. (1984). "Communism and clientelism: Rural politics in China." *World Politics* 37:238–266.

Pitt-Rivers, J.A. (1954). *The People of the Sierra*. London: Weidenfeld and Nicolson.

Popkin, Samuel L. (1979). *The Rational Peasant: The Political Economy of Rural Society in Vietnam*. Berkeley: University of California Press.

Rowen, H.H. (1978). "The master of patronage." Pp. 154–169 in *John de Witt, Grand Pensionary of Holland, 1625–1672*, Princeton: Princeton University Press.

Schmidt, Steffen W. et al. (eds.). (1977). *Friends, Followers and Factions: A Reader in Political Clientelism*. Berkeley: University of California Press.

Scott, James C. (1972a). "Patron-client politics and political change in Southeast Asia." *American Political Science Review* 66:103–127.

Scott, James C. (1972b). *Comparative Political Corruption*. Englewood Cliffs: Prentice Hall.

Shefter, M. (1977). "Party and patronage: Germany, England, and Italy." *Politics and Society* 7:403–451.

Singelmann, Peter. (1975). "The closing triangle: Critical notes on a model for peasant mobilization in Latin America." *Comparative Studies in Society and History* 17:389–409.

Sombart, Werner. (1906). *Warum gibt es in den Vereinigten Staaten keinen Sozialismus?*. Tübingen: Mohr.

Taylor, Michael. (1976). *Anarchy and Cooperation*. London: Wiley.

Walder, Andrew. (1986). *Communist Neo-Traditionalism*. Berkeley: University of California Press.

White, Harrison C. (1985). "Agency as control," Chapter 8 in John W. Pratt and

R. Zeckhauser, eds., *Principles and Agents: The Structure of Business*. Boston: Harvard University Press.

Willerton, J.P. (1979). "Clientelism in the Soviet Union: an initial examination." *Studies in Comparative Communism* 12:159–211.

Wolf, Eric. (1966). "Kinship, friendship, and patron-client relations in complex societies." Pp. 1–22 in M. Banton, ed., *The Social Anthropology of Complex Societies* New York: Praeger.

11

The Political Geography of Fascist Party Membership in Italy and Germany (1918–1933)

William Brustein

Both general, and case study explanations of the rise of fascism fail to account sufficiently for individuals' motivations for joining a fascist party.[1] First, neither type of explanation distinguishes between the motivations for *voting for* and the motivations for joining a fascist party. For instance, it is implicitly assumed that the "fear of socialism" (Snowden, 1972; Corner, 1975; Cardoza, 1982) or the "resistance to modernization" (Moore, 1966; Nolte, 1966) are sufficient to explain both voting for and joining a fascist party. While the fear of socialism or anxiety attributed to the modernization process may influence some individuals to vote for a fascist party, it is highly unlikely that these factors alone are adequate reasons for joining the party. Participation in a party, especially one that practiced extremism like fascism, should involve unquestionably higher personal risks than simply voting for it. Participants are called upon to give time to party activities and accept the consequences of being publicly labeled as a member. Voters, on the other hand, need not expend the energy involved in carrying out daily party tasks nor incur the costs of ostracism and repression that often accompany the public knowledge of membership.[2] I will argue that the reasons for voting for a fascist party in Italy between 1918 and 1922 and Germany between 1926 and 1933 were necessary but insufficient conditions for joining the party.

Second, the literature focuses on *irrational* rather than *rational* motivations to explain individuals joining a fascist party. In describing the kinds of individuals who were attracted to fascism, Arendt (1961:305) notes:

> It was characteristic of the rise of the Nazi movement in Germany and of the Communist movement in Europe after 1930 that they recruited their members from this mass of apparently indifferent people whom all other parties had given up as too apathetic or too stupid for their attention. The result was that the majority of their membership consisted of people who never before had appeared on the political scene. This permitted the introduction of entirely new methods of political propaganda, and indifference to the arguments of political opponents; these movements not only placed themselves outside and against the party system as a whole, they found a membership that had never been reached, never been "spoiled" by the party system. Therefore they did not need to refute opposing arguments and consistently preferred methods which ended in death rather than persuasion which spelled terror rather than conviction . . .

An emphasis on irrational motivations seems natural in light of the high degree of irrationality in fascism's collective result. But we should not conclude that individuals' calculations for joining were irrational simply because the collective result was irrational. I suggest, instead, that the irrationality of fascism as a collective result was not incompatible with the rational calculations of individual actors. Furthermore, the political geography of fascist party membership in Italy and Germany can be explained on the basis of rational calculations of individual actors.

How are we to explain the political geography of Italian and German fascist party membership during the interwar period (see Table 11.1)? To address the question of how individuals choose between alternative courses of action I present a theory that is guided by a version of subjective expected utility theory.[3] Following subjective expected utility theory each actor is faced with a choice between alternative courses of action; different actions are perceived to entail different sets of outcomes; associated with each outcome is a subjective evaluation and a belief about the likelihood of its occurrence for a given choice of a course of action. The subjective expected utility of a given alternative course of action is the sum of the utilities of the outcomes associated with that action, each weighted by its perceived likelihood of occurrence. Actors will opt for the choice for which the subjective expected utility is at its greatest. Thus, subjective expected utility theory should help to identify factors and processes in the Italian and German historical records that would explain the actual choices made by individuals. In particular, I argue that individuals' decisions to join the fascist party in Italy and Germany could be attributed to regional differences in (1) the extent to which the fascist party program was perceived to redress individuals' grievances, (2) the opportunities available to individuals to join the

Table 11.1. The Political Geography of Fascist Party Membership in Italy for 1922 and Germany for 1932, by Region

Italy	Party members to total population per 10,000 population	Germany	Party members to total population per 10,000 population
Piedmont	43	Bader	101
Liguria	66	Bayerische Ostmark	94
Lombardy	162	Danzig	223
Venetia	70	Dusseldorf	89
Emilia	170	Essen	95
Tuscany	177	Franken	74
Marches	20	Gross-Berlin	132
Umbria	85	Halle-Merseburg	109
Latium	60	Hamburg	108
Abruzzi-Molise	33	Hessen-Nassau	145
Campania	40	Koblenz-Trier	73
Apulia	88	Koln-Aachen	70
Basilicata	12	Kurhessen	172
Calabria	14	Magdeburg-Anhalt	133
Sicily	24	Mainfranken	65
Sardinia	24	Mecklenburg-Lubeck	174
Trentino-Alto Adige	18	Munchen-Oberbayern	106
Friuli-Venezia Giulia	209	Ost-Hannover	160
		Ostpreussen	118
		Pfalz	170
		Pommern	137
		Sachsen	168
		Schlesien	136
		Schleswig-Holstein	309
		Schwaben	100
		Sud-Hann. Braunschweig	208
		Thuringen	131
		Weser-Ems	140
		Westfalen-Nord	60
		Westfalen-Sud	93
		Wurttemburg-Hohenz.	78
Mean	73	Mean	129

Source: DeFelice. (1966:8–11); Mitchell (1981:73); *NSDAP Partei-Statistik*, 1935. Band II, pp. 10, 26.

party, (3) the degree of the party's control over the distribution of selective incentives, and (4) the degree of solidarity of individuals' social networks.

A necessary initial condition for joining the fascist party was the belief that the party offered solutions to people's grievances. Individuals are more likely to vote for a political party that promises to improve their situation than one that supports the welfare of others. However, shared interests by themselves cannot ensure that individuals will be attracted to the party. The party must be capable of skillfully projecting its position to individuals. Otherwise, individuals may remain unaware of the interest compatibility between themselves and the party. Moreover, a party that pays only lip service to individuals' demands may eventually encounter difficulty attracting individuals to its ranks. On the other hand, a party that directly involves itself in individuals' grievances should be in a better position to attract members.

The belief that the fascist party could redress individuals' grievances should have attracted individuals to the party and may have accounted largely for individuals' voting preferences. However, redressing individuals' grievances cannot, by itself, constitute the basis for joining a party. Jenkins and Perrow (1977) and McCarthy and Zald (1977) have argued that individuals will be reluctant to participate in a political party solely on the basis of shared interests. If shared interests were the sole condition for joining a party, rational individuals may just as likely choose to "free ride," that is, hope to consume the good without contributing to its production. In the case of joining the fascist party, the free rider would hope to receive the benefits of the party's coming to power (a public good) without incurring the costs of its production, which would entail active (and potentially risky) participation in the party. To explain fascist party membership we must look beyond those motivations shaping the voting choice; we must locate those factors which would have reduced the likelihood that individuals would have chosen to free ride.

What factors might explain why one group of individuals who voted for a fascist party decided not to join the party while another group of individuals who voted for a fascist party decided to join? The explanation may lie in regional differences in opportunities, selective incentives, and the solidarity of social networks.

Individuals may have decided to free ride because disincentives arising from the social environment raised the costs of participation. Disincentives frequently take the form of threats or punishments from an unsympathetic government (especially the police) and/or opposition movements (Salert, 1976; Oberschall, 1973; Tilly, 1978). Rational individuals are unlikely to risk involvement if they calculate that participation might result in the loss of employment, imprisonment, or physical harm. In addition, the belief that participation will be opposed may produce a reluctance among individuals to join since they may calculate that others would be unlikely to involve themselves for fear that they may incur high risks to their livelihood.

If individuals viewed membership in a fascist party as their sole means to maintain or gain access to selective incentives, they would have been less reluctant about joining the party (McCarthy and Zald, 1977; Gamson, 1975; Tilly, 1978; Olson, 1965). Selective incentives refer to goods that a party has the capacity to supply or withhold selectively, to members alone (Olson, 1965). These excludable goods include, among other things, jobs, property, information, behavioral confirmation, and social activities. If individuals require these resources, and the costs of obtaining them elsewhere are high, individuals will depend on the supplier. If the supplier is a political party, individuals are likely to join the party if membership will ensure an uninterrupted access to these resources. Individuals' dependence on the party for resources should correlate strongly with the party's monopolistic position in allocating these resources. If alternative parties or institutions possess valued resources and have the capacity to distribute them, individuals' dependence on any single group should be reduced. On the other hand, if the party is the sole provider of valued resources, it should be in a stronger position to demand participation by making this a condition for access to these resources (Hechter, 1987).

If a party's possession of selective incentives is a necessary condition for membership (a private good), is there any reason to include the fascist party's ability to redress people's grievances (a collective good) as a necessary condition? According to Tullock (1971), "the public goods aspects of a revolution are of relatively little importance in the decision to participate." But if this were true, individuals' motivations for joining the party would have little if anything to do with the political issues at stake (De Nardo, 1985:56). In the case of fascist party membership, we would expect to find socialists and communists joining if the party organizers simply provided coffee and donuts to the members (De Nardo, 1985:56). Yet we know this did not occur since the socialists and communists were never initially attracted to the party because their program did not address their particular constellation of grievances.

Individuals are unlikely to join a fascist party in the absence of the participation of members of their social networks, which include such institutions as family, friends, co-workers, and resource providers. They are a major source of solidarity and influence our action. The extent to which individuals are confident that members of their social network are likely to join the party should affect individuals' anxiety associated with free riding. If the confidence is high, individuals should have less anxiety; obviously, the converse is true. This follows because the personal costs in joining a fascist party were high in terms of public ostracism and expenditure of time. Since rational individuals want to share the risks involved in party membership, to have the party tasks divided among many people, and to gain behavioral confirmation from members of their social networks, they are likely to make their participation conditional on the participation of others. Thus rational individuals may decide to free ride unless they are confident that members of their networks are also likely to join. This is akin to what Taylor (1982) and Hardin (1982) refer to as conditional cooperation; that is, individuals make their cooperation conditional on the cooperation of others.

In what kinds of social situations should we expect to find a high degree of conditional cooperation? Taylor (1982) observes that conditional cooperation tends to emerge where there is a sense of community, that is, a social setting defined by shared values and beliefs, direct and many-sided relations, and reciprocity. Members of a community have the capacity to monitor the behavior of other community participants and can engage in a series of social sanctions in relationship to each other (Taylor, 1982). Monitoring is effective in a community because one's livelihood and social life depend on maintaining good relations with other members of the community.

A sense of community is often found in groups organized around traditional lines based on kinship, village, ethnic or tribal affiliations, but it can occur in secondary groups based on occupational, religious, and other special-interest associations (Oberschall, 1973; Fireman and Gamson, 1979). Moreover, a sense of community is more readily observed in small rather than large social settings. Taylor (1982:53) notes:

> as the size of the group increases, this mutual monitoring becomes increasingly difficult and the tacit contract of conditional cooperation becomes increasingly fragile. In a relatively small group, on the other hand, especially one with an unchanging or only very slowly changing membership, people come into contact with and can observe the behavior of most of their fellows so that conditional cooperation is more likely to be workable.

The existence of social networks also affects participation by producing social pressure, which can be an effective selective incentive. As Olson (1982) observes, individuals desire companionship, esteem of their colleagues, and a reduction of public ostracism. These are powerful selective incentives which a community can use to motivate individuals to participate in concerted action. But they can only be powerful selective incentives if individuals' social networks are tightly knit and thus capable of exerting social pressure.

In short, I argue that individuals' decisions to join the fascist party were shaped by their perception of the party's ability to redress their grievances, the opportunities available to them to join the party, the party's control over the distribution of desirable excludable goods, and the solidarity of individuals' social networks. I argue, furthermore, that since these conditions varied regionally, we should expect to find the highest fascist party membership in those regions where these conditions were present and the lowest fascist party membership in those regions where they were absent. In the following pages I will attempt to demonstrate the appropriateness of my argument through an examination of these four conditions in relation to various regions in Italy and Germany during the interwar period.

The perception that the fascist party could redress people's grievances appears to have played a crucial role in explaining the attachment of a sizable proportion of northern Italy's population to the Italian fascist party. Between 1919 and 1921 the socialist leagues succeeded in organizing many of the agricultural laborers employed on large capitalist estates in the Po Valley (Corner, 1975; Cardoza, 1982). Agricultural laborers who held out little hope of obtaining individual plots of land were attracted to the socialist leagues' call for higher wages and collective ownership of property (Corner, 1975:146–49). In contrast to these agricultural laborers, the Po Valley also contained a sizable number of smallowners, leaseholders, and sharecroppers who had, since 1911, come into the possession of land and were accumulating substantial cash reserves (Cardoza, 1982:321–22; Corner, 1975:145; Maier, 1975:310). The wealth of these smallholders, leaseholders, and sharecroppers had steadily climbed since 1914 because of the tremendous price rise in their major crops, hemp and sugarbeet (Corner, 1975:148–49; Maier, 1975: 311; Snowden, 1972:280). As Corner (1975:145) observes, the situation for Po Valley smallholders, leaseholders, and sharecroppers was especially encouraging in 1919 and 1920. Those smallholders who wanted to extend their holdings had capital to do so; leaseholders and sharecroppers who wanted to acquire property had the resources. The favorable economic conditions served to boost the hopes of many agricultural laborers as well. The day when they could finally own some land came nearer. The Po Valley smallholders, leaseholders, and sharecroppers saw little hope in the socialist leagues' program of collective ownership and higher wages. Collective ownership would destroy their dream of landowning or of increasing their holding; and since many leaseholders and sharecroppers employed hired labor, higher wages were not in their interests as employers (Snowden, 1972:277–78). Thus it was not surprising that some of the fiercest resistance to the socialist leagues came from these peasants (Cardoza, 1982:321–22).

Before 1921 the smallholders, leaseholders, and sharecroppers of the Po Valley lacked an established political party. In 1921, through its agrarian program, the fascist party emerged as a spokesperson for these peasants. In February 1921 Mussolini wrote:

> We want the land to belong not to the state but to the cultivator. Whereas social-communism tends to disinherit all, and to transform every cultivator into an employee of the state, we wish to give the ownership of the land and economic freedom to the greatest number of peasants. In place of the sovereignty of a central political caste, we support the sovereignty of the peasant (Snowden, 1972:279).

In other words, fascism promised to defend the newly acquired gains of the Po Valley smallholders, leaseholders, and sharecroppers. Furthermore, fascism proposed to liberate them from the economic restraints imposed by the socialist leagues such as the freezing of the provincial land market (Cardoza, 1982:321–22; Corner, 1975:162). Moreover, the Italian fascist party set out to win over the peasantry by promising "the land to him who works it" and "to every peasant the entire fruit of his sacred labor" (Snowden, 1972:279). Before long the *fascios* of the Po Valley had convinced large landowners to cede them land which they, in turn, made available to the peasants (Maier, 1975:314; Snowden, 1972: 279; Lyttleton, 1973:63; Tasca, 1966:102).

In short, those peasants who saw benefits in the capitalist expansion of agriculture and who saw the socialist leagues as the principal threat to their hopes found satisfaction in the fascist agrarian program. These peasants tended to reside in areas such as the Po Valley. By contrast, in regions of Italy where we find a predominance of landless agricultural laborers with limited prospects to become landowners, the socialist program of higher wages and collective ownership should have won adherents. In those regions of southern Italy marked by large, backward, and semi-feudal *latifondi* where absentee landlords leased minute parcels of land at usurious rates to impoverished peasants, neither the fascist program of land redistribution or the socialist program of higher wages were particularly appealing (Snowden, 1972:287–88). These peasants had slim hopes of ever accumulating enough capital to purchase a farm, and since they were not employed as agricultural labor, they had no personal incentive to favor higher wages.

The perception of the Nazi party to redress people's grievances seems to have also played an important role in this party's ability to attract supporters in the Geest region of the northern German states of Schleswig-Holstein and lower Saxony. The typical farmer of the Geest region was a smallowner engaged in the highly speculative activities of dairy farming and hog fattening (Heberle, 1951; Loomis and Beegle, 1946). In 1924 agricultural prices in the Geest region collapsed. Farmers were forced to remortgage their land with short-term high-interest loans (Noakes, 1971:114–15). The Geest dairy and meat farmers were again confronted with economic disaster after 1927. Much of the blame was laid on the shoulders of the Weimar government, which by concluding treaties with Denmark, Holland, Sweden, Belgium, and France had unleashed a flow of foreign dairy and meat products into Germany. One result of this policy was a sudden fall in the price of pork followed by a price collapse in beef and cabbage (Kater, 1983:39–40; Childers, 1983: 146–47). To make matters worse the Weimar government, in the hope of protecting grain production, placed import duties on fodder and feeds (barley, bran, and oil cake) which, while helping the East Elbian grain farmers, raised the price of animal feed for the Geest region dairy and beef farmers (Childers, 1983:147; Abraham, 1981:63). Between 1926 and 1932 many of these smallholders in the Geest region defaulted on their loans and lost their farms.

During the final years of the Weimar Republic many of the Geest farmers of Schleswig-Holstein and lower Saxony protested against what they perceived was the government's insensitivity to their economic plight. They demanded a German trade policy that would eliminate foreign sources of food, an immediate takeover by the state of mortgage interest payments, a law lowering the rate of interest, governmental financial assistance, lower taxes, and less expensive fertilizer and electricity (Tilton, 1975:52; Pridham, 1973:124).

The Nazis seemed to address the needs of these farmers. The Nazi agrarian program called for security of tenure, protection of German farmers from the vagaries of the world market (including drastic curtailment of imports of agricultural products), the institution of guaranteed prices for the full range of agricultural products, lower taxes and interest rates, lower prices for electricity and fertilizer, severe action against usury, and a reform of the inheritance law (Farquharson, 1976:13–15; Noakes, 1971:124–25; Pridham, 1973:124; Kater, 1983:41; Childers, 1983:149).

The Nazi agrarian program attracted the Geest farmers because it offered to improve their economic situation. However, farmers in other German regions were less eager to support the Nazis because their program did not respond to their needs. Many farmers in Germany's more prosperous regions who were less affected by price changes in the international market for dairy and beef were less susceptible to Nazi promises (Moeller, 1986:15–16; Kater, 1983:58). For example, in the state of Rhineland-Westphalia, the agricultural system was much more flexible than the system in the Geest region of Schleswig-Holstein and lower Saxony. In Rhineland-Westphalia farmers raised livestock and cultivated fodder crops for their livestock. They did not have to pay high prices for imports or for state-subsidized East Elbian animal feed. Moreover, the flexibility of Rhineland-Westphalian agriculture enabled farmers to avoid dependence on the sales of any single product: declining sales of livestock could be countered by increasing sales of rye (Moeller, 1986:15–16).

Moreover, the Nazi agrarian program did not win over many of the large East Elbian grain producers. In contrast to the government's apparent insensitivity to the plight of the Geest dairy and meat farmers, the government enacted a series of policies between 1928 and 1930 that exclusively benefitted the large grain producers in East Elbia (Abraham, 1981:91–92). If that was not enough, the East Elbian farmers became the beneficiaries of massive state aid in 1931 under the Eastern Assistance Program (*Osthilfe*) (Childers, 1983:217). These farmers continued to rely on the conservative DNVP as their political voice.

Many farmers in Germany's more prosperous regions had an additional reason to look unfavorably upon the Nazi agrarian program. The Nazi promise to halt the sale of a farm outside the family line meant that owners could not sell their property or offer it as collateral against a loan (Farquharson, 1976:63–68). While this policy should have received support in the economically depressed Geest region, where farmers were fighting to prevent foreclosure on their properties, it should not have been well-received by farmers in the relatively lucrative zones of Rhineland-Westphalia, Baden, and Bavaria where the sale of land was still a source of profit and where putting up one's property as collateral against a loan was seen as a suitable means to obtain capital to expand one's holding.

In southwestern Germany, farmers had a particular problem with the Nazi agrarian program. The Nazis called for a compulsory system of impartible inheritance. If implemented this would have terminated the practice of partible inheritance that had been in effect in much of southwestern Germany and had been guaranteed by regional laws (Farquharson, 1976:63–68). Since many farmers' children in southwestern Germany counted on their portion of fixed and moveable property as an inheritance, the Nazi pledge to eliminate partible inheritance had not elicited great enthusiasm. On the other hand, the Geest farmers of Schleswig-Holstein and lower Saxony had no problem with the Nazi position on inheritance since impartible inheritance was already in practice there. But what really won over the Geest farmers was that accompanying the Nazi policy on inheritance was the promise of a settlement program through which disinherited farmers' sons would receive land parcels in eastern Germany (Farquharson, 1976:13–15; Noakes, 1971: 124–25). The settlement program offered young farmers the hope of owning a piece of land. While there were other impartible inheritance areas in Germany, the Nazi settlement program had a special significance for the Geest farmers. Traditionally, in Germany's impartible inheritance regions, the noninheriting children received a monetary compensation. However, in the economically depressed Geest region, older peasants did not have enough cash to pay off their younger sons. By promising to set aside land in eastern Germany for the disinherited, the Nazi program offered both parents and children an appealing solution to their dilemma (Noakes, 1971:127; Farquharson, 1976:240).

Before concluding this section, I mention that the perception that the fascist party will redress people's grievances cannot ensure that individuals will vote for the party. The party must have an ability to skillfully project its positions to individuals, otherwise, individuals may remain unaware of the party's program. Moreover, a party that pays only lip service to individuals' demands may encounter difficulty in attracting individuals. On the other hand, a party that directly involves itself in individuals' grievances should be in a better position to attract individuals. This is clearly seen in the different approaches taken by the Nazis and the other Protestant parties in Schleswig-Holstein and Franconia in regard to peasant protests. Though other Protestant parties' agrarian programs differed little from the Nazis', these parties were reluctant to participate directly in farmers' protests. By contrast, the Nazis joined with farmers who aimed to physically prevent forced auctions from taking place (Richter, 1986; Farquharson, 1976).

Individuals may feel less likely to join a fascist party if their opportunities to participate are restricted. In the case of Italian fascism the social environment presented few disincentives. Opportunities to join the Fascist party abounded throughout Italy. Neither the state or opposition parties mounted a serious deterrent to Fascist political mobilization. In fact, the Liberal government indirectly enhanced the opportunities of individuals to join the Fascist party. Tasca (1966:121) and Maier (1975:316) observed that the police (*Carabinieri, Regia Guarda,* and *Questura*) displayed open sympathy for fascism while doing everything in its power to hinder the Left. Government sympathy for the Fascists received an additional boost once the Fascist party joined the National Bloc in national elections of May 1921 (Tasca, 1966:129). There was little fear that opposition parties would raise the costs of fascist political mobilization. The fear of socialist reprisal ebbed by 1921 as a result of the effective legal offensive against the socialist leagues' boycotts and the presence of fascist squads to protect nonsocialist peasants (Corner, 1975:157).

In opposition to the claims of many scholars that fascist strength was a direct consequence of socialist strength, my explanation posits that fascist strength may be more accurately attributed to socialist weakness. As the socialist tide ebbed and the likelihood of socialist threats diminished, individuals interested in the fascist program anticipated lower costs in fascist party membership and appeared less reluctant about joining the party.

On the surface it appears that the opportunity to participate in fascist political mobilization was universal throughout Italy. However, opportunities did vary regionally as a result of the role played by agricultural elites. In the Po Valley the agricultural elites generally held considerable local power (Maier, 1975:315). Since they sympathized with the Fascist party's agrarian program, they employed their resources to create a favorable climate for party mobilization. In southern Italy, agricultural elites also held considerable local power, but they tended to support the Liberals and Democrats. Consequently, they had little interest in enhancing the political mobilization efforts of the Italian fascist party.

In contrast to the Italian case, the social environment in Germany presented numerous impediments which limited fascist political mobilization. These disincentives were especially great in German states controlled by the socialist party (SPD), such as Prussia. As early as 1922, the Prussian minister of the Interior placed a ban on the Nazi party meetings (Noakes, 1971:28–9). Between 1925 and 1927 the states of Bavaria, Prussia, Saxony, Baden, Hesse, Oldenburg, Anhalt, Hamburg, and Lubeck banned Hitler's participation in public meetings (Pridham, 1973: 42). In 1930, several states implemented further bans on Nazi party mobilization. These included the ban on wearing Nazi uniforms in Bavaria, Prussia, and Baden and the Prussian prohibition against members of the civil service becoming members of the Nazi party. According to Prussian policy, membership in the Nazi party was incompatible with public service, and civil servants were obliged to sign declarations affirming that they were not party members (Abel, 1966:95; Childers, 1983:177; Pridham, 1973:126, 133). Moreover, the Prussian police unleashed a series of raids culminating in wholesale arrests of Nazis. Between 1930 and 1932, hundreds of party members were imprisoned for terms up to 10 years (Abel, 1966:95–96). The state governments of Bavaria and Baden stopped short of threatening civil servants with dismissal for joining the Nazi party. These governments simply advised their public servants to be cautious about belonging to extremist parties (Pridham, 1973:192). As late as 1932 the Bruning government placed a ban on *Sturmabteilung* (SA) and *Schutzstaffel* (SS) activities (Pridham, 1973:126; Abel, 1966:94). In the same year the Bavarian police compiled lists of members of the SA and SS and confiscated their weapons and propaganda (Pridham, 1973:189).

Disincentives to join the Nazi party came from other sources as well. During the Weimar regime, shops owned by Nazis were frequently boycotted and many members were fired by unsympathetic employers (Abel, 1966:99). In addition, many party activists fell victim to opposition party violence. Abel (1966:105) notes that between 1930 and 1932 Communists stoned, shot, or knifed to death several hundred Nazis.

However, not all German regions presented such obstacles to fascist political mobilization. In some states the Nazis had established influence over governmental policies thanks to the presence of Nazi deputies or sympathizers (Pridham, 1973:208). This was certainly true in the free state of Oldenburg where Nazis won 19 seats in the May 1931 Landtag election and a majority of seats in the June 1932 election (Noakes, 1971). Braunschweig, Thuringia, and Mecklenburg were other areas where the Nazis established early footholds in state governments. However, I emphasize the case of Oldenburg because the Geest region of lower Saxony encompasses the northern counties of Oldenburg. In states where the Nazis had influence over the government, we should expect to find fewer disincentives to join the Nazi party.

Participation in the Fascist party should also be affected by the extent to which individuals depend on a party for the allocation of selective incentives (McCarthy and Zald, 1977; Gamson, 1975; Tilly, 1978). Fascist political mobilization in Italy benefitted greatly from the party's key position as a provider of valued resources. An important element in the party's success in the Po Valley was its ability to obtain control over the distribution of land and the signing of new wage contracts. In the aftermath of World War I, with the general demobilization of the Italian army, land had become a highly sought-after good. While the socialists had substantial power over the issuance of wage contracts, they had virtually no control of land redistribution. Landlords resisted all attempts to hand over land to the socialist leagues. The crisis situation of 1919-1921 convinced many landlords that by ceding land to the fascists, they could erect an effective barrier to the further expansion of the socialist leagues (Tasca, 1966:109; Snowden, 1972:279; Lyttleton, 1973:63; Maier, 1975:316). Consequently, in many Po Valley districts the fascists came into exclusive possession of land. The intense market for land gave the Italian fascist party a prized resource which they could exchange for membership. In the province of Ferrara the fascist land office distributed 12,000 hectares to peasants on long leases (Lyttleton, 1973:63). Land was not, however, the only resource to fall into the hands of the Po Valley fascists. In the face of socialist boycotts, reprisals, and fines many nonsocialist peasants had no choice but to turn to the fascists as an effective guarantee of protection. The fascist guarantee carried credibility because the fascists demonstrated by example that they could effectively protect peasants from the socialist leagues (Cardoza, 1982:338-39). In some northern Italian regions, the fascists successfully eroded the socialist monopoly over employment opportunities and new wage contracts (Cardoza, 1982:338-39; Maier, 1975:316). For example, in Mantua (Lombardy) the fascist gained considerable control over employment. The Agrarian Association of Mantua announced that only those agricultural workers registered with the local *fascios* would get future work (Tasca, 1966:109).

In southern Italy, the Italian Fascist party's attempt to control valuable resources encountered stiff resistance from the principal landowning class. The clientelistic system imposed a quasitotal dependence of peasants on their landlords (Snowden, 1972:278–79; Tarrow, 1967:68, 169). Peasant dependence on landlords was reinforced by the absence of any horizontal solidarity that might have served as an alternative means by which peasants could obtain resources. The fascists could not break the landlords' stranglehold over resources, nor could they convince landlords to change their political allegiance from the Liberal and Democrat parties to the Fascist party. Consequently, the fascists had few resources to provide the southern Italian peasants.

The German Nazi party, in contrast to the Italian Fascist party, had little control over the redistribution of land and wage contracts. The potentially valuable resources the party could offer individuals were information, social activities, employment (within the party), and behavioral confirmation. An example of the Nazi dissemination of valuable information was the training of agricultural experts or consultants who were sent into the countryside by the *Gau* leadership to provide technical assistance to farmers as well as to explain the Nazi position on agricultural matters (Childers, 1983:151). In addition, the Nazis frequently sponsored "German evenings," a form of entertainment and propaganda. These "German evenings" might include speeches, concerts, sporting events, and parades (Pridham, 1973:105, 229–30). For many rural villages these Nazi-sponsored activities served as the principal form of information and entertainment. Another resource the Nazi party possessed was jobs. Within each *Gau* the party organization called for the creation of many party offices and specialists. In some rural communities party jobs provided the only viable opportunities for the unemployed (Orlow, 1969:158–59; Pridham, 1973:200–02).

In many rural areas, the strongest competition to the Nazi dissemination of resources came from the Catholic Zentrum and Bavarian People's Party. These parties had the financial support of the Catholic church (Childers, 1983:189; Hamilton, 1982:371; Pridham, 1973:233–34). After 1928, these Catholic parties became a greater competitor to the Nazis because, in addition to their resources, they shared with the Nazis similar positions on many key political and economic issues (Moeller, 1986:153).

In one highly significant respect the Nazi party's resources differed from those of the Italian Fascist party. The Nazi party held no monopoly over the resources in its possession and thus could not realistically demand participation in exchange for resources. The Italian fascists, by contrast, held a quasi-monopolistic control over land redistribution in the Po Valley and thus should have been in a better position to demand participation in exchange for land and agricultural employment.

The importance of the role of strong social networks in overcoming the reluctance to join the fascist party was apparent in the Italian Fascist party's mobilization success in the Po Valley and Apulia and its failure in southern Italy. In the Po Valley and Apulia peasants were concentrated in villages (Maier, 1975:306). Tasca (1966:117) notes that in the agricultural villages of Apulia everyone knew everyone else. Moreover, whether they were agricultural laborers or smallholders, Po Valley and Apulian peasants possessed a class organization and mentality (Tarrow, 1967:51; Cardoza, 1982:343–44). This may help to explain the high level of intra- and interclass organizational capacity in the Po Valley and Apulia. For instance, during 1902 there were 161 agricultural leagues in the province of Ferrara alone, with a membership of 32,000 peasants (Corner, 1975:9). In the aftermath of World War I, a plethora of agricultural unions, cooperatives, social clubs, and electoral schools blanketed the Po Valley. Many of these agricultural organizations, which held a large proportion of landless agricultural laborers, turned to the socialist leagues in 1919 and 1920. At the same time a sizable proportion of the wealthier peasants participated in the activities of the politically conservative Provincial Association of Agriculturalists (APA). Members of the APA came from all classes of agrarian employers, ranging from big commercial farmers to small peasant proprietors (Cardoza, 1982:278–79). Many APA members eventually would join the Italian fascists.

By contrast, the peasants of southern Italy were socially isolated and lacked a class organization and mentality (Rossi-Doria, 1958). Moss and Cappannari (1962:300) in their study of social solidarity in an agricultural village in the southern Italian province of Molise remarked "the solidarity of familial structure and the absence of any concept of community prevent mutual solutions to mutual problems. With the exception of those at the extremes of the social hierarchy, we find a complete absence of any conception analogous to neighborhood." This sense of low social solidarity is also echoed by Snowden (1972:288–89) and Rossi-Doria (1958). Rossi-Doria adds that the southern peasant possessed little class solidarity and infrequently participated in the life of the community (Rossi-Doria, 1958:23). Class solidarity in southern Italy suffered from the existence of many different occupational categories. For example, within the system of sharecropping there were eleven basic categories, each with a different duration and division of the product (Tarrow, 1967:52–53).

Furthermore, class solidarity fell victim to clientelist relations. In the South, clientelist relations between peasant and landlord were independent and vertical and thus hindered class organizations (Tarrow, 1967:

68). But the existence of a clientelist system need not always inhibit the formation of community. In an earlier study, I and a colleague argued that in particular subsistence regions of western Europe between 1500 and 1700 vertical solidarity between landlords and peasants was quite strong (Brustein and Levi, 1987). These peasants depended on their landlords for land, tools, and periodic loans of grain, seed, and corn. At the same time, the landlords depended on their peasants because the opportunity costs of finding alternative sources of labor were high in these areas of population dispersion and low population growth. The bond between peasant and landlord was further strengthened by the actual presence of the landlord, for a resident landlord is more capable of rendering assistance to a peasant in times of need than is an absentee landlord. And the landlord who, by his presence personally renders services in exchange for rents is perceived to be more legitimate than the landlord who, by his absence, renders no services (Stinchcombe, 1983: 160–61). However, clientelistic relations in southern Italy were quite different. The connections between landlord and peasant were tenuous, unstable, and rife with conflict (Snowden, 1972:288–89). The bond between peasant and landlord suffered since the majority of the *latifondisti* were absentee landlords, and the terms of their leases were crippling to the peasants. For instance, southern Italian landlords did not furnish their sharecroppers tools, living quarters, and other materials (Tarrow, 1967:52–53). All told, in the Po Valley and Apulia a tightly knit system of social networks was present while in southern Italy it was clearly absent.

The significance of strong social networks was also apparent in the German Nazi party's mobilization success in the Geest region of Schleswig-Holstein and lower Saxony and the party's relative mobilization difficulties in Rhineland-Westphalia, Baden, and Bavaria. The Geest region exhibited many prerequisites for conditional cooperation. Farms were generally small or medium and family-operated. A landless agricultural proletarian class was absent (Heberle, 1951:228; Noakes, 1971: 4). The absence of agricultural proletarians and large farmers produced a rather homogeneous social structure. Moreover, individuals in the Geest region resided in compact villages with close community ties (Passchier, 1980:290; Noakes, 1971:4). Village compactness and a homogeneous social structure nurtured social solidarity and social control.

By contrast, the preconditions for conditional cooperation were less apparent in many other German regions. Heberle (1951) and Noakes (1971) note that even within Schleswig-Holstein and neighboring lower Saxony there were districts where large and small farms coexisted and agricultural laborers were more common (Heberle, 1951; Noakes, 1971). These circumstances led to social heterogeneity. Noakes observed further that in contrast to the socially homogeneous Geest region, the level of social conflict was high in these socially heterogeneous villages. In the case of southwestern Germany, which also possessed a more heterogeneous agricultural population, the absence of common property, joint work, and impartible inheritance further hindered social solidarity.

Conclusion

In this chapter I have presented an explanation of the political geography of fascist party membership in Italy and Germany during the interwar period. Both general and case study explanations of the rise of fascism fail to distinguish between the motivations responsible for voting for and joining a fascist party and emphasize irrational rather than rational motivations for individuals support of fascist parties. Guided by a subjective expected utility approach, I have found that regional variation in fascist party membership in Italy and Germany could be attributed to regional differences in the extent to which the fascist party program was perceived to redress individuals' grievances, the opportunities available to individuals to join the party, the degree of the party's control over the distribution of selective incentives, and the degree of solidarity of individuals' social networks. These factors were important because they shaped individuals calculations regarding party membership. My explanation appears to help explain the German Nazi party's success in the Geest region of Schleswig-Holstein and lower Saxony and its relative weakness in Southwest Germany, and the Italian Fascist party's success in the Po Valley and Apulia and its failure in southern Italy. The reader is cautioned, however, that conclusions drawn from the evidence are more suggestive than definitive.

Acknowledgment

I would like to thank Barry Markovsky, Jurgen Falter, Karl-Dieter Opp, Harmut Esser, Michael Hechter, Siegwart Lindenberg, Karol Sołtan, Michael Loriaux, and Glen Perusek for helpful comments on earlier drafts of this manuscript.

Notes

1. For a more detailed examination of the problems associated with both general and case study explanations of the rise of fascism see Brustein (1988).

2. We may soon learn whether there is a strong correlation between voting behavior and party membership at least for the Weimar period. Jurgen Falter and Michael Kater are currently analyzing data on Nazi party membership and Nazi voting for a large sample of German communities.

3. For a more detailed discussion of the promise of subjective expected utility theory for the study of fascism's political geography see Brustein and Markovsky, (1988).

References

Abel, T. (1966). *Why Hitler Came Into Power*. New York: Prentice Hall.
Abraham, D. (1981). *The Collapse of the Weimar Republic: Political Economy and Crisis*. Princeton: Princeton University Press.
Arendt, H. (1961). *The Origins of Totalitarianism*, 2nd ed. Cleveland and New York: World.
Brustein, W. (1988). "The political geography of Belgian fascism: The case of Rexism." *American Sociological Review* 53:939–50.
Brustein, W. and M. Levi. (1987). "The geography of rebellion: Rulers, rebels, and regions, 1500–1700." *Theory and Society* 16:467–95.
Brustein, W. and B. Markovsky. (1988). "A subjective expected utility explanation of interwar Fascist Party membership in Italy and Germany." unpublished manuscript.
Cardoza, A.L. (1982). *Agrarian Elites and Italian Fascism: The Province of Bologna, 1901–1926*. Princeton: Princeton University Press.
Childers, T. (1983). *The Nazi Voter: The Social Foundations of Fascism in Germany, 1919–1933*. Chapel Hill: University of North Carolina Press.
Corner, P. (1975). *Fascism in Ferrara 1915–1925*. London: Oxford University Press.
De Felice, R. (1966). *Mussolini il Fascista: La Conquista del Potere 1921–1925*, vol. 1, Turin: Giulio Einaudi.
De Nardo, J. (1985). *Power in Numbers: The Political Strategy of Protest and Rebellion*. Princeton: Princeton University Press.
Farquharson, J.E. (1976). *The Plough and the Swastika: The NSDAP and Agriculture in Germany 1928–45*. London: Sage.
Fireman, B. and W.A. Gamson. (1979). "Utilitarian logic in the resource mobilization perspective." Pp. 8–44 in M.N. Zald and J.D. McCarthy, eds., *The Dynamics of Social Movements*. Cambridge, MA.: Winthrop.
Gamson, W.A. (1975). *The Strategy of Social Protest*. Homewood, IL.: Dorsey Press.
Hamilton, R.F. (1982). *Who Voted For Hitler?* Princeton: Princeton University Press.
Hardin, R. (1982). *Collective Action*. Baltimore: Johns Hopkins University Press.
Heberle, R. (1951). *Social Movements*. New York: Appleton-Century-Crofts.
Hechter, M. (1987). *Principles of Group Solidarity*. Berkeley: University of California Press.
Jenkins, J.C. and C. Perrow. (1977). "Insurgency of the powerless: Farm worker movements (1946–1972)." *American Sociological Review*. 42:249–68.

Kater, M. (1983). *The Nazi Party*. Cambridge, MA.: Harvard University Press.
Loomis, C. and P. Beegle. (1946). "The spread of nazism in rural areas." *American Sociological Review*. 11:724–33.
Lyttleton, A. (1973). *The seizure of power: Fascism in Italy, 1919–1929*. London: Weidenfeld and Nicolson.
McCarthy, J.D. and M.N. Zald. (1977). "Resource mobilization and social movements: A partial theory." *American Journal of Sociology*. 82:1212–41.
Maier, C. (1975). *Recasting Bourgeois Europe*. Princeton: Princeton University Press.
Merkl, P.H. (1975). *Political Violence Under the Swastika: 581 Pre-1933 Nazis*. Princeton: Princeton University Press.
Mitchell, B.R. (1981). *European Historical Statistics, 1750–1975*, 2nd ed. New York: Facts on File.
Moeller, R.G. (1986). *German Peasants and Agrarian Politics, 1914–1924*. Chapel Hill: University of North Carolina Press.
Moore, B. Jr. (1966). *Social Origins of Dictatorship and Democracy*. Boston: Beacon Press.
Moss, L.W. and S.C. Cappannari. (1962). "Estate and class in a south italian village." *American Anthropologist*. 64:287–300.
NSDAP Partei Statistik (1935). Band II
Noakes, J. (1971). *The Nazi Party in Lower Saxony, 1921–1933*. London: Oxford University Press.
Nolte, E. (1966). *Three Faces of Fascism*. New York: Holt, Rinehart and Winston.
Oberschall, A. (1973). *Social Conflict and Social Movements*. Englewood Cliffs: Prentice-Hall.
Olson, M. (1965). *The Logic of Collective Action*. Cambridge, MA.: Harvard University Press.
Olson, M. (1982). *The Rise and Decline of Nations*. New Haven: Yale University Press.
Orlow, D. (1969). *The History of the Nazi Party: 1919–1933*. Pittsburgh: University of Pittsburgh Press.
Passchier, N. (1980). "The electoral geography of the Nazi landslide." Pp. 283–300 in S.U. Larsen, B. Hagtvet, and J.P. Myklebust, eds., *Who Were the Fascists*. Bergen: Universitesforlaget.
Pridham, G. (1973). *Hitler's Rise to Power: The Nazi Movement in Bavaria, 1923–1933*. New York: Harper & Row.
Richter, M.W. (1986). "Resource mobilisation and legal revolution: National socialist tactics in Franconia." Pp. 104–130 in T. Childers, ed., *The Formation of the Nazi Constituency, 1919–1933*. Totowa, N.J.: Barnes & Noble Books.
Rossi-Doria, M. (1958). *Dieci Anni di Politica Agraria nel Mezzogiorno*. Bari: Laterza.
Salert, B. (1976). *Four Theories Revolutions and Revolutionaries*. New York: Elsevier.
Snowden, F.M. (1972). "The origins of agrarian fascism in Italy." *Archives Europeenes de Sociologie* 13:268–95.
Stinchcombe, A.L. (1983). *Economic Sociology*. New York: Academic Press.

Tarrow, S. (1967). *Peasant Communism in Southern Italy*. New Haven: Yale University Press.
Tasca, A. (1966). *The Rise of Italian Fascism 1918–1922*. New York: Howard Fertig.
Taylor, M. (1982). *Community, Anarchy and Liberty*. Cambridge: Cambridge University Press.
Tilly, C. (1978). *From Mobilization to Revolution*. Reading, MA.: Addison-Wesley.
Tilton, T.A. (1975). *Nazism, Neo-Nazism and the Peasantry*. Bloomington: University of Indiana Press.
Tullock, G. (1971). *The Logic of the Law*. New York: Basic Books

12

Incentives, Governance, and Development in Chinese Collective Agriculture

Anthony Oberschall

After their success in the civil war against the Guomintang in 1949 and following the largest land reform in history, the Chinese Communist Party (CCP) in 1953 collectivized agriculture for the next 25 years (Shue, 1980). Collective agriculture under CCP leadership was meant to liberate the forces of production previously stifled by exploiting landlords, a capitalist mode of land ownership and production, backward technology, and feudal peasant attitudes inimical to cooperation and production. At the same time, the social and economic leveling of the peasantry already accomplished was to be preserved. Within a basic institutional framework defining collective agriculture, important organizational changes were continually made which had a great impact on work incentives, the size of the basic production units, and the governance of the collective. These changes were a reaction to the lack of success achieved with raising agricultural productivity and output, and, as important, a reaction to ideological shifts and power struggles within the top leadership of the CCP (Perkins and Yusuf, 1984:78). From the mutual aid teams and cooperatives of the mid 1950s to the household responsibility system of the late 1970s, the 25 years of collective agriculture in the People's Republic of China (PRC) represent a vast social experiment which rivals in scope the organizational and institutional changes that manufacturing went through in the industrial revolution from cottage industry and the putting-out system to factory production and the scientifically managed assembly line in mass production industries. The purpose of this chapter is to explain the varying fortunes of Chinese collective agriculture with reference to a simple model grounded in recent social science thinking on institution building and the economics of organization. Chinese agriculture and village organization before the revolution will be described first; the basic design for collective agriculture in the PRC will be discussed next; following will be a simple model of the causal relationships between work incentives, team size, governance, and agricultural productivity and output; and, finally, I will examine the model against the evidence of a quarter of a century of collective agriculture in a single village, and draw some conclusions.

Peasantry and Village

Contrary to some views, landlordism on a large scale and heavy tax extraction by the state were not pervasive, nor were they primarily responsible for rural poverty and economic stagnation. According to Huang's (1985) detailed study of thirty-three villages in North China in the 1920s and 1930s, the basic unit of farm production was a small family farm of owner- and tenant-cultivators, with some combining both on different plots. The poorest peasants hired out some family labor to the larger managerial farms—the "rich" peasants—that needed more labor than family could supply. Still, much of the population was under- or unemployed during part of the year. Absentee landlords were rare. All farmers produced for their own consumption and some cash crops (e.g., cotton) for the market. Women from the poorer farming families supplemented farm income with weaving.

Reduced to wage labor, the poorest peasants could not afford to marry, and their families died out. Their ranks were replenished by small farmers who were victims of drought, floods, pests, poor health, indebtedness or incompetence. The more well-to-do farm families could afford to maintain the ideal of the stem family, with married sons living in their father's household. Because the more prosperous farmers had more children and practiced partible inheritance, their larger farms were broken up into smaller ones in the next generation. At the same time, some successful small farm families became prosperous, and in turn went through farm fragmentation in the succeeding generation. Beyond the low level of commercial agriculture, no breakthrough into more productive, more captial-intensive and technologically advanced farming occurred. For 150 years (up to 1949), farm technology, land tenure, and family institutions had remained almost the same, and, with them, the standard of life. The rural economy was stagnant.

As Huang describes them, the villages were insular, stratified, and atomized. Although villagers tended to belong to the same, or only a few lineages, lineage-based solidarity was in decline. For instance, the tradition of keeping village land in the lineage had ceased. Land for sale went simply to the highest bidder. Status competition among villagers was intense and was especially keen for marriage match-making, wedding feasts, and the amount of dowry. The poorer farmers who could only afford child brides were looked down upon.

There was no formal village leadership or headship. The state administration collected taxes from landowners through a village "head" nominated by the villagers and were unpaid. Although the head could manipulate village taxes and special levies to his and his kin's advantage, the position was shunned because it led to strained interpersonal relations with fellow villagers. In North China, the gentry had cut itself off from village roots and no longer exercised the role of patron, benefactor, and distributor of lineage land and resources. Some institutions of cooperation and solidarity had survived, notably collective defense against bandits and reciprocal help for house construction and for some agricultural tasks. Still, the dominant pattern was Malthusian competition for subsistence among nuclear families in a zero-sum resource setting, with many hovering on the brink of catastrophe. Little cooperation and low interpersonal trust was the rule. Only weak leadership was possible. Despite underemployment and idleness, villagers did not join in collective projects to improve their lot. Banfield (1958) discovered such an ethos of "amoral familism" in a poor village in south Italy. In a Mexican village, Foster (1960–1961, 1965) found that distrust and noncooperation were anchored in a zero-sum view of the world which mirrored the peasants' situation of limited and sharply competitive opportunity.

Fried's (1953) study of a county in central China in 1947–1948 has some useful information on social bonds and solidarity among peasants which differs somewhat from the situation in North China. There, too, the life of most peasants was taken up with the struggle for subsistence, securing a good tenancy, disposing of surplus family labor, and escaping from downward mobility into the class of poor wage laborers and of the outcasts who could not afford to marry. The poor peasants did not eat the rice they grew, but sold it and bought cheaper food instead. Landlords and share renting were more important than in North China. The tenant supplied his own seeds, tools, animals, and house and surrendered 40% of the staple grains after each of the two annual harvests and a variable amount of other crops.

Instead of short-term contracting with tenants and wage laborers, many landlord–tenant and landlord–hired hand relationships rested on longer term, diffuse contracts, not unlike patron–client ties found elsewhere. These relations were buttressed by the sentiment of "renching" (sympathy, mutual attraction), which expresses the ideal Chinese relationship between two persons of unequal social status. The relationship might entail small gifts and labor services to the landlord patron at important holidays. For the landlord, a long-term relationship and "renching" reduced the enforcement costs of the contract because the tenant was less likely to cheat him on the quantity and quality of rice owed. The tenant turned to the landlord rather than to money lenders in emergencies with an assurance of receiving help, and had good prospects of passing the tenancy to his son.

Market exchange in the county studied by Fried was thus tempered by some vertical solidarity. Horizontal, interpeasant competition was cushioned by some cooperation in work exchange for plowing and harvesting. Nevertheless, the struggle for survival at this low level of living strained social relationships even in the nuclear family: children who could not be fed were contracted out as laborers or apprentices in distant places, girls were sold as child brides, siblings disputed over inheritance and responsibility for maintaining aging parents, and widows were left to fend on their own. Many of the poor remained unmarried, itinerant casual workers and beggars. The rural economy was stagnant. These were the peasant villages inherited by the communists.

The Basic Design for Collective Agriculture

The "land-to-the-tiller" land reform equalized holdings among households, but redistributed the other means of production, such as farm animals and equipment, in more limited fashion (Shue, 1980; Chapter 2). At first, agricultural policy permitted buying, selling, and renting land, hiring labor, loaning money with interest, and setting up private enterprise for profit. The countryside recovered from the ravages of war and civil war. Soon there were signs of former poor peasants losing ground and of a growing inequality within the peasantry. After a brief period of experimentation with voluntary mutual-aid groups, the CCP turned, in 1955, to the collectivization of agriculture for achieving a number of objectives that included checking inequality (Shue, 1980: Chaps. 3, 4, 7).

The government abolished private grain markets and introduced a state monopoly of buying and selling grain. It sharply curtailed and controlled migration to cities and labor markets by issuing residency permits to all, and grain ration-books to city residents only. Henceforth, city residents were guaranteed access to food at subsidized and controlled prices, referred to as the security of the "iron rice bowl." The purpose of these measures was to finance industrialization by taxing peasants, restricting them to their villages, and curtailing their consumption of manufactured goods through a dual pricing system that made urban goods expensive relative to village-produced goods.

Thus in the 1950s and early 1960s, the CCP policy for rural development and increased food output through collective agriculture ruled out exogenous sources of change, such as state investment in agricultural technology, rural industries, transportation, and infrastructure. Development was to be based on the peasants' own labor under the leadership of party cadres. The key was internal reorganization of existing resources, both material and human, in which new styles of leadership, modes of social control, moral incentives, revolutionary fervor, cooperation and solidarity among peasants figured prominently (Perkins and Yusuf, 1984:73). Just as land reform broke the power of landlords, collectivization would liberate the forces of production.

Under the basic institutional design of collective agriculture in China, the means of production (land, tools, farm animals) were put under a single, centralized management (Shue, 1980; Chapter 7; Hinton, 1984: 114–125). The members were organized for collective work. Provisions were made to buy out draft animals and equipment from their owners in 3 years. Payment for labor was "to each according to his work," but in fact tended to include various leveling mechanisms based on need criteria and egalitarianism. Village craftsmen, villagers under temporary contract with an urban industry or assigned to public works projects, and those in village "sideline" industries (e.g., brickmakers) earned workpoints and were all paid in workpoints drawn from a common fund.

The collective was run by a chairman, a management, and a supervisory committee elected by the members. Within the collective, a number of year-round, equal-sized, production teams became responsible for cultivating a specific land area, and were assigned farm animals and equipment. Each team elected its leader and appointed technicians and administrators. Team leaders allocated work to team members and imposed labor discipline backed by criticism, fines, payment for damages, and reduction of workday credits.

The collective had to produce and sell its output according to the state plan, pay an agricultural tax, set aside a reserve fund for capital investment, and a welfare fund for needy members. The balance of income was distributed to members according to their earned labor shares or workpoints.

Two systems of earning workpoints were recommended. In the first, each worker would be assigned a workpoint rating based on skill and work capacity relative to a norm of ten points for an able-bodied adult male's output in a full day's work, subject to daily revision by the team leader and teammates.

In the second, piecework system, each task or job was assigned a number of workpoints, with ten workpoints per day for a job of average difficulty. Thus a particular plot of land to be used or ploughed by specified means (draft animals and equipment) was normed at a certain number of workpoints, with additional workpoint credits for overfulfillment and penalties for underfulfillment. The grain or money value of a workpoint was determined at the end of the harvest when the total income less taxes, reserve and welfare fund, production, and other expenses, was divided by total number of workpoints accumulated by all collective members during the year.

Despite frequent modifications, this remained the basic form of organization for collective agriculture until the "household responsiblity" system of 1978–1979. As one can tell from even this brief summary, the collective was a complex institution. Under this system, village output and peasant productivity were expected to increase. Small family plots were to be consolidated into large fields suitable for a single crop and mechanized agriculture. Elimination of boundaries and paths would increase crop space. The investment fund would finance technological improvements. Underutilized village labor in the slack seasons would be mobilized for collective improvements such as wells, irrigation canals, and sideline industries. The collective spread risk for innovations and offered some security to families deficient in labor through the welfare fund.

Productivity and Output

Within the basic institutional design, variations resulted from choices about the size of production teams and sharing groups, about work incentives, and about the governance of the collective. Team size refers to the number of farming households that pool and share productive inputs (land, labor, farm animals, tools, . . .) and periodically divide output. Team size might be as small as a single peasant household or a group of neighbors; the entire village formed into a "brigade," and several villages forming a "commune." Work incentives might vary. The division of the collective output might give more or less weight to work contributed and other merit criteria. Governance might vary as well. Farm management decisions and other aspects of governance could be apportioned variously among household heads, team leaders, brigade leaders, and higher authorities. How do team size, work incentives, and governance affect productivity and team output?

Among analysts of Chinese agriculture there is considerable agreement about the lack of economies of scale in crop production. Marshall (1985:55–56) writes:

> Chinese agriculture resembles horticulture in character. It is marked by an intensive, irrigation dominated pattern of farming, typical of many Asian countries. Chinese-type irrigation involves a multitude of variegated tasks . . . these operations do not lend themselves well to centralized management and decision-making . . . one would expect that an extremely decentralized organization of crop production would provide the best results. In this way, small groups of families who perhaps live in the same neighborhood . . . can make their own daily decisions concerning crop production.

Nevertheless, the efficient small team for crop production is not the most suitable for building an agricultural infrastructure. Building and managing water works and land reclamation requires decisions at the village or even higher levels. For collective agriculture, a two-tiered organization structure is suggested: daily farm management decisions to be made and implemented in households or small teams, and decisions about many collective goods to be taken and organized at the brigade and higher levels.

In transaction cost economics applied to the organization of work, incentives and the measurement of performance play a central role (Alchian and Demsetz, 1972; Williamson, 1985:Chapter 9). If peasants are rewarded according to merit criteria based on the amount of work performed or the contribution made to team output, they will work harder and will be more productive than if they are rewarded equally (regardless of work input) or according to need (e.g., the age, size, health, gender composition of their household). The greater the deviation from merit criteria, the greater will be the disposition to free ride and to shirk. In collective agriculture, Chinese peasants had an opportunity to do both. They had some discretion about how much household labor to contribute to team production and how much to their private family plots, and in team production itself they controlled the quality and intensity of their work.

These ideas can be more precisely stated. Assume team ouput is equally divided. If one assumes that team output is proportional to the input of labor, and if the average work effort in a group of size N is L units of labor, someone who puts in $L' > L$ labor effort will obtain only a fraction of the increased output resulting from his effort, i.e., only $(L' - L)/N$. Moreover, this fraction diminishes with group size (N). On the other hand, if someone puts in a below average labor effort $L' < L$, then his loss from shirking will only be a fraction of the diminished output, i.e., $(L - L')/N$, which also diminishes with group size. Thus there exist powerful disincentives for working hard and incentives for shirking, and both increase with team size (Perkins and Yusuf, 1984:79).

Assume now the more common situation of reward for work based on a mixture of merit and egalitarian criteria. Holding team size constant, it can be shown that as egalitarianism increases, a team member's share will *increase* if his contribution is *below average*, and will *diminish* if his contribution is *above average*. Such a perverse consequence of egalitarianism encourages shirking and free riding on other team members. To check shirking, one would have to supervise workers closely and continuously, and institute a system of fines and penalties, which is a backhanded way of giving more weight to "merit." Supervision, moreover, increases governance costs.

Governance cost in collective agriculture depends greatly on metering costs, i.e., how inputs and outputs are measured. If workpoints are awarded by days or hours worked, team members have to be closely and continuously supervised for the amount of time worked, the pace and intensity of work, and the quality of their work (e.g., planting rice at the proper depth, which requires more effort). Those who show up late or quit early have to be penalized by subtracting workpoints from their daily norm, as do those who loaf or work carelessly.

If workpoints are awarded by task, a major problem is the great variety of production tasks in diversified agriculture over the yearly cycle. In one village, piece rates were set for a normal day's work for some seventy tasks, and later for as many as 160 (Hinton, 1984:183). There were nine different workpoint norms for plowing per area since both quality and grade of soil, and the strength and health of draft animals varied. Hauling manure and compost had to be variously normed because distance from fields to manure tanks and compost piles varied, as did the size of the hauling equipment. Even after the tedious process of norming every task, there remained the daily cost of metering: inspecting the work done for quantity and quality. Both these input metering methods have high governance costs. Moreover, input metering based on workpoints does not reward quality of work nor the proper care of team animals, equipment, and common property (Shue, 1980:301–305).

Because of these undesirable consequences of input metering, there was experimentation with other forms of compensation, such as seasonal contracting for the care of a specified parcel of land (Perkins and Yusuf, 1984:76, and fn. 4, p. 101). A household or small group of households would be responsible for producing a given quota of grain on a specific plot in return for a certain number of workpoints, and assigned animals, equipment, and fertilizer to work with for an entire year. Grain in excess of the quota would fetch additional workpoints, and grain below the quota would result in workpoint penalties. Based on recent years' yields and adjusted for current weather, the quota would be set once a year. I refer to this method as "output" metering. The peasants had an incentive for high quality work and for caring for their animals and equipment. Governance costs were much lower since daily input metering and supervision by team leaders and workpoint recorders was unnecessary. The thrust of the analysis is that output metering entails lower governance costs than input metering. More people in the village would be performing agricultural rather than administrative work, and team leaders themselves had more time in a day to spend in production instead of supervision, planning, and record-keeping.

So far I have viewed collective agriculture as though it were an organizational variant for individualist peasants. Are there no gains then from freeing peasants from the pre-1949 competitive, limited opportunity environments which, according to Foster, sustains mistrust and lack of cooperation? What if greater "social consciousness" (Sen, 1966), "team cohesion," and "concern for other team members" (Chinn, 1979, 1980) are fostered in collective agriculture, and they, in turn, increase the productivity of peasants? What is a likely micro social process through which intense propaganda campaigns mounted from without the village about hard work and sacrifice for the common good actually take root in peasant consciousness?

Suppose that greater effort in collective agriculture depends on the assurance of fairness. One is likely to work hard if one is assured that others are working hard, and if one obtains a fair share of the team output. One is likely to slacken if others slacken and if some obtain more than their fair share of output. Social consciousness is a positive factor in productivity but only so long as there is assurance of fairness. What discourages free riding is peer pressure and sanctions against slackers on the negative side, and what stimulates work effort is social standing in the team and reputation based on contributing to the common good and for doing one's fair share in the team. But fairness is more likely assured in a small, "natural" team of interdependent households, e.g., neighbors, rather than a large team composed of strangers and households weakly dependent on each other (Perkins and Yusuf, 1984:79). In the small team, one's actions have a greater moral influence on others' actions; one is able to monitor personally how much effort others are putting out and what rewards they are getting; social standing in the group matters to each; and there is likely to be a consensus on the principle of distributive justice for defining fairness. Thus in large teams, or, on the other hand, when team size shrinks to a single house-

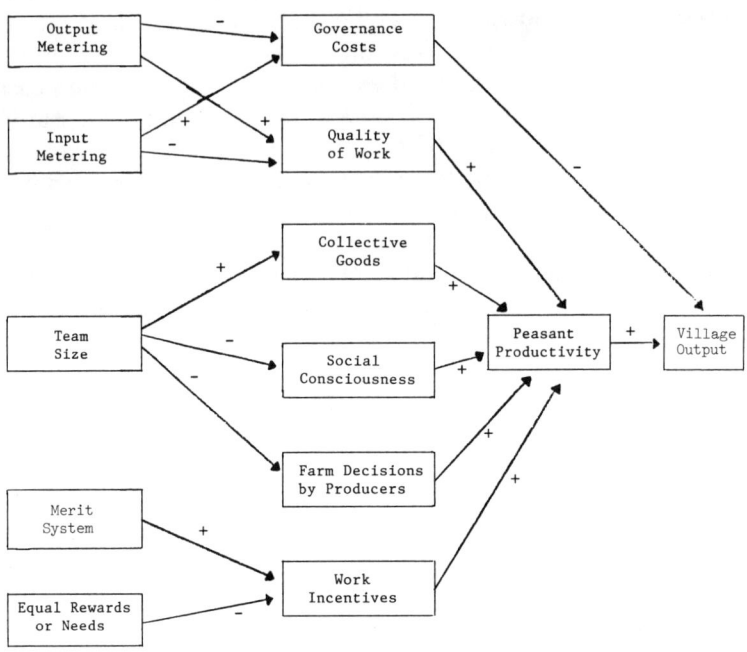

Figure 12.1 Determinants of productivity and output

hold or a few households whose resources, work, and output no longer depend on other villagers, social consciousness ceases to matter altogether for productivity.

These ideas about productivity and output are briefly summarized in Figure 12.1, where only the strongest and most direct causal relationships are entered. There is no need to review every single relationship. The most salient and readily observable variables are team size, output/input metering, and working incentives based on merit rewards as opposed to equal or need rewards. Social consciousness has to be inferred from observers' reports about trust, cooperation, disputes, theft, and the like. Output metering lowers goverance cost and encourages high quality of workmanship, and thus results in greater individual productivity and greater village output. Team size has one positive and two negative causal links to peasant productivity. Thus, on balance, there is a tendency for smaller team size to increase peasant productivity. Last, rewards based on merit motivate work effort and greater peasant productivity. These ideas and the model presented are applied in the section below to the experience of a single Chinese village with collective agriculture.

Chen Village and Institutional Experiments

Mutual Aid Teams

The following account is based on the superb case study of "Chen" village in South China by Anita Chan, Richard Madsen, and Jonathan Unger (1984). After the Revolution, in 1950, small work teams of cadres arrived in Chen village to implement land reform. Chen village consisted of about 1000 persons in 250 families, and was poor even by Chinese standards (Chan et al., 1984:14). The villagers owned only about 500 arable acres, more than half in distant small mountain valleys. The work team discovered only two landlords, neither of them with large land holdings, and five "rich" peasant households. Of the population, 80–85% were lower middle peasants who owned some land but also rented or labored for richer families, and poor peasants, who owned little or no land and were illiterate (Chan et al., 1984:21–22). Although the work team stripped the two landlords of all but the land needed to maintain their families and distributed the lineage lands among the poor peasants, land was far from equalized, since the poor peasants lacked tools and draft animals to work their land efficiently.[1] In keeping with the tradition of work exchange for plowing and harvesting, the work team urged friends and neighbors to cooperate in mutual-aid teams throughout the year (Chan et al., 1984:21–23).

In mutual-aid teams, members pooled and exchanged draft animals, equipment, and labor for some agricultural tasks. Each family made some farm decisions for its own fields and kept the output for itself. Elected team leaders planned each day's work, recorded the labor time of members, and credited farm animals and equipment used. When farm animals were not needed by the team, their owners were free to use them on their account. Several times a year, a balance sheet was drawn up and accounts settled in cash or grain (Shue, 1980: Chapter 4; Hinton, 1984:76–89). When teams were small, governance costs were low since team leaders participated full-time in team production. Work incentives were high: the more one worked on others' land, the greater one's share at settlement. Peer pressure to maintain quality of work was effective in small, face-to-face teams, and social consciousness was positive. The theory predicts high productivity under these circumstances.

A new tax system also provided positive incentives. Peasants who increased yields escaped additional taxes for the 3 initial years (Hinton, 1966:216–217).

The Commune

In 1954 and again in 1957, Chen village adopted a cooperative and "advanced" cooperative form of collective agriculture, which was so short lived that the authors provide little information about the outcomes.[2] Then, in 1958, at Mao's command, the new and more radical commune experiment was started all over China in the disastrous Great Leap Forward (Chan et. al., 1984: 24–26). Chen village was incorporated into a large commune of eight villages and 20,000 persons with whom it shared most of what it produced. The commune authority set targets and production quotas, although many daily farming and labor allocation decisions were delegated to the villages, now called "brigades." More radical was the abolition of the family household as the basic unit of consumption. Free public canteens were set up to feed the peasants. Consumption became decoupled from the peasants' productive inputs, including their own labor. The time saved from household chores was spent on irrigation projects, land reclamation, rural industries like the smelting of crude steel, and more labor-intensive methods of agriculture. With a large team size, many farm decisions made at higher levels, and rewards based on need, the theory predicts lower incentives to produce and more shirking, lower social consciousness, and thus lower productivity, although metering costs diminished when peasants were supplied food according to need and not according to work inputs or outputs. What also defeated the commune experiment was sheer incompetence of the commune and higher management. Some of the collective projects, e.g., steel smelting, failed miserably, and commune cadres enforced cultivation techniques that ruined the crops, e.g., by overplanting the rice fields. The commune experiment produced the Great Famine of 1959–1960.[3] It is estimated that as many as 26 million people died. In Chen village as well, the experiment was disastrous. Peasants scavenged the hillsides for edible plants and rested indoors to conserve their energy. People were so hungry they had difficulty sleeping (Chan et al., 1984:25).

Contracting Production to the Household (*Baochan Dao Hu*)

To repair the damage of the commune experiment, the government introduced a new agricultural policy in 1961, which restored production.

Chen village became a production brigade and was divided into five production teams of 40 families; later it became ten teams of about 20 to 25 households, with close kinsmen and neighbors sharing team membership. Each team was assigned an equal share of the village land and made its own production and labor allocation decisions. Elected team leaders were chosen for proven ability rather than class background and party membership. The state plan set rice, peanut, and sugar acreage for the entire brigade and a quota to be sold to the state at fixed, low procurement prices. In this fashion, the state assured a supply of cheap grains to the cities, lest peasants plant more profitable cash crops. Adherence to the state plan was the responsibility of brigade leadership. Brigade and team leaders then divided these quotas among the teams. Beyond these quotas and a tax on land, each team decided on how to dispose of its product and its resultant income. The brigade was responsible for village-wide projects, such as irrigation, and negotiated with the teams for funds and labor (Unger, 1985).

At first, the teams in Chen village chose to divide team land further, with each household getting some lowland paddy and some hill plots. Households also received fertilizer and seed from the team, and planted, weeded, and harvested their plots. Each lot had a grain quota, which was exchanged for workpoints (a fixed weight of rice per workpoint). Grain produced beyond the quota could be kept by households for food or sold at rural markets for a higher price than the state's. After a year, though, households had to deliver all grain to the team in exchange for workpoints. To stimulate production, households received workpoint penalties or bonuses for under or overfulfilling quotas. This system favored families with teenagers capable of work and was detrimental to families short of labor (Unger, 1985:120).

In addition, peasants were allowed small private plots for raising vegetables, pigs, and ducks, and also handicraft (sideline) production. These were an important source of cash for the bride price, building a house and providing a wedding feast when their sons married (Chan et al., 1984:194). The land allocated for these private plots depended on the size of each family. Private plots were fixed at 5% of cultivable land (Marshall, 1985:49).

This system of agriculture was popular and productive. Chan et al. (1984:26) report that "villagers began once more to work hard and in orderly fashion; and by the end of 1961, the village's famine was ended." It is evident why this would be the case. The basic unit of production was the household. Other collective farm and governance decisions were made by a small team of tightly knit kin and neighbors, which favored social consciousness. Incentives to produce were based on merit: the more each peasant produced, the more the family would eat and earn. Output metering had low cost. According to the theory, these factors all favored increased production and efficient resource use.

Bao Gong Contracted Work

Though *baochan daohu* served the villagers well, for China's political leadership it smacked too much of private enterprise and was not sufficiently "collective." Thus in 1963 a policy of collective team production and division of team revenue was imposed on Chinese villages, including Chen village. *Bao gong* was a complex piece- and task-rate system with every productive activity being assigned a certain number of workpoints. Metering costs increased tremendously. Unger (1985:121) writes that "most of the hundreds of chores required constant supervision by workpoint recorders—to record what each peasant accomplished." Conflicts developed with team leaders over the daily task assignments and with recorders over how many workpoints one deserved.

Many doubted the fairness of workpoint norms for some tasks, and social consciousness consequently suffered.[4] Given a gender division of labor in village work, women's work was systematically undervalued, as in dikes building, where men accumulated twice as many workpoints per hour dredging and digging mud from the river bottom than women did hauling mud buckets up the riverbank and packing dikes. This was resented by some women. Input metering led to a neglect of quality in work, which decreased crop yields. For transplanting rice seedlings, the roots have to be firmly secured, which takes more effort and more time, lest the plants later disengage. Each had an incentive to accumulate workpoints through quantity of rows planted, though shoddy quality diminished the total yield for the entire team.

According to the theory, input metering, neglect of quality, and fairness issues have a detrimental impact on productivity. Though the authors do not provide total production figures for the village and the teams, their account leaves little doubt that this system lowered productivity, elicited less cooperation, and led to growing mistrust and "selfishness" among villagers.[5]

Dazhai System

At Mao's call, 1966 saw another nationwide leftward lurch in agricuture with the shift to the Dazhai system, named after a village Mao was promoting as a model. Shoddy work and selfishness were to be eliminated (Chan *et al.*, 1984:91). Instead, self-sacrifice and social consciousness were to increase the peasants' work effort and the total pie to be divided up. Under Dazhai labor was rewarded for its overall quality and the "socialist" attitudes of workers, in addition to quantity. Dazhai used peer pressure for getting people to work hard, to cooperate, and to acquire social consciousness. At monthly meetings of each team, members were asked to make a self-appraisal of how many workpoints they were deserving. Teammates would then upgrade or downgrade the amount based on their personal knowledge of how each had performed. If people slackened, they would not only get fewer workpoints but suffer a public humiliation. And those who set a fast pace and put team welfare above private goals would be rewarded both with high workpoints and with a high standing in their team and village. Each had an interest that the others would be doing their fair share, and each had a simple and direct way of sanctioning their peers in the self-appraisal meetings. Moreover, an outside cadre group had come to the village to conduct a Mao study campaign. Villagers were going to be socialized into the appropriate Maoist attitudes that would make Dazhai a success. The cadres criticized peasants face-to-face for laziness and selfishness and praised them for public spirit on a daily basis during the midday meal break in the fields (Madsen, 1984:134). Social control and pressures were also tightened when particular villagers were praised and shamed over the public loudspeakers that had been installed in the village (Madsen, 1984:138–139). According to Unger (1985, p. 124) a "perfervid atmosphere somewhat resembling a religious revivalist movement was whipped up and put to the services of a new wage system."

From a theoretical standpoint, Dazhai eliminated the problems of quality neglect and of a fair standard for different tasks which had weighed on interpersonal relations. Team members would be each other's evaluators. Work incentives were increased with moral and social pressures. Sanctions would be meted out by team members themselves, thus cutting down on some metering and supervision costs. As long as each influenced the others to do their fair share by doing the same, social consciousness would remain high. But if the majority slackened and refused to diminish each other's workpoints, workpoint inflation would undervalue the contribution of those who worked hard. Eventually they would refuse being taken for a free ride. If they, in turn, slackened the pie would start diminishing.

Team appraisals not only allocated workpoints and thus economic well-being, but conferred a public definition of one's moral worth and social standing in the village. As is well known (Hirsch, 1978), status competition is positional and zero-sum: one can gain only at another's expense. Unless the peasants became fundamentally less status conscious, the status striving built into collective workpoint appraisals would weaken social consciousness.

Initially, the Dazhai campaign was successful.[6] By 1967, peasant income doubled compared to 1964. The weather had been favorable. According to Chan et al. (1984:93) "More rice shoots survived transplanting; people stayed out after dark to finish their chores; harvests were cut more efficiently and more quickly."

Madsen (1984:141) reports that "in some production teams, fields that used to take five days to harvest could now be harvested in three. During the agricultural slack season, team leaders found it easier to convince people to work on public works projects. There was less pilferage of collective night soil for use on private plots."

Beyond the new spirit of hard work and cooperation, production and productivity increased because Chen village joined the Green Revolution. Under prodding from the cadre work team, the villagers adopted high yield hybrid rice, new higher yield peanuts and sugar cane, and chemical fertilizers. They added water-pumping stations for increased irrigation, improved drainage and soil quality, and introduced many other innovations. Positive results convinced doubters about the superiority of the Dazhai system and of following Mao's thought.

In the next few years (Chan et al., 1984:214–221), the new prosperity of the village was translated into a higher standard of living. Chen villagers built new, two-story, spacious brick houses, bought bicycles, radios, and other urban consumer goods for the first time. But not all the additional income was cycled into consumption. In 1968, a brigade brickworks was organized, with each team sharing expenses and the assignment of a total of 30 fulltime workers to the project. In 1970–1971, the profits from brick sales and agriculture was invested in industries for semi-processed agricultural products: a grain mill, an oil press, a distillery, and sugar refining. Other collective goods were provided for the first time, such as a health clinic staffed by a barefoot doctor. Within a few years, one-sixth of the village workforce was employed in brigade industrial enterprises. The workers received the same number of workpoints as they would in agriculture—and when necessary at peak agricultural seasons helped plant and harvest in their original teams. This success was achieved despite the political turmoil of the cultural revolution which descended upon the country (and Chen village) and caused conflict and purges within the village.

As a result of purges and factional struggles in 1967, the authorities above the village level became incapacitated, and the brigade leadership was left without a higher authority for support. The teams started feuding over the allocation of the annual grain quota (Chan et al., 1984: 136–137) and the assignment of team labor to village-wide projects. As antagonisms in the village grew, the theft of chickens and ducks increased, and malicious rumors and gossip circulated the village (Chan *et al.*, 1984:138). In order to stop impending anarchy in much of China, People's Liberation Army teams were sent to the grassroots, including Chen village, to restore order. However, it was not until 1970 that the two main village factions reconciled and the wounds opened during the cultural revolution began to heal.

When social consciousness weakened during the divisive struggles and rivalries of the cultural revolution, the foundations of the Dazhai system were undermined. The self-appraisal meetings became contentious: participants gave inflated self-appraisals and others were afraid to criticize lest they be criticized, in turn. For the sake of avoiding conflict, meetings were called less frequently. The workpoint gap between best and worst worker narrowed from a 1966 high of 10 and low of 7.3 to a 1970 rating of 10 and 9, respectively, for men (Unger, 1985:132). This reduced the work incentives for the most able workers. As free riding increased, they felt "like live frogs dragging along dead frogs" (Chan *et al.*, 1984:248). The able workers slacked off and concentrated their energies on their family plots. In 1969, larger teams were introduced for achieving greater efficiency in irrigation and mechanization. Self-appraisal meetings became large and unwieldly, and eventually ceased altogether. By 1971 team heads simply awarded workpoints according to labor time without a link to performance.

Collective production in agriculture declined for a variety of other reasons. The cultural revolution had interrupted agricultural research and fertilizer production. When the hybrid crops became vulnerable to pests and rotting, new crop varieties were lacking. Fertilizer was more difficult to obtain. Thus, yields declined.

Of equal importance, authorities periodically forced teams to undertake wasteful and, at times, disastrous practices, such as surrendering family plots, fruit trees, and pigs (Chan *et al.*, 1984, p. 171), abolishing teams altogether (p. 174), planting crops unsuitable for local conditions (p. 279), undertaking huge capital projects that did not yield any returns, such as terracing mountain slopes that had no top soil (p. 239), and increasing state extraction with higher grain quotas sold to the state (pp. 241–242). In effect, the benefits of decentralized farm management were undermined by imposing a higher level authority for political reasons. Although all these policies were overturned, they constituted a huge, wasted effort that further demoralized the peasantry and undermined their faith in collective production. In Chen village, the value of workpoints earned by the best male worker in a day's work in team production declined from an all time high of 1.15 yen in 1968 to 0.80 yen in 1973 and 1974, and to 0.70 yen in 1977 (Chan *et al.*, p. 247). In 1973, the teams in Chen village decided to abandon the Dazhai system and reverted to the earlier task-, piece-rate (*bao gong*) system.

In the mid-1970s, collective agriculture was in a slump in much of China. In many places, peasant incomes did not diminish because village industry and private plots made up for the loss of earnings from collective agriculture. In Chen village, however, the brigade leadership made a disastrous investment in a paper-making plant that failed, thereby squandering village capital and labor (Chan *et al.*, 1984, p. 245). As the collective pie shrunk, distrust and noncooperation was manifest: theft of collective crops and farm animals (chickens and ducks), especially by youth (p. 254), large-scale illegal migration to Hong Kong (p. 266), again by young people, and petty corruption among village cadres and acts of sabotage and retaliation against them by angry villagers (pp. 258–259). In Chen village, the inner contradictions of the Dazhai system, the political excesses of the late 1960s, and the failures of the 1970s destroyed the social consciousness and faith in collective agriculture of the early Dazhai years.

The Responsibility System

After Mao's death in 1976 and the ousting of the Gang of Four by the Deng Xiaoping moderates, a "responsibility" system was introduced in order to increase work incentives and agricultural production and to check wasteful interference by higher authorities into village decision-making. According to Marshall (1985:144)

> ... teams conclude contracts with households. The contract includes the amount of land the household must till, the output to be produced, and what the brigade or team must provide. The contracted household organizes its own work and makes its own decision. The household sells its quota of output to the team and, depending on the crop, sells any remaining amounts in the free market.[7]

There is no private ownership of land. The team allocates land to each household by drawing lots, or by team leaders negotiating with households when grain quotas for delivery to the state are set for each field (Chan *et al.*, 1984:269). In effect, the state is everyone's landlord, and each farm household is now a tenant farmer. Security of tenure is high. Recently, the duration of contract was extended up to 15 years. Some allowances were made for a labor market and land use transfer between households, since the size of household farm labor force depends on the family life stage and on employment in nonagriculture production. By mid-1984, more than 90% of China's rural households had adopted the new system (Marshall, 1985:168–169).

Various arrangements were made for common property. In Chen village, farm tools, threshers, carts, etc., were auctioned off to the highest bidders (Chan et al., 1984:269–270) who could now rent such equipment to neighbors or set up a private business, as in transport. Some collective property vital for each family and too expensive for households to buy, like draft oxen, were provided by the team to sharing groups of households. Fruit trees, fishponds, and the village store were auctioned off for control to the highest bidders. In return for a yearly sum, the new managers gained total user rights over these collective assets (Chan et al., 1984:270). In Chen village, the peasants were eager to privatize the collective:

> The peasantry in Chen village . . . had few qualms about splitting up the fields. The fervent cooperative spirit of the Mao Thought period of the mid-1960s had been thoroughly eroded by the frustrations of the 1970s. They were now more willing to go it alone.

Team leaders had few powers and functions beyond collecting the rice quotas and distributing seed, fertilizer, and other agricultural supplies.

To make the new responsibility system a success, the government raised the grain procurement prices under which the state quota and surpluses were purchased, increased other agriculture prices, and froze the agriculture tax and the grain quotas at early 1970's levels (Marshall, 1985:166; Chan et al., 1984:263). Moreover, farm loans and consumer goods were increased to the peasantry. Important as well for the new rural prosperity that was ushered in by the responsibility system in Chen village was permission to sell foodstuffs directly to Hong Kong, and for Hong Kong wholesalers to buy fresh produce at higher than state prices (Chan et al., 1984:271). Last, but not least, some Chen villagers worked for urban wages in industrial employment in the county capital, and hired farmhands from poorer inland counties at lower farm wages to make up for the labor shortage in village agriculture (Chan et al., 1984:272).

The responsibility system has several advantages over collective production. Work incentives are based on merit. Governance costs are low because much of the team and brigade administrative apparatus is eliminated. There are no recurrent metering costs for inputs and outputs (piece rates, workpoints, attendance records). There is only a one-time division of land among households and the assignment of a tax and crop quota to each field, followed by a once-a-year delivery of the quota to the team.[8] Beyond these operations, households absorb governance costs during routine management of the household farm.

The potential flaw in the responsibility system is the weakening of the incentives and organizational capabilities for investing in agricultural infrastructure (irrigation, flood control, soil conservation, drainage, agricultural extension services, technological improvements) from local sources which made possible the advances of the late 1960s, and upon which contemporary rural prosperity rests (Kueh, 1985). The authority and administrative apparatus of team and brigade leadership in agriculture has been stripped to the barebones, which weakens the capability of investing in collective goods.[9] It is too early to tell what the long-term consequences might be.

Summary and Conclusions

Based on the various authors who have written about Chen village, supplemented by some other sources on similar villages, I have provided a summary presented in Table 12.1 of over 40 years' experience containing rough, qualitative measurement on the principal dimensions and variables of the theory. Although organizational changes were imposed from above by the party, peasants had a certain number of choices: they controlled the intensity and quality of their work; they often chose their team leaders and sometimes had direct input in evaluating each other, as with the Dazhai workpoints; they had some control over dividing their efforts between the private household sector and collective agriculture; they had, at times, some say over investing in collective goods like team and brigade equipment and small industry; and they also controlled the degree of cooperation with each other in collective agriculture and in other aspects of village life. From 1956 to 1979, three quarters or more of the peasants' income depended on how well collective agriculture was performing in the village, which is a high degree of mutual dependence by any standard. The table omits the impact of political events and of macro-economic policies on institutions and performance. The political turmoil of the cultural revolution created factions and dissent which had an impact on social consciousness and governance costs. The Green Revolution was brought in from outside the village and provided a foundation for the 1966–1969 output surge. Moreover, some infrastructure investment (collective goods) had long-term productivity benefits for subsequent periods. Tax changes helped mutual aid, and higher grain procurement prices helped the responsibility system.

By and large, transaction cost economics applied to the organization

Table 12.1. Chen Village Institutions and Performance

Institutions and Years	Farm decision unit	Collective control of village resources	Investment in collective goods	Governance costs: Input output metering	Governance costs: Other	Incentives in collective work: "Need" vs. "merit"	Incentives in collective work: Overall	Social consciousness: cooperation and trust in team	Output of collective agriculture	Standard of living
Pre-1949	Household	None	Low	NA[a]	Low	NA	NA	Low	NA	Low
Mutual-Aid teams 1950–57	Household and small team	Very low	?[a]	Low	Low	Merit	NA	Probably high	NA	Slow increase
Commune 1958–1960	Very large unit	Very high	Very high	Low	High	Need	Low	High, then low	Low	Decline
Baochan dao hu 1961 1962–1963	Household and small team	Low	?	Low; high	Low; low	Merit; both	High; high	Average	Probably average	Average improvement
Baogong 1963–1966 1973–1979	Small team	Hi gh	?	Very high	Average	Both	Average; low	Average; low	Average to low; low	Probably slow increase; no change
Dazhai 1966–1969 1970–1973	Small team Large team	Very high	High	Low	Average; low	Both; need	High; low	Very high; low	Very high; low	Great improvement; no change
Responsibility 1979–	Household	Very low	Very low	Very low	Very low	NA	NA	?	NA	Great improvement

[a] NA, not applicable; ?, insufficient information.

of work makes sense of the experience of Chen village. Small team size and farm decisions taken by the producers themselves enhance work incentives and lower governance cost. Complicated and comprehensive metering of inputs increases governance costs and makes for disputes over fairness and equity which weakens social consciousness. Rewarding need over merit lowers work incentives and productivity. The commune stands out as an especially unpalatable and counterproductive institution. In Williamson's words (1981, p. 562), ". . . to use a complex structure for governing simple transactions is to incur unneeded costs. . . ." *Baochan dao hu* featured small teams, decentralization of farm decision-making, low metering and governance costs, rewards based on merit; under this system collective agriculture performed at an average level. To realize the maximum productivity gains from these variables, China had to wait for the household responsibility system, which decollectivized agriculture. *Baogong,* favored on ideological grounds over *baochan dao hu,* performed somewhat worse because of high governance costs from input metering and lower merit rewards.

Yet, the model does not account satisfactorily for the short-lived surge of social consciousness and work effort in the first months of the commune, nor for the early Dazhai surge of work and productivity of 1966–1969 followed by the collapse of 1970–1973. Two possibilities come to mind. The theory makes a micro level interpretation of social consciousness. But surges of enthusiasm orchestrated by national mobilization campaigns might well be, at least for a time, macro level phenomena similar to waves of patriotism at the outbreak of a war or of revolutionary fervor at the overthrow of a hated regime when "everything seems possible" and private concerns are swept aside in a tide of public spirit (Zolberg, 1972). When high expectations are later disappointed, as they so often are, the rapid retreat to private pursuits lowers trust and cooperation below a minimum necessary for efficient transacting (Arrow, 1974). Apathy and demoralization are then difficult to reverse endogenously. As well, the theory is static. There is no feedback from performance back to incentives and social organization. Mismanagement or natural disasters can destroy enough resources to undermine otherwise efficient agricultural institutions, whereas a succession of good crop years allows gains in even inefficient systems. Outcomes must have both psychological and material consequences that a static model of productivity and performance fails to come to grips with. This chapter is only the first step in a satisfactory explanation of collective agriculture, which will entail a broader, more quantitative data base and a more sophisticated application of social theory and transaction cost economics to the organization of work in Chinese agriculture.

Acknowledgment

I wish to thank Karl-Dieter Opp, Gerhard Lenski and Jonathan Unger for comments on a previous version of this paper.

Notes

1. Elsewhere in China, this was also the case. Marshall (1985:34–36) suggests that nearly 40% of the cultivated land area in rural China was redistributed, indicating more redistribution than in Chen village.
2. Mutual-aid teams were quite successful in China as a whole (Marshall, 1985:56), and in Longbow village in particular (Hinton, 1984:76 ff. and 94). Elsewhere in China, the cooperatives were more successful than in Chen village. Indexes of irrigated acreage, multiple cropping of land, and grain output increased in the years 1954–1957. Success has been attributed to the cooperatives' mobilization of underutilized labor, intensification of cultivation practices, and investment in agricultural infrastructure (Marshall, 1985:38–41). In Longbow village, the average yield of 10 bushels of grain per acre in 1948 increased to 17.5 by 1958, and the standard of living had increased noticeably. According to Hinton, the cooperative worked "quite well . . . but quarrels about standards and quality of work never ceased" (Hinton, 1984:155, 300, 678–679).
3. Marshall (1985:48) estimates that China's grain output fell from 200 million metric tons (mmt) in 1958 to 143 mmt in 1960. Collective agriculture failed at Longbow Village as well (Hinton, 1984:233 ff).
4. Workpoint norms for each task were supposed to be based on the technical level required by the labor, intensity of labor, and the importance of labor in the production process (Marshall, 1985:50).
5. Madsen (1984:53) reports that "day-to-day life in the village seemed to involve constant squabbling over who was to get how many workpoints, who was to be assigned to which job, who would be allowed what small privilege, and so on." See also Nee (1985) on peasants' competitive strategies at the expense of the team.
6. Probably as a result of the Mao study campaign, the Dazhai system worked better and longer in Chen village than in many other villages. Where cadres intimidated ordinary team members in appraisal meetings, in the words of one peasant, ". . . there was the feeling that if someone didn't work hard yet finagled high workpoints, then I won't work hard either." (Unger, 1985:139).
7. Initially there were two additional decollectivization options. But by the summer of 1983 almost all peasants were farming in the least collectivized manner in which workpoints and the team as unit of account had been eliminated (Kueh, 1985:123–125).
8. To be sure, if and when there is a reassessment of the tax and crop quota for fields, there will be some additional governance costs (Kueh, 1985:130).
9. According to Oi (1985), production team leaders, though elected by villagers, had much power. They distributed the officially allocated grain rations to families. They assigned peasants to team jobs and thus controlled workpoints opportunities. They assigned private plots to families and authorized the loan of team tools and draft animals. They distributed team and state relief, and decided team loans of grain and money to households. Although no one could be expelled from a team, leaders had the power to assign team labor for infrastructure projects inside and outside the village in return for workpoints. Without these powers, the authorities must now persuade peasants to sign labor

contracts for capital construction projects. According to Kueh (1985:131), there is some evidence for increased problems with infrastructure maintenance and for a decrease in irrigated land. However, rural economic performance has been excellent since 1978 compared to the previous 25 years (Marshall, 1985:chapter 8).

References

Alchian, Armen and H. Demsetz. (1972). "Production, information costs, and economic organization." *American Economic Review* 62 (December):777–95.
Arrow, Kenneth. (1974). *The Limits of Organization.* New York: Norton.
Banfield, Edward. (1958). *The Moral Basis of a Backward Society.* Glencoe, IL: The Free Press.
Chan, Anita, Richard Madsen, and Jonathan Unger. (1984). *Chen Village.* Berkeley, CA: University of California Press.
Chinn, D. (1979). "Team cohesion and collective labor supply in Chinese agriculture." *Journal of Comparative Economics,* 3:375–94.
Chinn, D. (1980). "Diligence and laziness in Chinese production teams." *Journal of Development Economics,* 7:331–344.
Foster, George (1960–1961). "Interpersonal relations in peasant society." *Human Organization* 19(4), Winter. 174–184.
Foster George. (1965). "Peasant society and the image of the limited good." *American Anthropologist,* 67(2), April. 293–315.
Fried, Morton. (1953). *The Fabric of Chinese Society.* New York: Praeger.
Hinton, William. (1966). *Fanshen.* New York: Monthly Review Press.
Hinton, William. (1984). *Shenfan.* New York: Vintage.
Hirsch, Fred. (1978). *The Social Limits to Growth.* Cambridge: Harvard University Press.
Huang, Philip. (1985). *The Peasant Economy and Social Change in North China.* Stanford, CA: Stanford University Press.
Kueh, Y. Y. (1985). "The economics of the 'second land reform' in China." *China Quarterly,* No. 101 (March):122–131.
Madsen, Richard. (1984). *Morality and Power in a Chinese Village.* Berkeley: University of California.
Marshall, Marsh. (1985). *Organizations and Growth in Rural China.* New York: St. Martin's Press.
Nee, Victor. (1985). "Peasant Household Individualism." In William Parish, ed., *Chinese Rural Development.* Armonk, NY: Sharpe.
Oi, Jean. (1985). "Communism and clientelism in rural politics in China." *World Politics* 37 (2) (January):238–266.
Perkins, Dwight and Shahid Yusuf. (1984). *Rural Development in China.* Baltimore, MD: Johns Hopkins University Press.
Sen, A. (1966). "Labor allocation in a cooperative enterprise." *Review of Economic Studies,* October, pp. 361–71.
Shue, Vivienne. (1980). *Peasant China in Transition.* Berkeley, CA: University of California Press.

Unger, Jonathan. (1985). "Remuneration, ideology, and personal interest in a Chinese village, 1960–1980." In William Parrish, ed., *Chinese Rural Development*. Armonk, NY: Sharpe.

Williamson, Oliver. (1981). "The economics of organization: The transaction costs approach." *American Journal of Sociology* 87(3):548–577.

Williamson, Oliver. (1985). *The Economic Institutions of Capitalism*. New York, Free Press.

Zolberg, Aristide. (1972). "Moments of madness." *Politics and Society*, 2(2) (Winter) 183–208.

13

Toward a Theory of Union Emergence and Demise

Debra Friedman

Unions have grown and shrunk in fits and starts. American trade unionism was declared dead in 1815 (Perlman, 1923), and cries of its impending death resound once again (Lipset, 1986). Generally, but also across time, industry, and type of occupation, the rates of union formation and dissolution have been extremely uneven. Considering the proportion of the total workforce unionized, peaks of union membership are observed in 1945 and again in 1954 with a jagged but overall decline until 1980. Across industries, rates of union formation and dissolution are considerably more uneven: in the most recent decade, for instance, declines have been noted in traditionally heavily unionized industries (coal mining, automobiles, apparel, newspaper publishing, and printing); even more dramatic declines in union membership are seen in the service sector (notably eating and drinking establishments); and, in contrast, increases have been noted in hospitals, libraries, schools, and local and state governments (Kokkelenberg and Sockell, 1985).

Organic imagery applies poorly to trade unionism: resurrection is not only possible, it is common; age may bring vitality rather than decline. This fitful, nonlinear pattern best characterizes the emergence, growth, and decline of most individual unions, as well. A case in point is provided by the history of the International Seamen's Union of America

(ISU). I will present the details of this case, not because its history is so compelling, but because it provides a clear example of the uneven nature of institutional emergence, development, and decline.

The International Seamen's Union of America: A Capsule History

The origin of the Seamen's Friendly Union and Protective Society in 1866 has been lost in history, although the name of the association connotes its likely concerns. In 1880 this group became the Seamen's Protective Association, and this time the reason for the transformation is known. The principal employer in the Pacific, the Pacific Mail Steamship Company began a wholesale replacement of active, Caucasian seamen with Chinese sailors. The Seamen's Protective Association was, however, unsuccessful in fighting this move, and the organization disintegrated (a situation certainly not helped by the treasurer absconding with the funds). Soon thereafter, in 1885, following a reduction in already depressed wages, the Coast Seamen's Union (CSU) was organized in San Francisco. Several factors favored development of the union at this time: the isolation of the Pacific Coast together with the small number of West Coast ports; the ethnic homogeneity of the sailors; and the absence of alternative workers (seamen).

Within 1 year, however, a rival union, representing steamship deck crews, engaged in bitter jurisdictional quarrels with the CSU. These fights weakened both unions and, in 1891, the Steamshipmen proposed a merger. The CSU concurred and in this same year, the union amalgamation resulted in the Sailors' Union of the Pacific (SUP).

Expansion of control and membership were two of the SUP's early aims. First, they tried to gain control of the seamen's labor market by establishing a union shipping office. Then they attempted to organize worldwide in order to prevent inroads on wages and working conditions from foreign—especially British—seamen. Both of these efforts were ultimately unsuccessful. The effort to extend membership beyond the West Coast was successful nationally, however, and in 1892 the National Seamen's union was born. By 1895 the name had been changed to the International Seamen's Union (ISU) and the organization subsumed seamen's unions on the Great Lakes, the Gulf, and the Atlantic Coasts. The union was divided into semiautonomous regions and into separate deck, engine, and steward departments.

Once again the union expended efforts to gain membership, particularly on the East Coast. These efforts, however, were frustrated by the numerous ports, the heterogeneous workforce, and the centrifugal organizational structure of the union. By 1900 the membership stood at 3400, drawn mostly from the West Coast and Great Lakes.

Membership declined even further following an open-shop offensive undertaken by the Lake Carriers' Association in 1908. This was followed, 7 years later, by a surge in membership following the hard-won enactment of legislation designed to improve working conditions (the La Follette Seamen's Act of 1915). Another increase in membership took place during World War I; the peak was 115,000, of whom 80,000 were East Coast seamen. Despite these hearty numbers, in 1921, a depression in merchant shipping, increased foreign competition, and a surplus of seamen (from the war) all contributed to setting the stage for a serious confrontational battle among the U.S. Shipping Board, the private employers, and the unions. In particular, employers demanded an open shop, lower wages, and the elimination of overtime pay. The union was unable to withstand the onslaught, and membership fell to prewar levels.

As if these threats were not enough to challenge its survival, the ISU once again faced challenges from rival unions. The first challenge came from the Marine Transport Workers' Industrial Union (MTWIU), organized by the IWW, and then by the Marine Workers' Industrial Union (MWIU), organized by the Communist Trade Union Unity League. The MTWIU got its impetus from a minority constituency: first the Atlantic Coast Spanish firemen and then black longshoremen from Philadelphia. The MWIU offered challenges both to the ISU and to the MTWIU. After the National Industrial Recovery Act, seamen tended to affiliate with the less radical ISU, but in 1935 the ISU managed to lose the Pacific Coast seamen's branch of the union, spurring defections by the East Coast seamen to the NMU. Ultimately the ISU collapsed altogether. Its charter was revoked in 1938. Its death brought life to the Seafarers International Union (SIU).

The history of the ISU is not a unique one in its contours. Similar histories can be found. The International Brotherhood of Electrical Workers (IBEW), for instance, began organizing shortly after the Civil War, formed unions in the 1880's, formed a national association in 1891, was battered by the depression of 1893, suffered dual unionism between 1908 and 1913, lost membership again by 1925, took on the threat of a competing union (United Electrical Radio and Machine Workers of America), and, following World War II, steadily grew to become the second largest AFL-CIO affiliate. Masonry trades unions, organized in the 1820's, disappeared in the 1830's, reappeared in 1850, and disappeared once again in the late 1850's. Then in 1865, the Bricklayers' International Union was organized, grew until the 1870's, slumped following a downturn in construction and the formation of a rival organization, and grew again until the depression of 1893–1897. Membership surged once again, thriving in the face of an open-shop offensive. Institutional innovation—in the form of the establishment of rival contracting firms, as well as of a brickyard—led to the union's robustness. Changes in technology (the increased use of hollow tile, cement, and plaster) forced affiliation with the Stonemason's International Union and with plasterers, resulting in the establishment in 1910 of the Bricklayers, Masons and Plasterers' International Union of America (BMPIUA). By the 1920s the BMPIUA had a membership of more than 130,000; by 1933, membership decreased to 35,000 (the BMPIUA, like most unions, lost most of its members during the Depression); by 1955, and to the present, its membership level boasts 140,000.

It is probably correct to make the claim that no union's history can best be described as linear. The question then becomes whether or not a theoretical account can be forged that both honors these details and rises above them.

Six Propositions Toward A Theory of Union Emergence and Demise

In an early review and critique of the field of labor organization, Dunlop (1948) lamented the separation of historical and theoretical treatments of the emergence and development of labor organizations. He assigned the responsibility for the chasm to the theorists, and challenged them to build bridges: "despite all the epoch-making developments in the field of labor organization in the past 15 years, there has been virtually no contribution to the "theory" and scarcely a reputable narrative of this period exists" (Dunlop, 1948: 163–64). Reasons for lack of progress in this area to this day are well appreciated. First, such work is hampered by the absence of a general theory of the origin of organizations or institutions.[1] Second, the study of the origin of organizations is hindered by the lack of data; historical record-keeping belongs almost exclusively to the organizations themselves.

Nonetheless there are clues as to the direction to pursue in developing a theoretical account of union formation, growth, decline, and demise. If the rates of union formation or dissolution were associated in a linear fashion with rates of economic growth or contraction generally, or even specifically in given industries, we would not have to look far for an adequate explanation. A significant body of work has attempted to identify factors associated with economic trends, particularly those of decline: factors such as plant closures, layoffs, slower growth rates in basic manufacturing industries, and increased management resistance to union organization (Freeman and Medoff, 1984; Dickens and Leonard,

1985). Yet the empirical record does not lend much support to such an approach. None of the factors above are exclusively associated with decline. Layoffs and management resistance, for instance, can also serve to promote shared grievances that, in turn, bolster union strength. Furthermore, as noted above, it is the case empirically that periods of both economic expansion and contraction are associated with *both* union formation and demise.[2]

I will offer six propositions as a start toward a three-tiered theory of union emergence and demise. At the *individual level* it will be argued that agents are more likely to consider organizing when they can reach their goals only in concert with others and/or when their goals can be better realized by coordination to reduce (negative) externalities. At the *contextual* level I will argue that unions are most likely to arise and decline under conditions of objective uncertainty. This is because these conditions promote collective action. Once in place, unions will be threatened by objective contextual uncertainty because such conditions foster the rise of competitive institutions. At the *organizational level* I will argue that pre-existing, overlapping organizations may enhance the formation of unions, but when unions are nested within perfectly encompassing institutions, these may provide competition for membership in times of scarcity that unions cannot withstand. In addition, a union must choose either an inclusive or an exclusive membership strategy, and that once selected, the union will be vulnerable under different contextual conditions. Inclusive strategies tend to fail during times of severe contraction, whereas exclusive strategies tend to fail during times of prosperity. A summary of the key points of the argument is depicted in Figure 13.1.

Maximizing Income and Resisting Competition at the Individual Level

Proposition 1. *Individuals are more likely to consider the possibility of organizing or becoming involved in unions when (a) their goals cannot be attained through independent action; and/or (b) their goals can be better realized by coordination to reduce externalities (rather than by independent action).*

Propositions 1a and b are vacuous in the absence of goals, and so I will begin by assuming that individuals wish to maximize their income *over time* (and not necessarily at any given point in time). Straightforward rational choice reasoning would suggest that given this goal, individuals would generally be better off by *not* organizing. This is because individ-

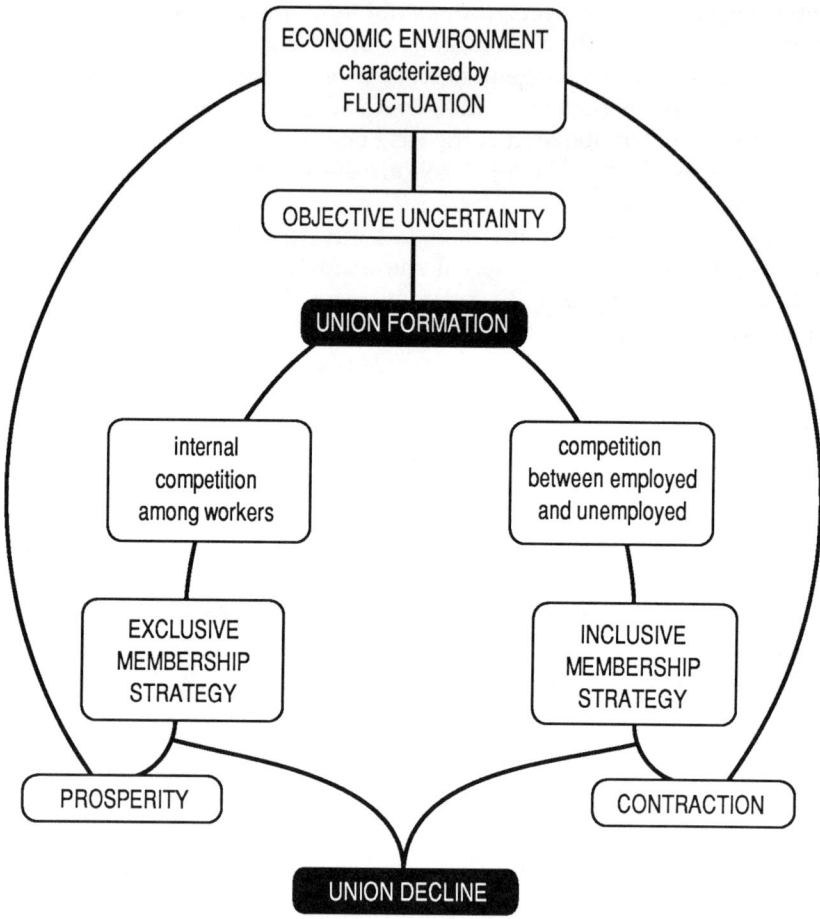

Figure 13.1. Principle factors contributing to union decline.

uals can expect to maximize their wages only if the means to do so are within their control, and control is maximized by acting independently, not interdependently. Why is this the case? First, individuals can try to tie their performance to their wages, and to the extent that they have control over their performance, they can maximize their wages. Second, during periods of labor surplus, they can attempt to make side payments to their employer to be kept on, or they can bargain with their employer to offer their labor at one penny less than the next bidder for their job. Third, during periods of labor shortage, they can negotiate to exact higher wages.

Each of these means to maximize wages, however, depends upon the employer's control capacity (Hechter, 1987). Should the employer be unable or unwilling to monitor—to gather information about individual performance—and then to reward exceptional performance, individuals have no incentive to modify their actions. When employers have poor control capacity, individual workers lose the means to maximize their wages. While the evidence of control capacity in the case of the Seamen is indirect, it is the case that employers were not present at the work site, and would have had to rely on the reports of agents regarding meritorious service, subject to all the usual problems of agency. Isolation and separation from employers served as contributing conditions for organization.

Poor monitoring also leads to another kind of consequence that has implications for union organization. In the absence of adequate monitoring, employers are more likely to use signalling devices (Spence, 1973) to hire, fire, and reward employees. Such devices promote corporate sentiment rather than individual initiative. The wholesale replacement of Caucasian seamen with Chinese seamen provides an illustration: this action ignored individual differences and served to promote renewed interest in organizing among Caucasian seamen. Thus, the *poorer* the employer's control capacity, the *greater* the individual's incentive to organize.

Proposition 1b is affected not only by the employer's control capacity but by the source of any competition, as well. Table 13.1 summarizes the relationship between labor supply and employer monitoring capacity. Competition for jobs can come from within the firm or from outside of it. In a firm composed of a hierarchy of positions with clear rules for mobility, in which individuals are not substitutable, competition arises because there are fewer positions at the higher levels than there are potential occupants of those positions at the lower levels. Should the employer's control capacity be high, union formation is unlikely; occupants of lower level positions have competitive interests, at least with

Table 13.1. The Relationship Between Labor Supply, Employer Monitoring Capacity, and Union Formation (Summary of Propositions 1a and 1b)

	Labor supply	
Monitoring Capacity of Employer	*Surplus*	*Shortage*
High	No org.	No org.
Low	Trade unions	Company unions[a]

[a]Or any employer-based associations such as Employee Protective Associations or Employee Representation Plans.

respect to mobility. Should it be poor, organizing becomes more probable.

However, competition can also come from workers outside of the firm. This may be conceived of as a situation in which there is little differentiation among most workers, and, especially during labor surpluses, fierce competition occurs at entry points. If workers outside are offering their services more cheaply as a group, workers inside have a motive to organize unless they can demonstrate their superior quality to their employer, or unless they can offer to lower their wage rate until the condition of surplus passes. Both of these possibilities again depend upon the control capacity of the employer: a greater control capacity will serve to dissuade organization while a poorer one will encourage it. Should the employer be unwilling or unable to reward individual performance or to make deals with individual workers, and should there be a condition of labor surplus, workers inside may well have an interest in organizing not only themselves (perhaps to pressure the employer through a strike), but also those who are offering the competition.[3] This last point demonstrates how individual interest can provide the impetus for a given organizing strategy (in this case, an inclusive one). This will be discussed in a later section.

Propositions 1a and 1b point to the importance of two factors—control capacity and competition—in understanding something about the factors that increase the probability of union organization. In the case of the Seafarers Union, control capacity was consistently poor and competition variable. Yet by themselves, these expectations are indeterminate, except when they are modified by the inclusion of some contextual factor (e.g., labor shortage). It is to these contextual conditions that I now turn.

Objective Uncertainty

Proposition 2. *Objective contextual uncertainty will tend to promote union formation, especially when that uncertainty is in conjunction with a loss.*

Proposition 3. *Once a union has been established, new kinds, sources, or magnitudes of objective contextual uncertainty will tend to threaten that union to the extent that such uncertainty leads to the rise of competitive organizations.*

Unions are conceived to be institutions that arise in the face of objective, contextual uncertainty. Uncertainty causes workers to band together to share risks as a means of blunting the unknown and potentially ill effects of shifting economic and political conditions. This perspective suggests that union formation occurs during periods of macroeconomic and/or political *fluctuation* when no other institutions exist to provide the kind of insurance benefits that workers demand. For instance, the 1860's and the 1870's were characterized by significant economic fluctuations as well as by dramatic increases in union formation. Decline in the number of unions and in the pace of union formation is expected either when alternative institutions (e.g., the state) come to provide such benefits, or when economic and political fluctuations abate.

If institutions are conceived to be principally concerned with meeting the assurance needs of their members (that is, reducing the untoward effects of uncertainty), then unions are but one institution among many alternatives. Instead of giving unions a hallowed status—as the only institutions devoted to meeting the needs of workers—they must be seen to compete with other kinds of institutions, such as the state and firms, that are also capable of providing valued benefits. Clues as to the past and future collective action potential of workers come in part from understanding the dynamics of that competition, and from appreciating the conditions under which alternative kinds of institutions might arise.

Elsewhere (Friedman, 1987), I have argued that uncertainty is a principal wellspring of collective action. Collective action is more likely when objective uncertainty is coupled with subjective uncertainty. Following Knight (1971), objective uncertainty is defined as the degree to which the future is predictable from the past, and exists as a supraindividual, emergent state. Sometimes objective uncertainty gives rise to subjective uncertainty—a state of indecision among alternative courses of action (Goldman, 1986)—among whole groups of actors. In so doing, it produces concerns and interests that are common to all who are so affected. Collective action becomes possible when objective uncertainty promotes a higher than average level of subjective uncertainty among a group of individuals.

When the future cannot be predicted with any confidence, individuals cannot know what value to attach to one course of action as against another as the consequences of those actions depend upon the future states. Deprived of their most valuable resource—information—rational actors are thereby motivated to seek the counsel of others, and in so doing, turn to the groups with which they are already affiliated.

Objective uncertainty can affect small or large numbers of people who are organized, or not. In addition, among those who are affected, the consequences may be more or less severe. For instance, uncertainty may be limited to a particular sector of the economy: fluctuations in the price of copper on the world market entail serious consequences for copper mine workers, but not for bricklayers. In general, the more specific the contextual uncertainty is to group boundaries, the more likely collective action is to occur. This happens for two reasons. First, pre-existing organizations help to foster collective action by eliminating many of the costs associated with establishing new groups, and by providing a store of resources for mobilization efforts (see McAdam, 1982). Second, small groups are more likely to succeed in providing collective goods than are large ones. This is due to the greater success that small groups enjoy in limiting access to collective goods and in providing selective incentives for participation (Olson, 1965; Oliver, 1980).

Even if all these conditions are present—if there is contextual uncertainty, and if it is accompanied by cognitive uncertainty, and if it falls along the fault lines of pre-existing groups—collective action still may not occur. Organizations and their leaders must choose collective action as the best solution to the assurance problems posed by uncertainty. There are alternatives. For instance, organizations to which people belong may already have mechanisms in place to blunt the ill effects of uncertainty. Second, other institutions—most frequently the state—may step in to override fluctuations by design (e.g., wage-price controls), or may raise the cost of collective action to prohibitively high levels by introducing sanctions for participation.

Finally, collective action is more likely to occur when the expected consequences of objective uncertainty constitute a loss. All collective action involves a certain amount of risk, for the outcome can never be known in advance, but loss encourages risk-seeking behavior (Kahneman and Tversky, 1979). Under the twin burden of uncertainty and loss, one might expect to more often observe the risky-shift—the tendency for groups to take more risky action than would be deemed acceptable by any one constituent member—necessary for plunging into collective action, particularly of the high-risk variety.

Thus, the expectation is that unions are most likely to arise under conditions of objective uncertainty because these conditions promote collective action. At the same time, it is expected that unions are most likely to decline under conditions of uncertainty as well. This is the case because objective uncertainty is likely to foster the rise of competitive institutions.

One kind of competitive institution is simply another union dedicated to representing the workers already unionized. The history of unions is replete with the rise of competing groups after a period of economic or political instability. These new periods of uncertainty may bring new types or magnitudes of uncertainty that existing unions cannot address. A union formed to protect wages (following a period of uncertainty in wage levels) may be unable to shift—following a period of vicissitudes in labor supply—to protect jobs themselves.

In addition, employers may well understand the power of an alternative union. Company unionism—in whatever guise—serves the purpose of providing an alternative. During the National Recovery Administration, a favorite tactic of those who employed cement workers was to create employee protection associations or employee representation plans. Farm equipment workers and chemical workers also had a difficult time keeping independent unions established in the face of such competition.

But competition does not have to be limited to alternative unions. The period of 1900–1930 not only boosted unions, but also marked the beginnings of the welfare state. The state provided benefits that had previously been the province of unions, and in so doing, robbed the union of a considerable portion of its cache of distinctive selective incentives. Given that membership in the welfare state is involuntary, duplication of benefits when the costs of maintaining dual membership becomes too high means that union membership will be spurned. This sort of competition is especially likely to threaten union survival. Hence, the next proposition:

> ***Proposition 4.*** *When unions are nested within other, encompassing institutions, these institutions may provide competition for membership in times of scarcity that unions cannot withstand.*

Exclusive and Inclusive Organizing Strategies

> ***Proposition 5.*** *Unions following an exclusive strategy, seeking to limit competition among workers within firms, are more likely to fail during times of prosperity.*

> ***Proposition 6.*** *Unions following an inclusive strategy, seeking to limit competition among employed and unemployed workers in the same occupation, are more likely to fail during times of economic contraction.*

Competition is one kind of externality that makes organizing worthwhile to workers, and, together with uncertainty, can result in the establishment of a union. Yet a union cannot address all kinds of competition and so must choose between an exclusive and an inclusive membership strategy. These are zero-sum options: the greater the commitment to an exclusive strategy, the lesser the commitment, necessarily, to an inclusive one.

An exclusive strategy attempts to limit competition among the employed. The seniority system—which might be seen as an imperfect substitute for a well-developed employer control system—is the principal mechanism that unions have devised to limit internal competition. A seniority system undercuts individualistic competitive efforts. A system that rewards the investment of time rather than investment in performance differentiates among workers as little as possible and on the basis of a characteristic over which they have no control.[4]

In general, we would expect that a union that emerged in a time of economic contraction would tend to follow an exclusive strategy. Yet, as noted above, it is not possible to invest in more than one strategy at a time, and once in place, the manifestations of exclusive strategies—like seniority—are quite difficult to dislodge without destroying the institution entirely. This suggests that unions following an exclusive strategy would be more vulnerable to failure during times of economic prosperity.

The reason is that prosperity is often associated with a decline in competition simply because more jobs become available. Increased employment opportunities bring previously excluded workers into firms with entrenched union employees who, during hard economic times, purposely pursued strategies designed to improve their own well-being at the expense of the unemployed worker. Furthermore, the previously excluded workers are, precisely because they are new, disadvantaged by the existence of the seniority system. Thus the new workers not only have no loyalty to the union, but can be expected to have antipathy toward it. They become possible allies for firms seeking to rid themselves of union partnership or for other unions seeking to unseat the established union. A greater than average failure rate for unions following an exclusive strategy is expected, therefore, during times of economic prosperity.

By contrast, an inclusive strategy is vulnerable during times of economic contraction. An inclusive strategy attempts to limit competition between the employed and the unemployed. There are several institutional mechanisms designed to do so. One is a system of job rotation in which the union acts as a hiring hall and attempts to spread the available employment across as large a number of workers as possible. The Seafarer's International Union, for instance, has an elaborate system of job bidding which specifies that people who have worked a given number of months in a 2-year period are queued behind those who have worked less.

The emphasis on welfare benefits generally is a part of the repertoire of an inclusive strategy. While the benefits of contractual terms won through collective bargaining apply only to those employed, welfare benefits offered as selective incentives for membership can easily be designed to cover both employed and unemployed members.

Inclusiveness makes unions vulnerable during times of economic contraction and often changes the balance of the unemployed and the employed such that the unemployed become a heavier and heavier burden for the employed to assume. Furthermore, the unemployed tend to pressure the employed more in times of economic stress and so the coalition between them is most likely to fail.

Conclusion

Taken together, these propositions suggest something about the emergence of unions. A period of objective uncertainty, especially one that results in loss for some group of workers, is a precondition for union formation. While necessary, it is insufficient: individual workers must gain benefits from cooperative activity. They are most likely to gain if their employer's control capacity is poor and if competition (either from workers inside the firm or outside of it) is significant. These propositions also speak to the issue of union demise. Unions can pursue exclusive or inclusive strategies. Different kinds of economic conditions will render each of these strategies dysfunctional. In addition, periods of uncertainty will threaten already existing unions, especially if the new period of uncertainty is different in scope or type than the period that gave rise to the union in the first place. Such uncertainties may well pave the way for the rise of competitive institutions—other unions or state welfare provisions—that seek to lure workers to their membership rolls and away from that of the initial union. Thus, in addition to being the precondition for the emergence of unions, uncertainty is also the precondition for their demise.

These propositions also focus attention on what, in the complicated story of the ISU, is probably similar to the stories of many other unions. The 1860's and 1870's were characterized by significant economic fluctuations, but the uncertainty that resulted, in and of itself, was insufficient to produce organization. Individual workers would first have to face losses before they would be tempted to participate in the establishment of unions: in this instance, to spur the Seamen's Protective Association (Caucasian seamen being replaced by Chinese sailors), and of the Coast Seamen's Union (a reduction in already depressed wages). There is no direct evidence regarding the control capacity of the employers, but the indirect evidence is highly suggestive. Seafaring work takes place far away from the eye—and therefore the monitoring and sanctioning capacities—of employers, so that this too provided an impetus toward organization among seamen.

Originally, the Coast Seamen's Union pursued an exclusive membership strategy, drawing on their comparative organizational advantages of isolation and racial homogeneity. But their exclusive strategy allowed another union—the Steamshipmen's Protective Union—to develop, and this union provided the CSU with bitter jurisdictional competition. The eventual merger of these two unions led the newly formed Sailor's Union of the Pacific to pursue an inclusive membership strategy (favoring establishment of a union shipping office, and the establishment of ties to international and national seamen). This inclusive strategy brought in terrific numbers of members but it could not withstand the economic contraction of the 1920's (depression in merchant shipping, increased foreign competition, and a surplus of seamen).

Last, it can be noted that uncertainty, competition, and choice of organizing strategy each contributes to the dynamism of the process of union emergence and demise. These propositions suggest neither a micro to macro model nor a macro to micro model; instead, they suggest a dynamic system that derives its impetus from macrosocial, organizational, and individual processes.

In the case of unions, and possibly of other institutions as well, the question of institutional emergence is not one that can be answered for one point in time. Unions do not emerge, mature, and die. They appear, change, disappear, reappear in a new form, grow, merge, and disappear once again. Thus, it would be a mistake to take the current trend of union dissolution as an indication that workers have ceased to be concerned with blunting the effects of future uncertainties. Instead, as these institutions become incapable of addressing the needs of their members, this becomes a period of great opportunity for innovative institutional solutions to those needs. Certainly the state has stepped in to meet concerns about continuing income and health care following retirement. Yet it has not addressed the principal assurance concerns of workers: those of steady employment and income stream during the working years. Note that these are the very same issues that led to the development of unions in the first place. It would be folly to assume that, in the absence of other institutional solutions, workers will never again engage in collective action to ensure themselves against the unpredictable losses of employment and income.

Notes

1. The most recent attempt to explain the origin of unions is that by Hannan (1987). He has a general theory of organizations—one based on population ecology models—and he applies it to the problem of union emergence.

2. Hernes (1972) quotes the Norwegian Labor Party leader, Finn Moe, speaking in 1937 on the subject:

> In many parts of the world, radicals have often proclaimed that, if we only had a depression, the workers will be prevailed upon to organize. The Norwegian labor movement long ago rejected the idea that the labor movement grows stronger in a period of increased economic misery. The experience of the world war clearly showed that so-called prosperous times strengthened the labor movement and increased the fighting spirit. Contrariwise, actual experience during a depression indicates that it is not only very difficult to conduct successful strikes, but that the organized workers are less willing to fight, as they are constantly afraid of losing their jobs. The best and most bitter proof of how depressed economic conditions weaken the labor movement was produced during the insurrection in Austria in February, 1934, when the members of the strongest and most valiant union in Austria, the railway workers, failed to follow the order of the union and refused to strike.
>
> Furthermore, depressions create the danger if not of a split, then of a clear cleavage within the labor movement itself, with the employed on the one side and the unemployed on the other.

3. It should be noted that there seems to be at least one major historical exception, namely, the continuing exclusion of nonwhite workers from many unions. It may be the case, however, that the usual telling of the story is reversed. It is possible that nonwhite workers would have gained nothing by joining unions, and may well have spurned such overtures. Then, white unionists' racism may be understood as, in part, sour grapes.

4. In addition to being well-suited to a situation in which there is poor employer control capacity, this is also particularly well-suited to occupations which require informal, on-the-job training (for example, most construction-related jobs). Seniority means that more experienced workers can share their knowledge with less experienced workers without fear of then being displaced by them.

References

Dickens, William T. and Jonathan S. Leonard. (1985). "Accounting for the decline in union membership, 1950–80." *Industrial and Labor Relations Review* 38(3):323–34.

Dryzek, John and Robert E. Goodin. (1986). "Risk-sharing and social justice: The motivational foundations of the post-war welfare state." *British Journal of Political Science* 16:1–34.

Dunlop, John T. (1948). "The development of labor organizations: A theoretical framework." Pp. 163–93 in Richard Lester and Joseph Shister, eds., *Insights into Labor Issues*. New York: Macmillan.

Freeman, Richard B. and James L. Medoff. (1984). *What Do Unions Do?* New York: Basic Books.

Friedman, Debra (1987). "Uncertainty and collective action." Unpublished paper.

Goldman, Alvin I. (1986). *Epistemology and Cognition*. Cambridge, MA: Harvard University Press.

Hannan, Michael. (1987). "The Ecology of Organizational Founding: American Labor Unions, 1836–1985." *American Journal of Sociology* 92:910–943.

Hechter, Michael. (1987). *Principles of Group Solidarity.* Berkeley: University of California Press.

Hernes, Gudmund. (1972). "Ideology and organization: The case of the Norwegian labor movement 1910–1940." Unpublished report.

Kahneman, Daniel and Amos Tversky. (1979). "Prospect theory: An analysis of decision under risk," *Econometrica* 47(2):263–91.

Keyssar, Alexander. (1986). *Out of Work: The First Century of Unemployment in Massachusetts.* Cambridge: Cambridge University Press.

Kokkelenberg, Edward C. and Donna R. Sockell. (1985). "Union membership in the United States, 1973–81." *Industrial and Labor Relations Review* 38(4):497–543.

Knight, Frank. (1971). *Risk, Uncertainty and Profit.* Chicago: University of Chicago Press.

Lipset, Seymour Martin. (Ed). (1986). *Unions in Transition.* San Francisco: Institute for Contemporary Studies Press.

McAdam, Doug. (1982). *Political Process and the Development of Black Insurgency, 1930–1970.* Chicago: University of Chicago Press.

Oliver, Pamela. (1980). "Rewards and punishments as selective incentives for collective action: Theoretical investigations." *American Journal of Sociology* 85(6):1356–75.

Olson, Mancur. (1965). *The Logic of Collective Action.* Harvard: Harvard University Press.

Perlman, Selig. (1923). *History of Trade Unionism in the United States.* New York: Macmillan.

Spence, Michael. (1973). "Job market signaling." *The Quarterly Journal of Economics* 87:355–75.

14

Intrafamilial Markets for Education in Japan

Mary C. Brinton

In recent years sociologists and economists have entered into an uneasy intellectual exchange with each other. Economists have become more interested in traditionally "sociological" topics such as the sexual division of labor in the home and in the workplace (Becker, 1981, 1985; Polachek, 1979, 1981) and sociologists have increasingly used the technical tools of economics to analyze a variety of problems. However, have sociologists and economists utilized their comparative advantages to synthesize their talents and contribute to richer theories of human behavior than either can produce on their own? This chapter begins with the premises that such an endeavor is just beginning, that it is most evident in the area of rational choice theorizing, and that it will be particularly important for topics such as social inequality that stand at the border of the provinces of both economics and sociology.

In this chapter, we take up the topic of gender stratification and argue for the utility of a rational choice-based model that combines assumptions from human capital theory (the economic input) with the social-institutional context (the sociological input).

Gender stratification in the economy, whether measured by the male–female wage gap, by occupational sex segregation, or by other indicators, is produced by a combination of at least three factors: (1) the differing amounts of human capital developed by men and women, (2) differing occupational choices ("preferences") on the part of men and

Table 14.1. Mothers' Aspirations for Sons and Daughters: A Cross-National Comparison[a]

	Aspire to university education	
	Sons (%)	Daughters (%)
Japan	73.0	27.7
United States	68.9	65.8
Sweden	87.3	84.5
West Germany	31.1	30.8
England	19.6	14.3
Philippines	48.1	44.1

[a] Table shows respondents' answers to the question, "What level of education would you like your son [daughter] to receive?" Countries were not purposively chosen by the author but are rather the countries included in the Japanese government survey. Respondents were a random sample of approximately 1200 women, aged 20–59 years, in each country.
Source: Office of the Prime Minister, Japan, 1982.

women, and (3) differential employer evaluation (in common parlance, discrimination) of the human capital of men and women. Neoclassical economists have focused mainly, although not exclusively, on the first two types of explanation, looking at how the conditions of labor supply influence job and wage determination for the sexes. Recently, sociologists have been particularly interested in the third factor, including how the structure of the labor market and the conditions of labor demand (via employer preferences) propel men and women into different jobs with correspondingly different wage scales (Roos and Reskin, 1984; Treiman and Hartmann, 1981).

We argue that a rapprochement between the sociologists' structural approach and the economists' voluntaristic approach can be effected by analyzing the types of social-institutional contexts that produce a gap between the human capital of the sexes. This is tantamount to asking: how does the environment structure the educational decisions of parents and young people?

We start with an interesting empirical observation from Japanese society. In Japan, men and women are highly differentiated in their levels of educational attainment. Over three times as many men (41.1%) as women (12.7%) graduate from 4-year universities. This social fact is mirrored almost perfectly by the ratio between parents' (specifically, mothers') university aspirations for sons vs. daughters, suggesting that it is not the case that educational behavior is simply lagging behind aspirations. Comparisons with a range of other nations (Table 14.1) show that Japanese mothers' educational aspirations are by far the least sex-egalitarian (Office of the Prime Minister, Japan, 1982). Lest this be dismissed as an Asian phenomenon or as a characteristic of an economic latecomer, comparisons of educational attainments with Taiwan and Korea indicate the gender gap to be larger in Japan, the country that leads Asia in terms of economic development. Why? In this chapter it is argued that under certain social-institutional constraints it is rational for parents to create an intrafamilial market for education. Japan is used as a model to explore what some of those constraints might be.

The Concept of a Human Capital Development System

The framework developed here to tackle the question of why the human capital of men and women differs widely in some cultural settings and not in others rests on the notion that societies have different *systems of human capital development* (Brinton, 1988). Such a system is based on the social-institutional configuration of household, educational system, and labor market in different societies. The social-institutional context of human capital development sets up the constraints and opportunities within which social actors—parents, educators, employers, and young men and women themselves—make decisions about investing in human capital. An adequate theory of why differences in human capital between men and women persist over time and vary across cultural settings should specify clearly the macro level, institutional context. This context can be used to determine the micro level and to predict the following:

1. Who are the key social actors in the human capital development process?
2. What are the principal motivations of these actors in making human capital investment decisions?
3. What informational inputs go into actors' decisions?
4. What resources do actors have access to, and how does this affect the decisions they make?

We begin by summarizing the nature of the human capital development system in Japan and for illustrative purposes contrast it with that of the United States. We then develop a number of hypotheses that are suggested by this macro level institutional environment. These go beyond the simple observations that Japanese men and women have varying amounts of education and that parental opinion supports sex-segregated educational outcomes. Within the space limitations of this chapter, we then examine these hypotheses using micro-level data on Japanese households.

Human Capital Development in Japan

A system of human capital development is comprised of two dimensions: (1) the way that the educational system and labor market fit together, and (2) the structure of intergenerational exchange in the family.

The first dimension of a human capital development system can be explained in the following way. In a society where the educational system is highly age-graded, highly competitive, and is the route by which young workers with general education are channeled into work organizations where they receive further training, educators and employers play relatively strong roles in deciding who will receive opportunities for human capital investment. We postulate that such choices will be made rationally, according to whether these social actors think that investments (time, emotions, or education and training resources) in men or women will bring greater "payoffs."

Firm-internal labor markets are highly developed in the Japanese economy, making it critical for young workers to succeed in the competition for entry-level jobs. Guidance and sponsorship are crucial to individual socioeconomic success; principles of sponsorship and merit operate to allocate young people into positions in highly ranked schools and into large firms where they can receive subsequent on-the-job training, promotions, and wage increases (Brinton, 1988). Individuals' opportunities to return to school or to otherwise invest in their own education and human capital development later in the life course are extremely limited. This type of systemic education–labor market connection presents difficulties for individuals who try to alternate energies across the life cycle among family responsibilities and work commitments. If these individuals are women, this educational system–labor market configuration is inherently (but not necessarily intentionally) sex-biased.

The education-work nexus described above characterizes the Japanese urban economy. The sharpness of age-grading in Japanese higher education and in managerial positions in firms contrasts with comparatively weak age-grading in American higher education and in managerial posts (Brinton, 1988). In Japan this demonstrates the importance attached to a rigid life-cycle schedule consisting of irreversible exit from education, immediate entrance into a work organization, and (if all goes according to plan) promotion through that work organization.

This first dimension of a human capital development system, the education–work nexus, is complemented by a second dimension: the structure of intergenerational exchange in the family. Japanese parents have a stronger degree of control over children's education than would be true in a society where the educational system is an institutional resource to which individuals themselves have access across their life cycle (in other words, where the individual is a relatively autonomous actor vis-à-vis schooling decisions). The investments parents make in their male and female children will influence the extent to which the two sexes are able to compete successfully in educational contests and in the contest for entry-level positions in the labor market, which critically determine eventual wages. But the flow of resources in the Japanese family is by no means one-way: parents hold expectations regarding the returns they will receive from the children. The structure of intergenerational exchange is dense and, as we will see, multifaceted.

Given that Japanese parents are crucial actors in the decision-making process regarding education, it makes sense to analyze education through the lens of parents' aspirations for their sons and daughters. Recalling the requirements outlined above for a theory of gender stratification, we can ask: what *perceptions, motivations,* and *resources* do parents call upon in the process of guiding the human capital development of their children? Clearly, these depend on the environment. Is the labor market sex-discriminatory? If so, is it more rational to hold high educational expectations for sons than for daughters, given that sons can, on average, garner greater monetary returns from their education? What educational requirements does society say are necessary to contract a "good" marriage? How does the environment shape the types of rewards (e.g., support in old age) parents expect to receive from highly educating their children? Is there a private schooling system, rendering a family's economic resources a variable in determining educational attainments of children? All of these possibilities suggest that parents respond in their aspirations for children to the social-institutional constraints and opportunities offered by the environment.

In general, Japanese parents overwhelmingly prefer a university education for their sons. In addition, Japanese parents (1) are generally *motivated* to invest in their children for old-age support of various kinds, (2) *perceive* the labor market to be sex-discriminatory, and (3) have a standard of living (produced by low fertility and rapid economic growth in the 1960s and early 1970s) that leaves some disposable income *(resources)* for educational investment. It is the thesis of this chapter that these factors all contribute to the maintenance of a large gap in Japanese parents' preferences for sons' vs. daughters' higher education. Figure 14.1 summarizes the theoretical framework developed in the chapter.

Perceptions, motivations, and resources will vary among families. The optimal way to test hypotheses will be to look at the micro level decisions of Japanese households that are subject to different sets of constraints. Before turning to the micro level data, we look in greater detail

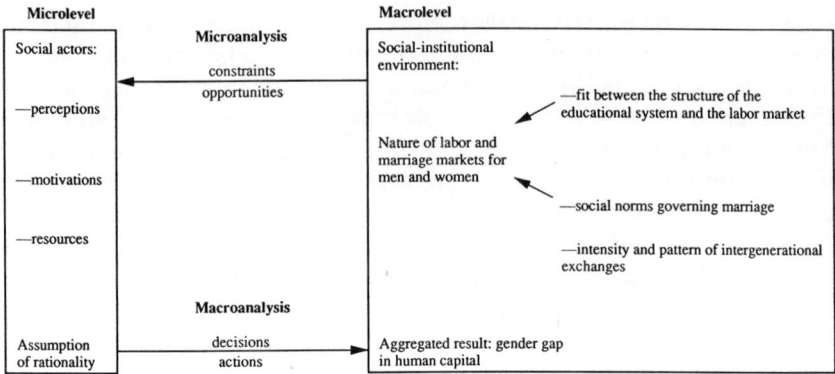

Figure 14.1. The micro-macro construction of intrafamilial markets for education.

at each of the three hypothesized inputs to parents' rational decision-making vis-à-vis the education of children.

Parents' Information Regarding Children's Future Probability of Success

We can think of education as preparing people for two principal markets in their adult life: the labor market and the marriage market. The argument presented above regarding Japan's human capital development system implies that the labor market is sex-discriminatory. Let us look for a moment at why this is so, and at how Japanese perceive the labor market.

The Japanese educational system provides general preparatory training and employers then take over the responsibility for training individuals for jobs. If most women move in and out of the labor market across the life cycle according to family responsibilities, it will be very difficult for them to participate in the now-infamous Japanese firm-internal labor markets (Cole 1979) with on-the-job training, promotions, and wage increases. Employers will find it rational to use a statistical discrimination rule, with sex as a screening criterion (Arrow, 1973; Phelps, 1972). The labor market thus becomes sex-discriminatory as a result of the structure of the education and employment system and of the "average" women's life cycle labor force participation pattern. Opinion polls indicate that the Japanese population indeed perceives a high degree of sex discrimination in the labor market. Table 14.2 shows that 22.2% of the public perceives women's position in the hiring process to be *very* dis-

Table 14.2. Attitudes Concerning Whether Women Are Treated Disadvantageously or Not in the Hiring Process[a]

Women are treated very disadvantageously	22.2%
Women are treated somewhat disadvantageously	57.4%
Women are not treated disadvantageously	11.7%
N.A.	8.8%

[a]Source: *Yomiuri Shinbun* (Yomiuri Newspaper) National Opinion Poll, May 14, 1984.

advantageous, and an additional 57.4% consider it to be *somewhat* disadvantageous. Thus, the majority of Japanese view employers as discriminating among potential employees on the basis of sex.

What do parents gain from preparing their children for the labor and the marriage markets? In a preindustrial society or a society in which the welfare function is borne mainly by families, parents can probably expect both prestige returns and pecuniary returns (although they may expect different returns from sons and daughters). A son with a high education may be able to command a higher salary, enjoy a job with higher status, and marry a woman from a "good" family—all of these presumably bring prestige to his parents. A daughter with a high education may be able to "marry up," or she may be able to command a higher salary. But a daughter's opportunities in labor and marriage markets are much more intricately linked to the specific environment than are her brother's. Is the labor market sex-discriminatory? To the extent that it is, parental investment in a daughter's education may be less rational, at least for economic reasons, than investment in her brother's education. Does the marriage market operate to effectively "discriminate" against women with high education, i.e., are there strong norms dictating that a man should marry a woman with somewhat less education than he, on the presumption that she will be a better wife and mother? In such a case, parents may maximize their prestige returns from a daughter by helping her to obtain a moderate, "acceptable" level of education—neither too low nor too high. These considerations give rise to several *perceptual* hypotheses:

1. Japanese parents will, on average, have higher educational aspirations for sons than daughters. This prediction can be made on the grounds that: (a) the majority of Japanese perceive the labor market to be sex-discriminatory, and (b) parents' common knowledge of marriage patterns would lead them to expect highly educated daughters to be "pricing themselves out of the marriage market" by reducing the number of potential partners with a higher education.
2. Parents will be more likely to have high educational aspirations

for daughters if they perceive the labor market to be sex-neutral (nondiscriminatory).
3. Parents will be more likely to have high educational aspirations for daughters if they feel that this will not hurt their daughter's chances of making a good marriage match.
4. Neither perceptions of the labor nor the marriage markets will significantly affect parents' aspirations for sons.

Parents' Incentives for Differentiating the Education of Sons and Daughters

In addition to their perceptions of the markets that children will face, parents also act on their preferences for the types of returns they would like to receive from different children. We do not delve here into the historical reasons why Japanese parents might prefer different returns from sons and daughters, but we use parents' stated preferences as input into the educational decision-making process. We specify three types of support parents may expect in old age: financial assistance, a joint living arrangement, and emotional help.

Japan does not have a well-developed social welfare system. Most companies set the retirement age in the late fifties, and pensions are paid in terms of a lump sum. Public pensions are available 5–10 years after retirement and many older Japanese search for second jobs during these years (Martin, 1987) and/or choose not to rely on public support. Preferences for living with a child are relatively strong. The most common preference is to live in separate but attached living quarters with a married son, preferably the eldest one. The emotional bond between parents and children, particularly between mother and children (Doi, 1973; Lebra, 1976), continues into old age and may increase in strength. Thus, financial exchanges, joint living arrangements, and emotional support are all possible types of returns parents anticipate in their old age. Given this, we make the following *motivational* predictions.

1. Parents will have higher educational aspirations for a son to the extent that they expect to rely financially on him in old age. If they expect to rely on a daughter, the strategy is more complicated: given that they almost certainly expect the daughter to marry, their returns might be maximized by her "good" marriage." But rarely is it the case that parents can hope to rely on a daughter financially if she marries out; it is more likely that their daughter and son-in-law will be relied on by his parents. Therefore, we might expect a curvilinear relationship between financial expectations of a daughter and educational expectations for

her. Financial expectations may be less likely from daughters who receive the most "proper" female education in Japan, junior college, than from daughters who receive a vocational school or university education that presumably prepares them for the labor market.

2. Parents who expect to live with a son will not necessarily have university expectations for him, because they will probably anticipate passing on the family property to him—the son thus has less need to "make it" in the labor market than he otherwise would. Few parents will anticipate living with a daughter (given the Japanese emphasis on the family line, through males) and it is not clear which direction the relationship between education and living aspirations would go for daughters.

3. The preference for wanting to rely emotionally on a daughter may somewhat dampen parents' educational aspirations for her, if they perceive that a very high level of education would make her less emotionally available to them. It is not immediately clear how the expectation of emotional reliance on a son would affect parents' educational aspirations for him.

Resources for Educational Investment in Children

Does household income have an effect on parents' educational expectations for sons and daughters? Income is an empirical indicator of a number of things, most importantly social status and resources. In its role as an indicator of social status, we could expect increasing income to lead to higher educational expectations for sons. Parents will want to maintain their social status by having a son who is highly educated and enters a good job and a good marriage. The resource effect of income should, at face value, also be positive: a higher income should facilitate higher education. The educational market in Japan is a complex one. The national universities are the highest ranked but are the least expensive. Many parents bear considerable monetary costs for tutors and after-school education to help their children pass the entrance exams to good high schools and universities (Hanley and Yamamura, 1975). Such schooling for exam preparation is increasingly regarded by Japanese parents as necessary for their children to get ahead.[1] Thus we would expect household income to be positively correlated with parents' university aspirations for sons; the status and resource effects of income should be consistent.

Daughters' education once again poses a more complex set of issues. While the resource effect should be positive, this would not be the case if parents perceive that a daughter's higher education will not be beneficial, either in terms of bringing prestige returns through promoting a good marriage or in terms of facilitating a good job in a sex-discriminatory labor market. We would expect the effect of household income on educational aspirations for daughters to be contingent on parents' perceptions of the marriage market and on their perception of sex discrimination in the labor market. The following specific *resource* predictions can be made:

1. Household income will be positively related to parents' educational aspirations for sons.
2. If parents perceive little or no sex discrimination in the labor market, household income will be positively related to educational aspirations for daughters.
3. If parents perceive that the marriage market disadvantages women with higher education, household income will have no effect on parents' educational aspirations for daughters.

Other Hypotheses

Several other factors may be related to educational aspirations. Certainly parents' own education is likely to influence the educational aspirations they have for their children. We hypothesize that mother's education will exert the most impact on parents' aspirations for daughters, and father's education will exert the most impact on aspirations for sons. Parents with a higher education will want a higher education for their children for status reasons. This link is likely to be strong between fathers and sons. Whether the respondent is the mother or the father, the stated aspiration for sons will be higher to the extent that the father is highly educated. Mothers' education may be less closely related to intentions for daughters' education than fathers' is for sons. This is because the effect of mothers' education, from a rational choice perspective, is based on how well a woman's interests were served by her education vis-à-vis the marriage and the labor markets. This makes the prediction somewhat indeterminate.

Sex of the respondent is used as a control variable. Given the strategic human capital development model there is no a priori reason to expect that mothers and fathers will differ from each other in their expectations of sons or in their expectations of daughters. Each sex probably has a better idea of what the marriage and labor markets are like for their own sex, but this does not necessarily mean that fathers, for example, will have higher aspirations than mothers do for sons.

The three cities where data were collected are in different regions of the country. Overall, educational aspirations may be higher in cities with highly educated, urban populations because of competition in the labor and marriage markets. In the present study, this would mean that educational aspirations would be higher in Kodaira (a Tokyo suburb) and Sapporo than in Toyohashi. The latter is the smallest of the three cities and has a larger proportion of population engaged in agriculture, either on a part- or full-time basis. This urban effect is more likely to exist for sons' education than daughters', as again, higher education for a son presumably helps him in both labor and marriage markets (in any environment, but especially in a large city). The outcome of higher education for daughters is less clear and is dependent on the specific labor and marriage markets in the environment.

In summary, the general predictions for factors that will raise educational aspirations for sons are much easier to make than the predictions for daughters—the "profitability" of higher education for daughters is more closely linked to the constraints and opportunities in the environment.

We predict that family composition will also be related to educational expectations for sons and daughters. If our strategic argument is correct in suggesting that parents "statistically discriminate" against daughters because they perceive the marriage market to favor daughters with moderate rather than high education, then daughters in families with sons will be particularly disfavored in educational terms. Conversely, a daughter who is the only child in a family or who has sisters but no brothers will be educationally favored compared to girls with brothers.

Parental aspirations for sons will also be affected by the sex composition and number of children. Aspirations should be highest for sons who are only children or who have sisters but no brothers. Among boys who have sisters, it is not clear whether a boy will be more educationally favored if he is the eldest child or not. In families with sons but no daughters, general educational aspirations for sons will be lower than in other families with sons because there will, in effect, be a very competitive market for education among sons in an all-male set.

Finally, some predictions implicit in the theoretical framework outlined here should be mentioned. Given that sons will *ceteris paribus* fare better in a sex-discriminatory labor market than daughters, a rational choice perspective would predict that parents are more apt to say that they plan to rely financially on sons than daughters. They also are more likely to plan to live with a son rather than a daughter. Given that a more affective role is typically assigned to daughters, parents may be more apt to expect reliance on a daughter for emotional support in old age. This expectation would be complicated by the fact that parents may expect to live with a son, however, and be in closer physical proximity to him. As mentioned earlier, we do not attempt here to explain the *origin* of these preferences and do not necessarily ascribe a rational choice basis to them. Rather, predictions are based on what would appear to be rational given the sets of constraints posed by the environment.

The sex-discriminatory nature of the labor market would also lead one to predict that parents will be more likely to report that education for daughters is less for the purpose of obtaining a good job than for obtaining a good marriage. For sons, the job-related purpose would probably rank first in parents' minds, with marriage close behind. It is important to point out that these particular findings would be consistent with a rational choice perspective but would also be consistent with a framework based on cultural norms. They thus cannot be taken as prima facie evidence for a rational choice model.

Data and Methods

Data for the analyses come from a survey conducted in 1984 by the author in the three Japanese cities of Sapporo, Kodaira (a Tokyo suburb), and Toyohashi. The survey was unique in that it asked a number of questions included in surveys carried out by the Japanese government and it also asked questions that generated variables necessary for testing the hypotheses outlined above. For instance, items included perceptions of sex discrimination in the labor market, educational aspirations for sons and daughters and the perceived purposes of education for each sex, and plans for old-age support.

The survey sample was collected by a stratified random sampling procedure that selected equal numbers of men and women aged 25–29 and men aged 40–44. Women aged 40–44 were oversampled in the survey design because a number of analyses (extraneous to the present chapter) involved female wages, and a labor force participation rate of approximately 60% for this age group of women suggested that oversampling was advisable. The overall response rate to the mailed questionnaire was 50.1%. Although this is a respectable rate for a mailed questionnaire in an urban population, in order to check for response bias a number of procedures were carried out. These are discussed more fully elsewhere (Brinton, 1989). Briefly, when each age/sex sample is adjusted to reflect the educational distribution of the sampled population, the total sample and the population are very similar on employment indicators (labor force status, employment status, and industry) reported in the population census.

The analyses presented here are restricted to men and women in the older (age 40–44) cohort who have at least one child. This yields 616 respondents. We use a model incorporating the theoretically relevant variables plus a number of control variables to predict the probability that a parent will have university aspirations for a son; the same model is also run for daughters. In these analyses, families of all sizes and compositions are examined. A second model incorporates the effect of perceptions of sex discrimination; this model is used to predict parents' university aspirations for daughters. Because the question on sex discrimination was asked of the Toyohashi sample only, the model is run only for that city.

All independent variables in the model are dummy variables scored as "0" or "1" with the exception of two variables: the logged income variable and the perception of sex discrimination in the labor market. Sex discrimination perceptions were originally measured on a four-point scale, with a score of "1" representing perception of considerable sex discrimination and a score of "4" representing perception of no sex discrimination. Scores of "3" and "4" were so infrequent that the two were combined, so that the three categories are: perception of considerable sex discrimination (1), perception of some sex discrimination (2), and perception of almost none or no sex discrimination (3).

The dependent variable in the model is also a dummy variable scored as "1" or "0" according to whether the respondent had university aspirations for a son [daughter] or not.

Descriptive Results

Table 14.3 shows the means and standard deviations for all variables. In families in the sample with at least one son, 73.1% of parents report having university aspirations for their son. In families with at least one daughter, 27.6% of parents hope to send a daughter to university. The most striking aspects of these figures are the wide disparity between them, and their nearly perfect equivalence to the national figures reported for Japan mentioned earlier: 73.0% of mothers reported university aspirations for sons and 27.7% reported university aspirations for daughters. This correspondence between the present and national samples is amazing, and lends credibility to the causal analyses. It is interesting to note that the figures are the same even though the national sample includes only mothers and ours includes both mothers and fathers (although women were oversampled). This suggests that men and women do not differ in their expectations of children. In our sample, virtually the same proportions of mothers (27.5%) as fathers (27.7%) aspired to university education for daughters. More mothers (75.3%) than fathers (69.1%) hoped for university education for sons. This sex

Table 14.3. Means and Standard Deviations of Variables

	Families with sons		Families with daughters	
	Mean	S.D.	Mean	S.D.
Sex of respondent	.353	.478	.338	.474
Household characteristics				
Wife's education				
Junior high school	.210	.468	.198	.399
High school	.522	.500	.532	.500
Junior college/vocational school	.169	.374	.163	.370
University	.077	.267	.081	.274
Husband's education				
Junior high school	.220	.414	.216	.412
High school	.389	.488	.399	.490
Junior college/vocational school	.046	.209	.041	.198
University	.325	.469	.322	.468
Household income (logged)	15.645	.525	15.569	.517
Region				
Toyohashi	.373	.484	.370	.483
Sapporo	.294	.456	.298	.458
Kodaira	.333	.472	.332	.471
Expectations for old-age assistance				
Expect financial help from a son [daughter]	.657	.475	.191	.394
Expect emotional help from a son [daughter]	.417	.494	.436	.496
Expect to live with a son [daughter]	.325	.469	.134	.341
Family composition				
Only child—son [daughter]	.103	.304	.079	.271
More than one child—all sons [daughters]	.198	.399	.147	.354
More than one child—son [daughter] is youngest or middle in a mixed-sex set	.416	.493	.495	.500
More than one child—son [daughter] is oldest in a mixed-sex set	.282	.451	.277	.448
Perception of sex discrimination in the labor market	—	—	1.542	.648
University aspirations for son [daughter]	.731	.444	.276	.447

Table 14.4. Differences in Parental Expectations of Support from Sons and Daughters in Old Age[a]

	Son	Daughter	T-value[b]
Anticipate financial help from a son [daughter]	.74	.06	−19.82***
Anticipate living jointly with a son [daughter]	.39	.08	−8.78***
Anticipate relying for emotional help mainly on a son [daughter]	.31	.44	2.66**
N=291			

[a](1) All *t*-tests are one-tailed. (2) Table is restricted to families with two or more children, where there is at least one son and at least one daughter. (3) Figures for support from sons and daughters do not necessarily sum to 100% because some parents report anticipating help from a combination of children or from none of their childrenn. The critical comparisons for our purposes are the two-way comparison between sons and daughters, on the one hand, and the two-way comparisons between the needs parents expect to have fulfilled by children of each sex (see text for discussion of the latter, not shown here), on the other.
[b]**T-value significant at .01 level. ***T-value signifiant at .001 level.

difference in expectations for sons is not statistically significant but does become significant in the causal analyses when we control for other variables. We will return to this point later in the discussion.

The univariate statistics demonstrate a number of differences in parents' expectations for children that were implied in our theoretical discussion. As predicted, more parents expect to rely on a son than on a daughter financially, and more expect to live with a son rather than a daughter. Slightly more expect to rely on a daughter than a son emotionally but the difference is not large, which, in fact, is what we predicted. These comparisons from Table 14.3, where families with sons and families with daughters are compared, are flawed by the fact that some of the families with sons may not have daughters and vice versa— thus we do not know what choice sets parents have in regard to reliance on sons and daughters. The valid comparison to make is reliance on a son vs. reliance on a daughter in families that have at least one son and one daughter, where parents have the option of choosing between the two sexes. Such a comparison is shown in Table 14.4.

As shown, in families with at least one child of each sex, parents are significantly more likely to state that they would rely financially on a male child, significantly more likely to state that they anticipate living with a male child, and significantly more likely to say that they would turn to a daughter for emotional support in old age. These sex differences are all statistically significant. For each sex there is also an ordering in terms of the needs parents expect to have filled. Parents are by far the most likely to turn to a daughter for emotional support rather than for financial or coresidence needs, neither of which is more likely than the other. (T-tests for differences in proportions indicate that anticipated emotional help from a daughter is significantly more likely than either anticipated financial help or coresidence. Expectations for the latter two do not vary significantly.) Parents' expectations of sons are clearly ranked: Foremost among parents' thoughts regarding reliance on sons is financial support, followed by coresidence needs and, finally, by emotional needs. Statistical comparisons between these needs show that the expectation for financial support is significantly stronger than expectations for the other two types. Expectations for coresidence with a son are significantly higher than expectations for emotional support, but this difference is significant only at the .05 level. These findings are consistent with the rational choice-based predictions we made.

As predicted, the purpose of higher education is viewed by parents as being different for sons and daughters. Parents who have one or more sons and who have university aspirations for at least one of them are significantly more likely to report that the goal of a university education for sons is to "give the necessary qualifications for a future job" than are parents who have one or more daughters and who have university hopes. The respective percentages are 72.9 and 55.5. In contrast, more parents of daughters (35.8%) than sons (20.6%) state that the goal of university education is "to gain a general educational background."

Multivariate Results

Tables 14.5, 14.6, and 14.7 show the results of multivariate logistic regression models that were run to predict the probability of university aspirations for sons and daughters. Most of our hypothesized relationships find support.

Looking first at the equation for sons, we find support for the motivational hypotheses: parents are more apt to have university aspirations for a son if they anticipate relying on him in old age, whereas anticipation of coresidence is not significantly related to educational aspirations nor is anticipation of emotional reliance. The resource hypothesis is also supported: household income is significantly related to university aspirations for a son. The family composition predictions are borne out. Sons who are only children are the most educationally favored, followed by sons who are the eldest in a family of daughters. In these two situations, parents are in a position of being able to single out a son in whom to place their aspirations. Parents who have sons but no daughters are less likely than these two groups to anticipate university education for

Table 14.5. Determinants of Parents' University Aspirations for a Son[a]

	Logit coefficients
Constant	−8.100**
	(3.542)
Sex of respondent	−.531*
	(.242)
Household characteristics	
Wife's education	
Junior high school	—
High school	.681*
	(.304)
Junior college/vocational school	.600
	(.405)
University	.105
	(.532)
Husband's education	
Junior high school	—
High school	.389
	(.316)
Junior college/vocational school	.807
	(.588)
University	1.147**
	(.385)
Household income	.465*
	(.230)
Region	
Toyohashi	—
Sapporo	.703**
	(.292)
Kodaira	.473*
	(.279)
Expectations for old-age assistance	
Expect financial help from a son	.550*
	(.297)
Expect emotional help from a son	.248
	(.762)
Expect to live with a son	.155
	(.274)
Family composition	
Only child—son	1.141**
	(.485)
More than one child—all sons	.067
	(.362)
More than one child—son is youngest or middle in a mixed-sex set	—
More than one child—son is oldest in a mixed-sex set	.528*
	(.284)
Maximum likelihood χ^2	510.30
D.F.	487

[a] All significance tests are one-tailed; *$p<.05$, **$p<.01$. The analysis was restricted to households with at least one son.

Table 14.6. Determinants of Parents' University Aspirations for a Daughter[a]

	Logit coefficients
Constant	−9.548**
	(4.081)
Sex of respondent	.121
	(.264)
Household characteristics	
Wife's education	
Junior high school	—
High school	1.028*
	(.461)
Junior college/vocational school	1.582**
	(.506)
University	2.436**
	(.603)
Husband's education	
Junior high school	—
High school	.423
	(.455)
Junior college/vocational school	1.578**
	(.658)
University	1.315**
	(.462)
Household income	.381
	(.263)
Region	
Toyohashi	—
Sapporo	.067
	(.315)
Kodaira	.763**
	(.291)
Expectations for old-age assistance	
Expect financial help from a daughter	.149
	(.431)
Expect emotional help from a daughter	−.159
	(.298)
Expect to live with a daughter	−.354
	(.399)
Family composition	
Only child—daughter	1.241**
	(.505)
More than one child—all daughters	1.524**
	(.440)
More than one child–daughter is youngest or middle in a mixed-sex set	—
More than one child—daughter is oldest in a mixed-sex set	.385
	(.308)
Maximum likelihood χ^2	446.25
D.F.	474

[a] All significance tests are one-tailed; *p<.05, **p<.01. The analysis was restricted to households with at least one daughter.

Table 14.7. Determinants of Parents' University Aspirations for a Daughter: Toyohashi Sample[a]

	Logit coefficients	
	(1)	(2)
Constant	3.672	.234
	(8.097)	(8.686)
Sex of respondent	.297	.198
	(.557)	(.576)
Household characteristics		
Wife's education		
Junior high school	—	—
High school	2.128*	2.291*
	(1.174)	(1.189)
Junior college/vocational school	3.246**	3.530**
	(1.236)	(1.270)
University	3.136*	3.328*
	(1.396)	(1.432)
Husband's education		
Junior high school	—	—
High school	.550	.287
	(.845)	(.862)
Junior college/vocational school	1.759	1.750
	(1.297)	(1.306)
University	1.617*	1.592*
	(.879)	(.894)
Household income	−.541	−.395
	(.532)	(.558)
Expectations for old-age assistance		
Expect financial help from a daughter	1.612	1.623
	(1.355)	(1.362)
Expect emotional help from a daughter	−1.101	−1.074
	(.744)	(.745)
Expect to live with a daughter	.609	.633
	(1.246)	(1.263)
Family composition		
Only child—daughter	−.137	−.008
	(1.519)	(1.512)
More than one child—all daughters	.799	.869
	(1.249)	(1.224)
More than one child—daughter is youngest or middle in a mixed-sex set	—	—
More than one child—daughter is oldest in a mixed-sex set	.399	.369
	(.599)	(.614)
Perception of sex-egalitarianism in the labor labor market	—	.717*
		(.387)
Maximum likelihood χ^2	115.38	111.94
D.F.	150	149

[a]All significance tests are one-tailed; *$p<.05$, **$p<.01$. The analysis was restricted to households with at least one daughter. Because the question on perceptions of sex discrimination was asked of Toyohashi respondents only, the analysis is further limited to them.

sons, supporting our supposition of a competitive market for education among sons.

University aspirations are more prevalent in both Kodaira and Sapporo than in Toyohashi, as predicted. The only level of fathers' education that is significantly related to university aspirations for sons is university education. Households in which the mother has a high school education are also significantly more likely to aspire to sons' university education. Although the coefficients for other levels of mothers' education are not significant, they show that university aspirations for a son decline as mothers' education continues to rise to junior college and university. Interestingly, the direct effect of respondent's sex is also significant: mothers are more likely than fathers to have university aspirations for sons. Mothers, especially those who did not go on to higher education, are more likely to actively invest their aspirations into sons' future than are fathers. This is consistent with the popular image that the mother–son bond is the strongest one in the Japanese family, and also is consistent with the image of the fervent *kyoiku mama* ("education mama") who urges her son to succeed in educational competition. If we think of this in the context of a society in which labor markets operate to discriminate against women and in which parental (especially maternal) reliance on children in old age is common, this finding seems to fit well with a rational choice approach.

Turning to the model predicting university aspirations for a daughter in Table 14.6, we see a general pattern of results that is consistent with a rational choice framework. Given that a woman's education may have quite different implications in marriage and in labor markets, coefficients that were significant for sons are not necessarily so for daughters. Because we have no direct measure of parents' perception of what the marriage market is like, we assume that most people have good general knowledge of the operation of the marriage market. About half of all marriages in Japan are arranged (Hodge and Ogawa, 1986). In the contemporary context this usually means that introductions are provided by relatives, friends, teachers, employers, or other trusted acquaintances of the family. In this type of context we can assume that families are quite conversant with the "market" value of education and of other achievements and attributes. We assume that Japanese parents generally perceive that a university-educated daughter would have a smaller pool of possible marriage mates than a daughter with a high school or junior college education, and we interpret the results with this assumption in mind.

The findings for old-age assistance are consistent with what was predicted: the signs for the coefficients were predicted but no significance was expected. Recalling the hypothesis that financial expectations will be related in a curvilinear fashion to educational aspirations for daughters, we tested this in a separate model (not shown here) that regressed financial expectations on all levels of educational aspirations for daughters. As predicted, parents are more likely to expect to rely financially on daughters if they expect them to go to a 2-year vocational school or to university than if they go to junior college. The coefficients for both vocational school and university were both positive and highly significant.

The resource hypothesis is also supported, in that household income does not have a significant effect on expectations for daughters. The effects of family composition are consistent with predictions. Daughters who are only children or who have sisters but no brothers are educationally favored over daughters in mixed-sex sets of children.

Parents in Kodaira are more likely to have university aspirations for daughters than parents in the other two cities. The effects of education of both mother and father exhibit a clearer pattern for aspirations for daughters than for sons: the mother–daughter link is particularly strong. Aspirations for daughters increase with each successive level of mothers' education. But mothers overall are no more likely than fathers to have university aspirations for daughters.

Table 14.7 shows the results of a separate analysis of the Toyohashi respondents only who were asked the question on perceptions of sex discrimination in the labor market. The basic pattern of coefficients in equation (1) is similar to the coefficients in Table 14.5, except that the coefficients for family composition are no longer significant. The variable measuring perceptions of sex discrimination makes a statistically significant contribution to explained variance. Parents are more likely to have university aspirations for a daughter to the extent that they perceive the labor market to be sex-egalitarian, supporting the rational choice-based prediction.

Because of the small number of cases it is not feasible to test in a multivariate model our hypothesis that household income will be positively related to educational aspirations for daughters in the absence of perceptions of sex discrimination. (The addition of an interaction term produced a number of cells with no cases.) The hypothesis was investigated in an exploratory fashion. Household incomes were grouped into four categories and the relation between income and aspirations for daughters was examined within collapsed categories of the sex discrimination variable (perceptions of high vs. little/no discrimination). Here, income was positively related to university aspirations in the case of perceptions of little/no sex discrimination and was negatively related to university aspirations in the case of perceptions of high discrimination. These results, though not statistically significant with this number of cases, were consistent with the hypothesis that the relationship between household resources and aspirations for a daughter is contingent on parents' information and perceptions regarding the labor market facing daughters.

Conclusion

This chapter has looked at an important theoretical issue for labor economists and sociologists: why do men and women develop different amounts of human capital? We have taken an interesting empirical case, Japan, where not only do men's and women's levels of educational attainment vary markedly but parental aspirations for sons and daughters mirror this gap. This case has been used as a vehicle to explore how a theory with rational choice assumptions can link the macro level of social institutions with the micro level of individual perceptions, motivations, and resources to produce decisions that aggregate to produce macro level outcomes. The theoretical analysis was thus initiated on the macro level and built down to the micro level of individuals, predicting what actors' rational behaviors would be in a given social-institutional context. These rational behaviors have implications for aggregate patterns of gender stratification in the economy. In this manner, the theory moves across macro and micro levels and builds social-institutional constraints into what otherwise would be a rather stark economic model with a large number of untested assumptions.

One of the unexpected empirical findings that is particularly interesting is that Japanese mothers are significantly more likely than fathers to hold university aspirations for sons. Why is this so? It may be that in a sex-discriminatory environment and in an environment where people expect to rely on their children in old age, women find it sensible to "invest" in the human capital of sons and in the mother-son bond. Given women's higher life expectancy, mothers rather than fathers are likely to be the recipients of old-age support from their sons. This interpretation would also be consistent with the fact that the sex differential exists in educational aspirations for sons but not for daughters. These findings will be interesting to explore in future work.

Acknowledgment

We would like to thank Thomas Voss for his helpful comments on an earlier version of this chapter. This chapter was written while the author was on a Spencer Fellowship from the National Academy of Education;

data were collected with support from the National Science Foundation grant #SES84-07208 and the Japan Foundation.

Notes

1. A recent survey conducted by the Japanese Ministry of Education reported rates of *juku* (after-school school) attendance of 53.3% for children in their final year of junior high school in cities of at least 100,000 population (Ministry of Education, 1985).

References

Arrow, Kenneth. (1973). "The theory of discrimination." Pp. 3–33 in O. Ashenfelter and A. Rees, eds., *Discrimination in Labor Markets*. Princeton, N.J.: Princeton University Press.

Becker, Gary S. (1981). *A Treatise on the Family*. Cambridge: Harvard University Press.

Becker, Gary S. (1985). "Human capital, effort, and the sexual division of labor." *Journal of Labor Economics* 3: S33–S58.

Brinton, Mary C. (1988). "The social-institutional bases of gender stratification: Japan as an illustrative case." *American Journal of Sociology*, 94:300–334.

Brinton, Mary C. (1989). "Gender stratification in contemporary urban Japan." *American Sociological Review* 54:542–557.

Cole, Robert. (1979). *Work, Mobility, and Participation*. Berkeley: University of California Press.

Doi, Takeo. (1973). *The Anatomy of Dependence*. Tokyo: Kodansha.

Hanley, Susan B. and Kozo Yamamura. (1975). "Ichi hime, ni Taro: Educational aspirations and the decline in fertility in postwar Japan." *The Journal of Japanese Studies* 2:83–125.

Hodge, William and Naohiro Ogawa. (1986). "Arranged marriages, assortative mating and achievement in Japan." Tokyo: Nihon University Population Research Institute, Research Paper Series No. 27.

Lebra, Takie Sugiyama. (1976). *Japanese Patterns of Behavior*. Honolulu: University of Hawaii Press.

Martin, Linda G. (1987). "The aging of Asia." Paper presented at the Annual Meeting of the Population Association of America.

Ministry of Education, Japan. (1985). *Jido, seito no gakkogai gakushu katsudo ni kansuru jittai chosa*. (Survey on students' extracurricular study activities). Tokyo: Ministry of Education.

Office of the Prime Minister, Japan, (1982). *Fujin mondai ni kansuru kokusai hikaku chosa*. (Comparative survey on women's problems). Tokyo: Office of the Prime Minister.

Phelps, Edmund S. (1972). "The statistical theory of racism and sexism." *American Economic Review*, 62:659–666.

Polachek, Solomon. (1979). "Occupational Segregation among Women: Theory,

Evidence, and a Prognosis." Pp. 137–57 in Cynthia B. Lloyd, Emily S. Andrews, and Curtis L. Gilroy, eds., *Women in the Labor Market*. New York: Columbia University Press.

Polachek, Solomon (1981). "Occupational self-selection: A human capital approach to sex differences in occupational structure." *Review of Economics and Statistics* 63:60–69.

Roos, Patricia A. and Barbara F. Reskin. (1984). "Institutional Factors Contributing to Sex Segregation in the Workplace." Pp. 192–232 in Barbara F. Reskin, ed., *Sex Segregation in the Workplace*. Washington, D.C.: National Academy Press.

Treiman, Donald J. and Heidi Hartmann. (1981). *Women, Work, and Wages: Equal Pay for Jobs of Equal Value*. Washington, D.C.: National Academy Press.

Biographical Sketches of the Contributors

Mary C. Brinton is Assistant Professor of Sociology at The University of Chicago. She is interested in applications of rational choice theory to social institutional issues, particularly those related to education, labor markets, and the family. She is currently completing a book on the role of women in the contemporary Japanese economy.

William Brustein is Associate Professor of Sociology at the University of Minnesota. He is the author of *Social Origins of Political Regionalism* (1988), a work that combines Marxist analysis and rational choice theory to explain variations in regional political loyalties in France since 1849. His current research focuses on the social bases of membership in the interwar Fascist parties in Italy and Germany.

James S. Coleman is Professor of Sociology and Education at The University of Chicago and member of the National Academy of Sciences, the American Philosophical Society, the American Academy of Arts and Sciences, the National Academy of Education, and the Royal Swedish Academy of Sciences. His books include *The Asymmetric Society* (1982); *High School Achievement: Public, Catholic, and Private Schools Compared* (1982); *Individual Interests and Collective Action* (1986); and *Public and Private High Schools: The Impact of Communities* (1987).

Hendrik Derk Flap is Assistant Professor at the University of Utrecht, and member of the Interuniversity Center for Sociological Theory and Methodology (ICS) of the universities of Groningen and Utrecht. His research interests focus on social networks and occupational attainment, and on the emergence of primary social networks. His chapter in this volume is part of a broader project that concerns the development of a theory of social capital. Recent publications include *Conflict, Loyalty and Violence* (1988) and "With a Little Help from My Friends" (*Social Forces*,

1988) (with N.D. De Graaf). Currently he is engaged in editing a book on network analysis, *Social Networks through Time* (with J. Weesie).

Henk de Vos is Associate Professor of Theoretical Sociology at the University of Groningen. His research interests include social processes in schools and classrooms, behavior in social dilemmas, altruism, labor market, and household production.

Bruno S. Frey is Professor of Economics at the University of Zurich. He is the author of several books, including *Modern Political Economy* (1978), *Democratic Economic Policy* (1983), *International Political Economics* (1984), and *Muses and Markets* (with W. Pommerehne) (1989). His books have been translated into German, French, Spanish, Portuguese, Italian, Japanese, and Chinese.

Debra Friedman is Assistant Professor of Sociology at The University of Arizona. She is the co-author (with Michael Hechter) of "The Contribution of Rational Choice Theory to Macrosociological Research" (*Sociological Theory*, 1988) and is the author of various articles on rational choice theory and collective action. She is currently working on a book on the change in presumptive child custody from fathers to mothers around the turn of the century in the United States and Western Europe.

Michael Hechter is Professor of Sociology and Director of the Research Group for Institutional Analysis at The University of Arizona. He is the author of *Internal Colonialism: The Celtic Fringe in British National Development, 1536–1966* (1975), *Principles of Group Solidarity* (1987), editor of *The Microfoundations of Macrosociology* (1983), and co-editor of *Towards A Scientific Understanding of Values* (forthcoming). His current research is on the social determinants of individual values.

Hartmut Kliemt is Professor of Philosophy at the University of Duisburg. He is the author of *Zustimmingstheorien der Staatsrechtfertigung* (1980), *Moralische Institutionen* (1985), and *Antagonistische Kooperation* (1986).

Anthony Oberschall, Professor of Sociology at the University of North Carolina in Chapel Hill, is the author of *Social Conflict and Social Movements* (1973) and of many articles on collective action and social movements. He has also taught, researched, and written about social change in sub-Saharan Africa and China, and is currently preparing a monograph to be titled *Social Inventions,* which contains a rational choice approach to social institutions.

Karl-Dieter Opp is Professor of Sociology at the University of Hamburg. His areas of interest include collective action and political protest, rational choice theory, and the emergence and effects of norms and institutions. His book, *The Rationality of Political Protest*, is forthcoming. He is currently engaged in an international panel study conducted in Israel, Peru, and West Germany testing rational choice models and competing propositions of collective political action.

Werner W. Pommerehne has been a Lecturer in Economics at the University of Zurich since 1977 and is currently Professor of Economics at the Free University of Berlin. His main areas of research are in the economic theory of politics, public sector economics, and the economic analysis of arts and culture.

Werner Raub is Associate Professor of Theoretical Sociology at the University of Utrecht. One of his central research interests is in the application of rational choice models in the social sciences.

Thomas Voss is Akademischer Rat, Department of Sociology, University of Munich. Among his publications are *Individuelles Handeln und Gesellschaftliche Folgen* (1981) (with Werner Raub) and *Rationale Akteure und Soziale Institutionen* (1985). His main research interests are in rational choice theory, the sociology of organizations, and labor market research.

Reinhard Wippler is Professor of Theoretical Sociology at the University of Utrecht and scientific director of the Interuniversity Center for Sociological Theory and Methodology. He has conducted quantitative empirical research on leisure behavior. Presently his research interests include the application of rational choice models to the study of organizations, the sociology of leisure, and the methodology of theory construction and model building.

Rolf Ziegler is Professor of Sociology at the University of Munich. His interests include organizational sociology, social network analysis, rational choice theory, and labor market research. He is co-author of a comparative study on interlocking directorships in ten countries (*Networks of Corporate Power* (1985) (with F.N. Stokman and J. Scott) and has recently published *Market, Power and Cooptation*, which analyzes the structure of financial participation and interlocking directorates among large German corporations. Currently he is engaged in research on the founding and survival of small enterprises.

Index

Accepting gift, 155
Aesthetic codes
  and artistic enjoyment, 196–199
  command of, 192–193
Agency theory, 237
Agrarian programs (*See also* Chinese collective agriculture)
  in Germany, Nazi, 252–256
  in Italy, 251–252
Ajzen-Fisbein model, 135
Akerlof's model, 89
Akerlof's theory of social custom, 137
American Sociological Association, 5
Anonymous situations, 128
Arousal potential, 190
Artistic enjoyment, 196–199
Assurance Game preferences
  adoption of, 102
  as effective preference, 100–101, 110
  interpretations of, 103
  order of, 91
  and social cooperation, 104–105
  valuation of, 88
Assurance problem, 18
Attenuation (*See* Customs)
Axelrod's repeated prisoner's dilemma, 146–148

Bad Homburg conference, 5
Bao gong contracted work, 278
Bargaining, 109
Barter (*See* Exchange)
Becker's theory, 207–209
Behavior (*See also* Morality)
  change-oriented action, 125–126

choice, 91
collective, 14, 126
  and customs, compliance with, 120–121
  in social institutions, 14
  in theater
    and government support, type of, 180–183
    quality, 177
    quantity, 176–177
    technology, 178–179
Behavioral confirmation, 190, 194–195
Bestowing gift, 155, 161
Bethnal Green
  institutional contexts of, 213–217
  social environment and work in, 211–213
Bilateral exchange (*See* Exchange, two-actor)
Binding commitment, 85
BMPIUA (Bricklayers, Masons and Plasterers' International Union of America), 294
Bricklayers' International Union, 293–294
Bricklayers, Masons and Plasterers' International Union of America (BMPIUA), 294

Caravans, 24
Ceremonial exchange (*See* Kula Ring)
Change-oriented action, 125–128
Character planning, 85–86
Chen Village
  bao gong contracted work in, 278
  commune in, 276

Index

household contracted work in, 277–278
mutual aid teams in, 275–276
Chinese collective agriculture in Chen Village
   bao gong contracted work, 278
   commune, 276
   household contracted work, 277–278
   mutual aid teams in, 275–276
  Dazhai system, 278–282
  design of, basic, 268–270
  effects of, 8
  organizational changes in, 265–266
  productivity and output of, 270–275
  purpose of, 265
  responsibility system, 270, 282–284
  before revolution, 266–268
  summary of, 284–286
Chinese Communist Party (CCP) (*See* Chinese collective agriculture)
Choice behavior, 91
Christmas-card sending, 120–121
Clientelism (*See* Patronage)
Coast Seamen's Union (CSU), 292, 304
Collective agriculture (*See* Chinese collective agriculture)
Collective behavior, 14, 126
Comfort, 190, 194
Communist societies
  collective agriculture in
   in Chen Village, 275–278
   Dazhai system, 278–282
   organizational changes in, 265–266
   productivity and output of, 270–275
   purpose of, 265
   responsibility system, 270, 282–284
   before revolution, 266–268
   summary of, 284–286
  patronage in, 227–228
Competition, 235, 295–298
Compliance, 135 (*See also* Customs, attenuation of)
Conditional cooperation, 104, 250–251, 260–261
Conjoint norms, 40
Conservatives, 131–133
Constraint hypothesis, 3–4
Constraints, in theater, 6–7, 171–172
Control capacity, 16
Conventional institutions, 15
Conventional norms, 40

Cooperation (*See* Cooperative institutions; Social cooperation)
Cooperative game theory
  in exchange, conventional, 62–63
  and Hobbesian problem, 64–67
  and Prisoner's Dilemmas, 63–65
  problems in, 62
  and rule creation, limits of, 68–73
Cooperative institutions (*See also* Theater)
  by-products of extant, 20–22
  control in, 19
  and conventional institutions, 15
  demand for, 16
  empirical applications of
   evidence about development, 22
   guilds and merchant leagues, 22–27
  explanation of origin of, 27–28
  goods produced in, 20–22
  monitoring, 19–20
  sanctions in, 20
  solidaristic approach to
   and first tier free rider problem, 17
   and fourth tier, 20–22
   and genesis of institutions, 20–22
   implications of, 20–21
   and second tier free rider problem, 17–18
   and third tier free rider problem, 18–20
Cooperative theater, 173–175
Coordination games, 122–124
Cost and benefits, 120, 123 (*See also* Payoffs)
Cost theories, 7
Co-worker relationships, 209–211
CSU (Coast Seamen's Union), 292, 304
Cultural institutions (*See* Theater)
Cultural resources, 191–192
Cultural resources and participation
  and educational attainment, 7
  rational choice theory in
   general assumptions of, 188–189
   goal assumptions of, 189–191
   resourcee assumptions of, 191–193
   social condition assumptions of, 193–195
  social conditions pertinent to
   aesthetic codes, 192–193, 196–199
   artistic enjoyment, 196–199
   educational attainment, 187–188, 200–202

Cultural resources (continued)
  physical well-being, 189–191, 195–196
  social approval, 189–191, 195–196
  social aspects of, 199–200
Customs (*See also* Norms)
  attenuation of
    alternative explanation of, 136–137
    in anonymous situations, 128
    assumptions about, 124–127
    Christmas-card sending, 120–121
    and compliance, 135
    endogenous, 127–129
    exogenous, 129–134
    explanation of, 134–135
    in intimate personal relations, 128–129
    problems in, 135–136
    reasons for, 6, 119
  Christmas-card sending, 120–121
  and compliance, 135
  as coordination games, 122–124
  examples of, 119
  purpose of, 119
  social, 137

Dazhai system, 278–282
Defection, 129, 134
Deficit coverage, 181–183
Delayed reciprocity, 143, 154–155
Differential defection, 134
Differentiation, 132–133
Disincentives, 248, 256
Disjoint norms, 40
Disparity (*See* Gender stratification)
Dual self models, 84–86

Economic resources, 191
Education (*See* Japanese education)
Educational attainment (*See also* Japanese education)
  and participation in high culture, 200–202
  as predictor of cultural participation, 7, 187–188, 200
Endogenous attenuation, 127–129
Epsilon–equilibrium, 101
Equilibrium theory, 13
Essential norms, 41
Exchange (*See also* Kula Ring)
  conventional, 61–63
  economic and social, 141–142
  Kula Ring as classic example of, 141
  social cooperation in, 61–63
  three-actor or more, 47–49
  two-actor, 45–47, 150–153
  value in, 49
Exogenous attenuation
  material incentives, changing, 133–134
  social network, changing, 129–133
Externalities, and interests in norms
  actions generating, 41
  and game-theoretic model, 45
  and market control, 41–42
  negative, 42–43
  positive, 42–43
  structure of, 43–45
  and three-actor or more exchange, 47–49
  and two-actor exchange, 45–47

Fascist party membership in Italy and Germany
  and conditional cooperation, 250–251, 260–261
  conditions for, 247–248
  and control of resources, 258–259
  and disincentives, 248, 256
  motivations for joining, 245–246
  of peasants
    in Geest region of Germany, 252–256
    in southern Italy, 251–252
  political geography of, 246
  and regional differences, 7–8, 246–248
  and selective incentives, 249, 256–257
  and social networks, participation by, 249–250, 259–260
First-order desires, 85
Focal actions, 39
Free ride, 248–249
Free-rider problems
  first tier, 17
  second-order, 51–53
  second tier, 17–18
  third tier, 18–20
Functional explanations, 136–137

Game **M**
  analysis of, 94–96
  conditions for application of, 107–109
  decision situation in, 92–93
  dilemma in, 106–107

Index

examples of, 96–100
extensive form of, 97–98
normal form of, 91–94
payoff for, 97–100
results of, 100–103
sensitivity problems in, 94
Game-theoretic model
alternative interpretation of, 110–111
assumptions of, 90–91
conditions for application of, 107–110
and externalities generating interests in norms, 45
game M
analysis of, 94–96
examples of, 96–100
normal form of, 91–94
results of, 100–103
implications of, 104–107
and Kula Ring, 6
and morality, 6
and repeated transactions, 145–146
and Sen's approach to morality, 86–89
Gender stratification
factors producing, 307–309
and human capital development system
concept of, 309
dimensions of, 310–312
parents' incentives for differentiating between sexes, 314–315
parents' information regarding children, 312–314
resources for investment in children, 315–316
study of
data and methods of, 318–319
descriptive results of, 319–322
empirical findings of, 328
multivariate results of, 322–328
other hypotheses, 316–318
patterns of, 8
Goals, assumptions about
empirical establishment of, 189
of physical well-being, 189–190, 195–196
of social approval, 189–191, 195–196
theoretical establishment of, 189
Government-supported theater, 179–183
Guilds and merchant leagues
and caravans, 24
development of, 26
Hanseatic League, 26–27

and joint ventures, 22–23
and parish guilds, 24–25
and partnerships, 23–24
and public goods, 25

Hanseatic League, 26–27 (*See also* Guilds and merchant leagues)
Heroic sanctions, 53–57
Hobbesian problem
and problematic social situation, 81–82
of social order, 65–67, 145
Human capital development system
concept of, 309
dimensions of, 310–312
institutionalized differences in amounts of, 8
parents' incentives for differentiating between sexes, 314–315
parents' information regarding children, 312–314
payoffs in, 310
resource investment in children, 315–316

IBEW (International Brotherhood of Electrical Workers), 293
Incentives, 123–124, 256–257
Income, maximizing, 295–298
Incremental sanctions, 53–57
Individual interests (*See* Preference changes)
Institutional genesis
analytical elements in, 6
cooperative
empirical applications of, 22–27
explanation of, 27–28
factors affecting, 16–17
and first tier free-rider problem, 17
and fourth tier, 20–22
implications of, 20–21
and second tier free-rider problem, 17–18
and third tier free-rider problem, 18–20
evolutionary explanations of, 74–78
interest in, current, 13
invisible-hand approach to, 13–14, 16
and noncooperative game theory, 74–78
and public goods question, 6
and rational choice theory, 5
and repeated game theory, 6

Institutional genesis (*continued*)
  and social institutions, concept of, 13–16
  solidaristic approach to, 13–16
Interactions (*See* Social interactions)
Intergenerational change, 133
Internalization, 134–135
Internalized commitment, 83
International Brotherhood of Electrical Workers (IBEW), 293
International Seamen's Union of America (ISU)
  history of, 291–293
  origin of, 292
  and propositions toward theory of unions, 303–304
International Sociological Association meeting of 1986, 5
Intimate personal relations, 128–129
Invisible-hand approach, 13–14, 16
ISU (*See* International Seamen's Union of America)

Japanese education
  and gender stratification, 307–308
  and human capital development
    concept of, 309
    dimensions of, 310–312
    parent's information regarding children, 312–314
    parents' incentives for differentiating between sexes, 314–315
    resources for investment in children, 315–316
  study of
    data and methods of, 318–319
    descriptive results of, 319–322
    empirical findings in, 328
    multivariate results of, 322–328
    other hypotheses in, 316–318
Joint goods, 16–20
Joint ventures, 22–23

Kula Ring (*See also* Exchange)
  and circular system of exchange, 150–153
  as classic example of exchange, 141
  functionalist interpretation of, 141–142
  and game-theoretic model, 6
  problems raised by, 164
  and social order

  as solution to problem of, 144–149
  as system to maintain, 153–155, 160–164
  social system of, 142–144

Labor organizations (*See* Unions)
Lopsided friendship, 226 (*See also* Patronage)
"Loyalty filters," 89
Lump sum government subsidy, 180–181

Marienthal community study, 206
Material incentives, changing, 133–134
Merchant leagues (*See* Guilds and merchant leagues)
Meta-preferences, 86
Micro/macro problem, 5
Middlemen, 151–153
Migration, 130–133
Mistrust, 155, 160–164
Moral entrepreneurs, 131–133
Moral institutions (*See also* Game-theoretical model; Morality)
  and preference changes
    conditions for modification of, 104–107
    model for modification of, 90–103
    problem of, 82–83
    rational action perspectives on, 83–86
    shortcomings of rational actions perspectives on, 86–90
  and social order, 82–83
Morality (*See also* Moral institutions)
  degree of, 84
  and game-theoretic model, 6
  via preference changes, 83–86
  and preferences, 90–91
  and self-interest, 84
  Sen's view of, 86–89
  sociological tradition of, 82–83
Multiple self, 84

National Science Foundation, 5
Neoclassical economic models, 13
Network (*See* Social network)
Noncompliance, 131–132 (*See also* Customs, attenuation of)
Noncooperative game theory
  and institutional genesis, 74–78
  and preference changes, 92
  Prisoner's Dilemmas in, 63–65

Index

Noninstitutional environment, 14
Nonsocial incentives, 123–124
Norms (*See also* Customs)
   classes of, 39–41
   concept of, 35–36
   conditions of occurrence, 37
   conjoint, 40
   conventional, 40
   disjoint, 40
   essential, 41
   examples of, 38–39
   and externalities, interests in
     actions generating, 41
     and game-theoretic model, 45
     and market control, 41–42
     negative, 42–43
     positive, 42–43
     structure of, 43–45
     and three-actor or more exchange, 47–49
     and two-actor exchange, 45–47
   and functioning of societies, 36–37
   prescriptive, 39
   proscriptive, 39
   in rational choice theory, 4, 36–37
   and sanctions, 37–38
   second-order public goods problem in, 51–53
   social structure of
     sanction problem in, 51–53
     sequencing problem in, 50–51
     in three-actor or more project, 49
     in two-actor project, 49
     and vest rights of control, 50
   in social theory, 35–36
   structure of, 37
   targets of, 39–41
   and value, 35–36

Objective uncertainty, 298–301
Organizing strategies, exclusive and inclusive, 301–303
Organizational economics, 237

Pareto optimal, 64, 151, 153
Parish guilds, 24–25
Partnerships, 23–24
Patronage
   in communist societies, 227–228
   as contract, implicit, 237–238
   decline in, 225
   definition of, 225
   empirical documentation on, lack of, 238–239
   future study of, 239–240
   importance of, 237
   intrigue of, 226
   in preindustrial, peasant societies, 226–227
   and social capital
     as explanation, 233–237
     theory of, 231–233
   as social network, specific, 7, 228–231
   as social organization, 226
   ties in, difference in, 225–226
Payoffs
   assumptions in, 126–127
   for compliance and defection, 130–133
   in human capital development system, 310
   structures of, 121–123
Physical well-being, 189–191, 195–196
Pleasure, 190, 193
Positive affect, 190–191, 194–195
Preference changes
   causal process of, 84
   and concept of person, 84–85
   conditions for modification of
     alternative interpretation of, 110–111
     application of, 107–110
     implications of, 104–107
   conflict in, 85–86
   intentional process of, 84
   model for modification of
     analysis of game **M**, 94–96
     assumptions of, 90–91
     examples of game **M**, 96–100
     normal form of game **M**, 91–94
     results of game **M**, 100–103
   morality via, 83–86
   and noncooperative game theory, 92
   in problematic social situations, 82, 90
   rational action perspectives on
     and Akerlof's model, 89–90
     character planning, 85–86
     dual self models, 84–86
     "self-command," 84–85
     and Sen's approach, 86–89
     shortcomings of, 86–90
     "sour grapes" mechanism, 84
   social interaction in, 90
Preference hypothesis, 3

Prescriptive norms, 39
Prisoner's Dilemmas
  complaince to customs as, 135–136
  in cooperative game theory, 63–65
  in noncooperative game theory, 63–65
  social cooperation in, 15–16, 63–65
Problematic social situations, 81–82, 90
    (See also Preference changes)
Production rules, 17
Profit-oriented theater, 175–179
Property rights, theory of, 136
Proscriptive norms, 39
Public goods
  in cooperative institutions, 20–22
  and guilds and merchant leagues, 25
  and institutional genesis, 6
  and market control, 41–42
  theory of, 136

Rational choice theory
  advances in, 2
  applications of, 2
  common elements of, 3
  in cultural resources and participation
    general assumptions of, 188–189
    goal assumptions of, 189–191
    resource assumptions of, 191–193
    social condition assumptions of, 193–195
  hypotheses under
    constraint, 3–4
    preference, 3
    utility maximization, 3–4
  and institutional genesis, 5
  norms in, 4, 36–37
  origins of, 2
  as research program, 8
  social cooperation in
    and evolutionary explanation of emergence of institutions, 74–78
    problems in, 73–74
    switching model in, 78–79
  social institutions in, 4–5
Reciprocity (See Delayed reciprocity; Exchange)
Relationships (See Social interaction)
Repeated game theory, 6, 15–16
Resources, assumptions about, 191–193
Responsibility system, 270, 282–284
Ricardian law of association, 63

Ring structure, 150–153 (See also Kula Ring)
Ritualism, 154
Rule creation, limits of, 68–73

Sanctions
  in cooperative institutions, 20
  examples of, 38–39
  heroic, 53–57
  incremental, 53–57
  and norms, 37–38
  problem of, in social structure of norms, 51–53
  second-order public goods problem, 51–53
  term of, 40
Schelling points, 27
Seamen's Friendly Union and Protective Society, 292
Seamen's Protective Association, 292
Second-order desires, 85
Second-order free-rider problem, 51–53
Second-order public goods problem, 51–53
Selective incentives, 249
Self-command, 84–85
Self-interest, 84
Sen's approach to morality, 86–89
Sensitivity problems, 94
Sequencing problem, 50–51
Shadow of tomorrow, 232
Social approval, 189–191, 195–196
Social capital
  acquisition of, 232–233
  components of, 231–232
  and cost theories, 7
  in explanation of patronage, 233–237
  theory of, 231–233
  value of, 232
Social codes, 192
Social conditions
  assumptions about, 193–195
  and cultural participation
    aesthetic codes, 192–193, 196–199
    artistic enjoyment, 196–199
    physical well-being, 189–190, 195–196
    social approval, 189–191, 195–196
    social aspects of, 199–200
Social cooperation

Index

and Assurance Game preferences, 104–105
conditional, 104, 205, 250–251, 260–261
in exchange, conventional, 61–63
in Prisoner's Dilemmas, 15–16, 63–65
in problematic social situations, 81
in rational choice theory
  and evolutionary explanation of emergence of institutions, 74–78
  problems in, 73–74
  switching model of, 78–79
and rule creation, limits of, 68–73
Social cost, 41–42
Social environment, 211–213
Social incentives, 123
Social institutions (*See also* Cooperative institutions; Institutional genesis; Morality institutions)
  analysis of, 1
  behavior in, collective, 14
  concept of, 13–16
  from economic point of view, 171–173
  emergence of
    essays on, 6–8
    from noninstitutional environment, 14
    questions centering on, 1–2
    and rational choice theory, 4–5
  in equilibrium theory, 13
  and micro/macro problem, 5
  in neoclassical economic models, 13
  in rational choice theory, 4–5
Social interactions
  Becker's theory of, 207–209
  in preference changes, 90
  in social structure of norms, 51–52
  and unemployment, 7
Social network
  changing, 129–133
  and fascist party membership, 249–250, 259–260
  patronage as specific, 228–231
Social order
  Hobbesian problem of, 65–67, 145
  and Kula Ring
    as solution to problem of, 144–149
    as system to maintain, 161–165
  and moral institutions, 82–83
Social organization, 49, 142–144
Social relationships (*See* Social interactions)

Social resources, 191
Social theory, 35–36
Sociology, 1
Solidaristic approach
  to cooperative institutions
    and first tier free-rider problem, 17
    and fourth tier, 20–22
    and genesis of institutions, 20–22
    implications of, 20–21
    and second tier free-rider problem, 17–18
    and third tier free-rider problem, 18–20
  to institutional genesis, 13–16
"Sour grapes" mechanism, 84
Status, 190
Stonemason's International Union, 294
Supergames, 146, 155, 161–165
Switching model, of rational choice, 78–79

Targets, of norms, 39–40
Theater
  behavior in
    government support on, type of, 180–193
    quality, 177
    quantity, 176–177
    technology, 178–179
  constraints in, 6–7, 171–172
  cooperative, 173–175
  economic point of view of, 171–173
  government-supported, 179–183
  profit-oriented, 175–179
Theory gap, 238
Tit-for-tat (TFT) rule, 146
Transaction costs approach, 136
Transaction cost theory, 237
Transactions, 234
Trust, 155, 160–164

Unemployment (*See also* Welfare state)
  in 1930's and 1980's, 205–207
  consequences of, 213
  and social contacts, opportunities to purchase, 217–218
  and social interactions, 7
  voluntary, 218–220
Unions
  BMPIUA, 293–294

Unions (*continued*)
  IBEW, 293
  ISU, 291–293, 303–304
  patterns in, 8
  propositions toward theory of
    clues for, 294–295
    exclusive and inclusive organizing strategies, 301–303
    implications of, 303–305
    maximizing income and resisting competition, 295–298
    objective uncertainty, 298–301
    problems in forming, 294
  rise and fall of, 291
Utility maximization hypothesis, 3–4
Utility theory, 246

Value
  in exchange, 49
  and norms, 35–36
  of social capital, 232
  of work, 209–211
Vertical integration, 237

Weak ties, 210
Welfare state (*See also* Unemployment)
  in 1930's and 1980's, 205–207
  Becker's theory of, 207–209
  in Bethnal Green conditions, 211–213
  debate over, 206–207
  institutional contexts for
    pre-welfare states, 213–217
    welfare state, 213–217
  and social contacts, opportunities to purchase, 217–218
  and social environment, 211–213
  and unemployment, 213
  and voluntary unemployment, 218–220
  in Woodford conditions, 211–213
  and work, social value of, 209–211
Werner Reimers Foundation, 5
Williamson's hostages model, 110–111
Woodford
  institutional contexts of, 213–217
  social environment and work in, 211–213

Work
  and social environment, 211–213
  social value of, 209–211